DAPHNE DU MAURIER

BIOGRAPHY

The Rash Adventurer
The Rise and Fall of Charles
Edward Stuart
William Makepeace Thackeray
Memoirs of a Victorian Gentleman
Significant Sisters
The Grassroots of Active Feminism
1839–1939
Elizabeth Barrett Browning

POETRY

Selected Poems
of Elizabeth Barrett Browning (Editor)

FICTION

Dame's Delight
Georgy Girl
The Bogeyman
The Travels of Maudie Tipstaff
The Park
Miss Owen-Owen is At Home
Fenella Phizackerley
Mr Bone's Retreat
The Seduction of Mrs Pendlebury
Mother Can You Hear Me?
The Bride of Lowther Fell
Marital Rites
Private Papers
Have the Men had Enough?
Lady's Maid
The Battle for Christabel

DAPHNE DU MAURIER

Margaret Forster

Chatto & Windus
LONDON

Published in 1993 by
Chatto & Windus Ltd
20 Vauxhall Bridge Road
London SW1V 2SA

A CIP catalogue record for this book is
available from the British Library.

ISBN 0 7011 3699 5

Index by Hazel Bell

Phototypeset by Intype, London
Printed and bound in Great Britain by
Mackays of Chatham PLC, Chatham, Kent

For Joyce Blake (who first aroused
my interest in biography) and
in memory of Phyllis Wynne (who first
aroused my interest in the novels of
Daphne du Maurier).

Contents

Daphne du Maurier

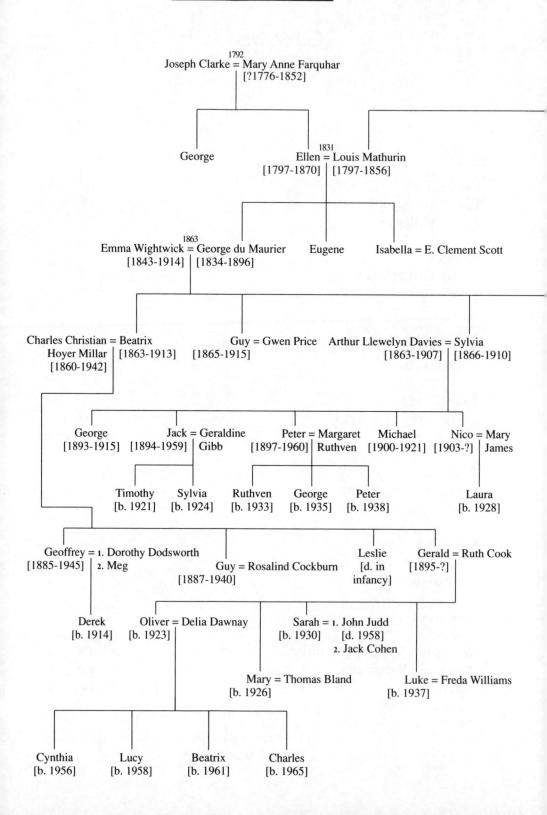

Family Tree

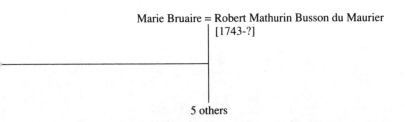

Marie Bruaire = Robert Mathurin Busson du Maurier
[1743-?]

5 others

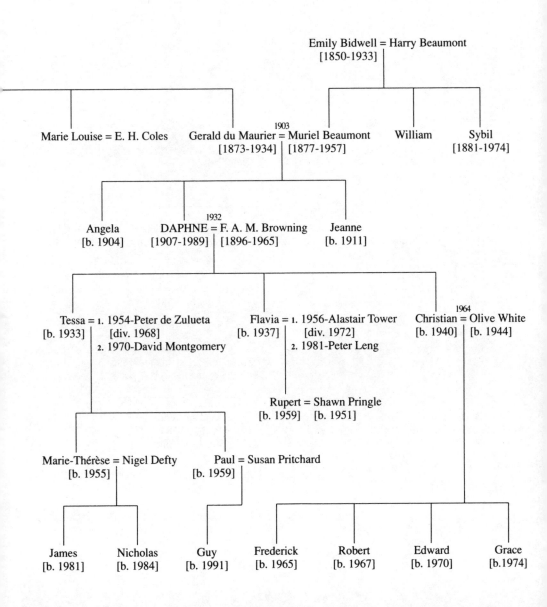

Emily Bidwell = Harry Beaumont
[1850-1933]

Marie Louise = E. H. Coles   Gerald du Maurier ¹⁹⁰³= Muriel Beaumont   William   Sybil
                           [1873-1934]   [1877-1957]   [1881-1974]

Angela   DAPHNE ¹⁹³²= F. A. M. Browning   Jeanne
[b. 1904]   [1907-1989]   [1896-1965]   [b. 1911]

Tessa = 1. 1954-Peter de Zulueta   Flavia = 1. 1956-Alastair Tower   Christian ¹⁹⁶⁴= Olive White
[b. 1933]   [div. 1968]   [b. 1937]   [div. 1972]   [b. 1940]   [b. 1944]
         2. 1970-David Montgomery   2. 1981-Peter Leng

Rupert = Shawn Pringle
[b. 1959]   [b. 1951]

Marie-Thérèse = Nigel Defty   Paul = Susan Pritchard
[b. 1955]   [b. 1959]

James   Nicholas   Guy   Frederick   Robert   Edward   Grace
[b. 1981]   [b. 1984]   [b. 1991]   [b. 1965]   [b. 1967]   [b. 1970]   [b.1974]

List of Illustrations

Every attempt has been made to trace sources of photographs but in some cases this has proved impossible. Where sources are not credited above, photographs have been supplied by the Browning family and are reproduced with their kind permission.

Acknowledgements

Since Daphne du Maurier's letters and papers are all in private hands, with the exception of a small collection of some correspondence with her publisher Victor Gollancz during the fifties (which is in the Modern Records Centre, University of Warwick), these acknowledgements also act as source material notes.

The full co-operation of Daphne du Maurier's children has been essential. Between them they possess documentation for the whole of their mother's life, including her letters from the age of five, and also letters of Gerald du Maurier's, together with many covering the life of their father Lt.-Gen. Browning. Apart from those letters written to each of them by their mother, they hold letters to Maud Waddell (Tod), Daphne's governess; to Mlle Fernande Yvon; to her mother Lady du Maurier; to her sister-in-law Grace Browning; and to Augustus and Ina Agar.

There are also important collections of letters belonging to people outside the family, and I am grateful for access to them. For access to the correspondence between Daphne du Maurier and Ellen Doubleday special thanks to the latter's daughter, Ellen M. Violett, Curator of the Ellen Doubleday Collection (Princeton University); thanks to Guy Symondson for letters to his mother's cousin Foy Quiller-Couch; Garth Lean for his own letters from Daphne, covering the MRA years; Michael Thornton for his own letters; and John Williams for letters to his mother Evie Williams, Gertrude Lawrence's secretary in England.

Other people who have kindly shared their letters from Daphne, and often their personal memories, with me are Bunny Austin, Henrietta Stapleton-Bretherton, Elizabeth Divine, Antonia Fraser, Bridget Graham, Doe Howard, Cynthia Millar, Lord Montgomery, John Prescott (to his mother Karen Prescott), Œnone

Acknowledgements

Richardson (neé Rashleigh), Laila Spence (to her late husband Kenneth), Dorothy Sheppard, Douglas Symington (to his father J. A. Symington), Ellen M. Violett and Lady Wolfenden.

Daphne du Maurier's publishers Victor Gollancz Ltd have generously allowed me to study their extensive files, and I thank Livia Gollancz and Stephen Bray for this permission. Curtis Brown Ltd, Daphne's agent for virtually the whole of her career, have also allowed me access to their files, and I thank Anthea Morton-Saner for arranging this. Jane Holah, Group Librarian of the Octopus Publishing Group, has kindly supplied me with publication details, from the Heinemann files, of Daphne's first three novels.

Apart from these letters I have learned a great deal of importance in conversation with members of the du Maurier and Browning families and with Daphne du Maurier's friends and those who worked for her. Angela and Jeanne du Maurier have helped me with early memories, and Daphne's grandchildren with more recent ones. But it is to her three children, Tessa (Lady Montgomery), Flavia (Lady Leng) and Kits (Christian Browning), that I am most indebted. They have spent many hours answering questions and have provided me with introductions to people in their mother's life whom it would have been otherwise quite impossible for me to track down. Their role has not been an easy one. I have exposed events in their mother's life which were unknown to them and which have proved painful for them to discover. But they know that their mother believed that if biographies are written – and she never at any time banned a biography about herself, once she was dead, though she had a great aversion to any during her lifetime – they should try to tell what she called 'all truth'. What she detested were biographies that were 'stereo-typed, dull-as-ditchwater, or very fulsome praising'. She realized the truth was 'often hard for the family to take', but saw no point in biography otherwise.* The particular truths revealed in this biography have been hard for her own family to take, but they have stayed loyal to their mother's directive, and taken them.

* Letter to Ellen Doubleday, 3 February 1949.

Acknowledgements

I am grateful to the following people who have given me so much of their time to talk about Daphne and about her husband: Michael Bossiney, Sheila Bush, Liz Calder, Lord Carrington, Maj.-Gen. C. M. F. Deakin, Lady Donaldson, Margaret Eglesfield, Richard Elsden, Rena M. Fairley (who talked to me about her cousin Maud Waddell), Mary Fox, Patricia Frere, Joanna Goldsworthy, Giles Gordon, Anne Griffiths, Brian and Pauline Johnston, John Knight, Garth and Margo Lean, Dr Martin Luther, Oriel Malet, Lord Montgomery, Margaret Netherton, Mike Parker, Janet Puxley (who talked to me about her late husband's family and the background to *Hungry Hill*), Gladys Powell, Veronica Rashleigh, Margaret Robertson, A. L. Rowse, Elizabeth Spillane, Guy and Kate Symondson, Alastair Tower, Mary Varcoe, Ellen M. Violett, Sir Brian Warren, Major (retd) S. Weaver and Noël Welch.

Others who answered questions by letter are H.R.H. Prince Philip; Canon Denys and Mr Hubert Browning (from New Zealand); and Terry Jones (from Canada); George Bott, Lavinia Greacen, Ian Hamilton, Patricia Hastings, Ken McCormick, Sir Oliver Millar, the late Matthew Norgate, John Reece, Mrs Milton Runyon, Michael Thornton, Michael Trinick, Nicholas Wapshott and Oscar Yerburgh.

I thank the following people for permission to look round the houses where Daphne du Maurier lived: Angela Hodges (Cumberland Terrace, Regents Park); Jane Simpson (Cannon Hall); Angela du Maurier (Ferryside); Veronica Rashleigh (Menabilly and Kilmarth).

Special mention should be made of Esther Rowe, Daphne's housekeeper for thirty-one years, who has been unstinting in her help both by letter and in interviews.

Daphne du Maurier's literary executors are her son Kits, and Monty Baker-Munton, husband of Maureen Luschwitz, General Browning's Staff Officer (PA), who returned with him in 1946. Daphne had implicit trust in Monty and involved him in her business affairs from 1960 onwards. Both he and Maureen became close friends and were depended upon to a great extent. I am deeply indebted to both of them for the time and trouble they have taken to assist me.

Acknowledgements

Finally, I would like to say how much it has mattered to me to have an agent, a publisher, an editor and a typist all as enthusiastic about a project as mine have been. Tessa Sayle, Carmen Callil, Alison Samuel and Gertrud Watson have shown a curiosity about, and interest in, the life of Daphne du Maurier which has very nearly matched my own and has been far beyond the call of any duty. It has greatly added to the pleasure of writing this book.

DAPHNE DU MAURIER

PART ONE

The Golden Girl
1907–1932

Chapter One

Sheet-lightning split the sky over London on the evening of 12 May 1907 and thunder rumbled long into the night. All day it had been hot and sultry, the trees in Regent's Park barely moving and a heat haze obscuring the new growth of leaves. Then, towards dawn the next day, the weather began to change. A wind picked up and by afternoon the rain had begun, light at first, but by 5.20, when Muriel du Maurier gave birth to her second daughter, heavy and persistent, bringing with it the relief of much cooler weather. The theatres, which had played to poor audiences because of the heat, were once more almost full. Marie Tempest starred in *The Truth* at the Comedy, Sir Herbert Beerbohm Tree in *Julius Caesar* at Her Majesty's, and at the Hicks Theatre in Shaftesbury Avenue Gerald du Maurier was scoring an immense success, the night his new daughter was born, in a light comedy entitled *Brewster's Millions.*

But his success, in the kind of part which had made his name, had begun to bore him. Gerald's whole life was the theatre, in which he had always seemed extremely happy and confident, but during the last few years he had decided that he had come to hate both acting and the theatre itself. In July 1906, while his wife Muriel was staying on the Isle of Wight with her two-year-old first child Angela, Gerald confided in a letter that he 'loathed acting and actors'. He longed to join his little family on holiday and could hardly bear to be without them – 'I hate living alone . . . it is dreadful waking up and no blessed angel.' He could never sleep when his wife was away – 'I thought I would be a good boy last night, so I had a mug of cocoa and went to bed early. Never again. I slept for five minutes between four and five . . .' He thought of Muriel all the time, swimming and sunbathing, concerned that she might be 'getting brown – don't you go and overdo it – I love you most looking fragile'. She was, he wrote, 'the only real thing in this world and I get a sort of pain in my heart when you're not near'. This pain made him reluctant to allow even the briefest of separations, and every reunion was ecstatic. When he joined Muriel in August 1906 he wrote he would 'faint when I see you', so overwhelming was his passion. The thought of this love ever fading made him feverish – 'I only pray from my soul that I may make you always happy and keep your wonderful love to the end.'

Supremely conscious that he had at last been fortunate, after two ill-fated liaisons,[1] he was always anxious that Muriel should know she was appreciated. 'Muriel, I love you,' he had written when they married in 1903. 'It is a splendid thing that has happened to us both, dearest, and I do hope the Great Spirit will bless us. It's by our truth, loyalty and devotion to each other that we shall accomplish a beautiful life and with such love as we have for each other, dear dear Muriel, it should not be difficult ... I seem to love you in all ways, as a child, as a boy, as a grown man – simply, passionately and sensibly, and with it all there is a sweet sense of security.'

The most telling phrase of all was Gerald's longing for 'a sweet sense of security', so vital to his well-being. His upbringing as the youngest of the five children of George and Emma du Maurier had been utterly secure, but suddenly, in April of this very year, 1907, fate had dealt the first of several blows to the du Maurier family. Arthur Llewelyn Davies,[2] husband of Sylvia, Gerald's second eldest sister, had died, after months of agony, of cancer of the jaw. The anguish of this death, and Sylvia's grief, had obliged Gerald to be more of a 'grown man' than the boy he preferred still to think himself.

He was thirty-four years old when this tragedy happened, but until then had always managed to go through life in an entirely light-hearted way, his mother's 'ewe lamb', everyone's favourite. He was Gerald the joker, Gerald the debonair, Gerald the charmer, a man who had been spared responsibility in life and had always taken advantage of this. But with Arthur's death, Sylvia's misery and the pathos of five young nephews left fatherless, Gerald had just begun to see the world differently. His own new-found happiness was threatened by the evidence of what had happened to Arthur, and when, in 1910, Sylvia herself also died of breast cancer, he discovered it was not, after all, going to be so easy to preserve the 'beautiful life' he had promised Muriel. Golden lads and lasses also came to dust, and rather sooner, and much more terrifyingly, than he had ever imagined.

So Daphne du Maurier was born at a time when her father's personality had begun to change. This manifested itself in small ways at first – sudden, brief moments of 'moodiness', as it was called – then more markedly. Gerald could now seem uncharacteristically 'low' for days at a time, when he was not actually on the stage, and he would sometimes openly sigh and confess he felt unhappy, but so lugubrious was his expression that his family were convinced he was being intentionally funny. After all, what did he have to be depressed about? He was successful in his work, happy in his home life at 24 Cumberland Terrace, Regent's Park, where Daphne was born. Up to the outbreak of the First World War in 1914, Gerald was leaping ahead, moving from being primarily an actor to being an actor-manager, who shared in the profits. He went into partnership with Frank Curzon and stamped his mark on their productions at Wyndham's Theatre. There was nothing at all for him to worry about.

And yet Gerald did worry. He worried about what he was doing with his own life, where he thought he was going, now that middle age was in sight. He was a highly successful actor, credited with developing a new naturalistic style of acting, but he doubted the value of this. There was a restlessness in him and a desire for greater things, which few guessed at – he seemed, outwardly, so buoyant and optimistic. There was a yearning in him to which he could give no name and which he covered over with apparently inexhaustible high spirits, only to feel a sense of despair about himself because he could not be more serious. When tragedies like his brother-in-law Arthur's death happened he was more than normally overwhelmed with their pointlessness and cruelty. Lacking any religious beliefs, he had no answers to the questions with which he plagued himself – what was the meaning of his life, was death the end, was there any *point* to it all? Silence, emptiness, being on his own were a horror to him and made him panic – he wanted always to be busy and surrounded by people so that he would not have to think. Fortunately, his wife Muriel appreciated this and worked hard at ensuring Gerald's 'boredom' was kept at bay. She was a superb organizer, easily able to entertain the hordes of people her husband needed about him to distract and occupy him. An actress herself – Gerald had met her in a production of J. M. Barrie's *The Admirable Crichton* in 1902 – she gave up the stage, without appearing to regret it, before the birth of her third daughter, Jeanne, in 1911, and devoted herself to running Gerald's life. On the surface, she was successful. As a hostess she excelled, never appearing to weary of providing Gerald with the endless social gatherings which he required. He was put first at all times. Even her mother-in-law, to whom Gerald, as the youngest of her five children, had always seemed most precious, was satisfied with Muriel's devotion.

But Muriel was by no means the cipher this exaggerated respect for Gerald's needs might suggest, nor was her own family insignificant beside the du Mauriers. She was named after her maternal great-grandfather, Charles Muriel Bidwell, whose son founded a prestigious firm of chartered surveyors in Cambridge. Her father, Harry Beaumont, came from an East Anglian family of lawyers. He himself was a solicitor whose practice ran into difficulties after he had moved from Cambridge to Battersea. It was unusual for a young woman of Muriel Beaumont's background to go on the stage at the turn of the century, but nobody meeting her ever doubted her refinement and she was admired for seeking to earn her own income and contribute towards her family's. She had a brother, Willie, who was a literary agent and journalist, and a sister, Sybil, known as 'Billie', who was a secretary. All three Beaumont children showed some strength of character in the ways in which they reacted to their father's comparative ill-fortune, and they shared a familial devotion equal to that of the du Mauriers. Gerald, visiting Muriel's home before they were married, was instantly impressed by the warmth of the Beaumont family life and by the sweetness of her parents.

For a decade, Muriel, known as 'Mo', gave Gerald what he needed: stability, adoration, the comforts of a well-run home. But as he became more dissatisfied with himself Gerald began to grow restless. He could not do without Mo, still loved her, but he felt a new lack. What Mo could not respond to was the mercurial side of Gerald's character, the side of him which was quick, a touch wicked, even a little crazy. Mo was sensible, calm and, although always charming, never original or challenging. Gerald loved to talk, to tell stories, to indulge in repartee, delighting in responses quicker than his own, loving the excitement of risqué raconteurs whom he would dare to go further. All of this was beyond Mo. She was the centre of Gerald's life, but increasingly he liked to travel away from it, though ever dependent on knowing it was there to return to. His affairs with young actresses were known to her – they were known to everyone in their theatrical circle – but she seemed to cope with this knowledge by appearing to ignore it. The image of Gerald and Mo as utterly devoted was not the façade this attitude might suggest – they *were* devoted but sexual fidelity on Gerald's part was not essential to the devotion. So long as Mo was not publicly humiliated, so long as she knew no other woman could ever claim a place in her husband's heart, then she tolerated his transgressions. But to deduce from this that she was a weak character would be wrong. On the contrary, she was in her own way strong, even formidable, possessing great dignity and always impressing with the authority with which she ran her home. Gerald seemed to depend on her a great deal, especially returning late from the theatre when the two of them would sit talking while he wound down from whatever part he had been playing. Gerald was a family man, a husband and a father above all else, whatever the impression others received.

When Angela, Daphne and Jeanne du Maurier were young they thought their father was perfect. Their childhood memories enshrined a father so caring and affectionate, so energetic and jolly, so inventive and enthusiastic and so overwhelmingly protective that they were sure there could be no other like him. The sun rose and set with Gerald – his world was made their world, a world of action, a world of living in great comfort among colourful people, a world of the theatre. Their own little nursery world on the top floor of the Cumberland Terrace house might be staid

7

and traditional, but downstairs was the ever-thrilling presence of Gerald, who would swoop and enfold them and draw them into his own exciting existence. He played marvellous imaginative games[3] with them, read to them, took them with him to the theatre, involved himself in their lives totally when he was with them, and they saw themselves blessed with such a father. As indeed, until adolescence, they were.

In an era when fathers were by no means common in the nursery, and certainly not fun-loving figures when they did put in an appearance, Gerald du Maurier stood out. He gave time to his daughters, and saw to it that this time was rich. Above all, he spent hours talking to them, not in a patronizing way, but treating them, if not as equals, at least as people whose words were worthy of serious consideration on any topic. Gradually, as the three girls grew up, it was the talk which fascinated them most. Their mother was not part of it. She would withdraw and let Gerald and the girls converse, never quite sure what enthralled them so, though she understood the language perfectly well. This language was full of du Maurier code words, impenetrable to an outsider, code words which changed and were added to all the time and gave to any discussion a delicious sense of secrecy. To outsiders, it could sound affected and even downright silly and annoying, but just as the English upper classes of the era loved to have their own private language, which excluded anyone not belonging to the magic circle, so the du Mauriers loved having theirs. For the girls it was all an extension of the theatre: they acted in real life just as Gerald acted on stage, and the code words were like scripts which must be perfectly learned. It made them feel quite triumphant to be able to communicate in public, as well as private, in a language no one else could exactly penetrate. Some of this language was easy to understand: to refer to someone being 'on a hard chair' meant they were easily offended, being 'menaced' was being attracted by another person (and 'a fearful menace' was a very attractive person), while indulging in a 'tell-him' was to be boring. But it was harder to trace the derivation of others: 'wain', for example, was to be embarrassed, but nobody could remember why. Usually, some incident in family life had given rise to a code word and then the incident itself was often forgotten. It was the same with names. The girls themselves had different nicknames, religiously adhered to for a while, then suddenly changed when a better one presented itself. New people coming into the family circle were invariably given nicknames, until it seemed no one ever had their proper name or spoke in plain English.

The girls loved it and entered into the spirit of it quite naturally. They were encouraged, even expected, to use their imaginations, to make their conversation as amusing and colourful as possible. What was rather more dangerous was the way in which they were also pulled into Gerald's own style of mockery. Mockery was his favourite weapon and he used it mercilessly. Everything and everyone could be mocked and not to enjoy this sport was to have no sense of humour. Yet at the same time – which was confusing for children – good manners were essential. Gerald could mock someone until they seemed completely ridiculous, but should that person later appear they had to be treated with absolute respect with never a hint of what had gone before. So the children learned very early that nothing was ever what it seemed – a kind of complicated double standard was operated by their beloved father both on and off the stage.

Gerald himself saw no contradictions in his role as father. He openly loved his daughters – he was very affectionate, carrying them round long after they had outgrown this stage, and cuddling them all in the most demonstrative way – and felt he inculcated in them the highest values and standards. The most important of values was family pride. As he grew older, Gerald loved and revered his family more and more and talked endlessly about its history, both recent and long past, to his children. In 1916, when he purchased Cannon Hall, Cannon Place in Hampstead, the return to the area where he had been born[4] reinforced his passion for tales of his father, the artist and novelist George du Maurier, and every walk from their new home became for the girls a lesson in family history. Gerald was extremely proud of his father, of his ability both as an artist (he illustrated the work of Hardy and Henry James as well as being a famous *Punch* cartoonist) and as a writer. The three novels his father had written – *Peter Ibbetson*, *Trilby* (introducing Svengali), and *The Martians* – were adored by Gerald and he never tired of talking of them. The girls listened

9

dutifully but at that stage were rather bored by all this emphasis on the past. Family meant to them, as to all children, those who were alive and who featured in their everyday existence. Grandparents came first and contrasted strongly with one another. Their paternal grandfather, about whom they heard so much, was dead, but their paternal grandmother, Emma du Maurier, was alive and a touch formidable. The girls called her 'Big Granny', because she was tall and majestic. They had lunch with her at her flat in Portman Mansions once a week, but, although she was always kind to them, they were in awe of her black clothes and the little lace cap on her head. Visits to her were formal and a little tense, whereas those to their maternal grandparents were quite the opposite.

By the time Gerald had moved his family to Hampstead, the Beaumonts had also moved to nearby Golders Green, so convenient for grandchildren to visit. Daphne in particular loved to go and stay the weekend at 45 Woodstock Avenue, where everything was so humble, quite markedly different from the splendours of Cannon Hall. This was a large Queen Anne house, only a hundred yards from Hampstead Heath, with a small courtyard in front and an enormous walled garden at the back from which there were magnificent views over the whole of London. The house was imposing but not austere, pleasantly rambling in character, though rather formally decorated and furnished by Muriel. Part of the attraction of the tiny Woodstock Avenue house where Daphne's maternal grandparents lived was its ordinariness. It was one in a row of new semi-detached houses, with the railway line running along nearby, and seemed like part of Toytown with everything on a small scale. Daphne liked, too, her grandparents' routine, such a contrast to the excitement and glamour which so often filled Cannon Hall. Her grandfather did little except potter about and listen to the wireless while her grandmother baked and sewed and shopped in Golders Green High Street without the help of any of the servants needed to run Cannon Hall.[5] Daphne liked to go shopping with her for everyday necessities and was curiously content to play on her own in the tiny back garden and sleep on a camp-bed in her Aunt Billie's room.

But then Daphne, alone of the three du Maurier girls, had a

fascination with lives different from her own. She had a great rapport with the Cannon Hall servants and her curiosity amused them. Dorothy Sheppard, who started work as a between-maid soon after the du Mauriers bought Cannon Hall, was rather startled by Daphne's eager interest in her. Only sixteen herself, Dorothy came straight from her home in a village near Sandringham to the imposing Hampstead house, half-terrified by the prospect. But within a week she was counting herself lucky and had decided she could not have landed anywhere better. Not only did she like all the other five servants, but she thought the family 'lovely', especially ten-year-old Daphne. Dorothy slept in the night nursery with Daphne and six-year-old Jeanne, and was from the first plagued with questions about her family, her home, her village, about how she felt, was she lonely? . . . Daphne could hardly wait for the light to be put out before subjecting Dorothy to an inquisition. Once Dor, as she was known, had begun walking out with Jack, the boy who brought the fish from Nockles, the questioning became more searching: did Jack hold Dor's hand, did he kiss her, and if he did what did it feel like and what was going to happen next? This was the same child who shrank from facing visitors, who had to be persuaded to talk to them, who seemed always ill at ease in company, but then that was precisely the difference: with Dor, with her Beaumont grandparents, Daphne did not need to perform. She did not feel she was being examined and scrutinized, her remarks analysed and pronounced upon so disconcertingly. To these people she was able to be herself without worrying about being found wanting or thought curious: they sensed nothing strange about her. But to those many others who visited Cannon Hall, particularly the theatrical crowd, she did seem 'odd'. Clever, yes. Pretty, certainly. Talented, possibly. But silent, watchful and, most peculiar of all in that household, *shy*.

It was the kind of shyness most frequently misunderstood, especially by Gerald's friends. If young Daphne had blushed and trembled and looked appealingly nervous then she would have caused no comment, but instead her shyness came out as haughtiness, her chin held aggressively in the air, her mouth set, and she would glare and toss her head with what was mistaken as defiance.

Her eyes, which were a startlingly clear blue, were beautiful, but they were apt to appear hostile and when she looked away, as she frequently did through embarrassment, she could seem sly. The contrast with her sisters was marked. Angela was direct and extremely sociable, and Jeanne, the baby, although also quite shy, was used to being petted and cooed over. Taken to their father's dressing-room at the theatre, as they so often were, Angela was in her element, Jeanne happy to accept attention, but Daphne hated it. Gerald's dressing-room was always full, she felt, of 'gushing fools' whom even as a child she despised. It needed only one voice to cry 'Oh, the darlings' to freeze her with horror. She would be struck dumb backstage, hating the atmosphere there as much as she loved it front-of-house. She found herself suddenly clumsy, knocking things over and behaving in general like some Lower School boy.[6]

She wished often that she was a boy, not only because, like so many young girls throughout the ages, she envied the greater freedom and opportunities of a boy's life, but because she and her sisters were well aware how passionately their father had longed for a son to carry on the du Maurier name. Gerald's obsession with family grew stronger with every year, and after his only brother, Guy, was killed in action in 1915, leaving no children, he knew he was the last of the male line.[7] He did not in the least regard his daughters as being of the 'wrong' sex – daughters were the thing – but, like his parents, he would have liked two sons as well as three daughters. After the birth of Jeanne, his disappointment developed and, since this in no way affected his love for his girls, he was able to be perfectly open about it. All three daughters wished their beloved father could have had a son to make him happy, and Daphne wished it most of all. She was the one most like Gerald himself and could imagine herself as the boy he had been. She did not look like him, but relatives noticed not only that she walked and moved in the way Gerald did but that she shared his quick thinking. There was an empathy between the two of them which was quite unmistakable.

This was certainly something Gerald acknowledged himself. He wrote a poem to her:[8]

My very slender one
So brave of heart, but delicate of will,
So careful not to wound, never kill,
My tender one –
Who seems to live in Kingdoms all her own
In realms of joy
Where heroes young and old
In climates hot and cold
Do deeds of daring and much fame
And she knows she could do the same
If only she'd been born a boy.
And sometimes in the silence of the night
I wake and think perhaps my darling's right
And that she should have been,
And, if I'd had my way,
She would have been, a boy.

My very slender one
So feminine and fair, so fresh and sweet,
So full of fun and womanly deceit.
My tender one
Who seems to dream her life away alone.
A dainty girl
But always well attired
And loves to be admired
Wherever she may be, and wants
To be the being who enchants
Because she has been born a girl.
And sometimes in the turmoil of the day
I pause, and think my darling may
Be one of those who will
For good or ill
Remain a girl for ever and be still
A Girl.

It was a confused message for a girl to interpret: on the one hand her father seemed to be expressing strong regret that she was not a boy, and to be telling her she was more suited to being a boy than a girl, and on the other to be rejoicing in her femininity, so long as she never grew up. In her own mind Daphne had no doubts: everything about being a boy appealed to her more. She hated dressing as a girl while she was growing up and most of the time did not do so. She and Jeanne wore boys' shorts and shirts and ties and thick schoolboy socks and shoes – they liked to dress *exactly* as boys in an era when young girls did not wear trousers. She hated having her hair put in ringlets and having it endlessly brushed and was quick to adopt a short bob as soon as she had any choice. Her alter ego, 'Eric Avon',[9] in whom she believed implicitly, went to Rugby and was bold and fearless and did all the things she would have done if she had been a boy. In a family where flights of fancy, and fantasy, were positively encouraged, there was no objection to Daphne's passion for all things masculine. But the truth was that even clad in the most boyish of clothes and doing the most boyish of things Daphne looked indisputably and very fetchingly feminine. She was always a little girl playing at being a boy with no confusion whatsoever possible in the eye of any beholder. It was all rather charming and nobody was disturbed, nobody realized quite how much Daphne genuinely hated being a girl.

What her family also did not realize, and this was much more serious, was that Daphne actually convinced herself she *was* a boy. Her outward form was a mistake: inside, she was a boy, with a boy's mind and heart and ambitions.[10] Everything she did, she did as she judged a boy would do. This made the onset of puberty at twelve absolutely devastating for her. It was for the first time impossible for her to be a boy once menstruation had begun. The shock was profound and she took a long time to recover. She hated her periods – given the code name 'Robert' – and saw them as signifying 'the end of being boyish'. The level of her distress was so acute that she retreated even more into her fantasy world, the one place she was truly happy. The only person who recognized how fiercely Daphne resented her own gender was her governess, Miss Maud Waddell, who came into the du Maurier household in 1918 when Daphne was eleven. Maud was a Cumbrian, born at Head's Nook near Carlisle in 1887, and was as far from being a timid, subservient governess figure as it was possible to be. She came from a comfortably off family, of some standing in the area where they lived, and had been well educated at the Carlisle and County High School for Girls. Maud had a great desire to travel and after a brief spell teaching took herself off to Paris where she suddenly decided to train as a milliner. She served her apprenticeship with a Madame Paulette and then, with equal suddenness, went to Australia to visit her sister Winifred who had emigrated. But Maud disliked Australia and returned to England where she found lodgings in Hampstead and a job as governess to the du Maurier girls.

Daphne was from the beginning greatly intrigued by the new governess, who quickly, du Maurier fashion, became known as 'Tod'.[11] Tod was a strong character who talked a lot and had decided opinions. Since she had never been trained as a teacher her methods were a little haphazard, but she was a naturally disciplined person and very firm with her pupils. She was appalled by Daphne's handwriting and particularly by her spelling – both gave her sleepless nights – but impressed by her wide reading. The best thing about Tod, from Daphne's point of view, was her love of literature and her ability to feed her with the right books at the right time. They read Browning together and Keats and Shelley and then moved on to more difficult poets – Donne, Dryden, Swinburne. Tod was very much the teacher, with no taste for familiarity, but this was what appealed to her young pupil. Daphne hated people who were anxious to curry favour or who showed too great a desire to be friendly. She preferred those who were clearly independent and could not care less whether they were going to be liked, were even a touch aloof and critical. Tod's direct, confident manner, and the fact that she had been fairly adventurous in her thirty-one years, were all marks in her favour and within a very short time Daphne was devoted to her. The age gap of twenty years was immense, but then a younger governess would have lacked the authority Daphne craved.

The relationship with Tod was the first, outside family relationships, which Daphne developed and it was very important to her. The letters she wrote to Tod from family holidays were confessional in nature, revealing a great need to express herself to someone she could trust and who understood her. From Birchington-on-Sea, where the joint du Maurier and Freddy Lonsdale[12] families holidayed when she was thirteen, Daphne wrote to Tod of how she had been unable to bear being part of a big gang and had gone off on her own for long walks, which had led to scoldings, because she was presumed lost. She felt restless and discontented and did not even have a good book to console her. She'd been reduced to a 'soppy book' from which she quoted a sentence to show her disgust at 'romantic slush' ('One glimpse only had she of his eyes and it was as if she was looking into the deep, deep heart of the fire unquenchable'). She longed to be off on a European Grand Tour just with Tod – 'we would live in a Bohemian way (baths, of course), talk French and you'd do a lot of painting.[13] I think I should take up writing or poetry!! Life might be romantic in Rome.' It was certainly far from romantic in Birchington-on-Sea, where the popular playwright Freddy Lonsdale and Gerald played energetic games and forced their daughters to compete with each other. 'Life is a curious problem', wrote Daphne soulfully to Tod, 'and always will be. One is so selfish about one's own happiness . . . I have become an idealist, realism is so earthy and sometimes sordid – very often in fact.'

From another holiday venue Daphne wrote to Tod, feeling even more disillusioned: 'You don't know how I long to have a good talk with you and pour everything out. I never tell anyone anything and there is no one to talk to. I must be an awful rotter, as we have a ripping time always and no kids could be more indulged and made more fuss of, yet I long for something so terribly and I don't know what it is. The feeling is always there and I don't think I shall ever find it. It is no good telling the others things like that, they would only laugh . . . everyone thinks I am moody and tiresome . . . I really don't know why I feel like this. People say I am acid and bitter . . . it's terrible at my age to get bored with life.' She was echoing her father's restlessness without realizing it and, since she was so extremely sensitive to his moods, it is always possible she was reflecting them and not simply suffering from teenage *Angst*. What made these feelings worse was that Angela never seemed to suffer from them. Angela adored the 'ripping time', lapped up the travelling and parties, and was enjoying the crushes she had, usually on actors. Daphne was disapproving of these – 'Angela's got a crush on Ronald Pertwee,' she told Tod, 'she is quite hopeless over crushes.'

Daphne herself was wary of crushes. She permitted herself 'a sort of crush' on Ivor Novello, whom she and Angela had met backstage after a performance of *Betrothal*, but her only real admiration was reserved for Gladys Cooper. It was often remarked that Daphne bore a startling resemblance to Gladys, and encouraged by this she used to 'work up in my mind that I *was* her daughter, smuggled at birth into Mummy's care (except that Mummy would never have stood for it)'.[14] But it was the done thing to have a crush on some male actor, so for a while she fixed on Basil Rathbone until the development of a genuine crush wiped him from her memory. This crush, when it hit her, was something more serious.

When Daphne was fourteen and on another family holiday she was suddenly and violently attracted to her thirty-six-year-old cousin Geoffrey Millar, who had joined the du Mauriers, together with his second wife. Geoffrey held her hand and she felt, for the first time, a physical thrill which she identified immediately as quite different from any feeling she had had before – dangerous, exciting, having little to do with schoolgirl crushes. What disturbed her most was the confusion between the physical and the emotional: she felt towards Geoffrey something like and yet quite different from what she felt towards her father. Her reaction was to be both elated but also a little frightened. For a long time, as she had written to Tod more than once, she had been searching for something nameless and now she wondered if this was 'it', and if 'it' was love. But she was controlled and analytical in her response to Geoffrey, and most alert to the effect his attentions to her had on Gerald. Even before this holiday she had noted and seemed to relish her father's agitation if she appeared attracted to any man or boy. Once, on holiday in Dieppe, she wrote to Tod that there had been 'a young French officer, who I see on the front every day . . . Daddy thinks he is an awful bounder and I pretend I like him very much just to annoy him'.

In the case of his nephew Geoffrey Millar, Gerald had every right to be alarmed. Geoffrey had a reputation, established in his own adolescence, for being dangerously attractive to women and taking great advantage of this. He treated his women badly once he had lost interest in them and, though his charm and good looks made him popular, everyone in the family was well aware how far he could go. Gerald, knowing of his history, watched him not as he had watched the harmless French sailor, but with real dread. It was no good assuring himself that Geoffrey would surely never even think of seducing young Daphne: nobody could be sure what Geoffrey would or would not be capable of. Nor, for that matter, could anyone know how Daphne herself would respond. She had a great desire to be *daring*, as Gerald knew, and might, at her tender age, prove more susceptible to the kind of flattery, not to mention expertise, Geoffrey could subtly employ. Both of them had a streak of wildness in them, shared the 'devil' that Gerald knew to be in himself. The potential for catastrophe was there. 'I am feeling rather depressed at the moment,' Daphne wrote to Tod, 'I am always having rows with the parents. The latest is about Geoffrey . . . Daddy overhears certain conversations, the rest I leave to your imagination.' When Geoffrey left to return to London, Gerald was vastly relieved, not knowing that Dorothy Sheppard, the maid, carried notes between Daphne and Geoffrey when she made the journey backwards and forwards from Cannon Hall during the holidays. Once Geoffrey had gone, Daphne turned to Swinburne's poetry for consolation and found a verse in *The Garden of Prosperine* which summed up what she felt (it begins: 'I'm tired of tears . . .'). It was, she wrote to Tod, 'foul' for a girl her age to be in such a state.

Her sexual awakening – and that is what it was, even though Geoffrey had only held her hand – left her more dissatisfied with life than ever. 'The future', she announced to Tod, 'is always such a complete blank. There is nothing ahead that lures me terribly . . . If only I was a man.' And yet even as she wrote this, she wondered why on earth she wanted to be a man when 'I like women much better than men'. She was coming to the conclusion nevertheless that 'I may as well run the race with the rest of the pack instead of being a damned solitary hound missing the game'. But 'the game' itself she was beginning to believe was primarily about sex, and playing this game with a vengeance was her own father. Sex, she now knew, did not take place only within marriage, but she was not sure whether it had anything to do with love either. 'Daddy says love is the only thing worth while,' she wrote to Tod, 'real, ceaseless love. I don't know.' For years she and her sisters had heard Gerald mock those young actresses who made up his 'stable', and though it had always seemed such fun she was, at almost fifteen, less sure. She watched Gerald carefully – became 'beady', in du Maurier code – noting his flirtatious behaviour and her mother's apparent indifference, and wondered. 'Father has been playing golf with Eileen,' she told Tod, adding, 'she likes him, doesn't she?' She set Gerald little tests and reported to Tod the result. One arose from reading Somerset Maugham's volume of short stories, *The Trembling of a Leaf*, especially one story, 'Rain'. This is the story about a missionary who reforms and converts a prostitute only to succumb to her himself. 'It had', wrote Daphne, 'finished men forever in my eyes,' but she gave it to Gerald to read and invited his comments. Predictably Gerald was 'horrified . . . said it was terribly *pas pour les jeunes filles*'. Daphne agreed it was 'foul'. What she thought foul was the missionary's lust, his inability to resist sex, and what she saw in her father's life was the same inability to resist young actresses. If 'the stable' really was kept for sex, where did that leave love, and most of all where did it leave Mo?

Her mother's attitude puzzled Daphne. She could not understand, at that stage of her life, how her mother could seem to love her father so much, and be loved by him, and yet know, as she must, how unfaithful he was to her. She watched her mother and saw no sign of anger or distress. This made her think that what this might signify was that sex itself was unimportant – her parents could love each other without it. If this were so – and she was by no means convinced it was – then it surely made marriage a sham. But this did not make sense to her either: Gerald and Muriel's marriage was clearly not a sham but very real and enduring. It was all very confusing and so was her mother's treatment of her. She felt not only unloved by Mo but actively disliked. She craved her affection, the same affection she saw given to her sisters, particularly Jeanne, and did not receive it. The lack of it inhibited her and drove her further into herself. Gerald, she knew, did love her and gave her all the affection she wanted, and which was not available from Mo, but this now only added to her confusion.

Disturbed by her own newly recognized sexuality, and puzzled about her father's, Daphne was still at this stage very close to Gerald. In public, people saw his pride in her grow all the time. She went to the Eton and Harrow cricket match with him, to first nights, to lunch at famous restaurants and hotels and occasionally (because she was not yet officially old enough) to dances. Daphne loved to dance, losing all her social inhibitions once she was on the dance floor, especially if the dance were a foxtrot. 'When I hear a foxtrot I go mad for want of dancing,' she wrote to Tod. Dancing was the only form of socializing she relished and when her parents gave a dance at the Piccadilly Hotel, during the Christmas season of 1921, Daphne, aged only fourteen but allowed to attend as a special favour, was ecstatic. She took part in a tableau with Ellen Terry 'and my adorable Gladys', and enjoyed herself thoroughly. Her life that night seemed privileged in the right kind of way and when, soon after this event, she read Katherine Mansfield's *Bliss and Other Stories* she found they filled her with 'a helpless pity for the dreariness of other people's lives . . . a sort of feeling life is merely repetition and monotony'. She appreciated how fortunate she was that her own life was so varied and exciting, and yet could not work out why her good luck did not make her happier, why she always seemed to appear ungrateful when she was not.

The measure of contentment she did have was shattered at the end of that year when Tod left to take up an exciting sounding new post as governess to the children of a Sultan, Prince Abdul Madjid, in Constantinople. Almost as soon as she had departed, Tod was begged to return by Daphne, who wrote, 'I miss you awfully, sweetest.' Tod's departure was like an act of betrayal and, though Daphne could well understand her governess's desire to travel again, she did not like to think this was preferable to being with her at Cannon Hall. In fact, though Daphne lost a close confidante – except, of course, by correspondence, which was continual – she did gain something from Tod's desertion. Miss Vigo, the new governess, lived, as Tod had done, in lodgings nearby, but was in many ways a better teacher. 'Vigo . . . is not bad', Daphne reported grudgingly, 'but different.' She was not a kindred spirit and their relationship was formal. To her annoyance, Daphne was set French homework out of the *Oxford Junior*, a standard she felt she had long since passed, but not in Miss Vigo's opinion. It was difficult to settle down with someone new, not only from the teaching point of view but because, without Tod, she had no close friend. Angela, three years older and a debutante, had many friends of her own, and Jeanne, aged eleven, went to school locally and was part of a quite different world. But to Jeanne's schoolfriends, Daphne was a figure not of pathos, wandering about on her own, always with a pencil stuck behind her ear in case she had a sudden urge to write, but of awe. She looked haughty and rather fierce.

Her urge to write was known about by her family and encouraged but not at this stage taken seriously even by Daphne herself. She reported to Tod that her spare time, without Tod to talk to, was 'taken up with writing a book. It's great fun. It is about a boy who is searching for happiness, at least not exactly happiness, but that something that is somewhere, you know. You feel it and you miss it and it beckons and you can't reach it . . . I don't think anyone can find it on this earth.' The book she mentioned was a story she called 'The Seekers'. She wrote it in a beautiful Italian sketch book which fastened with dark green ribbons. The writing, in ink, is her very best effort, incomparably superior to her normal scrawl in letters, and covers twenty-six of the large folio pages. As a piece of juvenilia, 'The Seekers' is impressive but its autobiographical significance is greater. Into this tale of a boy called Maurice, aged six at the beginning, Daphne worked all the *angst* about which she wrote to Tod: Maurice is clearly herself. It was an obvious, even crude, device: if she wrote about a boy she felt free to write about herself.

Maurice, who 'began to think' at six, has problems. The first is his Nurse, who thinks Maurice is 'soft-headed'. Maurice doesn't laugh at things others find funny, such as the clowns at the circus. Instead, he laughs when Nurse slips on orange-peel and crashes to the ground hurting herself. But a bigger problem is the lack of a father. Maurice's father is dead. His mother – bearing no resemblance whatsoever to Daphne's own mother – pines not for her dead husband but for another man she once loved, called Tommy.

It is hard to see the direction the story is going to take until the day Maurice gets lost and is befriended by 'the man with the pipe'. He has merry brown eyes and thrills Maurice by telling him: 'You are a lonely traveller in mexico [sic] who has lost his way in a terrific storm. You have come to me for shelter and do not know I am a brigand who will take your life.' They play this game for hours then the man takes Maurice home. Later, on holiday, Maurice's mother meets him and the story ends with their reunion: the man is Tommy, her long lost lover. Tommy is forty but 'it didn't matter very much ... you see, he'd never grown up'. Even his daughter, Maurice's age, is said to be 'in reality' years older than her father. Tommy, who sounds exactly like Gerald (though physically like J. M. Barrie), is described with great affection as a show-off, brilliant at imaginary games, but also with a slight edge of contempt. Maurice, although he loves him, sees through him – 'he was like a very little boy', like Peter Pan in fact, about whom his mother told him stories.

The influence of J. M. Barrie in this first story was strong. Barrie was 'Uncle Jim' to the du Maurier girls just as he was to the Llewelyn Davies boys, their cousins, for whom he had written *Peter Pan*. He and Gerald were great friends[15] and he was in the habit of coming home with him to play with the girls in the nursery. Daphne not only liked Uncle Jim but identified totally with his creation of fantasy lives. His imaginary islands and woods, which featured so heavily in the stories he told the children, were real places to her and she had no difficulty at all in matching his invention. But what gives this little tale merit as a literary effort is the feeling for landscape. Maurice loves to be alone, beside the sea, where there was 'no sound of roaring traffic nor the sight of dingy chimney pots and wet grey roofs'. He runs barefoot on the sand and lies for hours listening 'to the winds [which] whispered of romance and strange tumultous [sic] seas where bleak lands lie'. There is a real feeling of the sea evoked and his pleasure in it – 'Oh! The never-ending glory of the day in such a place!' Maurice, in this story, does not find what he is seeking nor does he identify what it is.

In the same letter to Tod in which Daphne mentions this book she is trying to write, she repeats that she herself is searching for something, but does not know what exactly. Once, she had thought it was love, but now she had decided 'it isn't love or anything like that'. What she suffered from was that familiar adolescent yearning to give some meaning to life, that sense of a lack of purpose which can drive sensitive teenagers mad. Over and over she asked herself the question 'What am I going to do with my life?' It was not enough to reply: 'Live – enjoy the easy, good time given to you.' But that was the point: she hardly ever *did* enjoy these good times. Her own restlessness both disgusted and frightened her. She observed Angela becoming increasingly religious, heard her voice her growing attraction to Roman Catholicism, but she knew that was not the answer for her, any more than it was for her father. 'Angela', she told Tod, 'is emotional and sentimental. I am matter-of-fact and hate sloppiness.' 'Churches', she reasoned, 'would never comfort me' (though she did not reject religion itself, stating she was not an atheist).

All this introspection exhausted her but she could not help it. She told Tod her absorption in herself nauseated her – 'I only think of myself and pity anyone who likes me.' So far as she could judge, few people did. She felt Angela and Jeanne were popular, but she was not, and they both appeared to her to relish their lives. Angela, in particular, always seemed to be having fun and was surrounded by other girls, also enjoying life as débutantes, who were in a permanent state of excitement about who was engaged to be married. This brought forth all the seventeen-year-old Daphne's scorn – she might long to have friends but she certainly had no yearning to be engaged or married. 'Tod, have you noticed', she wrote indignantly, '(I think it is vile) that if one marries it's considered awful if one doesn't do it thoroughly (you know what I mean) and yet if one does certain things without being married it's considered awful too. Surely that's narrow-minded and disgusting. Either the act of – er – well, you know, is Right or Wrong. A wedding ring can't change facts. An illegitimate child is looked upon as a sort of "freak" or "unnatural specimen", whereas a child whose parents are married is wholesome and decent. Yet they both came into the world by the same means, they weren't conjured up by a wedding ring.' She wanted Tod to agree with her that it was ridiculous for people to say, on the one hand, 'Isn't it lovely, so-and-so is married' and yet on the other 'My dear, have you heard, so-and-so is living with some man.' Both people, she fumed, were doing exactly the same thing, 'yet one is praised, the other banned. It is extraordinary.' The hypocrisy of it all revolted her, and into this revulsion came doubts about her own father. He was married, and loved his wife and children, and yet, as she now knew, 'things went on' with other women.

Naturally, with her head full of such thoughts and her behaviour sullen, Daphne was often difficult to live with. Her parents never openly criticized her but, on the contrary, did everything possible to occupy and amuse her and in spite of some arguments remained long-suffering and concerned. What became obvious to them was that their middle daughter needed a life other than the one they indulgently offered her, and they broached the idea of a finishing school abroad. Angela had already been to a French finishing school and had not been happy, but since Daphne was very unlike her sister it was felt this might almost be a recommendation. In the spring of 1925, just before Daphne's eighteenth birthday, arrangements were made for her to go to Camposena, a village near Meudon, outside Paris, to a school run by a Miss Wicksteed, with Doodie Millar, another girl the same age. This met with Daphne's enthusiastic approval. It was not the thought of going to finishing school which attracted her so much as being near Paris, which she had visited on holiday with her family once and had adored. She was sure she would be able to find ways of getting to know Paris, perhaps even of finding that nameless 'something' she was conscious of looking for.

Chapter Two

'Life is queer,' Daphne wrote to Tod, soon after she arrived at Camposena.[1] 'I can't make it out, I worry about things here that wouldn't occur to me at home, and vice versa.' Among the things she worried about was her own standing. At home, and in the circles in which the du Maurier family moved, she had never had any doubts about her own position. At Camposena, one of twenty-five girls, and together with Doodie the newest, she felt displaced. Most of the girls were English, with one or two Poles and Canadians, and so they knew what the du Maurier name stood for, but this gave Daphne little prestige. Nearly all the girls were the daughters of people of note, and the daughter of an actor-manager, even the most famous one of all, and one recently knighted, was nothing special. All her young life Daphne had thought she disliked her father's fame, and the attention it brought her, but now she discovered with something of a shock that she loathed being virtually anonymous. What also worried her was that her French was not as good as she had believed, and she was deeply insulted by being put into the third of four classes.

Another unpleasant surprise, and rather a rude awakening, was the discomfort of the school. Daphne liked to think she despised luxury – but then, to her, hot baths on demand and warm beds and a fire in her bedroom were necessities. In her first letter to her mother from Camposena she had reported how, on the journey over – with Miss Wicksteed herself acting as chaperone for Daphne and Doodie – she had been sure to 'bag the best couch of course and poor old Wicksteed had to lie humped in a tiny space'. Once at Camposena, Miss Wicksteed had her revenge. Daphne was appalled by the cold. The place was 'full of weird conservatories' which were freezing and her bedroom was 'bare and very cold just like a servant's, and the drawers creak'. During the first week she did exercises to warm up before getting into bed wearing her fur coat. She had not slept because 'cocks seemed to crow all night and the clock chimed every quarter of an hour'. Getting up in the mornings she was horrified that she was expected to wash in cold water and that the wash-basin was cracked. With dismay, she discovered girls had to make their own beds, some-thing she had no idea how to do and had no intention of learning. Using all her du Maurier charm she soon had 'a nice girl in the next room' making hers. She didn't like the food – 'I scarcely eat anything without wanting to retch' – but acknowledged this might be her own fault for being 'too faddy' and that really the food was perfectly palatable. But the biggest deprivation, worse than the lack of home comforts, was that she was only allowed to walk on her own in the not very extensive grounds of the school. It was quite a pretty garden, with statues in odd corners, but she felt confined in it. Wandering round it when she arrived she felt curiously depressed and it took a telegram from Gladys Cooper – 'Fondest love darling, thinking of you, Glads' – to cheer her up.

It was her first experience of any kind of institutional living, of being part of any community other than her family. Most of the girls had come on to Camposena after boarding school and were used to all the things so disturbingly new to Daphne. They were also used to relating to one another. Daphne noted, derisively, how most girls went around in twos, 'some soppy, with their arms entwined'. She wrote to her mother that 'I'm a most objectionable girl to the others, I expect, because I make myself pleasant to the mistresses, especially Miss Wick. There's nothing like currying favour if you want things done for you.' She herself always saw through anyone who did that, and despised them accordingly, but she had no hesitation in doing it skilfully, and with great effect, herself. In no time she did indeed get things done: a fire in her bedroom, hot baths, and all on the grounds of precarious health. 'I expect', she wrote blithely to her mother, 'the bill for extras will be huge.' But what currying favour and exerting charm could not change were the rules and the timetable. These, she com-mented, were 'absurd', 'OK for girls from boarding schools' but not for her. It was ridiculous to have to get up at 7.15, report for prayers at 7.50, breakfast at 8, walk or practise music until 9.45 when lessons began, and lunch at the unbelievable hour of midday, and be summoned everywhere by the 'great clashing of bells'. If it had not been for the regular trips to Paris – to the Comédie Française, the Opera, the Louvre, Versailles and so forth – she would not, she wrote, have thought it worth enduring these rules.

Those outings meant everything to her. 'Don't you love Paris?' she enthused to Tod, 'with its cobbled streets, shrieking taxis and wonderful lights and chic little women and dago-like men[2] with broad-brimmed trilby hats? I think that the Place de la Concorde at night, after it's been raining, with all the lights, is too wonderful . . . it's all quite divine.' Paris was where she wanted to be, not stuck in school 'with its petty intrigues and rather narrow outlook' which made it 'boring'. Not completely boring, however. From the moment she arrived Daphne had quickly detected that the teacher who seemed the most powerful was not Miss Wicksteed, so easy to curry favour with, but Mlle Fernande Yvon. At first, she described Mlle Yvon to her mother as 'an alarming old hag'. She noticed how all the other girls seemed to have crushes on this teacher and therefore decided 'I shall avoid her'. She wrote, darkly, 'I know the type, she has favourites,' and it certainly was not in her own character to compete to be a favourite. Within a month, she had reconsidered. It had become obvious to her that, hag or not, Mlle Yvon's approval was vital if one was to have any prestige at all; and prestige, Daphne was mortified to acknowledge, mattered rather more to her than she had ever imagined.

The plain truth was that although she judged most of her fellow pupils as 'brainless types' the few who were not sat at Mlle Yvon's feet. She taught the top class and in the evenings they sat with her, an exclusive little group apart from the rest. It was an indication of how, in spite of being shy, Daphne could also be bold (and force herself to the kind of behaviour most shy people would not be able to contemplate) that one evening she simply took her place with this group though she was not entitled to. Mlle Yvon, amused, and sensing behind the superficial arrogance a great eagerness to be given her due, allowed Daphne to become part of the charmed circle. Soon she was the favourite, a position she greatly enjoyed. She wrote to Tod, 'By the way, I've quite fallen for that woman I told you about, Mlle Yvon. She has a fatal attraction . . . she's absolutely kind of lured me on and now I am coiled in the net.' In case Tod should be in any doubt as to the meaning of this melodramatic announcement she was forthright in her estimate of Mlle Yvon's sexual designs: 'Venetian, I should think' ('Venetian' being du Maurier code for 'lesbian'). 'She pops up to the bedroom at odd moments . . . and is generally divine. She's most seductive when coming back from the opera. I get on the back seat with her and she puts her arm round me and makes me put my head on her shoulder, then sort of presses me! Ugh! it all sounds too sordid and low, but I don't know, it gives one a sort of extra-ordinary thrill! I only hope I haven't got Venetian tendencies.' In fact, 'Venetian tendencies' were precisely what she realized she did have, though the reality was more complex than this. For six years, ever since, at the onset of puberty, she had had to acknow-ledge that there was no escape from being a girl, she had forced herself to lock up in a box the boy she had at heart thought herself to be.[3] Attracted by Mlle Yvon, and feeling herself respond to her advances, she worried not only that she was 'Venetian' but that, after all, she was really a boy. Having 'Venetian tendencies' could only, in her opinion, mean just that: a woman who loved and was physically attracted to another woman *must* really be a man. This scared her and she fought her 'tendencies' hard. She might want to be male but she did *not* want to be 'Venetian'. Her attitudes then were distinctly homophobic and she was repelled at the idea of being associated with homosexuals. The fact that her father despised homosexuals,[4] who he felt were infiltrating the theatre, made her even more frightened of admitting she had any 'Venetian' feelings at all.

The frankness of her letter to Tod illustrates very well Daphne's remarkable ability to stand outside herself and realize exactly what was confusing her. She knew she was not 'in love' with Mlle Yvon, any more than she had been with Cousin Geoffrey, but she acknowledged the sexual implications of both encounters. Her body and her emotions seemed to her, as to many adolescents, quite separate. The strength of her physical reaction to being touched by Geoffrey or Mlle Yvon, even if they only 'sort of press me', surprised and excited her, but she knew that in her mind she felt quite cool and undisturbed. She wrote to Tod that she could see some of the girls were jealous and suspicious of her growing closeness to Mlle Yvon, and this made her uncomfortable, because she knew they were making the wrong assumptions. 'When I next write,' she promised Tod, 'I expect the woman will have entirely dropped me, and I shall be languishing in despair!' But there was no risk of that whether Mlle Yvon dropped her or not. It was all a game with nothing to lose. 'It will be fun,' she assured Tod, 'when I get back for the holidays, imitating everyone here and laughing at it all. Even when I'm feeling most "épris" of Mlle Yvon, there is always something inside me laughing somewhere. I hope I never lose my sense of humour – it's the saving of me here.'

This sense of humour was of the du Maurier variety: mocking, sometimes jeering, often merciless, a touch cruel, and very easily misunderstood by those outside the family circle. Daphne's contemporaries at Camposena were never quite sure whether some of her actions were funny or not. One day, a young curate came out from Paris to give religious instruction to those being prepared for confirmation. It was a hot afternoon and the class was held in the garden. Daphne stood on the fringe, listening avidly. Occasionally she would throw some clever question at the curate, who stammered in reply and found it difficult to cope. Suddenly, Daphne seized a wrought-iron chair and, advancing towards the curate, shouted she was going to bash him on the head and kill him. The young man cowered in front of her and Daphne started to laugh, saying that it was just as she had suspected – he had told them they were all going to Heaven when they died, but when he himself was threatened with death he was afraid. This proved, she laughed, that everything he said, all this promise of life eternal, was rubbish. The girls had hysterics, and Daphne's daring was admired more than ever. But at the same time incidents like this did little to endear her to the others and she continued, though not unhappily, to be without close friends except for Doodie with whom she had arrived and who soon had new friends of her own. Certainly no one at Camposena thought of her as the shy girl she believed herself to be. On the contrary, the other girls, while admiring Daphne's beauty – she was slim, blonde and strikingly attractive – never for one moment thought her solitary state was anything but her own choice. They saw no element of nervousness in her and had no idea how much it had cost her to force herself into Mlle Yvon's circle.

Originally, the plan had been that Daphne would spend only a term at Camposena but she stayed for three. This was entirely due to her growing dependence on Mlle Yvon who, by the end of that first term, had become 'Ferdy'. When the school closed in July at the end of Daphne's second term, for the long summer vacation, she was given permission to accept Ferdy's invitation to accompany her to La Bourboule, in the Puy-de-Dôme, a quiet place in the Massif Central where Ferdy herself was going to take a 'cure'. Daphne had always loved and thrived in the country and it would, both parents judged, be as good for her health as for her teacher's. Muriel in particular had it firmly fixed in her head that Daphne was delicate and needed building up. She was far too thin and had regular bouts of bronchitis which were always worrying and suspected of being something more sinister. They were sorry Daphne would not be with them on their own family tour of northern Italy, but rather impressed that she had chosen instead what sounded like a studious vacation.

The holiday with Ferdy was on the surface every bit as studious as it seemed. Daphne read almost the entire day, every day. What she read were the short stories of Katherine Mansfield and Maupassant (both in French and in translation). Katherine Mansfield influenced her enormously – she told Tod she probably would not have thought about trying to write at all if it had not been for reading her – but since coming to Camposena, Maupassant had become her greater love. The only diversion other than reading was taking the funicular up to Charlannes and having tea there. Otherwise, she wrote letters to her family and Tod, and talked to Ferdy.

Talking to Ferdy was not like talking to Tod. Ferdy was thirty to Daphne's eighteen, and therefore the gap in age was not so great, and though not attractive, any more than Tod was physically attractive, she had an allure lacking in the down-to-earth English governess. Her charm was tremendous and her personality flamboyant – she had a giggly sense of humour and a most seductive way of talking in her heavily accented but perfect English. But what intrigued Daphne most about Ferdy was wondering how much of a poseur her sophisticated teacher was. She listened carefully, much more carefully than Ferdy realized, to all the tales told of her past life and she thought she detected hollow notes. Ferdy was extremely fond of insinuation – she would drop hints of certain exciting events in her background – but Daphne had not been reading so much fiction without picking up a thing or two. Some of Ferdy's innuendoes were decidedly novelettish and, though she never challenged her teacher, Daphne privately had her doubts. Although from the first, as she had told Tod, she was sure Ferdy was 'Venetian', she noted that references to male lovers who had died or been killed dramatically were frequently made. Why, she wondered, did Ferdy do this? Was it to make her pupil feel safe? Was it just boasting? Was it a desire to pretend she was not a lesbian? Was it to make herself seem more interesting? Daphne was not sure, but all that holiday she was absorbing everything Ferdy said and filing it away to mull over afterwards. Never, at any time, was she so infatuated with Ferdy that her innate scepticism deserted her. Ferdy had secrets, she put on a great performance, but until she had fathomed both, Daphne reserved judgement. What she did not reserve judgement on was Ferdy's attraction for her. The boy was out of the box and in love and, though she kept this hidden from all but Ferdy herself, she felt the greatest sense of relief imaginable. She loved Ferdy, and was loved by her, 'in every conceivable way',[5] and, though she intended to conceal this from her family, it gave her a new happiness and joy.

Once back at Cannon Hall for the rest of the holidays, she was more content than she had been for a long time. Her family were delighted to find her more appreciative both of home life and of the social opportunities it offered, which she had previously scorned. She went with her father, quite willingly, on the kind of visits she had always loathed. She and Gerald went to Trent Park, the home of Philip Sassoon, a wealthy patron of the arts, for a weekend. 'Ha! Ha!' she joked to Tod, 'it's dollars gets me! he's terribly attractive, most oriental (you'd probably shudder!) the sort of person that ought to lay on [sic] divans and have naked black girls to dance before him – and – er! – that's not all!! Anyway, he fascinated me.' He also gave her more of those 'strange thrills' she had already felt, and in the light of her love for Ferdy she was nervous of what else this told her about herself. She played tennis – Gerald was an indefatigable tennis player – with 'Russian princes and English earls' and generally led, for once, the life of the socialites she despised. Half of her descriptions were clearly for Tod's benefit – Tod was a great snob – and consequently exaggerated, but there was no mistaking her genuine enjoyment. It might sound as if, at eighteen, she was now more sophisticated, but in the same letter mention of her note to the actress Gwen Farrer – 'Dear Gwen, I think you are quite perfect' – gave the opposite impression. She confessed to Tod that she was worried Gwen might show it to someone and they might 'think things', but that was a risk she was prepared to take, because 'life's no fun, unless there's a danger in it'. Considering the real 'danger' she was running in her affair with Ferdy, expressing 'a pash' for Gwen Farrer was mild in the extreme.

The summer of 1925 was not just devoted to socializing. Tod was treated to several accounts of how Daphne had been 'really trying' to write and discovering she lacked the necessary application. What she was trying to write, and had been doing so intermittently since she wrote 'The Seekers' at fifteen, were short stories inspired by her three favourite short story writers, Maugham, Mansfield and Maupassant. She found it easy enough to select her subject matter, and even to decide how to begin and end – the plot of a story came to her complete – but the difficulty lay in executing her intention. Story after story remained unfinished in spite of Aunt Billie's lending her a typewriter and heavy encouragement from Gerald. She wished, sometimes, she had never mentioned she was trying to write, especially when she no longer seemed to be able to complete anything. 'I try to write,' she told Tod, 'but I find it boring.' Thinking of the story was absorbing, the actual writing of it too laborious to appeal. By the time she returned to Camposena in September she had not one story finished to her satisfaction.

That last term was a disaster. The autumn mists which enveloped the school made it look mysterious in the way Daphne liked, but they were not good for anyone with a tendency to chest colds. In the spring, Daphne had found the place cold enough but now, at the beginning of winter, she found it almost intolerable. Her appetite, never good, faded and she ate frighteningly little. In spite of all the 'extras', her special exemption from the worst rigours of the school, she became ill with influenza and had not the resistance to throw it off. The matron was alarmed, the parents informed, and they, who had always panicked over every minor illness of any of their daughters, arranged for a chest specialist to come out from Paris to examine Daphne. A spot on the lung was diagnosed, to Gerald and Muriel's alarm. Their instinct was to have Daphne brought home at once, but they were told it would be unwise for her to make the Channel crossing. Instead, she was moved to Paris, to the luxurious Crillon Hotel, where an American friend of the du Mauriers was living at the time. She offered to supervise the care and medical treatment Daphne needed.

There followed a period of several weeks in which Daphne languished in the grand surroundings of one of Paris's most opulent hotels, receiving treatment more appropriate to the previous century. It was a mixture of sal volatile injections, deep heat and a bizarre diet, none of which are demonstrably beneficial to someone with a spot on the lung. Daphne cried a great deal (which was very unlike her), half from weakness and half from boredom. Visits from Ferdy, for which she pleaded, helped a little but not enough. By December, Muriel du Maurier had had enough of Daphne's tear-stained letters and of her friend's reports of the lack of progress in her recovery. Accompanied by the fourteen-year-old Jeanne, she travelled to Paris herself and, as well as seeing her daughter and the doctor, inevitably encountered Ferdy. This meeting worried Daphne greatly. Up to then, Ferdy had been hers entirely, but now she would be scrutinized by her mother, and Daphne knew Muriel to be shrewd: if she sized up Ferdy and suspected anything, then the friendship would be abruptly terminated. Fortunately, Muriel gave her approval, and even welcomed the suggestion that, after spending Christmas at home, Daphne should return to Paris for more treatment and this time live in a small hotel near the doctor's clinic with Ferdy supervising her until the start of the Camposena term. Should Daphne not be fully recovered by then, Angela could come over to replace Ferdy. But whatever happened, Daphne herself would not be returning to school: she was now 'finished'.

No one was more aware of this than Daphne herself. She saw 1926 as a crucial year in her life and dreaded it. There could be no more pretending, if she wanted to do something with her life. She could not bear to think of resuming the old routine of before Camposena on a permanent basis – it was all very well to enjoy the social round while on holiday, but the prospect of making it her life appalled her. Her illness was real, but she knew it was providing her with an excuse to carry on in the indulgent way encouraged by her parents and she was determined to reject this. The return to Paris in the New Year was a relief, and so was the realization that, thanks more to Ferdy's care of her than the doctor's injections, she was getting better; but her anxiety about her own future increased. She loved Paris, but how could she justify staying there? She was doomed, at the end of January, to go back to Cannon Hall and then there would be no escape. A kind of self-disgust at the thought of the pampered existence which lay ahead of her set in. She wanted to reject it but had nothing to put in its place. Nobody needed to tell her how lucky she was – she knew it – but what nobody guessed at was how, knowing she was so privileged, she felt worse, rather than better.

The following months were wretched. She was moody and sullen and ashamed to be so. Her parents were, as ever, tolerant, but failed to divine that amusements would solve nothing where Daphne was concerned – it was simply no good offering more outings to theatres and parties and expecting her to 'cheer up'. Unfortunately, the du Mauriers did not move in circles where, in the mid-1920s, any form of higher education was thought suitable for a girl, so the idea of Daphne perhaps going to university was never considered. She had a good brain and a love of literature, was happiest when reading, and it was the kind of intense reading nearer to studying than mere amusement; but she herself never, at that stage, contemplated such an outlandish solution to her problems. Instead, it was suggested she should learn to drive, which she duly did. The Cannon Hall chauffeur taught her in Muriel's little car and she was soon whizzing round London on her own, not at all deterred by the odd small collision. Her parents were pleased at the success of this scheme to give Daphne an interest but, inevitably, the novelty wore off and she was once more disconsolate. The next proposition was that she should be given a dog.

Dogs were not new in her life.[6] The du Mauriers loved dogs, but since the defection of Brutus, a mongrel fox-terrier, who had opted to live mainly with the local vet before Daphne went to Camposena, the family had not had another dog. Now Daphne was invited to choose one to be her very own. She chose a West Highland terrier, named Jock after another West Highlander the family had had at Cumberland Terrace. Jock was even more of a success than learning to drive, and she enjoyed her long daily walks on the Heath more with him; but still she saw everything through what she described to Tod as 'a mist of hate'. What she hated was her own by now familiar sense of aimlessness. The only way to deal with it, she decided, was to try harder to write, because it was the only talent she felt she might possess. So she began on short stories again, but then suddenly veered off in the direction of poetry. She tried her hand at both long, mostly descriptive, narrative poems, which rhymed conventionally, and at shorter pieces of a satirical bent. One, entitled 'Lunch', revealed only too clearly what she thought of the theatrical world:

'Please pass the cream – yes – that's enough'
('I knew her years before the war')
'I'd love some of that sugary stuff'
('She must be at least fifty-four')
'I can't believe your dress is true'
('He said his lines in an appalling way')
'It's almost a delphinium blue'
('To me he ruined the entire play')
'The whole thing's such a terrible disgrace'
('Surely he was the Duke's adopted son!')
'If I were in Winston Churchill's place . . .'
('My dear, you're thinking of another one')
'I always loathed the girl, she drinks and swears'

And everyone was thinking – 'Christ! Who cares.'

Sometimes, listening to this kind of chatter, empty and idle, Daphne wondered whether she would only manage to write if she could get away from London, if she could be by herself somewhere quiet and empty. In March 1926, she and Jeanne and Muriel went on holiday to Cumberland, to a farm in the Newlands Valley, the other side of Derwentwater, and more than any place she had ever been in, the Lake District attracted her strongly. The countryside was not of course something with which she was unfamiliar – all her childhood she had loved the many family holidays in different country locations – but the Lake District was remote and wild and she loved climbing Catbells, Causey Pike and roaming for miles with Jock up the streams to the valley head, never meeting a soul. The weather was poor, but this did not deter her. She knew she felt happier there than anywhere else she had ever been.

The arrival of Ferdy was meant to put the seal on this happiness. It had been Muriel's idea to invite Ferdy, to thank her for her kindness to the convalescent Daphne earlier in the year, but when she finally accepted and made her way north, in April, it turned out to be a mistake. The Lake District was exactly the wrong kind of place for this sophisticated Frenchwoman. She made no attempt to go on walks in the rain with Daphne, preferring instead to sit by the fire and talk to Muriel. This would not have been too upsetting, if it had not been for Ferdy's new obsequiousness. Thinking back, Daphne remembered how she had admired her teacher because, like Tod, she was her own person; but now she saw signs of the toady in Ferdy. She was heard boasting to the farmer's wife about her friendship with the famous du Maurier family, and Daphne began to wonder if, after all, Ferdy had liked the status and possible wealth of her family rather more than her pupil. It was always abhorrent to Daphne to think she had been exploited or fooled, and she could hardly bear her own suspicions. Nor was it easy to have the woman she 'loved in every conceivable way' with her and yet be unable to demonstrate this love.

Once they were all back in London, it turned out that Ferdy had lost her job, for no reason – or no reason that could safely be communicated to the du Mauriers. Immediately, Daphne jumped to a likely conclusion: Ferdy had been sacked for her too-close relationship with her. It seemed perfectly feasible that Miss Wicksteed had not approved of any teacher favouring one particular pupil to the extent of spending holidays with her and helping to nurse her. Schools had to be careful about rumours, and this was the kind of thing which could so easily give rise to them. (In fact, there had been rumours circulating round the school and, if Daphne had not been quite so solitary, she would have heard them.) She felt she had to ask Ferdy whether her deduction was correct, but Ferdy denied it. Daphne's relief was immediately replaced by another anxiety when Ferdy asked if Gerald might give her a job – she had, apparently, always felt she was an actress *manquée*.

Daphne found it difficult, and embarrassing, to credit that the woman she loved could ask this of her. What did Ferdy think acting was? It seemed not just a form of conceit for her to suppose she could jump on a stage and act without either training or experience, but also an insult to Gerald himself. She responded coldly. Her father, she said firmly, was not in a position to help and she refused to ask him. What she cared about was not so much that Ferdy would be humiliated – she knew her father would let her down lightly – but that in watching Ferdy be rejected she would feel humiliated herself. Her beloved teacher, about whom she had boasted, would be exposed as the worst kind of hanger-on and she herself as someone who had not the wit to see she was being used.

Ferdy took this refusal to intercede on her behalf very well. She did not attempt to plead or, worse still, become upset, but simply accepted the verdict. The subject was never mentioned again. But what was more significant was that the incident did not lead to the termination of the friendship or even to any serious cooling. When Ferdy returned to Paris, with the intention of investigating the feasibility of starting her own small school (in which she subsequently succeeded), she and Daphne were devoted to each other, if secretly, even if the teacher had had a warning and the pupil was now on her guard and still trying to rationalize what had happened.

Reliable old Tod was treated to a particularly long letter in which Ferdy was not mentioned. Instead, Daphne waxed lyrical about the Lake District – 'one looked at sheep and thatched cottages and wondered about Wordsworth and daffodils and talked to old bearded shepherds about the rain, and I was sorry to come back and experience the boredom of the General Strike'. Whereas other girls with Daphne's affluent background were experiencing doubts, for perhaps the first time, about the justice of their own privileged lives and finding out, often to their astonishment, what the strike was about, she not only found it boring but had the temerity to tell Tod that 'nothing much happened beyond the fact that buses and tubes were driven by good-looking undergraduates in plus-fours ... what is really happening and what it is about nobody has the slightest idea'. There was more naïvety than arrogance in this kind of foolishly flippant remark, but it did indicate how shallow was Daphne's concern for those who led the 'dreary lives' she worried about in other letters. Her affinity with servants, and her preference for ordinary people rather than grand ones, had not led her to learn anything about the social conditions of her time, of which she was totally ignorant. But then, at the du Maurier table, politics, and the situation in the country in general, were not popular topics for discussion. There was no tradition of concern about such matters in the du Maurier household, and if Daphne was going to develop it she would have to do so on her own. She was familiar with charity work – Gerald was very active on behalf of several theatrical charities – but not with campaigning for a different kind of world. As the streets of London filled with marchers, the du Mauriers talked not of what had caused these men to march so far, but of how the box-office returns of the latest play would be affected.

The play they were so concerned about was Edgar Wallace's *The Ringer*, which opened on 1 May at Wyndham's Theatre. Gerald was producing and acting and had partly rewritten the play itself. There was a strong possibility that the 'beastly General Strike' might ruin everything – but it did not. In spite of hot weather as well as the tense political situation, *The Ringer* was rapturously received and settled down to a long and immensely popular and profitable run. Daphne might have little interest in the strike, but she was passionately interested in her father's new friend. What fascinated her – she, who found it so hard to complete any short story – was Edgar's productivity. How had he turned out so many successful books, how had he made himself stick at it? That summer of 1926 Daphne and Gerald spent a great deal of time with Edgar and his daughter Pat, who was the same age as Daphne. They were all in the habit of lunching together at the Embassy, the men sticking to Gerald's favourite cold beef and cos lettuce and the girls indulging themselves with chocolate profiteroles, and the four of them vying with one another in the telling of anecdotes and jokes. But in the middle of all this banter Daphne was studying Edgar closely, as well as reading his books carefully, and trying to divine in him the force which kept him working, which actually got him to sit down and transfer his imagination to paper. She did not doubt the strength of her own imagination, or even that she possessed just as much ingenuity, but what she wanted was to discover the secret of Edgar's amazingly prolific output.

He convinced her it was all a matter of iron discipline and she vowed she was going to impose a rigid working routine on herself. But, apart from jolly lunches at the Embassy, the summer brought a more tempting and dangerous distraction. No real work was done, because she had a suitor in whom she was interested. The suitor was male. Daphne, in spite of her love for Ferdy, which had by no means ended, could not suppress an interest in men too. She found that she was so attractive herself that men flirted with her and that, when they did so, she often felt the beginnings of a sexual response similar to that she had felt with her cousin Geoffrey. The boy could sometimes be shut up in the box inside her, it seemed, without causing any strain. In the summer of 1926 her mysterious suitor certainly believed her to be attracted to him and had no suspicions that there was any boy in her at all. What he saw was a young woman of nineteen who had about her a strangely appealing air of vulnerability. She was pretty in a classic English way – perfect complexion, enormous blue eyes, thick fair hair, delicate features, slender figure – and yet there was something elusive and secretive about her which decidedly did not belong to the average girl. She was tremendous fun to be with – quick, intelligent, responding instantly to jokes and easily able to share in witty repartee. She was too original and unusual to be labelled sophisticated – though her clothes at the time, heavily influenced by her mother's excellent taste, were very chic – and yet she was too well versed in the theatrical life to be naïve. In du Maurier code, she was undoubtedly 'a menace' (attractive), and her unidentified suitor was very 'menaced' indeed.

At the end of June, this man sent Daphne a letter dated '3.20 am, Tuesday' to say that he had 'just got home from leaving you to your bluebells – very late – very quiet – I never want to wake up from the trance into which I shot suddenly. Don't ever wake me and don't put it in your diary – oh, that diary! Dangerous, indiscreet and stupid.' This mysterious gentleman expected, it seems, to meet Daphne on Wednesday, by which time he vowed his longing for her would have made him 'forty years older, stumbling along'. Rather curiously, he begged her to 'be happy – rather young, than old and wise'. He knew she was off to France soon, to Trébeurden, in Brittany (where she was to join Ferdy for a holiday), and he could hardly bear the thought of this separation.

Once in Brittany, safe with Ferdy, she wrote a poem on the notepaper of the Grand Hôtel de la Plage in which her feelings about the man she had left behind were neatly analysed. It began:

> If to be happy one must needs be chaste
> Dull and neglected, middle-class and kind,
> Surrounded by a garden and four walls
> Croquet, and a tennis court behind,
> Surely one would choose then to be sad . . .

and ended:

> I fear you are too faithful to be false
> And that I shall see you in a while
> Fashioning for children nursery rhymes
> Or listening to a sentimental waltz.
> However, you have a certain twisting smile
> That forces one to think of you at times.

What she was thinking about in particular was the day she had spent in June with him-of-the-twisted-smile, the day at the end of which he had written her that unsigned letter. On the back of this letter, Daphne wrote another poem, entitled 'Richmond Park':

> 'Oh, we played halma,⁷ talked, and read,
>   After all, one has to live.'
> This is what I vaguely said
>   To those who were inquisitive.
> But more beautiful, less drear,
>   Was the vision in my mind
> A greater risk, a happy fear,
>   Halma of another kind,
> Crushed ferns amidst a haze of blue –
>   The sun, egg sandwiches – and you.

What precisely had happened among the bluebells and ferns of Richmond Park that June day was never elaborated upon, but Daphne's desire for excitement, for 'a greater risk', for life to be something other than 'middle-class and kind' was obvious. But no sooner had she involved herself with this man, however lightly, than she was off to be with Ferdy. She spent her time swimming, often naked as she preferred (always having a complete lack of self-consciousness in this particular respect), walking and reading: the mixture as before but with one vital difference. Removed from London, with Edgar's advice ringing in her ears, she was determined to finish a short story which satisfied her before she went home. And she did so. By the time she returned to London she had three stories completed, and felt quite triumphant that she was on her way to achieving something at last.

Chapter Three

The short stories Daphne wrote in Brittany, and for the next three years, all have one striking thing in common: the male characters are thoroughly unpleasant. They are bullies, seducers and cheats. The women, in contrast, are pitifully weak creatures, who are endlessly dominated and betrayed, never capable of saving themselves and having only the energy just to survive. The settings of these first stories, most of which were published in magazines, are often Paris, but a Paris the author did not know well. The tone of all the stories is cynical and there is an obsession with the life of the working-class girl, often a prostitute. The thread that binds all the early stories together is one of total disillusionment with the relationship between men and women – they are bleak, bitter and sad, not at all the sort of stories which might have been expected to come from someone with Daphne's early history. Yet, in a way, these cynical stories could be said to reflect very accurately her secret feelings about her parents' marriage which had troubled her for so long. Gerald was no bully but she certainly saw him as a cheat. Mo was not a pitiful weak creature, but it seemed to Daphne that she was indeed betrayed. Her anger with her father went into these stories, however obliquely, and so did her despair at her mother's position, even if it was a position Mo herself did not acknowledge. There was nothing, by the late 1920s, that Daphne did not know about Gerald's philandering and, though tales of his exploits, which were common currency among the theatrical set, did not make her despise him, or turn against him, they did make her believe that sex was the cause of all the difficulty she saw in the relationships between men and women.

But if these stories were cynical in tone they were also atmospheric, with a strong sense of place. This, from the beginning of her writing life, fascinated Daphne. If she was describing a scene, she wanted readers to be *there*. 'La Sainte-Vierge', the first story she completed in Brittany (though it was not the first published), has atmosphere, if little else, to recommend it. The setting is the countryside, near the sea, and in the very first paragraph its atmosphere is strongly established:

It was hot and sultry, that oppressive kind of heat where there is no air, no life. The trees were motionless and dull, their drooping leaves colourless with summer dust. The ditches smelt of dead ferns and long-dried mud, the grasses of the field were blistered and brown. The village seemed asleep. No one stirred among the far scattered cottages on the hillside, strange uneven cottages, huddled together for fear of loneliness, with white walls and no windows, and small gardens massed with orange flowers.

The story itself is about a young woman married to a fisherman who is ignorant, unintelligent and betraying her without her knowledge. The reader's sympathy is hardly engaged at all because the woman herself seems as despicable as her husband in her avowal that there are no 'depths of degradation' to which she would not sink for his sake. In the end she is tricked by her husband and her intense religious faith, but rather than pitying her the author appears to invite scorn.

As soon as she arrived home, Daphne showed this story, and the other two, to Gerald. There was no doubt that she wanted his approbation, but showing him her work was another little test along the lines of showing him 'Rain'. Would he think 'La Sainte-Vierge' 'sordid' too? Would he pronounce it not the sort of thing a *jeune fille* should write? Gerald, although dismayed by the cynicism of the story, had the sense to realize that what was important was that Daphne had completed something to her satisfaction and might well be launched on the writing career he had wished for her and to which she herself aspired. He launched into a familiar paean of praise of his father, emphasizing once more how like George du Maurier Daphne was, and predicting that she, too, would one day write novels as great as *Trilby*. But novels were

not something his daughter felt she could yet attempt. She resolved
to go on with the short stories until she had enough to form a
collection, and at the same time tried to write a play in blank
verse.

It annoyed her that, just as she was settling down to writing
for at least an hour a day in the little room above the Cannon
Hall garage, she was required to go with her mother and sisters
on a tour of Cornwall in an attempt to buy a house which could
be used for holidays. Normally, she would have jumped at this
opportunity to get out of London, but for once she was reluctant
to go. It seemed to her that whenever she tried to discipline herself
her family worked equally hard to distract her, and it could only
mean that nobody took her writing seriously. What was more to
the point, if a holiday home was to be bought she would rather
it were in France. Much as she had loved Cornwall on the family's
two holidays there, when she was five and ten,[1] she wondered
what it could have to offer compared with France.

What it had to offer was Fowey. Daphne's first view of this
little town was dramatic. The du Mauriers drove down the startlingly steep hill into Bodinnick and saw Fowey across the estuary,
spread out along the waterfront with woods behind. The houses,
painted grey and white, with the occasional touch of blue and
pink and yellow, were all different shapes and ages and, hugging
the sea so closely, gave a first impression of some Mediterranean
village. The sky was blue, the clouds moving swiftly across it, and
there was an exuberance about the scene which immediately lifted
Daphne's spirits. Fowey is a working port and she could see ships,
some of them enormous, chugging their ponderous way up the
estuary from the open sea with all the white-sailed boats scattering
before them. The whole scene, from the top of the Bodinnick hill,
was vibrant and exhilarating. By the time the du Mauriers had
reached the bottom and found that opposite the inn in Bodinnick
there was a house for sale, Daphne's fascination was complete.

Fortunately, Muriel was equally charmed. The house, which
had once been part of a boatyard, was bought that autumn out of
the proceeds of *The Ringer*, and renamed Ferryside, since it was
literally beside the ferry across to Fowey. Compared to the houses
Daphne had already lived in, Ferryside was modest and small. It

was, in fact, rather ramshackle and needed a great deal of work, but far from being daunted, Muriel saw this as a challenge she would enjoy. It was the position of the house which was its chief attraction: it stood almost *over* the water which rushed dangerously past the front wall. There was virtually no garden beyond a strip of grass, which bore traces of being regularly submerged, and a few lilac bushes. The house is cut into the hillside behind, and anyone could have told at a glance that damp would be a major problem. But the romantic appeal of this unusual house far outweighed practical drawbacks for the du Mauriers, and they were thrilled with the views of the sea from all the windows. The timbers of the floors and ceilings were ancient, and the shape of the rooms, spread out on two floors connected by small staircases, and with additional bedrooms under the eaves, was irregular. Muriel saw at once the possibility of converting it into something original. Daphne saw the possibility of escape: she was filled with an absolute conviction that, if only she could live at Ferryside on her own, she could be both successful and happy.

It was three years before that escape came about, and during those years Daphne changed considerably. On the surface, back in London, life went on as usual that winter of 1926. Daphne went on trying to write for an hour a day – still the short stories and blank-verse play – but there was the same constant pressure to enjoy herself and become caught up in the parties, first nights, and holidays abroad. Some of these holidays were too tempting to refuse. Who could stay in a dismal little room above a garage trying to write if invited, begged and even half-bribed into going to join the Edgar Wallace family on a skiing holiday in Switzerland? There was a side of Daphne, as there is of even the most studious and earnest nineteen-year-old, which longed for fun – and fun was what the winter sports party staying at the Palace Hotel in Caux promised. To her own surprise and pleasure, Daphne discovered she had no problems fitting in – this was not, after all, school, and she got on well with the young people the Wallaces had so generously gathered together. She and Pat Wallace were already good friends, both with quick minds and a relish for mockery. Pat saw very well how, in this new environment, Daphne blossomed – she was more relaxed, not so defensive, more light-hearted, less reflective and aloof. She and Pat spent hours practising conversations to have with young men, very 'ATP' – anxious to please. It was all a delicious game, and without Gerald waiting for her to come home, ready to cross-examine her, it was a game Daphne was prepared to play with a new zest.

She had realized, of course, that Pat's relationship with her father Edgar was very different from her own with Gerald. Both fathers doted on their daughters, but there the similarity ended. Edgar adored Pat, cared about her deeply, loved to be with her, but he was not possessive nor did he brood over her in the suspicious way Gerald did over Daphne. Life at Cannon Hall for both Daphne and Angela had become increasingly difficult over the last few years, ever since they had reached the age when they were of interest to, and interested in, the opposite sex. Gerald, in the tradition of his great friend J. M. Barrie, did not want his girls to grow up. This reluctance to face the fact that they would was not the normal, rather touching feeling of any father, but a much more violently experienced emotion, especially towards Daphne's transition from child to woman. In *Dear Brutus*,[2] the play in which Gerald took the part of the father, Will Dearth, who has a fantasy daughter, Barrie caught exactly the nature of Gerald's infatuation with his daughter. Daphne was only ten when the play was first performed in 1917, but even then she had found it unbearable to watch her real father's pain as he enacted Will Dearth's part. 'Oh! How you do love me, daddy!' cries Margaret, the fantasy daughter, and when she considers her own future life, grown up, she says knowingly, 'It would be hard for me if you lost me, but it would be worse for my daddy! I don't know how I know that, but I do know it. What would you do without me?' Her father immediately tells her not to be 'wicked and stupid and naughty' – the mere thought of losing her is unbearable, and when the moment in the play arrived at which this daughter is revealed as the fantasy she always was, the entire theatre sobbed.

But by 1926, after experiencing once too often Gerald's fury and misery every time she was invited out by a young man, Daphne no longer wept in sympathy. She bitterly resented both her father's desire to know absolutely everything about her private life and also his unpleasant insinuations as to her supposed behaviour. There was nothing amusing or sweet about Gerald's jealousy, which was ugly and ridiculous. Waiting for his daughters to come home he could work himself up into such a lather of rage that he would hurl at them quite shocking accusations which they hardly understood. This was a different father from the one they had always known, the father who had always been such fun and so kind, who had endlessly entertained and educated them with infinite patience. They hardly recognized him in this man who now was so unreasonable and shouted. Angela, the most innocent of girls, was once accused of being a whore, and when she had pains in her stomach, from what turned out to be appendicitis, was suspected of being pregnant.[3] But what had begun to tinge Daphne's great love for her father with disgust was the hypocrisy involved in his attitude. Who was he to be such a puritan, such a prude? The double standard he was operating brought her near to hating him at times, and it coloured her own already ambivalent attitude to sex. Gerald's 'stable' was no longer such a joke. The latest favourite, Audrey Carten, was only a few years older than Daphne herself and she was clearly not playing with Gerald as he was playing with her, but was profoundly in love with him. It was disturbing to witness and so was the first overt sign of her mother's resentment. Gerald had broken their implicit understanding by parking his car outside Audrey's house for all to see, and Mo was outraged at this humiliation. Her reaction – so very rare – made a deep impression on Daphne. She looked at her father more critically and came to the conclusion that his chief problem was his refusal to grow old gracefully. He was a true Peter Pan, who never wanted to grow up, and now, at fifty-three, was refusing to do so. Part of this refusal was his determined resistance to the fact that his daughters were growing up too – he wanted them all to stay young and innocent, and never reach the stage where they could have been members of his own 'stable'.

In Caux, however, there was no Gerald. Daphne felt free, and at the same time began to believe that she was attractive. In spite of her obvious prettiness and the compliments she had been paid, she had never rated herself highly and had had little confidence in her looks, but now she began to recognize her own power. Then there was the dancing – she had always loved to dance and now, at Caux, there was dancing every night, all night, with young men queuing up to partner her and no Gerald waiting at home to glare and storm and subject her to loathsome questions. She was greatly admired as she whirled round the floor, and, though on the one hand never susceptible to flattery, and completely lacking in vanity, this admiration made her feel better about herself than she had done since early adolescence. The result was that she looked less fierce and allowed herself to have a good time without end-lessly analysing her own behaviour.

Yet at the same time as enjoying this social life more, Daphne was also always on the look-out for conversation of a more serious kind than holiday banter. She was a listener and an observer rather than a talker, and what she liked to listen to was not idle chat but people she admired discussing issues they cared about or literature they knew and in which she was interested. She read voraciously herself – an average of four books a week, with heavy emphasis on R. L. Stevenson, Walter Scott, and W. M. Thackeray at that time – and liked to discuss what she read. Any conversations of a philosophical as well as a literary bent engaged her instantly, even if she did not always contribute towards them; and though these were in short supply at Caux, or indeed at Cannon Hall generally, she had that autumn become acquainted with a man she greatly revered both as a writer and a person. This was Sir Arthur Quiller-Couch, known as 'Q', who lived half the year at The Haven, in Fowey, and half in Cambridge where he held the chair in English. J. M. Barrie, a great friend of his, introduced the du Mauriers, who were now going to be his neighbours in Fowey, to him.

Meeting 'Q' was rather different from meeting Edgar Wallace. Daphne had met few intellectuals in her life and was from the first greatly in awe of this eminent scholar, who had also written a vast amount of fiction, verse and literary journalism, not to mention having edited in 1900 the first *Oxford Book of English Verse*. She had read 'Q's *Troy Town*, a novel about a barely disguised Fowey, and also *On the Art of Writing*, one of 'Q's influential volumes of lectures. 'Q' was a Victorian, strictly conventional, holding the highest possible standards and wanting to see any aspiring writer hold them too. To 'Q', language was more important than content, and language 'should be kept noble'.

Sitting at 'Q's feet on a visit to Cambridge in the autumn of 1926, Daphne was fascinated by him. His appearance was idiosyncratic – he looked like a weather-beaten sailor and dressed in a strange collection of brightly coloured garments[4] – and his speech, with its West Country pronunciation (he was born in Cornwall), was most attractive to listen to. 'Q' put ideas of excellence into her head which she was almost afraid to think about and made her re-examine what she had already written with some natural anxiety. Was her language noble? She did not think so. And had she striven to emulate the literary greats? She did not think that either, and it was all rather depressing.

Unfortunately, when she brought herself to show the poems and blank-verse play she had now completed to her cousin Gerald Millar (Geoffrey's brother), who was a reader for the Heinemann Publishing Company, he had to share her own doubts. As yet, he told her, she had not turned out anything good enough for publication. She wrote to Tod that she was glad her cousin had told her the truth, because she knew herself that her stuff was not yet up to much. What was odd was that she had chosen to submit to Gerald Millar her poems and play and not her short stories. This was because she felt that her short stories were too trivial and lightweight, whereas her poetry, however poor, was at least an attempt at something 'noble'. Writing poetry, whatever the quality, came easily, whereas writing stories was work. It needed sustained effort and she was still shamefully aware at the start of 1927 that she simply was not making enough effort for enough time – pleasure constantly beckoned and she succumbed too readily.

The outstanding pleasure of that year was the completion of the Ferryside conversion. In May, the builders and decorators moved out and Muriel and the girls moved in (Gerald was in London directing Gladys Cooper in an adaptation of Somerset Maugham's *The Letter*). Muriel, who had a flair for interior decoration, had seen to it that the essential character of the house was kept – it remained simple and plain – but that it was made comfortable and colourful. There was nothing fussy or grand about the result.

Whereas Cannon Hall, with its imposing period furniture and valuable old pictures, struck some people as a little over-formal, Ferryside had a country feel about it. Daphne loved it at once. The room she shared with Jeanne was the kind of room she had always wanted, with windows facing west over the estuary and south-west towards the open sea. There was a door leading onto some small wooden steps which went down to the garden, so that one did not even have to go through the house to get outside – it was perfect. She lay in bed, hearing the hooting of ships' horns and the constant cry of the seagulls, and she found that instead of clinging to sleep, as she had done all her life, she was eager to be up and out at once.

The walks directly from the house satisfied her in a way that Hampstead Heath had never done. Immediately above Ferryside, starting halfway up the Bodinnick hill, is the famous Hall Walk along the cliff top, winding inland round the Pont river and then back once more to the cliffs and eventually to Polruan. Striding along this path with her dog Daphne could look to the right, over the rooftops of Fowey, and there spread out were all the yachts and steamers and rowing-boats filling the estuary. If she wished, she could walk even further, on to Lanteglos church, hidden in a little valley with the high hedges along the lanes shutting out all sight and sound of the sea. Then there was the Fowey side – she only had to take the ferry over and she could walk through Fowey all the way to Readymoney Cove at the end and up into the woods to the cliff path which ran right round the Gribbin headland to Polkerris and beyond to Par. There were hours and hours of walks to be had, and even in bad weather she loved them. The mist might hide the magnificent views but it made everything sinister and mysterious, just as she liked it.

But walking was not her only passion. Daphne now began to learn how to sail. Not to do so was foolish, when she was living practically on the water, and she was eager to identify herself with a universal way of life in Fowey. She bought a fisherman's jersey and boots – the kind of clothes she loved best – and started learning immediately, taught by a local boatman, Adams, who told her stories about his family and his wife's family as he showed her how to handle a boat. 'My time', she wrote ecstatically, 'is spent in a sort of fatuous state of bliss and ridiculous concentration.' On the day after her twentieth birthday, 13 May, Muriel, Jeanne and Angela returned to London and she was left alone for the first time in Ferryside (but with a woman coming in to cook and clean for this one solitary girl). The obliging Adams taught her how to helm, how to tack, and how to handle rough seas, all the while encouraged by her to carry on talking about the past. Always inquisitive, Daphne questioned him about the old schooner, *Jane Slade*, its figurehead still intact, which she had seen lying up the Pont river, and listened attentively as he told her that Jane Slade was his wife's grandmother. By the time Daphne had learnt to sail adequately enough to go out on her own, she knew the Jane Slade story off by heart and knew, too, that some family letters still survived which one day she might persuade Adams to show her. In her mind, though very vaguely, was the idea that she might somehow make something of them.

The summer seemed long and wonderful, every day filled with sailing, swimming and walking, and even when the rest of the family returned, and Ferryside was filled with people, it was always possible to slip off with her new dog, Bingo, half spaniel and half sheepdog, and see nobody at all. But one person she did want to see, and who she arranged should visit her, at his request, when she was on her own, was Cousin Geoffrey, who was back in England after touring in a play abroad. At twenty, Daphne considered she was now capable of dealing with Geoffrey's advances rather better than she had done at fourteen, and she did not see why she should not have the pleasure of his company even if he was a married man. Geoffrey spent only a day with her, but that was long enough for him to discover that his outrageous flirting now only made his cousin laugh. He had the grace to laugh himself, giving up all hope of conquering the little schoolgirl of six years before. But they liked each other, and Daphne was foolish enough to tell her parents about Geoffrey's visit – foolish because she well understood how unbalanced her father could be on this subject. There was no need for Gerald ever to have known about this fleeting visit, but Daphne told him and was subjected to the usual inquisition, this time by telephone. She was so irritated by her father's absurd and quite unfounded suspicions, and also by the way he continued to treat her as a child and wanted to control every corner of her life, that she promptly invited Geoffrey again and was sorry when he could not come.

She was even sorrier when October arrived and Ferryside was shut up for the winter. The return to London was terrible, not only because she lost everything she loved in Cornwall, but because she had once more to face living with her father. Her love for Gerald, no longer a simple emotion, did not blind her to the change in him. The intimacy they had shared when she was a child, that complete empathy which had bound them together, had changed into something else. He still claimed the same closeness, but she felt stifled by his growing dependency on her – their roles seemed reversed and she did not like it. Nor did she like observing how much more depressed Gerald was than he had ever been before. He seemed suddenly to be verging on the pathetic and Daphne loathed pathos, hated anyone who made an open show of their distress. And now here was the once fun-loving Gerald drooping about the house waiting humbly for her to go for walks with him and, even worse, succumbing to tearful appeals for her company on any terms. Even his appearance, off stage, had changed. Once, he was vitality itself, never still, but now he lacked energy. He was no longer able to relax by playing the energetic games of tennis and golf which had kept him occupied when he was not working, and he had nothing with which to fill the gap. This lack of physical activity depressed him and he was visibly slipping into a state of apathy. There were mutterings, too, about financial worries, which no one took seriously (though these were serious), and she knew Gerald's career was in the doldrums. He had a run of plays which failed and his only successes seemed to be in revivals. He wandered about Cannon Hall with books on psychology under his arm, and though there was nothing new in his obsession with family history there was something new about his frantic determination to trace every one of his own characteristics back to his ancestors.

It was all difficult for a young woman to handle just at the stage when she was attempting to assert her own independence. The more Daphne tried to slip out of her father's orbit, the harder he worked at keeping her at the centre of his universe. He wished aloud that he was her brother and not her father – since he could see his paternal role rapidly waning – and most upsetting of all told her that when he died he hoped he could come back as her son.[5] Mixed up with this panic that he was losing his favourite daughter was a deeper terror that he was going to find himself old and would have to confront the fact that he had wasted his life. It was no good anyone pointing to his enormous success in the theatre – this was dismissed as worthless. He felt himself sliding into decay and ruin, and just when he needed his daughters most, they were leaving him spiritually if not in reality. The quality of his visible emotion was so overpowering that it inhibited Daphne – she found herself incapable of reacting spontaneously with true warmth, and felt towards him the same paralysing shyness she had always felt towards strangers. When he, who had always been a tactile person, clung to her she found this almost unbearable and was afraid he would sense this. 'Oh! I am *so* unhappy!' he would wail, and no longer was it possible to laugh and consider it a joke.

In November, Daphne could stand no more of this without some respite. She took her quarterly allowance out of the bank and went to visit Ferdy, whose new school at Boulogne-sur-Seine was flourishing. A month later, she returned to find Gerald no better. To her alarm, she found Muriel and Angela had already gone to Fowey, to open Ferryside up for Christmas, and that she was effectively in charge of her father with sixteen-year-old Jeanne for company. It seemed to her that he must be going through some kind of breakdown, and he was certainly drinking too much, but it was difficult to make any sense of what he said. He had always had a rambling way of talking – someone once remarked that he spoke in telegrams, abruptly, in short, choppy sentences – but now the rambling was wilder. The effect on Daphne was to make her want to be alone more than ever. Once, Gerald had been so tolerant of that urge, had understood exactly, but now he demanded her presence virtually all the time they were both in the house. She found herself pitying her mother, having to endure this newly sad, demanding husband, and felt even more disillusioned about marriage as an institution. It was well known that Gerald, before this particular collapse, had taken up with an old flame again, and this seemed to Daphne particularly contemptible:

that her mother should suffer this kind of whining at home and then, when Gerald recovered, he should go off to his mistress. Meanwhile, once at Ferryside, after the rest of the family had returned to London, she put all her cynicism into completing more short stories.

All the stories she wrote at that time, as earlier, were fuelled by disgust. She was repelled by the way men used women, and women allowed themselves to be used. She wrote not about the society, and its manners, which she knew, but about what she suspected went on, what she heard talked about. In all of her stories, girls suffered because of men's lust and always the men got away with it. One of the strongest stories was 'And Now to God the Father', in which a fashionable vicar is sought out by a young aristocrat who has made a lower-middle-class girl pregnant. The vicar is sympathetic – young men will be young men – and says he will take care of everything. He sends for the girl, telling her not to bother her seducer and that he will arrange for her to be taken care of. The girl drowns herself. There is no remorse on the vicar's part when he learns of her death: the reader is meant to despise him, and does, but is left in no doubt that this is how the world works and that nothing can be done about it. Men triumph over women; wealth and breeding over poverty.

The rest of the stories continued in the same vein. In all the stories, eleven of which were finished by the spring of 1928, there is no trace of the charmed life Daphne led. Her view of the world is dark and dismal, and the overriding influence is clearly that of her father's amorous relationships. None of the men in these stories is even remotely like Gerald du Maurier – none has any charm, none is witty, none talented or attractive – but in all of them is the unmistakable flavour of what Daphne found it so hard to accept: all men were like her beloved father, unfaithful and not what they seemed. No other topic interested her so much as the relationship between men and women. What she was doing was emphasizing over and over again her own pessimism as she surveyed what she believed to be the truth about these relationships. She concentrated on the interchanges between couples, often not bothering to give either man or woman a name, and made no attempt to build up their characters or to set them securely in any context. One story, 'Tame Cat', about a girl who has suddenly grown up and arrives home for the holidays to find her mother's lover desires her instead, seemed to express succinctly what the author was saying repeatedly: 'Being grown-up was this, a sordid tissue of intimate relationships, complicated and vile.'

But the way in which these stories were written went some way towards making them less dismal than the subject matter dictated. Most were written in a taut, almost cinematic way, in short scenes with distinct breaks punctuating the text. Although she frequently acknowledged the influence of Katherine Mansfield and Guy de Maupassant there was no sign of this influence in Daphne's own stories. Her style was slightly more akin to Somerset Maugham, and she shared some of Maugham's preoccupations, but even then nothing was recognizably derivative. Aunt Billie typed them out for her and this time she decided not to send them to her cousin Gerald, but instead to try a literary agent.

Feeling that this would be a real test, Daphne could not bear to hang about waiting for the verdict and so she arranged to go to Paris, saying goodbye before she left to Geoffrey, who was going to Australia. She found this a strangely unemotional experience and tried to analyse why. She liked Geoffrey so much and when it came to kissing him goodbye – the first and last time he really kissed her – she found this very agreeable. It was, she wrote, like kissing her father used to be – pleasant, familiar, comfortable – making her think how strong family similarities were, seeming to show Gerald and Geoffrey, uncle and nephew, inextricably linked both with each other and with her, daughter and cousin. What worried her, though, was how quickly she forgot Geoffrey once he had gone. Did this mean she did not after all care very much for him? Or did it mean she was selfish and cold, caring only for people who were actually with her? Either way, she was relieved to find she did not miss her cousin, and instead found herself embarrassed by the evidence in his letters that he missed her. She had a horror of sloppiness, and Geoffrey's letters were full of the kind of phrases she used to copy out of bad novels and send to Tod with her own caustic comments alongside.

She liked, all the same, to make a story out of Geoffrey's devotion to her. While in Paris she visited Ferdy, as usual, and related to her, with much mocking, her cousin's adoration. Understandably, Ferdy was not amused. She thought it disgraceful that a married man of forty-two should carry on like this with a girl of twenty. Daphne said she could not see that Geoffrey's being married mattered, especially as nothing had happened between them. She liked to tease Ferdy, to push her into defending her moralistic point of view, and there was more than a whiff of titillation about it all. She knew perfectly well that this admission of an interest in men hurt Ferdy, whom she still professed to love, but she could not resist displaying her own power. She wanted Ferdy, and Tod for that matter, to see that she had this 'power' and that even if she did not choose to use it she was aware of it and it excited her. In a sense both these older women were substitute mothers, people who would forgive her anything and to whom she could tell anything, and with whom she enjoyed a closeness she did not have with her own mother. If her relationship with Gerald was now causing her considerable anguish, hers with Muriel had, of course, always done so. She had adored Gerald, which made her new, confused feelings about him painful; though she had never adored Muriel, she was finding it almost equally painful to observe that instead of growing closer to her mother now she was an adult, she was growing even further away. This disturbed and hurt her. She needed Muriel now as an ally, needed her to act as a kind of buffer between herself and her father, but her mother remained distant.

She thought a great deal while she stayed with Ferdy in Paris about the fate of her eleven stories, hardly daring to hope that at least some would find favour. Then a letter arrived in Paris saying that the agent A. P. Watt liked them and, if she could add another half-dozen or so, was sure he could find a publisher for them. The relief was enormous. But in spite of the encouragement given to her by A. P. Watt, Daphne did not at once settle down to producing the extra stories that would make up a collection.

Instead, she was side-tracked by another summer at Ferryside. The new excitement was that she now had her own boat. Two boats, in fact. One was a 13-foot rowing-boat which she named *Annabel Lee*, given to her for her twenty-first birthday, and the other a fishing lugger, 32 feet long, built in the Polruan boatyard and called *Marie-Louise*. The whole summer was spent rowing in *Annabel Lee* and watching *Marie-Louise* being built. She made very little attempt to write any more stories. She excused her laziness on the grounds that Ferryside was too crowded for her to have peace to work – and it was indeed full of an endless stream of guests invited to keep Gerald amused while he was there – but when September came she was ashamed of her lack of effort. What was it 'Q' said? Literature needed practice, and she was not practising. She wished she could stay by herself at Ferryside and work all winter – which she swore she would do – but she was obliged to return to London.

There was, however, a chink of light: her parents said that *if* she could sell her stories and earn enough to keep herself, then she would be allowed to stay at Ferryside. Never having earned a penny in her life, nor having been required to, it was a rather unreal condition, but one Daphne accepted at once. She did not *want* to be dependent financially or in any other way on her parents – it would fill her with joy to have her own money and this was the incentive she needed. She resolved to go back to Hampstead and apply herself as she had never done before, then return to Fowey with her own income and never leave it.

But before she left Cornwall, she had become fascinated by Menabilly.

Chapter Four

Menabilly[1] was always more than a house to Daphne du Maurier. Its chief attraction for her was its secrecy, not its size or beauty or history. She loved the way it was so cunningly hidden from prying eyes, buried among trees in the middle of the Gribbin peninsula. Again and again in her early letters and her diaries she had craved perfect solitude, so hard to find as a member of a sociable family – 'it is so awful to be part of a big family', she once wrote to Tod. Solitude not only made her happier but in some strange way excited her. It had always puzzled her that, without in the least wanting to act, she found herself acting all the time. Every word she spoke, every gesture she made seemed to her rehearsed even when she was most at ease. Alone, with no one to act for, the relief was great and with this relief came a sense of exhilaration: *now* she knew who she was, could be herself. Large houses in extensive grounds presented endless opportunities for getting 'lost' and she loved them.

Once Ferryside was bought, the du Mauriers naturally became interested in the history of Fowey. They quickly learned that there were two important local families, the Treffrys, ensconced in Place, an extraordinary folly of a house situated in the very heart of Fowey, and the Rashleighs, who owned most of the Gribbin peninsula upon which the town was built. The Treffrys were still prosperous and in residence, but the fortunes of the Rashleighs had varied. Guidebooks which the du Mauriers consulted always listed Menabilly as the principal home of the Rashleighs but, in fact, no member of the family lived there full time. Nothing of the original Tudor house was left, and of the seventeenth-century replacement only some stone mullioned windows and some panelling and underground cellars had survived a nineteenth-century fire. The house had been deliberately built so that there was no view of it from the sea, except from one secret point, to keep it safe from unwelcome enemy attention.

By the time the du Mauriers came to Fowey it was owned by Dr John Rashleigh, married but with no children, who did not live there but came for two or three days every quarter to collect the rents of the farms and cottages he owned on the estate. The house was kept furnished and was aired once a week by a woman who came up from the nearby village of Polkerris. It was variously rumoured that Dr Rashleigh did not himself live at Menabilly because his health would not permit it – the location was damp – or because, having found his first wife in the arms of her lover there, he could not abide the place. All this was common gossip which the du Mauriers soon picked up. They heard that the house, in spite of being still furnished and used, was neglected and falling into serious disrepair. All this, of course, made it even more attractive to Daphne.

Trying to find Menabilly with the help of a map soon became a favourite pastime. Daphne and Angela first attempted to reach the house by setting off from the lodge at the Four Turnings crossroads, but they found the path so overgrown that by the time it was dark they had to give up. Their next attempt was by the more obvious route. They drove to the West Lodge and began walking across the open parkland, still unable to see even a chimney of the house, and feeling apprehensive because they knew they were trespassing. Eventually, penetrating a thicket of shrubs and trees, they came out on to a huge unkempt lawn and there before them was Menabilly.

Seeing it at last gave Daphne a physical thrill – it was so very much more satisfying than she had imagined, with the walls covered in thick ivy, almost obliterating the windows, and betraying no sign of human occupation. It was not the enormous stately home she had half expected – in fact, in comparison with many houses in which she had stayed, Menabilly was modest. Only two-storeyed, it was long and low, unadorned, a quiet-looking house. She thought of it immediately as being asleep, an image strengthened by the way in which she and Angela had stolen up on it. She felt she could awaken this lovely house and with it awaken something in herself.

Instead, she was obliged to return to London. At least she now felt she had a target: to finish sufficient short stories to enable A. P. Watt to show publishers a collection substantial enough to publish. But in spite of good intentions she found she could settle to nothing. She sat in the rather dark, sparsely furnished little room over the Cannon Hall garage, not writing but daydreaming, seeing herself walking along the cliffs at Fowey, standing entranced before the shuttered Menabilly. Aunt Billie was obliged to report to A. P. Watt that the eleven stories they had already would have to do. These were accordingly shown to several publishers, though without success. Uncle Willie, who, as well as being a literary agent, edited the fashionable *Bystander*, was prepared to come to the rescue. He had read Daphne's stories and liked one of them enough to offer to publish it in his magazine if she would agree to some cutting. Deeply suspicious that she was being humoured, and well aware that this was the most blatant piece of nepotism, Daphne reacted to the offer gracelessly. She said she was not prepared to have the story in question, 'And Now to God the Father', cut and certainly not for the offered fee of £10. Fortunately, Uncle Willie was amused and said he would think about it. His magazine only published one story per issue, in a set space which included a large illustration, and he would have to see what could be done.

Meanwhile, Hampstead life went on and Gerald's depression worsened. His business manager, Tom Vaughan, had died and there was now something for him to be seriously depressed and worried about. His financial state was parlous. Gerald had always worried about money even when spending it with the apparently careless generosity and extravagance for which he was famous. He had taken out insurance policies as soon as he married, and several of his early letters to Muriel showed anxiety about his solvency. But as he became more successful and the money rolled in he had begun to spend with abandon, always depending on Tom to keep him straight. Once Tom died, Gerald found himself having to deal with vexatious things like income tax returns, just at the time when his earnings had begun to drop most seriously. Hannen

Swaffer, in an article on the decline of actor-managers, commented, 'Gerald du Maurier, after several consecutive failures at the St James's, must be wondering about a future fraught with peril . . . actor-managers were for a time very uppish . . . they are not uppish today. They are downish.' And none more downish than Gerald, who could see disaster staring him in the face. Drastic action was called for, and the only solution he could think of which would bring in the money he needed was to go into films, an idea he loathed.[2]

He was drinking heavily, which increased his depression, and the atmosphere in Cannon Hall was oppressive. Daphne's own discontent and restlessness matched her father's and they made uneasy companions. She felt trapped, and thrashed about, sulky and furious with herself, resenting Gerald's heavy dependency on her and his need for the support she failed to give. When she was once more invited to Caux for winter sports by the Edgar Wallaces she accepted at once. This was not the answer to her problems but a very agreeable way to escape them for a while, and she had been brought up to divert herself at every opportunity.

Caux that year, 1929, proved more significant than she had expected. It was there that Daphne met Carol Reed,[3] the illegitimate son of Herbert Beerbohm Tree and half-brother of Viola Tree, a great friend of the du Mauriers. Apart from her fleeting interest in the man with whom she had dallied in Richmond Park, Daphne at twenty-one had had no love affairs with men. But Cousin Geoffrey had awakened her to the existence of sexual desire and Ferdy had shown her that there was more than one kind of sexual advance to which she responded. But no man had made love to her, whatever her father suspected. All that his gross suspicions had done was to fuel in her a rebellious desire to commit the act of which he accused her: since Gerald thought she had lovers she might as well have one.

Carol Reed, only six months older than she was, presented himself as the ideal candidate. In many ways he was as unconventional as she believed herself to be and this attracted her greatly. He was not smooth and sophisticated but instead very casual and even Bohemian in manner. He, too, disliked social occasions and liked to be by himself. He was given to spur-of-the-moment adventures, like dashing off in his fast car to look at the moon from some unlikely vantage point, and he appeared daring, even a trifle insolent, with a tendency to daydream in company. His clothes were the sort of clothes of which Daphne approved – pullovers, big coats, nothing smart. He was tall – she liked men to be tall and strong-looking – and had eyes nearly as blue as her own. His background was her own background and they had scores of theatrical friends in common.

The affair did not begin at Caux. Daphne threw herself into a hectic type of socializing, of the sort she usually scorned but which seemed right in Caux. She danced until dawn every night, kissed freely and meaninglessly and was generally part of the happy, frenzied crowd. While there, she wrote an entertaining letter to Ferdy, wildly exaggerating all the fun she was having and perfectly calculated to upset her, and when she returned home it was to discover that Ferdy had actually written to Aunt Billie, with whom she had become friendly during her stay in London, saying that Daphne was on the road to ruin and should be watched. Billie felt obliged to tell Muriel, who, of course, told Gerald, and the reception committee awaiting Daphne was formidable. Her parents' readiness to believe that she had seriously compromised herself at Caux enraged her, as did Ferdy's interference, which she, not unnaturally, interpreted as jealousy. More and more it seemed a waste not to be wicked if, in the pursuit of harmless fun, that was how she was to be branded. When Carol returned and contacted her she was more than ready for him.

He was at that time working for Edgar Wallace as an assistant director on a film and was leading a haphazard existence, sometimes working long hours in the studio, sometimes with whole days free. He and Daphne discovered at once that they had one thing in common they had not known about in Caux: they both loved frequenting unpretentious cafés in unfashionable districts where they could sit and observe people and eavesdrop. They would spend hours over cups of coffee, sitting silently smoking, building up theories about the strangers around them, and then, afterwards, comparing fantasies about them. Carol cared no more for fine food and wine than Daphne – a sandwich was more to their liking – and had a similar passion for wandering the streets trying to imagine the lives of those who lived there. A favourite with both of them was the dockland area, where the sight of foreign ships would stimulate wilder flights of fancy. Sometimes Carol would do silly, even dangerous things like suddenly climbing scaffolding or jumping on to statues, but Daphne loved these touches of eccentricity. She loved, too, Carol's evident ambition – she liked people who wanted to do things in life and Carol had great plans. He was not boastful but was full of a quiet conviction that he would achieve something in the theatre or film world, and he had every intention of dedicating himself to the job. Those who observed Daphne and Carol at this time thought what an attractive couple they made and how happy they seemed. Daphne in particular was light-hearted, always on the edge of some joke shared only with Carol, her former watchful expression quite gone. The only thing that threatened to spoil this charming romance was Gerald's hostility.

Now that Gerald had someone upon whom to fix his jealousy, and giving weight to his suspicions, he went on the attack. Seeing Daphne brought home very late, night after night, by Carol, he assumed they were lovers long before they actually were. His reaction was crude. He would stand at the top of the Cannon Hall stairs, from which point there is a clear view through a high window into the courtyard below, so that he could see Carol embrace and kiss Daphne when he brought her home. Knowing he was spying, Daphne took care that he should see nothing, but this only made her father angrier. He would ask her what she had been doing with Carol so late at night, and when she said they had simply been driving about, this seemed to enrage him more than if she had said they had been in bed. But Gerald's anger was easier to face than his misery, and Daphne, though distressed, found herself better able to withstand it. His new bullying manner did not intimidate her – it only made her more reserved and cold towards him and more determined than ever to go her own way. But what she found harder to handle was her mother's disapproval. Muriel looked at her with barely disguised hostility and this she could not fathom. Her father's possessiveness was one thing, her mother's angry disapproval another. If, as she had begun to suspect, her mother's attitude was dictated by a feeling that Gerald and Daphne were too close and that he loved her more than he loved his wife, why, now that he was angry with her, and the relationship had altered, was Muriel not more sympathetic? Why did she not take Daphne's part and act as mediator between husband and daughter? It seemed to Daphne terribly unfair and she resented her mother's unfriendliness as much as her father's jealousy.[4]

It was resentment as well as real attraction which drove her to consummate her affair with Carol in the summer of 1929, soon after her twenty-second birthday. She had come to the conclusion that the boy within her had no chance of survival and must be locked up in his box forever. She was a woman and must live as a woman and that, to her, meant suppressing her attraction to Ferdy and allowing her growing attraction to Carol to develop into a proper love-affair. But once Carol had become her lover, she was troubled to find that she thought of him with more affection than passion. In a way this was a relief. What was important to her was that no love-affair should interrupt her plans to be free of her parents and live as she wanted down in Fowey. Her diary was full of entries at this time about the value of independence and the desire to be utterly irresponsible. Carol was part of this defiant irresponsibility, but she was never sure that she loved him.

Geoffrey turned up again and she was aware once more of a rival pull towards him, but knew that this, too, was not necessarily love. With great candour, she admitted to her diary that she felt Geoffrey was like an attractive brother and Carol like a son and that neither seemed 'a dashed-off-my-feet thing'. Never at any time did she wonder if her lack of deep feeling for either man might mean that suppressing her 'Venetian tendencies' had failed. She was determined to forget about the boy-in-the-box. She had committed herself to Carol at least temporarily, and Muriel guessed instantly. It was she, not Gerald, who told Daphne she had had enough of her wanton behaviour: she was writing to Carol to tell him what she thought of him. The mere thought of such a letter was so embarrassing that Daphne could hardly bear it. Bitterly, she confessed to her diary that her parents were impossible to please. She was, she wrote, 'getting horribly fed up with sitting in that bedroom at home and being sort of supervised'.

Carol did what he could to calm the situation down. He replied to Muriel with a note of apology for how late he had kept Daphne out and said he would bring her home at a reasonable hour. But, of course, all this curfew did was make the lovers meet in the afternoon instead, which had an excitement all its own, and the affair carried on exactly as before. Carol, who was genuinely in love, began to suggest marriage and even to assume it was inevitable, which alarmed Daphne greatly. She wanted to be irresponsible and marriage was the most boringly responsible step anyone could take. But it was easy to placate Carol by pointing out that neither of them had any money and that their two lives could not for the moment be permanently united. Carol had to be in London, where the theatres and film studios were, and she wanted to be in Fowey, writing. Not knowing how cool was Daphne's view of her own love-affair, her parents were determined to get her away from Carol. They pressed her to accept an invitation to go on a cruise of the Norwegian fjords with a select party organized by the millionaire Otto Kahn.[5] She went, succumbing as ever to this kind of family pressure, but three weeks later was back in Carol's arms. Soon he was going on tour with Edgar Wallace's *The Calendar* and she would be off to Fowey for the summer, so she knew a natural break would follow.

But, as it turned out, though Carol did indeed go off on tour, she did not go to Fowey until later in the summer, which grieved her greatly. Her parents had changed their plans and she was reminded again that, however comfortable and indulged her life seemed, she was powerless without money of her own to do what she wanted. On the surface, she was well off, had her own generous allowance, even in these comparatively hard times for her father, but she had no true independence, could control nothing, not even a simple thing like the date for going to Fowey.

The fact that on 15 May, two days after her twenty-second birthday, her first published story had appeared at last, earning her £10, seemed to show her the way. Ten pounds was miserably little but it was a start. Uncle Willie had made the most of the billing for 'And Now to God the Father'. In the 8 May issue a little inset box announced with something of a fanfare for what was only a short story: 'Miss Daphne du Maurier is the author of *The Bystander* short story which will appear in next week's issue . . . Miss du Maurier, as our readers will realise, has inherited the genius of her grandfather George du Maurier, and in our opinion, in "And Now to God the Father", reveals herself as a writer and stylist of the front rank.' Daphne co-operated for publicity purposes, agreeing to pose for a cover photograph. She dressed herself in an elegant tan-coloured suit and polo-necked sweater, had her hair done, and wore a gold bracelet. The result was an eye-catching colour photograph, in which Daphne looked both haughty and mysterious as well as beautiful. The only detail marring the general effect was that owing to the poor colour-printing her famous blue eyes came out as brown as her suit. No one could have had a more auspicious start, not even with an uncle as editor. Daphne knew this, and knew, too, that *The Bystander*, read for its society, fashion and sports pages, was hardly a literary magazine in which it was a matter of pride to appear. She had no illusions: both her name and her relationship with the editor had given her this start.

But it was a start and she allowed herself to feel pleased. The real benefit resulting from this début was that Uncle Willie introduced her to Miss Nancy Pearn of the literary agency Curtis Brown (A. P. Watt, having been given their chance, were now discarded). Miss Pearn in turn introduced her to Michael Joseph, who ran the book side of Curtis Brown, and he was immediately smitten by Daphne both as a woman and as a potential author. He encouraged her to start thinking of a novel, and when she admitted she thought she had an idea for one, if only she could get down to Fowey to write it, he became quite excited. But first came some more short stories.

On one of her by now regular visits to Ferdy, who appeared to have accepted that, though Daphne still loved her, she was no longer to be her lover, Daphne wrote several more. She thought she had done rather well to apply herself so successfully even though the weather was lovely and it was tempting to sit in the sun all day, and she was extremely irritated when Ferdy criticized her for being 'weak'. Ferdy scoffed at the short stories and said she could see Daphne was never going to achieve anything really worthwhile. Furiously, Daphne denied this. Perhaps she was lazy, but she knew that within her she had a strength and determination no one guessed at. What people saw – a girl drifting aimlessly, living a life of leisure without purpose – was not really her. Her real self was a tough, inner person, watching, absorbing and feverishly creating in her head a wildly different world from the one in which she lived. But Ferdy's accusation made her work harder than ever before, and by the time she returned to London she had completed five more stories.

These were all still on deeply depressing themes. Again and again she stressed masculine heartlessness and feminine helplessness, and the general tone of disillusionment was stronger than ever. Even when she tried to balance male and female responsibility for love going wrong, as she did in 'A Difference in Temperament', the woman still emerged as the victim. The man in this story is full of resentment because he can never be alone, the woman equally frustrated because she can never persuade him to share everything. She thinks he is cruel and selfish, he thinks she parades an imagined suffering. But – and this was a new departure from everything Daphne had previously written – this couple do love each other. What she tried to work out in the story was why people who love each other do not also instinctively understand each other. It puzzled her greatly. Love, she concluded, caused more problems than it solved and nothing between men and women was simple.

On 26 June *The Bystander* ran 'A Difference in Temperament', bringing the grand total of Daphne's earnings to £20 by the time she finally went down to Fowey. Unfortunately, the weather was poor. It rained constantly, the mists swept in from the sea, the fog horns hooted miserably and, though Daphne loved it, Gerald was wretched. He had arrived at Ferryside exhausted after filming *Escape*, a disastrous experience, and was in no mood for bitter winds and grey clouds. Golf was impossible most days, and he was bored to death, even though the house was full of entertaining guests. He began muttering about selling Ferryside, even of having to sell it to meet tax demands, a catastrophe for Daphne only narrowly averted by shipping Gerald back to London with the greatest speed. Once he had gone, Daphne wrote to Tod that winter was almost upon them and once more she, too, would be obliged to go back to London. Not even the thought of Carol eagerly awaiting her eased her anguish. In fact this increased it. She was still fond of Carol but he was becoming too dependent. Whereas other women might relish being told how much they were missed she did not like it. It smacked too much of Gerald and Muriel's relationship. The last thing she wanted was a man telling her he could not do without her. With her passion for people who didn't give a damn what one thought of them, for people strong and independent, it was anathema for her to be told she was needed. She had no wish to hurt Carol, but neither had she any intention of becoming what she saw as some kind of surrogate mother.

The regular arrival of Carol's letters did her an unexpected favour, however. Her parents suddenly gave her permission to stay in Ferryside for the winter, provided she would sleep in one of the cottages opposite, lodging with a Miss Roberts, and only going into the house during the day to write. It was a tremendous concession, and though Daphne could see the reasoning behind it – better to have her in Fowey than up to no good with Carol Reed in London – she was grateful. This, she knew, was her big chance. For three years she had sworn that if only she could be alone down in Fowey she would be able to write properly. She must discipline herself, work regular hours and not succumb to diversions. But, of course, in Fowey in winter, there would be no diversions, only walks. There would be no first nights, no cinemas, no cafés, no parties, no excursions and virtually no company. If she failed now she would never succeed.

Once everyone had departed, Daphne settled into The Nook, Miss Roberts' tiny cottage. It had no bathroom and an outside lavatory, both of which convinced Daphne she was leading a truly spartan life. 'It takes courage', she wrote solemnly to Tod, 'to crouch in a hip bath and use the outside lav.' It was Miss Roberts, of course, who filled the hip bath, toiling up the stairs with buckets of hot water. She also cooked Daphne's evening meal and washed her clothes, performing all these tasks with the greatest cheerfulness and willingness. Daphne's great advantage in such situations was her lack of any superior manner. It is true she allowed herself to be waited on hand and foot, but she was always appreciative and never acted as though it was only her due. She liked listening to Miss Roberts, encouraging her to talk, and rapidly became acquainted with all the local gossip, quickly learning the names of everyone involved and showing genuine interest in them. She was easy and friendly to have in the cottage and inspired great devotion.

On 3 October 1929, Daphne went across to Ferryside to begin the new routine. It rather pleased her that it was a terrible day, with the wind howling round the empty house, the rain driving against the windows and the sea lashing the quay. She settled down at a table feeling the weather was symbolic of the kind of book she wanted to write – a story about a seafaring family in which atmosphere and a sense of place would dominate. She wanted to give the story a mystical background, quite different from the down-to-earth nature of her short stories, and she wanted to take her time, to build slowly on the foundation she had in mind. Her preparatory work had been to read the Slade family letters, which the boatman Adams had found for her, and to consult old boatyard records. She had investigated the history of the ship *Jane Slade*, launched in Polruan in 1870, and had carefully absorbed how shares in the ship operated. She knew the details of Christopher Slade's life (son of the original Jane) and the fortunes of his children. But more important than this basic research was the way in which over the past three years she had steeped herself in the atmosphere of the local landscape. Day after day she had walked the Hall Walk and along the cliffs both sides of the estuary and up the river until she was familiar with every view and knew the countryside in all its moods. She had observed the sky so acutely that she could predict the weather as surely as any local – and all of this feeling for the place itself she wanted to bring into her story.

Once begun, the new regime proved satisfyingly easy to follow. In the mornings she wrote, broke for lunch with Miss Roberts, then in the afternoon walked or rowed before returning to Ferryside at four o'clock to resume writing until she locked the house up at about seven o'clock and returned to The Nook. In the evenings, she read and retired early. As she had known, there were few distractions. On Sundays she had supper at The Haven with the Quiller-Couches and sometimes she went riding with Foy Quiller-Couch, who became her great friend. Foy was eight years older than Daphne and led the life of a Victorian daughter at The Haven, very much under her father's influence, which was rather repressive. But behind the dutifulness Foy was an independent spirit and Daphne quickly came to appreciate her finer points. Foy took her off to meet Lady Vyvyan,[6] who lived at Trelowarren in the Helford district, a place Daphne described as 'the most beautiful imaginable'. Soon she was thinking of Foy and Clara Vyvyan as her two dearest friends, reflecting at the same time 'what curious friendships I make . . . how I hate "nice" girls. Nobody could describe me as that . . .' The three women were all slightly unusual, not to say eccentric, in appearance, with Daphne in her (for the times) daring red slacks, Foy in a jumble of old clothes, and the much older Clara in the inevitable beret over hair she had never cut in her life.

Apart from these outings with Foy, there was only the Women's Institute to amuse her. Daphne went with Miss Roberts, to please her, and to show a willingness to be part of the community, and was half mystified, half horrified by the gathering. She described 'Mrs Burghard at the piano, eyes fixed feverishly on a piece of music, demanding in frantic tones that some unseen presence should bring her her chariot of fire . . . My spirits sank as Mrs Morten from Truro announced that all over England a quarter of a million women were meeting together as we were doing . . . and finally reached zero when Mrs Burghard told us of a competition next month when every member was to make a lady's handbag, the materials of which must not cost more than a shilling . . . half an hour later, you would have been gratified by the spectacle of twenty-five ladies standing in rows opposite each other passing tennis balls to one another in a strange form of race . . .' But such excitements were only monthly and did not disrupt the pattern of work.

Within two weeks, working six hours a day on average, Daphne had completed 45,000 words of her novel. After another three weeks she had completed Part Two, of roughly the same length, but by then, in mid-November, she could sense that the main impetus of the story was over. This worried her. In her notes, she had ambitiously sketched out a story covering four generations, bringing it up to very nearly the present day, but the further she went from the original Jane Slade background the harder it became to write with the same conviction and fluency. She was learning that just beyond the middle of a long novel was the hardest place to be. She was also missing the wealth of actual detail she had had in the first two parts. Confiding this to Miss Roberts she was rescued by a local man, Richard Bunt, who lent her books about life at the turn of the century to use as the basis for Part Three. By 17 November, Part Three was finished, after a good deal of labour. It was significantly shorter than the first two parts, but she was happy to have completed it. Just as she was looking forward to the last part, her mother ordered her home for Christmas and she knew she could not possibly finish the whole novel before she went. It would have to wait until her return in January because she would not be able to write in London. But this return to Fowey, it now transpired, was by no means to be counted on. In her mother's letter there was a scarcely veiled threat that permission to return to Ferryside would be dependent on good behaviour over Christmas. This made Daphne so anxious that she resolved to take no chances: she would stay in every evening and go out of her way to be charming. Leaving her dog with Miss Roberts, together with her almost completed novel, she left for London determined her conduct would be exemplary, even though, she commented to Foy, London was 'a definite hell'.

Chapter Five

The knowledge that back at Ferryside she had left an almost completed novel gave Daphne the energy to join in the Christmas festivities at Cannon Hall with more enthusiasm than she had shown for several years. Christmas itself was always a big affair with the du Mauriers – they celebrated it in Dickensian style with a magnificently dressed tree, lavish meals and generous presents. That year Daphne had 'got a marvellous thing for changing into every night. Black evening trousers, cream satin shirt and black velvet jacket . . . I rather fancy myself,' she wrote to Foy, 'and try to look like Shelley!' She enjoyed herself and it was not until the New Year that she began to grow restive.

Since she was trying so hard to be 'good' she could not go off with Carol too ostentatiously, nor stay out with him late at night, but in a way these restrictions added excitement to their assignations and at the same time gave her the excuse not to become too intense. She still thought of Carol as a very special friend with whom she had a sexual relationship, rather than as a lover who was also a friend: the distinction was clear in her own mind if not in his. What she liked best was not the love-making, but the talking and the listening and the hanging around cafés, speculating about strangers. Since it was January and cold, they spent rather more time in cafés than usual and visited not only insignificant places but also the Café de Paris in Coventry Street. They would sit upstairs, smoking, but sipping nothing stronger than orangeade, listening to the singers and watching the floor shows. These were often daring – 'at the Café de Paris', reported *The Bystander*, 'an extraordinary dancing display is given by Roseray & Capella . . . both dancers being almost nude'. One night Daphne reported to Tod that she almost had her breath taken away when she heard 'a negress sing a couple of songs . . . "I Like The Way He Does It" and "Put it Where It Was Last Night" '. The sensual side of her nature, which she was still unsure about, sometimes thinking it did not exist, responded so strongly to these suggestive songs that she was afraid her expression would betray her feelings and people would know.

Carol certainly knew, but he knew also that, whatever the appearances to the contrary, he was no nearer winning Daphne over completely. She was adroit at side-stepping his urgent requests to put their relationship on a more permanent basis, to become at least officially engaged. But she prevaricated, telling him she had work to do and must finish her novel before she thought about anything else. If he did not understand this, then he did not understand her. Another person who continued not to seem to understand her was her mother. Often, when they happened to be alone together in the house that January, Daphne felt she and Muriel might as well be on different planets. Memories of thinking, when she was a child, that her mother was like the wicked stepmother in 'Snow White'[1] flashed into her head. She knew this was silly, that her mother was very far from being wicked, and she was honest enough to acknowledge that, whatever the reason for her less-than-warm relationship with her mother, it could not be all Muriel's fault. Angela and Jeanne enjoyed a perfectly harmonious relationship with her, found her affectionate and caring, and were quite at ease. The obvious explanation – obvious not only to Daphne but to everyone who knew the family – was that, since Daphne was Gerald's favourite, Muriel saw her as a rival. It was a neat theory, and one Daphne had accepted while she was an adolescent, but now she was not convinced of its truth.

Daphne was envious, in a wistful rather than a raging sort of way, of her sisters' relationship with their mother, but this did not create a barrier between the sisters themselves. The three of them were very unalike, both in appearance and personality, but they got on well together even if they were not exactly close. Angela was in the habit of confiding in Daphne about her 'pashes', and both of them had suffered together from Gerald's suspicions which made a strong bond. Neither criticized the other: Angela respected Daphne's need to be alone and Daphne was indulgent over Angela's need to be surrounded by friends. Towards Jeanne they were both affectionate, but there was not the same involvement. Jeanne not only seemed much younger – four years younger than Daphne, seven than Angela – but she had a much closer relationship, as Daphne had observed, with Mo. She was Mo's 'ewe lamb', just as Gerald had been his mother's, and was treated, the older sisters felt, with more latitude.

It seemed to Daphne that increasingly, over the last few years, Jeanne had in many ways reigned supreme in Gerald's affections. She, too, now reminded him of his father, but whereas he believed Daphne to have inherited George du Maurier's talent as a writer, he believed Jeanne had inherited his talent as an artist. This pleased him, and so did another of his youngest daughter's talents: she was surprisingly athletic. She did not yet play golf, Gerald's chief sporting passion, but she was good at tennis, his next love, and adored hockey and riding. He was terrified she would get hurt and once, when she was hit by a hockey stick and slightly concussed, he forbade her ever to play again. But Jeanne easily got round him – she was, at this time, the darling of both parents.

Daphne, by contrast, felt that at home she was now nobody's darling, and though she did not exactly want to be – if you were someone's darling, their chief concern, you sacrificed at least a measure of independence – she felt a little displaced. None of her friends seemed to be available, and she realized that, in fact, Foy Quiller-Couch was now the person she was closest to, with the exception of Tod and Ferdy, who were in a different category and with whom she could only, on the whole, correspond. Yet she was careful to control her dissatisfaction and restlessness, fearing that if they became obvious she would be thought ungrateful and there would be no chance of returning to Ferryside. Mid-January arrived and she dared to enquire if she might return to her dog and her novel in Cornwall. The gracious answer was that she might, at the end of the month.

She was elated but, when the time came, bewildered to find how painful the parting from Carol proved to be. Exactly what she had hoped to avoid had happened: Carol needed her and said so. His distress at the news of her departure touched her deeply, but not so deeply that she was unable to analyse her feelings. When Gerald had made it plain he needed her and looked to her for support she had been, and still was, upset, but her distress over Carol's misery was different. She discovered that whereas she resented her father's demands she felt responsible for Carol's expectations. To her own surprise she felt moved to tears, though confessing to Foy 'I am not generally given to tears', and confused over what Carol actually meant to her. What was this emotion which so unexpectedly overcame her? She tried to work it out in a poem:

> We should remember this little room.
> Pale flaky walls a dusty sun lays bare;
> Tumbled blankets, rough and warm, the smell
> Of tenderness, all wrapped for one sharp moment
> In an air of love, and held within
> A drop of time; a womb-world unassailable
> In day or place forgotten by the mind,
> A dividend of love for two to share
> And miser-like set by a hoard for distant memories.
> Yes, we should remember this room, but we forget
> That a sadness lies in the creeping of time
> When two are no longer one; when one heart flies
> And the other is left in the empty hell of remembering.

It was Carol who was 'left in the empty hell', and her heart which flew not to another person but to Fowey and the other self she became when she was there alone with her writing.

All the way down to Cornwall she worried about Carol, but once she was there her anxiety lifted and, in registering this, she wondered about its significance. Every time she thought she loved a man, he had only to go out of her sight for her to discover he faded from her mind. Instead of absence making her heart grow fonder, it made it grow cool. It was, she wrote to Tod, 'queer' and she did not altogether like to wonder too much what it meant, in case she came to the conclusion that she was shallow and heartless. Once back at work she threw off these worries and devoted herself to the troublesome Part Four of her novel. It was a struggle. Part Four brought her almost up to her own times and she felt there was something strained in the writing which had not been there before. It was the end of March before she completed Part Four.

The agreement with her parents had been that once her novel was finished she would return to London, which she did, leaving her manuscript to be typed out. She felt curiously depressed and exhausted and Hampstead did nothing to improve her mood. Far from hopes of instant success, she worried that what she had written might be 'hopeless' and prepared herself for her agent Michael Joseph shaking his head and telling her to stick to short stories after all. The completed typescript arrived a month later.

She shut herself up in the room above the garage and read it. Even then, she had no confidence. All she knew was that what she had written was very different from anything she had tried before. She was cautiously optimistic that she had succeeded in capturing the sense of place for which she had striven. Plyn, the village modelled on Fowey, seemed to her real and that pleased her. The character of Janet Coombe, based on what she knew of Jane Slade, but containing many facets of her own character, was also satisfactory. Janet emerged as strong, she felt, just as she had intended. One half of Janet wanted to be a conventional wife and mother, the other to be 'part of a ship . . . and the seas'. Janet is always aware, even when appearing to settle down, that she is searching for something, though she does not know for what and feels there is 'something greater waiting', just as Daphne herself had confessed to Tod. Even nearer to what she herself felt was Janet's inner rebellion against being a woman – 'Please God, make me a lad afore I'm grown,' Janet had prayed as a girl, and even after she had become a wife and mother she is saying 'I'd been a man . . . if I had my way' and 'Why wasn't I born a man?' But what troubled Daphne, as she tried to judge her own work, was the visionary element. Had it worked? Was Janet's yearning towards a future, when she would be dead, but in which her spirit would communicate with and sustain her beloved son Joseph, credible or just silly? Did it weaken the novel? She had no means of knowing and did not trust her own critical faculties.

What she did feel, as she parcelled the book up and sent it to

Michael Joseph, was that she had succeeded in one vital respect: the reader, any reader, would surely want to know what happened next and how it all ended. And in this she was not mistaken. The narrative drive in *The Loving Spirit* is strong even in the less convincing parts of the novel. Between the first two and the last two parts the fire goes out of the story. Once Janet and then Joseph die the other characters seem mundane but, even so, curiosity is kept alive, that very desire to find out what happens afterwards, which Daphne wanted. The real difficulty, which the author suspected without being able to define it, lies in a shift of tone. The first two parts, those parts she had so enjoyed writing and had written so quickly and easily, with their inspired descriptions of the landscape and feeling for the atmosphere of Plyn, belonged to an older tradition of romantic (in the wider, artistic sense) writing. Daphne had been reading Mary Webb over the winter and there were touches of that kind of fervid prose in *The Loving Spirit*. Sometimes it worked and sometimes, particularly in some of the dialogue – of the 'we'm cleft together you an' I, like the stars to the sky' variety – it became ludicrous, and it was only the passion in the writing which saved it from bathos. The third and fourth parts of *The Loving Spirit* are in a quite different tradition, more in the *Kipps* style of H. G. Wells, full of social observation and detail. There were really two novels here, determinedly lashed into one, with romanticism drifting into realism and both suffering from confusion.

Once the novel had gone to Michael Joseph, Daphne took herself off to Paris again. 'Paris', she reported to Foy, 'has an electric thrill in the air you can't mistake,' and it made her feel happier. While she was there, staying with Ferdy, she received a letter from an elated Michael Joseph saying he loved her novel and was offering it immediately to Heinemann. Daphne was thrilled – she and Angela, when young, used solemnly to discuss whom they would choose as their publisher when each had written her *magnum opus*, and Heinemann was top of the list. Heinemann's verdict was equally swift. While still in Paris, Daphne heard that they would publish *The Loving Spirit* with some minor conditions about cuts. They reserved the right to delay the publication date until they were satisfied, but publish it they would. This news was 'wonderful' and had an immediate effect. Success made her want to start writing another, better, novel at once. No longer would she drift. She was now a proper accredited author and she was eager to capitalize on her initial success – not for one moment did she consider waiting to see how her first effort was greeted.

What was remarkable, and certainly made Ferdy eat her words, was the discipline and commitment Daphne now showed. She returned to London and, under Michael Joseph's direction, made the alterations (none drastic) required by Heinemann then, after a brief sojourn in Fowey, returned without complaint to London where she began at once on her second novel. All the encouragement she needed was the certainty of *The Loving Spirit* being published. The trappings of success – seeing the finished book, seeing the cover with her name on it, receiving reviews, notching up sales – meant little to her. What was important was that she had not deluded herself: she could write. Charles Evans of Heinemann was not Uncle Willie, and even if, as she realized, her name and age made her a tempting bet for any publisher, she had enough common sense to know that this would not have been quite enough without some evidence of talent. The thing was, she was launched and it was up to her to consolidate her position.

Her second novel, finally entitled *I'll Never Be Young Again*, was startlingly different in both style and subject matter from *The Loving Spirit*. She no longer felt that being at Fowey was essential before she could write. She worked instead in Orchard Street, off Leicester Square, in the office her Aunt Billie used as Gerald's secretary. She organized a working day every bit as disciplined as she had had at Fowey, with the difference that instead of afternoon breaks walking or sailing she 'nipped out for lunch with Carol' whenever he was free. Their affair continued, with Carol still pressing for the commitment she continued to refuse him. She felt exactly the same about him as before – when she was with him it was fun and she was fond of him, but when she was not she did not miss him. What she had always liked about Carol was the way he lived for the moment, the way he didn't want to be tied down and become staid and boring. But now, with regard to her, he seemed to want to do just that. His tendency to daydream, so like her own, showed signs of disappearing and he was becoming practical in a way she resented. Whatever he meant to her she was not prepared to become as serious as he wished. She felt each day, as she went from home to Orchard Street, that she had a proper job which she did not want interrupted by Carol or anyone else. Writing was work and it was her life. Such was her application – a deaf ear turned now to all family attempts to ensnare her in delightful distractions – that she finished her second novel in two months, long before her first was out. There was no need this time for research. The research was all her own recent experience, partly of the Norwegian fjords, which she had seen on the Otto Kahn cruise, and more particularly her affair with Carol. Since this still continued she was living as well as writing part of the novel and no experience was wasted.

The story Daphne chose to write this time was highly contemporary and was intended to deal – bravely, for 1930 – with sexual issues. The relationships between men and women, especially sexual ones, had been the stuff of her early short stories, but always she had preserved an authorial detachment. Now, though her theme was the same, she dropped the cynical, world-weary approach and devoted herself to examining what sexual passion was all about. She wrote in the first person as a man, a bold step to free herself to write about her own experience: if the 'I' were masculine, then it would not automatically be suspected that this character voiced her own opinions and feelings. But he did. He was the boy-in-the-box, allowed out in her imagination. Dick, the young narrator, is far more Daphne than is Hesta, the girl with whom, in the second part of the novel, he has an affair. Dick's pronouncements about sex match very closely Daphne's own to Tod in her letters and, though Hesta shares some of Daphne's own reactions to Carol, it is Dick who commands the attention, though it is not until the first part is over that Dick actually merits much attention at all. In this first half credibility is strained so far that it all but snaps. Dick is saved from suicide by a wholly unbelievable character, just out of prison, called Jake. Together, the two of them work their passage to Norway where they leave their ship and travel on horseback through the country. There is an implicit, though never realized, homosexual relationship between the two men, but there is also more than a hint that they are each a half of the same man. This makes for an uneasy read. Dick and Jake do not have conversations but make speeches to each other, they pontificate and make grand but banal statements about the meaning of life ('Being young is something you won't understand until it is gone from you'). The only redeeming feature lies in Dick's relationship with his famous father in whose shadow he lives. As Dick reminisces, the narrative ignites briefly, but it takes Dick's affair with an American girl during his travels to bring any real fire to a strangely wooden story.

Suddenly, the whole point of the novel becomes apparent. Dick is appalled by his first experience of sex – 'the ugliness of passion . . . my own sense of inexplicable degradation' distresses him beyond measure and he wonders why 'desire should turn into degradation and from degradation into nothing'. Then, once Jake has been conveniently drowned and Dick is having a real love-affair in Paris with Hesta, his ideas about sex change. The novel begins to grow in strength, with the glory and then the death of sexual passion cleverly caught. Dick has to work hard to woo Hesta, but once converted to the joys of sex, she can think of nothing else just as Dick's own interest wanes. What troubles Dick most is his wish to separate Hesta as a woman from Hesta as a source of sexual gratification. He says to her at one point, 'I wish you were a prostitute,' because then he could just use her. When, under his tuition, she begins 'to do things' when they make love, he tells her she is 'wicked'. He cannot bear the discovery that she loves sex and 'must have it, that's all, it doesn't matter [who] with'. Inevitably, they part, with Hesta despatched to a debauched life and Dick to a puritanical one as a bank clerk, glad that all passion is spent and he is no longer young.

Throughout this revealing novel, Dick has all the strong lines. He is determined that Hesta should realize sex is only a game, even if a dangerous and exciting one – it must not be confused with the serious ambition to do well with whatever talents one possesses. He tells Hesta 'sex should be like a game of tennis'[2] and should be practised as such until one becomes expert. At the same time, it is 'natural' and should not be repressed. But most important of all is the need to distinguish between sex and love. Sex is a step on the way to love, perhaps, but it is not to be thought of as the goal itself. In a conversation in a café with some rakish friends he has made, Dick is told 'you'll have to surrender to sex before you purify yourself'. He rejects this, deciding the whole crowd are 'dirty, fusty little moles' and he hates them. But when his need to have full sexual intercourse with Hesta overwhelms him he begins to think the 'dirty moles' were right. He overcomes her reluctance and then almost immediately 'I had to deny passivity and be her lover'. She wants to 'wander into my mind, to share that with me, to be part of this as well', and he cannot stand this assumption that because of their sexual relationship they must also have a complete emotional and mental one. This he will not give her. He is a writer and knows 'this power of writing [is] more dangerous than adventure, more satisfying than love'. Nothing horrifies him more than Hesta's new sexual appetite – 'Sweetheart,' he tells her, 'it's beastly . . . it's, it's unattractive. It's all right for me to want you, but not for you – at least, never to say. It's terrible, darling.' When she says she cannot help it – 'I never cared to, and you used to beg and beg me . . . and now that I want you . . . you say it's beastly' – he is appalled.

Daphne felt shattered when she had finished this second novel and extremely nervous about what kind of reception it would have. *The Loving Spirit* might have its faults – she knew it did – but it would not shock. *I'll Never Be Young Again* was almost certain to. People she admired, people like Sir Arthur Quiller-Couch, might be disgusted. But she was defiant, feeling she had tried to write honestly about something that mattered, something not written about openly, and this justified perhaps upsetting some people. *The Loving Spirit* was still not to be published for six months, but she submitted this second novel as soon as it was ready. Both her agent and her publisher were surprised by it. They were fairly certain it would not have the appeal of the first, but on the other hand amazed to find that in this new young author they had someone more versatile than they had suspected. If Daphne du Maurier, aged only twenty-three, could in the space of nine months produce two such radically different novels, then the future looked bright indeed for all of them.

Heinemann, secure in this knowledge, put a great deal of preparation into the publication of *The Loving Spirit* on 23 February

1931.[3] Naturally, much was made of the du Maurier name and of the author's youth and beauty – newspapers and magazines then, as now, liked to brighten their pages with photographs of lovely girls, especially lovely girls from famous families. The publicity drum beat loudly and the book was a great success in every way. It was widely reviewed by eminent critics – including Rebecca West – and sold well, for a first novel.

In America it had a tougher but equally prominent reception. Rebecca West's quote – 'a whopper of a romantic novel in the vein of Emily Brontë' – which was used in the publicity by Doubleday, may have worked against it. The influential *Saturday Review of Literature* was rather scathing about the Brontë comparison, though conceding that *The Loving Spirit* was indeed in the romantic tradition and as such 'interesting'. But it was the *New York Herald Tribune* which, either side of the Atlantic, proved the most perspicacious and prophetic. 'When some literary historian comes to survey the first third of the twentieth century,' it suggested, 'he will have fun tracing the roots of the flourishing young romantic revival that is growing up among us.' It went on to claim that after the First World War there had been a deluge of realism, 'sparing no ghastly detail', followed now by 'a surprising number of long leisurely books to be savoured quietly'. It predicted that these 'modern romantics' would gain ground steadily because the public desperately needed not just the escapism offered, but the 'sense of continuity' these 'saga novels' gave. It noted, too, that in the bestseller list together with *The Loving Spirit* was Hugh Walpole's *Judith Paris* (the second volume of his hugely popular *Herries Chronicle*) which supported this theory.

No first novelist could have had more attention, but Daphne was more impressed by the cheque, which arrived from Heinemann, and by her father's delight. She hoped this delight would not be short-lived and prepared herself for it to turn to disapproval on the publication of *I'll Never be Young Again*. Heinemann paid her more for her second novel – £125 as opposed to £75 – but to her surprise and disappointment printed three hundred fewer copies. The reaction of her family and friends – all so delighted with and proud of *The Loving Spirit* – was expected but none the less a little depressing. Tod hated it, as did Sir Arthur Quiller-

Couch and Aunt Billie, but Angela, who was writing a novel herself[4] at the time, was fascinated by it, and Gerald managed to say carefully loyal things.

Already Daphne had an idea for a third novel, which she started in Paris in January 1931 and continued in Fowey in March, as soon as *The Loving Spirit* was out. Rather to her surprise, this third book, *The Progress of Julius*, took nine months to complete. It was yet another departure, as different from *I'll Never Be Young Again* as that novel had been from *The Loving Spirit*. By the time all three novels had been published it was impossible to predict which way this young writer would go, how she would develop.

The Progress of Julius is a powerful, if flawed novel, with a vigour in the writing absent from Daphne's first two novels. This time she had an overall vision of one character, Julius Levy himself. This is a man whose whole life is dedicated to getting 'something for nothing', but who discovers, in his daughter Gabriel, his only true pleasure and satisfaction. But his joy in this daughter comes to an end when he finds he cannot possess and control her as he has possessed and controlled everything else in his life, even his wife. The murder of Gabriel by Julius, a murder he gets away with, is a horrifying but absolutely logical end to the story.

The story, since it covers the whole of a man's life, compresses a great deal of material. Julius' childhood, in the Paris of 1860-1872, and his youth in Algiers are sketched with great zest and written at a great, galloping pace. He is unmoved by the sight of his father murdering his mother (found in bed with another man because the child Julius has betrayed her), and by the girl prostitute who adores him so much that she is willing to endure any humiliation at his hands. On and on Julius goes, richer but uglier by the minute.

Daphne keeps his character perfectly consistent, and though there are many highly melodramatic episodes, sometimes teetering on the edge of the ludicrous, never for one moment is Julius' single-mindedness doubted. She sees him as a type, but there is a wealth of detail in her observations on Julius' behaviour. She knew how self-made Jewish millionaires conducted themselves and knew, too, the kind of prejudice which existed against them in the first quarter of the century. But it was in Julius' relationship with his daughter that she developed her main theme and put into it her strongest personal feelings. What makes this novel startling is its clear autobiographical content.

Julius has 'a voracious passion' for his daughter, who is 'exactly [like him] . . . in their supreme blind egotism'. When Julius sees his adolescent daughter playing the flute he finds he is overcome by 'an odd taste in his mouth, and a sensation in mind and body that was shameful and unclean'. He cannot resist asking her 'Do you like me?' and her evasive answers enrage him. She tells him not to be silly and he asks her if she is a child or does she torment him on purpose? 'I don't know what the devil you're talking about,' says Gabriel, to be told, 'You're a bloody liar.' The tension between them mounts, only to be diffused by the entry of Rachel, Gabriel's mother.

This is one of many scenes in which Daphne puts into Julius' mouth sentiments very near to Gerald's own and, into Gabriel's, words she herself had thought or written, if not uttered.[5] Julius, told by his daughter that his wife Rachel is jealous of her, at first finds this 'funny' and then 'the idea excited him'. Gabriel is not so excited. She tells him not 'to harp at me, it bores me' and he calls her 'a bitch'. When she starts to have boyfriends and Julius' own jealousy begins there are scenes closely matching those Daphne had endured with Gerald. Gabriel is so angry with Julius' ridiculous snooping that she tells him to go to hell. She almost begins to hate him – 'he was relentless, he was like some oppressive, suffocating power that stifled her . . . it was too much for her, too strong'. Yet at the same time she knew ultimately 'she would be the victor . . . she held him between her hands and he did not know . . . Papa would be hurt.' Just as in J. M. Barrie's play *Dear Brutus*, she, the daughter, would do the hurting. It comes as a great shock to find that, although Gabriel does indeed do the hurting, she pays with her life. Unable to bear the thought of her with a lover, her father strangles her. She was lost to him, but nobody else could have her.

What Daphne put into *The Progress of Julius* in the last two parts was remarkable enough in its confessional content, but what she left out was even more revealing. The novel was handwritten in exercise books and contains extensive crossings-out. Whole pages are scored through, but are still legible. In the first rejected version the hatred of the mother goes much further than it does in the final novel. Julius' father tells him he has always loved him better than his wife – 'I will love you better than anything in the world and we will always be together.' Julius is entirely happy and glad his mother is out of the way. He enjoys his father holding him close and 'patting his body, pressing his little behind'. This is heavily crossed out, and so is the child's assertion that 'we are happy because we are the same, Papa' and the father's assurance that his wife had only been of value because she was 'nice to touch'. Julius is nicer, though. There is no record that Daphne herself at any time experienced the kind of fondling Julius received from his father, but the whole imagined relationship in this draft, first between Julius and his father, and then between Julius and his daughter, certainly suggests a strong indication that the physical contact between fathers and children fascinated if not troubled her.

Parts Two and Three, in which Julius' rise to fame and fortune are recounted, suffer little change, but in Part Four, when Gabriel is growing up, some drastic cuts are made. They are mostly about the mother. Julius' passion for Gabriel is said to have come 'at a critical time to husband and wife . . . She must fade and dim and dissolve away . . . a woman with a grievance . . . not positively unhappy but negative, a shadow . . .' When Rachel watches husband and daughter together the sexual tension between them is immediately apparent. She is reminded, looking at Julius' face, of a drawing she had seen of 'a satyr . . . with a look of yearning on his lascivious face . . . hands stretching to lose themselves in the hair of a wild bacchante [sic] who lay curled upon the branch of a tree'.

Strangely, Daphne had no qualms about Gerald reading *The Progress of Julius*. Her confidence may have been an indication that what she had written about this relationship bore no resemblance to her relationship with Gerald (though, of course, the more startling passages had been removed from the final draft), but Julius' possessiveness, and the distress this caused his daughter, is undoubtedly Gerald's, and everything Daphne writes about the darker side of Julius' obsession echoes what she had recorded herself as feeling. The fact that she felt able to write about it at all showed she had to a great extent broken free of her father's emotional demands. She loved him deeply, but his ability to torture her with his need for her had gone. She knew herself to be moving out of Gerald's emotional reach. She was moving out of Carol's far weaker claim on her too – she knew now that she would never marry him, although she had not yet told him. What filled her thoughts, in 1931, was her career.

And at that point she met Major 'Boy' Browning.

Chapter Six

Major Frederick Arthur Montague Browning, known as 'Tommy' to his family and 'Boy'[1] in his regiment, was thirty-four years old when he sailed with his friend, John Prescott, a West Country man, into Fowey harbour and was observed by the du Maurier sisters. He was captain, and cook, of *Ygdrasil*, his 20-foot cruiser, and his fellow officer John was engineer, navigator and crew. They had spent their leave sailing from the Isle of Wight, stopping off at various points along the South Coast until they reached Fowey, where the boatman, George Hunkin,[2] an old friend of John's, had reserved one of his moorings for them off the old pilchard factory by Polruan. They arrived on 3 October 1931, just as the du Mauriers were on the verge of closing up Ferryside for the winter and returning to London. Angela saw the two good-looking officers first, as they cruised past Ferryside in their boat, and called Daphne's attention to them. She was immediately impressed by the helmsman, who was soon easily identified from local gossip as 'Boy' Browning. He was tall – six foot – with dark hair and grey eyes, very alert and energetic, and with a confident but not arrogant bearing.

Browning made no attempt, on that visit, to introduce himself to the du Mauriers, even though he knew they owned Ferryside and he was interested in Daphne. Unusually for a Grenadier Guards officer, Browning enjoyed reading novels, and had read *The Loving Spirit*, attracted by reviews which described it as a story set in a small sea-town with a strong seafaring background. He had found the novel appealing and not only for the sea setting. To his contemporaries and to those who had served under him he was known as a ferocious disciplinarian who set the highest standards for his men and for himself. He demanded total dedication and was renowned for his smart appearance. His army career had begun at eighteen when he went from Sandhurst to join the 2nd Battalion Grenadier Guards in France in the second year of the First World War. In December 1917, the month of his twentieth birthday, he won the DSO for his part in the capture of Gauche Wood. By the time the war ended, he had become a Captain, and when he sailed into Fowey harbour he was a Major.

This exemplary record tells very little about Browning's real personality and character. Clearly, he was brave, hard-working and efficient. What very few people knew, or were ever to know, was that his courage was of different kinds. His DSO for outstanding bravery was won only after a miserable spell when he was invalided home, after barely two months, with what was entered in the records as 'nervous exhaustion'. Those two months in 1915 had been an appalling experience for any new recruit – the weather in France was bitterly cold, with snow and raw winds, the casualties heavy, the sniping and bombing continual.[3] There was no real rest, in spite of the official policy of keeping troops for only two days in the trenches then two days out, because the Germans were using high-explosive shells. But the battalion which the young Browning joined fought in no major battle during these two months he was with them, and he was not attached to any of the small groups who went on raids and were engaged in skirmishes. He was not wounded or shell-shocked and yet he was sent back to England as 'unfit'.

This was an unusual and rather ignominious return for a soldier in 1916. Most soldiers were treated in field hospitals unless they were so badly wounded they had to be sent home never to return. The doctors who examined those declared 'unfit' were strict and unsympathetic – it was almost impossible to hoodwink them. But Browning had no desire to trick anyone or to get out of the war, so the eight months of enforced rest he was given were neither easy nor welcome. 'Nervous exhaustion' in a new young officer, who had not taken part in any major campaign and had not been physically injured, was an unwelcome label to be saddled with. Every month he appeared before a board of three army doctors at Caxton Hall and was declared still to be suffering from this embarrassingly vague condition. His family believed the trouble was his old complaint, known as 'Tommy's tum'. Every now and again, starting in childhood, Tommy would experience violent stomach pains which defied medical diagnosis. His mother Nancy would soothe the pains away, when he was little, by gently rubbing his stomach.[4] By the time he was at Eton, and had developed into a superb sportsman, Tommy had learned how to deal with 'me tum' himself. He was quite incapacitated during the attacks, but if he kept very still and quiet they eventually wore off. They did not prevent him from becoming an Olympic high-hurdler and bob-sleighing for England.

But in France, or so his family believed, the stomach pains returned with a vengeance. Nobody appears to have suggested they were psychosomatic and there is no mention of them in the army records. It seems likely that 'nervous exhaustion' and 'unfit' were terms used to describe a condition nobody could fathom, but in the circumstances of those times they carried a hint of some kind of breakdown under pressure. Whatever the cause, Browning had to struggle to get 'fit'. He finally passed the Caxton Hall board in September 1916 and rejoined his battalion in France.

During the next year, his stomach pains, or whatever had caused him to be 'unfit', did not return. He wrote home to his only sister (he had no brothers), Grace, that his morale was pretty good, though he expected to be wounded soon if not killed. On his return he had found there were only six men still alive who had been with him before he was sent home, and, like every soldier then, he knew the casualty rate stood so high the odds were overwhelmingly against survival. The war was 'beastly', the pace 'too hot', and every leave seemed an eternity away. He was a man whose comforts were extravagant too – he liked expensive cars, drooling over the Peugeot catalogues he had Grace send him, and good food and wine, all unobtainable for the moment. He had to make do with a hundred cigarettes a week and playing his drum. It was all dreary, wretched and in spite of the fear also 'boring for long stretches'.

At the end of 1917, the boredom vanished. Browning's battalion was ordered to take a wood, Gauche Wood, on the top of a hill. It was in an open field, without cover, and the Germans were known to have machine-guns in the wood. Three companies, including one led by Browning, were to attack the wood while a fourth was held in reserve. All night the men hid on a railway embankment and then, at dawn, with the mist not yet lifted and the light poor, the onslaught began. Up the hillside the soldiers went, straight into machine-gun fire. The promised tank support never materialized. Those who reached the wood were picked off by German snipers, and those who escaped were engaged in hand-to-hand bayonet fighting. The whole wood was soon full of screaming, wounded men and within a short time 'Boy' Browning was the only one of seventeen officers left alive. The reserve company, led by Guy Westmacott, came to the rescue. Browning gathered up the remnants of all three companies – a hideous task, involving abandoning those too wounded to move and dragging others out who could move but were in terrible pain – and with the reserve company dug in on the left flank of the wood.

The ordeal was not over. After several more hours, the shelling began and then the Germans started a counter-attack. This was repulsed and the Germans shelled the wood again before retreating. For this engagement, both Browning and Westmacott were awarded the DSO, Westmacott commenting that Browning deserved his far more because he had had 'to cope with all the nasty hand-to-hand fighting in the wood for five hours'.[5] Browning was now a hero, if one of many, and any stigma, real or imagined, of being once classified 'unfit' was forgotten. He was proud, as he had every right to be, mainly for his family's sake. The King's secretary wrote to Browning's father saying that in any other campaign his son would have been awarded the VC. But though this bravery earned him the DSO and a lifelong reputation for being fearless, it also shattered the young soldier emotionally. The nightmares about Gauche Wood began as soon as the battle was over, and at the time Browning met Daphne, fourteen years later, they had not stopped. Nobody knew about them except those other soldiers with whom he had shared quarters, and to them, in the context of the war, they were commonplace. Like so many men, Browning never fully recovered from his horrific experience at the age of nineteen. What he learned to do was to control his reactions so successfully that people thought of him as the perfect soldier.

When the war ended he was not quite twenty-two. His father wanted him to go into the family wine business, but he decided to stay in the army. He remained with the Grenadiers, becoming Adjutant of Sandhurst in 1924. In a regiment famous for the smart appearance of its officers Browning stood out as the most immaculate of all. His period as Adjutant, which lasted four years, established even more securely his reputation as an officer with the highest and most exacting of standards. By 1931, when he was commanding a Grenadier battalion at Pirbright, he had been a Major for three years.

But in spite of his good looks, his elegance and his decoration, 'Boy' Browning had not been successful in love. Women were greatly attracted to him, and he to them, but at the age of thirty-four, when Daphne first saw him, he was not married and had begun to worry about this. He had had countless girlfriends and two serious attachments, but he had not been able to find 'the right girl'. The nearest he had come to doing so was in Jan Ricardo, a dark-haired, rather exotic young woman, beautiful but highly strung. They became engaged, but then Browning broke it off.[6]

This, then, was the man Daphne saw in the autumn of 1931, just as she finished *The Progress of Julius*. When, in the following April, the two of them finally met,[7] Browning's looks made an immediate impression. Men had to be tall and handsome and preferably athletic in appearance to attract her. If they were short, ugly and, worst of all, fat, they had little chance of interesting her, no matter how great their talents or how attractive their personality. So Tommy's looks – he was soon 'Tommy' to her – were vitally important, as was his supremely alert and confident manner. Daphne, with her respect for people who 'sort of chuck one', liked an independent spirit and, though it had been lacking in Carol Reed, she also liked an air of authority. But then that, among other things, had been the trouble with Carol – he was not commanding enough, he was like an equal, and she had always felt the stronger. This was why, she reasoned, her affair with him had lacked real passion.

Confronted with Tommy, she saw the difference at once. He was so definite, so sure, so dominant. She found him exciting at the wheel of his boat. She was attracted to him sexually in a way she had never been attracted to a man before, and made up her mind very quickly that she wanted to have an affair. To her astonishment, Tommy, though equally attracted to her, was shocked – he was very much of the opinion that affairs were 'sleazy' and that 'nice girls didn't'. Daphne, always proud of not being one of those nice girls she despised, was taken aback and found she had rapidly to revise her ideas on sex and love and even marriage. Tommy clearly had standards – standards not unlike 'Q's – and he expected her to have them too. It was no good arguing with Tommy, as Dick had done with Hesta in *I'll Never Be Young Again*, that sex was like a game which must be practised to be made perfect.

In her own mind, Daphne knew she had at last resolved all doubts about whether sex was inseparable from love, or love from sex – she understood now that the two could be perfectly fused. She also felt relieved that her decision to lock the boy in her in a box had been the right one, and even came to believe that perhaps she had been mistaken in the existence of this 'boy' at all. Her feelings for Tommy were strong and unmistakable. 'I am in love!!' she wrote to Tod after she'd known him only three weeks. 'But hush, not a word to anyone. He is the best-looking thing I have ever seen, 35, lives for boats and all the things I live for, and came to Fowey in his boat, because he had read *The Loving Spirit*.' She had no doubt of what had happened – 'directly we met it was a case of mutual love at first sight. How's that for romance?!' She was self-conscious about what Tod, and everyone else who remembered her many condemnations of love and romance, would think, and anxious to assure Tod that 'this time it is real'. But she acknowledged it was 'early days yet . . . he is one of these people with terrific "ideals" and I'm scared of giving him a shock'. She assured Tod also that although 'in love' she would not now become 'sentimental . . . no sighs and gazing at the moon for me, thank you', though she was 'all for the spice of passion . . . which is a different thing from slop'.

To Foy, a few weeks later, she confessed: 'I never thought this would happen to me, or if it did I would have lived carelessly in Walmsley fashion.'[8] But Tommy would have none of this gay abandon, she told Foy, 'he is trying to teach me that those ways of living are messy and stupid and very, very young'. Foy's father, 'Q', had 'unwittingly pushed me a step further in the right direction when he spoke to me . . . about a code of living, and a standard, and that marriage and children meant more in life than all the novels and successes ever written'. It was, she wrote, 'going to be a bit of a job at first to change all my old ideas and to have a shot at living "unselfishly" for the first time in my life'. She only hoped that 'having by a queer stroke of fate, been "picked" by someone with . . . ideals and principles . . . maybe it won't be so difficult'. What impressed her most about the man who had 'picked' her was his integrity: Tommy knew the difference between right and wrong and explained it to her. Instead of laughing, she began to re-examine all her previous notions of marriage. There was something she described as 'true' in Tommy and she felt in awe of it. The way she had behaved with Carol suddenly seemed shabby and not the 'gloriously irresponsible' fun she had thought it was.

By the middle of June – two months after Tommy had first introduced himself, when she had gone to Fowey in the spring of 1932 to recuperate after an appendix operation – she knew she would have to agree to marriage. 'It will take at least five brandy-and-sodas, sloe gin and a handkerchief of ether to push me to the altar rail', she told Foy, but in the end she not only agreed with Tommy that they would have to marry but she proposed to him herself.[9] This startled Tommy – if 'nice' girls did not have affairs, nor did they take the initiative and propose – but he, of course, accepted, only feeling guilty that he had not asked her first.

It was significant that Daphne broke the news first to her mother, not her father or both together, and that she did so by letter. 'Darling Mummy,' she wrote on 6 July, ' . . . We think we will be married. I hope you don't mind. We decided last time he was down it would be nice. I don't want to be all pompous though, with engagement rings and things, so I think it will be time enough to tell everyone when it happens, don't you?' Since Muriel and Gerald were arriving at Ferryside on the 11th, this would be convenient for a wedding. She hoped her mother would not be 'awfully staggered . . . don't know quite what I'm doing myself, it all seems so extraordinary and I never thought I was the sort of person who would get married ... How Puff and Queenie[10] will jeer ... and Geoffrey will get a laugh out of it, won't he?' Her great fear was that, far from laughing, her parents would not approve, or would try to force a 'proper' wedding upon her, which she was determined to resist. But there was no need for nervousness. Muriel and Gerald, who had met Tommy in London and been as impressed by him as Daphne herself, were delighted, though Muriel regretted such a short engagement and no prospect of a real wedding. (Aunt Billie wrote and told Daphne how selfish she was being, denying her mother this day of glory, a reprimand which was dismissed as 'typical' and ignored.) The story was quickly related that, on receiving this news, Gerald had burst into tears and cried that it was not fair, but to his friends he enthused. Bunny and Phyllis Austin, who lived near Cannon Hall and were regular Sunday visitors, asked if Gerald was pleased that Daphne was to marry a Guardsman and, knowing his great affection for his daughter, awaited the answer with some trepidation. 'Pleased?' said Gerald. 'My dears, I am *delighted* – I thought she would have had a baby by a Cornish fisherman by now!'

Exactly when she would be married, Daphne was not sure, but she wrote to Foy that it would be 'early one morning in Lanteglos church before anyone is awake, with the grave-digger for witness, and so out and away to Helford and beyond'. But first she had to meet Tommy's family and visit Pirbright, where his battalion was stationed, both of which she dreaded. 'I've now got to pluck up my best manners,' she told Foy, but, in fact, when she reached Tommy's home and met his widowed mother Nancy and his sister Grace, she realized at once she had nothing to fear. His home, at Rousham, near Oxford, reminded her of Slyfield, where she had been on holiday as a child and which she had loved. It was an 'old Rectory on an estate' and the garden was lovely. Mrs Browning was 'charming and sweet', a gentle woman and not at all the strong, dominant mother-in-law-to-be Daphne had feared. Grace was a surprise too – 'ripping, very hearty and jolly, but a good sort'. Mrs Browning honoured Daphne by giving her her own treasured engagement ring – 'diamonds and sapphires, rather heavy' – which she did not at all want, but was touched to be given.

Less successful was the visit to the military camp at Pirbright, where Daphne stayed with the Dorman-Smiths (and made a great impact on Eric Dorman-Smith, known as 'Chink',[11] who had become friends with Tommy at Sandhurst). It was the first time she had seen Tommy in uniform – he had always, down in Fowey, dressed in old trousers and jumpers – and she was astonished by the display of 'ribbands starting with a DSO in the middle of his chest to a French *Croix-de-Guerre* somewhere near his shoulder. I felt a bit subdued . . .' Her glimpse of army life that weekend, which Tommy had insisted she should have, also slightly lowered her spirits. She wrote to her mother that she 'couldn't see the sense in military life . . . bugles and khaki and people yelling all the time and saluting'. It seemed to her both silly and comical and she could not believe anyone could take it seriously. But she saw that her husband-to-be did. Desperately seriously. She learned, to her alarm, that he was 'the officer who sets the highest standard of efficiency in the whole Brigade of Guards, that at 32 he had been the youngest major in the entire army!!!' She did not like to imagine what kind of life the wife of such a person would have to lead, but assured Tod that 'an officer in the Brigade of Guards doesn't lead a petty army life . . . he is a class apart'. It was just as well, because 'I can't see myself giving away prizes to the troops'.

Tommy himself, knowing his professional life was far more 'petty' than Daphne airily supposed, was worried about how she would adapt. It was not only a matter of where they would be required to live – no Cannon Halls or Ferrysides – but the duties she would be obliged to undertake. It was, he knew, asking a great deal to expect the wayward, always indulged Daphne to accept the restrictions which would inevitably be imposed upon her style of living. He had no wish to turn her into something she was not, nor to curb that streak of wildness in her which had so attracted him, but he knew some measure of conformity would be called for in the wife of a Major in the Grenadier Guards.[12] He knew already that Daphne's hatred of formal socializing was genuine and so was her particular brand of shyness, but she would have to concede something, she would be obliged to entertain and be entertained, and must accept some responsibility for the wives and families of the men who served under him. Then there was the problem of money. Tommy was not wealthy. His father[13] had died two days before the 1929 stock market crash in which most of the family money was lost, leaving his widow and daughter a very small income to live on. Tommy had only his army pay and though, by the standards of the thirties, that was not to be dismissed, it left little to spare for a man with expensive tastes in a regiment full of men with handsome private means. Tommy, extravagant and generous himself, knew Daphne had no more idea about budgeting than he did, and he was deeply apprehensive about how they would manage. The fact that Daphne did not share his worries concerned him even more – he knew the reason for her confidence was that she had no idea what anything cost. She had never worried about money, simply because she had never had to, and, like many people with her background, fondly thought her tastes simple and easily financed.

But, though he was right in thinking Daphne did not understand money, Tommy was wrong to think she did not appreciate its importance. She did. She knew money was power, it brought independence. Earning money, even if, so far, not much, from her novels, had brought her a feeling of independence from her parents, which had deeply satisfied her. She wanted that independence to grow, and she relished the idea of supporting her marriage with her own money rather than her husband's. Right from the beginning of her literary career she was more interested in financial transactions than in plans for publication. Writing to her mother about Tommy's anxiety over his own solvency, she said that 'considering I do well with the books and hope to do better' she did not think he should worry. *The Progress of Julius* was not yet out, but *The Loving Spirit* and *I'll Never Be Young Again* had done quite well, especially the first. She had no means of estimating how much she could earn with future books, but she felt absolutely confident that she could keep producing them and was proud that she had so quickly established a reputation as a young writer to be watched, and in whom a publisher could invest. Her only qualms were over what direction she should take next. It had not escaped her notice that *I'll Never Be Young Again* was not popular with many people she respected – they urged her not to write 'that sort of book' and, though she stood by her own book, she listened to them. When 'Q' read *The Progress of Julius* he considered it vulgar and cheap. Some of the dialogue in *I'll Never Be Young Again* appalled him too – 'Are you a sodomite?' . . . 'No . . . I haven't sufficient rhythm' – and for a father to call his daughter a bitch, as Julius did, was completely unacceptable. Both books were banished from his bookshelves, Daphne taken to task (defending herself staunchly) and his great-nephew Guy forbidden to read them in case his mind was polluted.

Nevertheless, the books sold and the fact of being able to earn her own money mattered greatly. She felt she was a genuine writer, unable now *not* to write, loving it, feeling it came naturally, that it rose within her spontaneously and could not be denied. Marriage would not be able to sap her ambition or make her deny her vocation – she was sure enough of her own talent by then to be able to forget how she had thought of marriage as 'a kind of death'. So she faced her wedding day more philosophically than she had ever thought she would be able to, though sticking to her firm intention that the whole business should be as simple and discreet as possible. The day fixed on was 19 July, giving neither Angela nor Jeanne, both on holiday, time to be there. More surprisingly, neither Mrs Browning nor Grace was present either, and Tommy had as his best man the boatman George Hunkin. The only family members on either side present were Gerald, Muriel and Cousin Geoffrey.[14] At half past seven in the morning Daphne got up and dressed in a blue suit, not new but pressed the night before by a resigned Muriel, and set off with her parents and Geoffrey by boat to Pont bridge from where they would walk to Lanteglos church. It was a hideously early hour for any du Maurier, but necessary to catch the tide. Tommy followed with the Hunkins in *Ygdrasil*. At Pont, the boats were moored and everyone then had to walk up the narrow path and on to the steep country road to the church, half a mile away. It was a walk Daphne loved. The sun shone, casting thick shadows on one side of the lane, the hedgerows were thick with wild roses and dark, scented honeysuckle. The little church, standing lonely in the midst of farms and fields, a long way from the villages it serves, pealed its six silver-tongued bells as the small bridal party entered its plain interior, where Jane Slade had been married too. Daphne was more moved than she had expected – she had wanted her wedding to be quick and quiet, but found she had after all staged it most romantically.

Afterwards, there was a breakfast at Ferryside before the bride and groom changed into their beloved old clothes, jumped into *Ygdrasil*, and set off for the open sea. They sailed to the Helford river and moored for the night in Frenchman's Creek, where on a summer's evening the trees are so dense it seems a mysterious place. They were hidden away, just as Daphne wanted. The only sounds were the slapping of the slow running water against the side of the boat and the screeching of the seagulls. It struck her as extraordinary that she was there at all, that her life had changed so dramatically within the space of three months. She had made her mind up so quickly, perfectly realizing how terrifying this was, but excited to be following her own instinct. She was proud of her own daring and proud of her husband. The deed was done. The stars glittered through the thick overhead canopy of leaves hanging over the boat, and the slim crescent of a new moon wavered above. It was all quite perfect.

PART TWO

Marriage, Motherhood & Rebecca
1932–1939

Chapter Seven

'My husband', Daphne wrote to Tod, after three months of married life, 'is the most charming person in the world.' Life was 'a whirl', divided between Fowey and Hampstead, and only a very little of it devoted to the army camp at Pirbright where Tommy spent most of his time. Never slow to ask her parents for favours, in spite of her desire to be independent, Daphne had suggested they let her have one of the two cottages at the foot of the Cannon Hall garden – 'we would love one of the little Providence corner cottages, if not all knocked into one' – and this had duly been given to her as a wedding present.

She was finding housekeeping, which had come so easily to her mother, 'a bit of a cope'. Any kind of cooking was beyond her – 'it is a bit of a strain when one sits and thinks how to do up the beef sort of thing' – so she had to have a cook, especially since Tommy, though 'easy', liked good food. Fortunately, Tommy had an excellent batman called Richards, who had a wife willing to help the young Mrs Browning with 'the agony of linen and pans'. She was relieved, distrusting her ability to hire servants and, even more nerve-racking, to keep them. She told her mother that she still got a shock every time her eye fell on her wedding ring and another when sharing a double bed. Double beds, she commented, were most uncomfortable – 'we keep waking up and barging into each other . . . then the other person seems to make such a noise breathing'.

She was extremely happy, but it was to her mother that she chose to confess a few doubts. The change in her attitude to her mother began as soon as she was married – their entire relationship shifted from being hostile and difficult to being most harmonious, with the impetus for this coming from Daphne. She saw her mother as someone who would sympathize, whereas before sympathy was what she had needed but had never found forthcoming. Now she was married, now Gerald had been obliged to let her go, she drew her mother into a little conspiracy against the trials and tribulations of being a wife. 'One realises the trials of being married,' she wrote solemnly, 'the way you never leave Daddy. Rather awful. One must be a bit firm and not give way to them . . .' Enough to make Muriel smile with amusement, but what followed was more serious. 'I feel I mustn't leave Tommy too much, all the same,' wrote Daphne, 'he has these awful nervy fits of misery, ten times worse than Daddy's old horrors,[1] all harking back to that beastly war.' In her innocence, she could not believe that the events of fourteen years ago, however hideous, still had the power to make a man like Tommy wake up screaming. She was frightened by the violence of these nightmares and distressed when she found 'he clings to me just like a terrified little boy, so pathetic, it wrings one's heart'. Watching him go off in the mornings, so smart and strong, and listening to him barking out orders at Pirbright, so fierce and confident, the young wife could hardly reconcile this soldier with the creature whose sobbing she sometimes comforted in the middle of the night. It was like possessing a terrible secret which she had no wish to know, and mixed up with her compassion was an unmistakable alarm. She had never wanted a dependent husband, one who needed her. She wanted what she thought she had married, an utterly self-reliant war hero, somebody calm, solid and stable. 'Whenever I've imagined being married,' she wrote to her mother, 'I've imagined someone who knew about horses and dogs and the country and wore smelly tweeds, but . . . he is so exactly like the husband Ralph in *Portrait of Clare*, who got killed in the Boer war.' Nor did she like what she termed Tommy's hypochondria – 'he gets irritable . . . and sorry for himself if he gets a cold'. Since this was exactly how all du Mauriers reacted to colds her annoyance was surprising, but then she found that the real trouble was her husband's need to be looked after and ministered to. The nurturing side of Daphne was almost non-existent and it horrified her to have any kind of care demanded of her.

When Tommy left Fowey or Hampstead to go back to camp,

Daphne described him with dismay as 'like a miserable boy being sent to school' and commented again, 'how awful if he gets like Daddy about being left'. It was rapidly dawning on her that whereas she thought she had married a man who was the opposite of her father (except for the charm, and it was a very different kind of charm) she was discovering disquieting similarities all the time. Tommy's need of her was blatant. He yearned to be with her all the time, whereas she could tolerate small separations very well. It was like the situation in her early short story 'A Difference in Temperament', though not so extreme, and of course, unlike the couple she had imagined, she and Tommy still loved each other and were happy. But she felt already, in the first months of marriage, that in some curious as yet unproven way she was stronger than Tommy; and she did not like that feeling. She never, ever, wanted to find herself in the position she had found herself in with her father, with him desperate for support and demanding a complete devotion of body and soul, which she did not want to give. She had seen her mother devote her life to upholding Gerald during his bad times and appearing to bear no resentment. Daphne knew she was not like Muriel – no matter how deep her love for her husband, and it was deep, she had no intention of becoming indispensable to him. She was not going to be a *motherly* wife: men who were like children did not appeal to her.

Children themselves she expected to have, six of them, all sons. By November, four months after her marriage, she was reporting to Tod that there was 'no sign of the pattering of tiny feet' with what reads like regret and certainly an acknowledgement that the tiny feet were anticipated. Two months later she knew she was pregnant. The thought of her son being born was exciting and during her pregnancy she dreamed of him as Janet did of Joseph in *The Loving Spirit*. She felt serene and placid and also, which came as a surprise, found she had the urge 'to wax' (du Maurier code for making love) very strongly. So these were happy months. Waiting for her son to be born was an occupation in itself and she had no desire to write. *The Progress of Julius* came out that spring (1933) and, though the two newspapers whose reviews she most valued at the time – the *Observer* and *The Times* – found some praise for it, the general reception was much more critical than she had expected. It did not sell as well as *The Loving Spirit*, but then neither had *I'll Never Be Young Again*. She was puzzled that nobody seemed to appreciate that her second and third novels were, in her own opinion, actually better books than the first and that no one gave her credit for attempting more ambitious and relevant themes.

In idle moments, she made lists of what she should prepare for her son's arrival, aware that this was what one did. She was amused at her own vagueness as to what would be needed. 'One yard of flannel,' she jotted down, wondering what on earth one did with it, 'four vests (luxury weight chillprove [*sic*], four flannels, four neighties [*sic*], four dresses, two small shawls . . . baby's chamber pot'. But she knew all this was playing and what she would really need was a nanny to put her right. The thought of having to have one bothered her – she disliked the idea of any personal relationship being forced on her and yet did not know how to keep such relations impersonal. It was one of the most attractive sides of her character that she was never haughty, never treated servants as inferiors or exerted any authority over them, even if her expectations of them were high and invariably disappointed. She advertised in *The Lady* and the *Daily Telegraph* for a nanny who 'need not be highly trained', hoping that this would protect her from the kind of fearsome, dominant character she dreaded. The young woman she liked the sound of, and whom she selected for interview, was two years younger than herself – she thought if she had a young nanny she might feel less intimidated. Margaret Eglesfield had had one previous job and had been trained at Putney Nursery Training School. Confronted with her, Daphne was at a loss for words. She had no idea how to conduct an interview and in desperation asked Margaret what they should talk about. Startled, Margaret replied that they should discuss Mrs Browning's requirements. But Daphne could not think how to be specific about these, so Margaret interviewed herself and agreed to £42 a year, all found, the standard rate. She noticed, when she asked to see the nursery which had been prepared, that everything was in blue and the boy's name 'Christian' was painted on the cupboard doors. She commented that this might be a little awkward if the baby turned out to be a girl. 'Heaven forbid,' said Daphne.

The baby was due at the beginning of July. 'I still go for long walks on the heath every morning, even when it is 90° in the shade,' Daphne wrote to Foy. She wished she was down at Ferryside, walking by the sea, but Hampstead was so much more convenient for the birth. She had no fear of childbirth, but when the time came the reality shocked her. On 15 July, four days before her first wedding anniversary, Daphne gave birth not to the son she longed for and confidently expected, but to a daughter. She found the pain excruciating – 'a hundred times worse than an appendix – real hell' – and wrote to Tod, 'all the old wives' tales about childbirth are true! Of all the hellish performances – so beastly degrading too, lying on a bed with legs spreadeagled and feeling exactly as though one's entire inside plus intestines and bowels were being torn from one! Pheugh! It makes me sweat to think back on it.' It also made her sweat to think of going through it again. 'Let's hope I shan't be like the rhyme about the poor Queen of Spain, how does it go? "What a life for the Queen of Spain / Two minutes' pleasure and nine months' pain / Three weeks' rest and she's at it again." ' She was determined to 'take steps' to safeguard herself from this fate – 'a good two and a half years, I hope, before I make an effort to get a son'.

Her disappointment was intense, nor did it disappear quickly, and she made no attempt to hide it. But in spite of the pain she had suffered and her dismay at being the mother of a daughter some pride did come through. 'The child is flourishing,' she wrote to Tod. 'Exactly like Tommy, but fair hair and blue eyes. Very well-formed body, though I say it myself. Strong limbs and nice skin, never red or pasty. Name of Tessa.'[2] She was also proud that she was 'by way of coping with feeding her myself', though this did not last long. By the time Margaret Eglesfield took over from the monthly nurse, Tessa was being bottle-fed. Daphne wrote to Tod that she was not only disillusioned with childbirth but also with breast-feeding – 'have always heard it left one in a state of ecstasy, but can assure you that the pastime leaves me unmoved. The child hiccups most of the time and kicks me in the stomach. But then I never was sentimental.' She was nevertheless more devoted than she was sometimes prepared to admit. Although in every letter Tessa was referred to in a detached, ironic way as 'The

Child', Daphne was reluctant to leave her. Tommy had a month's leave after Tessa's birth and was keen that Daphne should go with him down to Fowey, but although she longed to go she resisted the temptation, because 'I wouldn't like to leave The Child at so tender an age'.

Once the nanny was installed, Daphne's life went on much as before. Her involvement with her baby was minimal. The nanny had complete charge and Daphne had nothing to do with the care of the baby – she was prepared to put her total trust in the nanny. When Margaret arrived it was August and still very hot, but she was disconcerted to find that, although there was a yard of flannel, there was no pram and evidently no thought of one being needed. She could not bear to be inside on such beautiful days, with Hampstead Heath so near, and decided to take short walks carrying the five-week-old Tessa in her arms. On one such walk, she wandered along to the nearby Vale of Health pond on the heath, where she sat on a seat. It was cool there, beside the water, shaded by a tree and she was perfectly happy until a man came and sat beside her. He asked her how old the baby was. She replied, but then turned pointedly away to make it quite clear she did not speak to strange men. The man would not be put off and persisted in questioning her – was it not tiring carrying a baby, did her arms not ache, would it not be better to purchase a pram, and so on. Margaret decided this had gone far enough. She got up and began walking home. To her alarm, the man followed her. She walked more quickly. So did he. By the time she reached the Cannon Hall cottage she was running. She banged on the door and when Richards opened it told him a strange man was following her, who seemed suspiciously interested in the baby. Richards looked past her, saw the man who was now coming up to the door and, smiling, said, 'This is Sir Gerald du Maurier, the baby's grandfather.'

Feeling extremely foolish, Margaret apologized. Gerald sighed and said it was typical of Daphne not to have thought of a pram and that one must be bought at once. Next morning, a Harrods van arrived at the door and six prams were wheeled out for Margaret's inspection. An hour later, a Selfridges van arrived with a similar cargo, followed by a third from Milson's. Quite overcome, Margaret chose a big grey Osnath, for which Gerald paid, instructing her to come to him should she need anything else for his granddaughter. But there was nothing else she lacked. Her days settled into a pleasant routine with no interference from, and not much contact with, her employer. Daphne got up late, went for walks, visited her parents and sisters. Angela and Jeanne were still living at home, just round the corner, and Angela in particular loved Tessa and adored playing with her. Since neither sister worked, though Angela, too, was trying to write, and Jeanne had begun to take her painting seriously, they had plenty of time, still leading the privileged life which had made Daphne so discontented, to see a great deal of their sister. Daphne and Tommy went to theatres with them and dined out with various friends of their own, including Bunny and Phyllis Austin, known as 'Mr and Mrs A' to their 'Mr and Mrs B'. Margaret had no idea she was working for a writer and saw no writing being done. Every now and again there would be visits to Fowey, which sometimes included her and Tessa, and sometimes not. After nearly six months of this, Margaret realized that, though her days were perfectly easy, and life in the Browning household extremely pleasant, she had not had a single day off and Mrs Browning appeared not even to have noticed or thought anything of it. But Major Browning did. One evening he came bounding upstairs to the nursery, asking if it was very hard to give a baby its bottle. Margaret assured him it was simple. Encouraged, the Major then suggested Margaret should have a night off, going with Richards and his wife Lily to the theatre, for which he would get tickets, and he and Mrs Browning would take care of Tessa.

Tickets were duly provided and off the three of them went. They had a wonderful time, but as they arrived home, Richards pointed out that all the lights were blazing in the nursery and as they entered they could hear piercing screams. Margaret rushed upstairs to find the Major pacing the floor and shouting 'Oh my God!' and Daphne sitting with a look of agony as she tried to force a bottle into the mouth of her blue-faced baby, while Bunny Austin sat watching, helpless. Within seconds, Margaret had calmed Tessa, brought up the wind that was troubling her, cleared the hole in the bottle's teat, which had become clogged, and all was well. But it was from then onwards that she began to insist the young mother should become more involved in the care of her own baby. Dutifully, Mrs Browning agreed. She was perfectly aware how incompetent she was, and anxious to do her best whatever her feelings towards her baby.

It was rather too clear by then what these feelings were. Daphne had still not got over Tessa being a girl, and Margaret went so far as to consider that she was rejecting her own baby. She did not cuddle or kiss her, she did not talk or sing to her, she did not in any way appear to dote on her or want to be with her. She seemed, in fact, to have difficulty with the whole idea of being a mother. But Margaret could see that even if Mrs Browning was no earth-mother, she was also no socialite, however idle her days appeared to be. There were 'words' over various engagements Major Browning wished to accept and Mrs Browning did not. It turned out there was a side to Tommy that Daphne had not known about.

It was true that, as she had told Tod before they were married, he liked nothing better than to mess about in boats, wearing old clothes, just as she did; but it was also true, which she had never suspected, that he could occasionally also enjoy a kind of socializing she loathed. Her idea of socializing, if she had to be sociable, was to be among like-minded people in a relaxed and casual setting, all being what she called 'jam-a-long' – easy-going, informal, with no need for any pretence. But Tommy had been in the habit before he met her of accepting invitations to rather grand country house weekends, and now that he had a lovely young wife he was eager for her to share this pleasure with him. Daphne did not find such experiences a pleasure – in fact, she hated them. Reluctantly, she was sometimes obliged to accompany him, but put up great resistance. She wrote to Grace, Tommy's sister, in the autumn of 1933, after such a visit to Leeds Castle, that she had 'never known anything like it'. There were twenty-one people to dinner every night and to her amazement the dinner was held in a different dining-room each of the three nights. The footmen were 'like cabinet ministers' and her bedroom 'like a stateroom at Versailles'. She vowed she needed opera glasses in bed to see the dressing-table across the room and that the marble lavatory, disguised as an armchair, was distinctly insanitary. 'I am afraid they are a dreadful set,' she commented to Foy, ' . . . the sort of people one would gladly see guillotined.' She found such opulence distasteful and wished herself at home with a hot-water bottle. Nor did the sight of Tommy enjoying himself, and proving an obvious hit with every woman present, make her feel any happier. She came back from such weekends feeling furious.

There were signs that she was suffering from a mild post-natal depression. She confessed to Grace that a 'shameful weakening of the eye-duct' kept coming over her. She found herself weeping for no reason and was horrified – she was not that sort of woman and did not want to be. She despised tears as weakness and was proud that only rarely, under extreme stress, did she give way to them. Though she had nothing else to do in Hampstead but rest, if she so chose, she wondered in her letter if she might come to her sister-in-law's home, where Grace lived with her widowed mother, and rest. All she would need was 'a glass of water and a lettuce leaf every now and again', and she would only need the sheets changed every two weeks. Maybe, she suggested, Grace would like to swap places – a switch for them both 'might be amusing and act as a tonic'. Apparently the energetic Grace, tireless worker for the Girl Guides and countless other organizations, had no need of a tonic.[3]

Daphne went home to her hot-water bottle. Tommy, concerned over her weepiness and general low spirits, reacted much as her parents had done: he thought she needed amusement and bought her 'a little Morris . . . in a frenzied fit of divine generosity, for me to go about in'.[4] But 'going about' did her little good, and she was disturbed to find herself feeling as restless as she had done before she got down to her first novel at Ferryside in the winter of 1929–30. Being a wife and a mother ought, she felt, to fulfil her, but the truth was that it did not; it was writing which made her content. But there was more to her restlessness than that. Not only did she miss writing, she missed being alone, far away from everyone, walking on the Gribbin or sailing. And now she could not indulge herself exactly as she wished – she had a husband and a baby to think of, even if her duties were minimal. Instead of making her unselfish, as she had hoped, marriage had made her desire to return to being more selfish again in spite of her love for Tommy.

Things got worse in the New Year of 1934. Tommy was now second-in-command of the 2nd Battalion Grenadier Guards (he became commanding officer in January 1936) and had to take up residence at Frimley, in Surrey. The Cannon Hall cottage was given up and the Brownings moved, though not to any army quarters – they rented a beautiful Queen Anne house, the Old Rectory, and though Daphne had groaned at the thought of sub-urban Surrey, she was charmed with it. The country round about was pleasant and afforded some tolerable walks which were better than Hampstead Heath. Tommy was very busy which left her with more time on her own, and she quite frankly relished this. Margaret looked after Tessa, except for an hour a day, which she insisted Mrs Browning should devote to her daughter, and she began to see that if she wanted to she could begin to write again.

But then Gerald became ill. He was to go into hospital for an exploratory operation, and though she was told there was no cause for alarm, the entire family shared her fear. Gerald hated hospitals – which, in du Maurier code, were always called 'slaughterhouses' – and was always frightened of illness. Daphne did not want him to have any kind of operation. She was, she wrote to Tod, 'against all operations on principle, believing, as I do, three-quarters of them to be unnecessary'. But the week after his sixty-first birthday Gerald went into a clinic in Devonshire Place and was operated on. Cancer of the colon was diagnosed. The malignant tumour was removed and everyone informed that the operation had been a complete success. But on 11 April, his thirty-first wedding anniversary, Gerald died.

The shock for his wife and daughters was profound. None of them had had the faintest inkling that Gerald would die, and they had had no time even to adjust to his being seriously ill. For Daphne this was grief of a kind she had never experienced, but she gave no overt signs of it. She was controlled and fatalistic: what would be, would be. She quickly convinced herself that 'death has come at the right moment for him, like a way of escape'. She thought of Gerald as someone who could not possibly face the horrors of old age, who was simply not equipped to age gracefully. He was the sort of person who 'ought always to be young', just like Peter Pan, and to condemn him to a gradual decline would have been too cruel. Hand in hand with this determined philosophy went another: she was sure that in some way Gerald was *not* dead. She was no more religious than he had been himself (in spite of her new habit, since her marriage, of saying prayers at night because Tommy did so) but she had a strong presentiment, from the moment she was told of her father's death, that he was somehow around her. She concentrated hard on keeping this strange sensation alive and managed successfully, except for the moment when she had to witness her mother's appalling distress. Then, seeing the placid, dignified, always elegant Muriel devastated by grief 'broke me up'. She wrote to Foy that this utter wretchedness of her mother's, the sight of her lying on her bed, her face obliterated by tears, racked by sobs, unable to speak, was 'the worst thing of all'. She knew that, for all Gerald's womanizing, it was Mo he had truly loved, and now he was dead she was utterly bereft. Daphne suffered for her and in doing so a compassion completed the softening of her attitude to her mother which had already begun. She felt close to her for the first time, even physically close, able to embrace her as she never had done before, and she felt instantly protective. There had never, or so she had thought, been any role for her in her mother's life, but now that she could see how much support was going to be needed she was eager to acknowledge her new responsibilities. A kind of love for her mother touched her for the first time.

But she did not go to the funeral.[5] Gerald was buried with the other members of his family in Hampstead churchyard after a ceremony kept very simple and held in the evening to ensure privacy. Daphne went on to the Heath instead and released some pigeons. She was perfectly aware that this might seem an extravagantly romantic gesture, but she thought it in keeping with the spirit of Gerald and it comforted her to watch the birds soar into the sky and imagine Gerald equally free of the earth. Since she was persuading herself Gerald was not really dead, she saw this as a celebration and she felt reassured and almost happy. Then she helped her sisters deal with all the letters of condolence and found 'it helped an awful lot, because we were able to do it in a sort of rather ruthless cold-blooded way, and we kept thinking how many of them would have made Daddy laugh, and so they made us laugh too. We kept thinking how Daddy would say "Good God – what the hell is old so-and-so writing for, he's hated my guts for years", or "Listen to this one – I never knew what's-her-name had a bent for religion", and though a lot of people might have thought us heartless and cursed with a mordant beastly type of humour, I don't think we were – we were really being much closer to Daddy than all the people with the solemn faces.'[6]

This feeling of closeness to Gerald stayed with her when she returned to Frimley, and instead of being depressed she found herself curiously expectant. One day she went into the local church and sat down, not to pray but simply to be quiet. She closed her eyes and an extraordinary conviction that Gerald was there came over her. She did not hear his voice or see his body, there was nothing ghostly or visionary about the experience, but she simply had the knowledge that he was with her. At the same time she had a sudden desire to begin to do what, at the back of her mind, she had been wanting to do ever since she heard of his death: write about him. She had only ever written fiction, but she knew this could not be fiction. It would have to be, she supposed, though she shied away from the word, a biography, but a biography intent on telling the story of Gerald's life and catching the essence of him rather than a record of his theatrical achievements. The idea excited her, but at the same time made her nervous. She had all the du Maurier horror of being 'wain' (embarrassing) or 'see me' (showing off) or committing a 'tell him' (being boring). All three would have to be avoided. Then she was not sure if any publisher would be interested, and she felt she could not embark on such a venture without some assurance that it would be looked kindly upon. For two weeks after her visit to the church, she turned the idea over in her mind, wondering whether she should act on it or not. Was the challenge too great? Would Gerald have approved? Was it too near to his death to be decent? Would she be able to tell the truth without being disloyal or hurting anyone still alive? She felt hesitant and yet inspired and finally decided that there was no harm in trying, and seeing what resulted.

In May 1934, she signed a contract for a biography of her father, but she signed it with Victor Gollancz, not with Heinemann, the publisher of her first three novels. This naturally caused everyone at Heinemann great concern. They felt they had done well for her and certainly did not want to lose her. John Frere, then a director of Heinemann and married to Daphne's old friend Pat Wallace, rang her up, puzzled and hurt, when he heard the news, to find out what had happened. Daphne's explanation was that Victor Gollancz had approached her with the idea of doing a biography of her father, immediately after Gerald's death, and she had felt she therefore had to do it for him. This was untrue but a typical way of avoiding any confrontation, which she hated, or unpleasantness. In fact, the agent Curtis Brown himself had suggested Victor Gollancz[7] as a more suitable person to publish it than Heinemann, who he did not think had done so well with Daphne's second and third novels as he would have liked. Since the new book would be non-fiction there was no need for Daphne to feel disloyal. What was significant was Daphne's own eagerness to try Gollancz – she might genuinely hate publicity, if it meant exposing herself personally to it, but at the same time she wanted to make an impact and see her books do as well as they possibly could, especially now that she was married and living on Tommy's pay. She had shrugged off his worries about money, saying what she earned from her books would make up any deficit; but, now that she had been married over a year and produced nothing new, and the income from her last two novels was shown to be considerably less than that from the first, she was beginning to see that she would have to do better. According to Curtis Brown, and everyone else in the literary world, there was no one more likely to help with self-advancement than the dynamic head of a publishing house only six years old, Victor Gollancz.[8]

Within a very short time Victor had developed a relationship with Daphne which she had never enjoyed with anyone at Heinemann. The strange thing was that, although she had a horror of any 'showing off' kind of behaviour, and was herself very reticent, Daphne greatly admired Victor's vigorous approach to his work. In an era when advertising books was a discreet affair he had startled other publishers with his huge (some said vulgar) splashes in the serious newspapers. His first bestseller, after he set up on his own, was Isadora Duncan's *My Life*, and true to his style he had immediately celebrated with a lavish party at Claridge's, which became an annual event. By 1934, when Daphne contracted to write *Gerald*, his list was already impressive: A. J. Cronin, Joyce Cary, and Ivy Compton-Burnett were among the names. There was nothing Victor liked better than having a young author full of potential to promote, and in Daphne du Maurier he saw he had a gift: a talented, pretty young woman, already known for her novels, writing about her famous just-dead father. It was irresistible, a natural for the bestseller lists. And the bestseller lists were where Daphne wanted to be, not because she craved glory, not that she was greedy, not because she valued such a thing in itself, but because she wanted to fulfil her promise to be the breadwinner. She would write only what came naturally, but once she had done so her aims were practical and she saw no contradiction in that.

Gerald: A Portrait was written in four months, in the summer of 1934. 'The book was finished this morning,' Daphne wrote to Victor on 31 August. 'I am going to correct it with a severe blue pencil and you shall have it next week. I am glad to have done it up to time – never expected I would. Shows one can do anything if one tries hard enough.' Victor, realizing the urgent need to bring out the biography while Gerald was still in everyone's mind, had stipulated she must hand in the manuscript by the last day of that same year. He was delighted to have it ready by mid-September, and pushed ahead immediately for publication on 1 November to catch the Christmas trade. His enthusiasm thrilled Daphne – she recognized it as genuine and treasured her new publisher's intelligent appreciation of what she had done. He praised the pace of the biography, the way it read like a novel, and this was exactly what she had aimed at – she wanted all the facts in but she did not want these to weigh the narrative down and get in the way of conveying Gerald's spirit. This made for the lively style she wanted, but it also made the book a curious hybrid. It was written in the third person, even when Daphne was referring to herself, and yet it covered certain events in an intimate way more suited to the first person. Daphne struggled to be objective, hence the third person, but when she wanted to demonstrate the psychological insight only she possessed, she was constrained by her own style. Those passages in the book where she described Gerald's character, are by far the most interesting and brave. She was not in the least afraid to be critical, pointing out that however successful her father had seemed, he was a man 'whose soul cried out for a goal in life' and that he ended his life 'still without his creed'. She did not dwell upon his affairs with women, though she managed to make it clear these existed, but his depressions were the subject of her most piercing analysis. She saw him as a man whose 'brain and his entire nervous system' yearned for work of 'a more intensive kind' and who, when it failed to appear, became 'stagnant and discouraged'. She stressed how spoiled he had been all his life and what a fatal effect this had had, and yet she rejoiced, too, in Gerald's *joie de vivre* in his younger days and in a humour which had remained utterly childish. His work as actor and manager she praised, seeing as the pinnacle his performance as Will Dearth in *Dear Brutus* in 1917.

Gerald rises out of this portrait wonderfully real and colourful, with all his charm intact, his eccentricities amusingly portrayed, and with the dark side of his nature sensitively drawn. About his relationship with her, Daphne's character study was astute, but she pulled back from revealing the full extent of her own very mixed feelings about him. The book states frankly that he could not cope with the adolescence of any of his daughters and that the 'very quality of his emotion' made them all shy and made them want to distance themselves from this father to whom they had been so close in childhood. It also tells of Gerald's constant refrain of 'I wish I was your brother instead of your father', and what a burden this at first amusing desire became. But the real misery Gerald had caused her, much of which went into *The Progress of Julius*, is lacking – Daphne wanted to keep faith with her father, to tell the truth, but only so far as she thought acceptable at that time. It was a shock to her to discover that a great deal of what she had so lovingly written was regarded on publication as, on the contrary, quite unacceptable. Many of Gerald's contemporaries regarded the book as a betrayal of a father by a daughter and thought the descriptions of Gerald's depressions distasteful, the exposure of his weaknesses crude, and the mention of his extra-marital relationships outrageous.

Fortunately, the reviewers did not agree. Michael Joseph, Daphne's agent at Curtis Brown, had prophesied that *Gerald* would be hailed as 'the most vivid, original and sincere biography for years' and he was right. *The Times*, the newspaper Daphne revered most, called it 'A remarkable book . . . some brilliant comic writing . . . the description of the family's start for a holiday cannot be read . . . without laughing and then . . . the laughter dies and the reader's heart sinks into sadness.' Other reviews were equally laudatory and the sales were excellent. But from Daphne's point of view what was even more encouraging was what she had earned. On publication day she received £1,000 and 20 per cent of the home sales up to 10,000 copies sold. Beside that, the disapproval of some old men sitting in the Garrick Club was nothing, and in any case the only people who really mattered, her family, had all read the book before publication and thoroughly approved.

But after all the excitement was over, reaction set in. December found the triumphant biographer reporting to Tod that she felt 'distinctly off colour'. All her insides felt mixed up and she was terrified she was pregnant again (though she wasn't). She had come to the conclusion in Frimley, as she wrote to Foy, that she was only really happy 'in the middle of Dartmoor in a hail storm within an hour of sundown of a late November afternoon'. Instead there were rumours that she might soon find herself in the boiling heat of Egypt where Tommy's battalion might be posted. This dismayed her, but luckily the rumour turned out for the moment to be untrue. Her spirits remained low over Christmas – the first without Gerald as master of ceremonies – and though she had never expressed any affection for Cannon Hall, she was upset that it had been sold. Her mother and sisters moved for the time being into the Cannon Hall cottage she and Tommy had vacated, but there was talk of withdrawing from Hampstead entirely and moving to Ferryside. Unmistakably, an era had ended and, though she had always prided herself on not being sentimental, Daphne now found herself wallowing in sentiment and, something else more worrying, she found herself thinking more and more about the past, even the past beyond her own memory, just as Gerald had done. This was perhaps, she reasoned, what everyone did on the death of a parent, it was perhaps an inevitable rite of passage, but what puzzled her was how attractive the past already seemed, more attractive than the present; and yet she was not only happy in the present but knew that a great deal of this past had *not* been happy.

The truth was that, although fundamentally happy, quite a large slice of her life was far from satisfactory and this irritated her. With Tommy as second-in-command she could not always shut herself up, as she had just done while writing *Gerald*, but was obliged to show some interest in the wives and families of the soldiers. She found this agonizing. 'Can you picture me', she wrote to Tod, 'going round the married quarters and chatting up forty different women? "And how is the leg, Mrs Skinner?" and "Dear little Freddie, what a fine boy he is", (this to a swollen-faced object obviously suffering from mumps, who comes and breathes over one.)' She could not understand how the wives put up with their miserable existence – 'I must say, though, the poor things are very cheerful on the whole, and clean.' This apparent acceptance of their fate by the soldiers' wives fascinated her – how could they bear such awful living conditions? It was her first glimpse of any kind of deprivation, since the only 'poor' she had come into contact with had been people like Miss Roberts, about whose cottage in Bodinnick there was nothing dreary in spite of the outside lavatory, and the Cannon Hall servants, who she had always felt lived rather well. But when she went into the army married quarters she was easily thrown by what she observed. 'There was one wretched woman', she told Tod, 'whose husband was only a private and she had *nine* children under *nine*! They live in a room half the size of yours . . . and three of them wouldn't walk and had a skin disease and they were all propped up on chairs round the room while the poor woman cooked the rather unsavoury stew for midday dinner.' It disturbed her to witness such scenes and she knew she ought to try to do something about the more pressing problems these women had, so she dutifully tried to do her bit. She found out that several wives were entitled to certain benefits they were not getting, and on their behalf filled in forms and corresponded with the appropriate authorities. This, she knew, was the least she could do, but she shrank from any more serious involvement. She shrank, too, from other duties as an army officer's wife, loathing any kind of social gathering and hating things like the presentation of prizes. Once, she got lost in the barracks and ended up in the middle of a group of soldiers who never guessed that she was the wife of the officer second-in-command of the battalion – 'I had to run the gauntlet of wolf whistles,' she told Foy, and thought of the scene with extreme embarrassment, dreading the men's eventual discovery of her identity. Part of the trouble, she knew, was that she did not look like the received image of an officer's wife. She looked like a slip of a girl, blonde and pretty enough to whistle at, always with a rather diffident air, someone who blushed easily and had no air of authority whatsoever.

Getting away from army life was her prime object throughout 1935. She went down to Fowey as often as possible and even when it poured found the place 'too lovely' and felt better at once. A trip to Bodmin Moor put her in mind of a previous visit with Foy and she began to make notes for the new book she had contracted in February to write – for Victor Gollancz. Heinemann were still supposed to be her publisher for fiction, but Victor was determined to keep her and suggested to Curtis Brown: 'A way out of this situation occurs to me. Why not suggest she signs an agreement for *one novel* with no tie-ups or options.' It would be, he argued, 'inefficient to have *Gerald* with one publisher and then a novel with another' (but not, apparently, inefficient to have had three novels with one publisher then to have come with *Gerald* to him). This, he thought, would 'enable her to satisfy herself about my suitability . . . as her novel publisher before committing her destinies rather more permanently to my hands'. Given this chance 'I feel sure that when the time comes she will want to go with me'. He was prepared to pay an advance of £1,000 with the same royalties as for *Gerald*, and Daphne had been glad to accept. She had promised him another kind of novel from the ones she had already written – 'a tale of adventure . . . set in Cornwall, full of smugglers and steeped in atmosphere'. On Bodmin Moor again, she felt it take shape.

It was annoying that almost as soon as she had begun, she had to return to Frimley and, worse still, waste time preparing to be presented at Court. She resented all the fuss this involved and thought it silly, but told Tod that Tommy wanted it. Yet in spite of this assertion there is no doubt that if she had really objected to the Court presentation – as she had vehemently objected to a formal wedding – Tommy would never have been able to persuade her. There was, whatever she said, a respect in her for such conventional honours and she was a confirmed royalist as well as a lover of pageantry. But it was true, she found it an interruption she could have done without, though it was a good excuse to go to Tod's Baker Street flat, where she was now trying to make a living as a milliner, and 'have a good laugh' getting ready.

Victor kept enquiring how the novel was going, and by November she was able to tell him it would soon be finished and she thought he would like it. Once she had started she adopted a strict regime of writing for three hours in the morning, another two in the late afternoon after her walk and, if Tommy was not home from his duties with the battalion, another hour in the evening. She had a typewriter now and had taught herself to type (very badly). Margaret looked after Tessa, she had a cook to look after meals and a woman to clean, and there were neither interruptions nor calls on her time. When she finished the novel, at the beginning of 1936, and sent it to Victor, he liked it very much, recognizing at once that this was by far the best fiction Daphne had yet produced and that he could do great things with it. It was called *Jamaica Inn* and was a completely new departure.

Chapter Eight

Jamaica Inn was intentionally a melodramatic tale, in the manner of R. L. Stevenson's *Treasure Island*, and, as Daphne had promised, full of smugglers and stirring, mysterious happenings. She wanted the atmosphere of Cornwall to be impressed upon every page, and it was. She wanted to excite her readers with a plot full of suspense, and she succeeded. This was no saga novel, slow, always edging towards fantasy, like *The Loving Spirit*, but a tightly plotted thriller containing some ingenious and unexpected twists. The writing showed a new tautness, and that sense of pace for which she had always striven was finally there. It had not been arrived at without a great deal of hard work – the structure of this Gothic tale was firmly put in place before she wrote a word. Beside these successes – of plot and atmosphere – the failures did not seem to matter, but they were there, to be exposed in all its subsequent dramatizations.

The characters, with the exception of the heroine, Mary Yellan herself, and the sinister Vicar of Altarnun, are dangerously near to caricature, particularly the all-important Joss Merlyn. He is, rather unfortunately, compared within one paragraph to a horse, a gorilla and a wolf and described as being not only nearly seven feet high but having fists like hams. In a similar way, much of the dialogue verges on the ludicrous, especially between Mary and her Aunt Patience. This only has to be spoken aloud to destroy the atmosphere of menace which is captured so easily in the written word and communicates itself to the solitary reader. But what is more interesting than the story itself, and what cannot be spoiled by any clumsiness of characterization or conversation, is the subtext to this tale of adventure. In her delineation of Mary Yellan and her plight Daphne was entirely consistent with her aim in all her previous fiction: to demonstrate the unevenness of the relationship between the sexes, to show the man as brute and the woman as victim. And this time she took the theme further.

From the first chapter Mary is a victim, first of circumstance and then of her uncle. She is full of 'gallant courage', but is told a girl cannot live alone and must have, after the death of her mother, the protection of a man, her uncle. Right from Mary's first meeting with Joss his brutality revolts her. 'Had she been a man', we are told, she would challenge him, but as a woman she cannot. She is disgusted by her own weakness, but even more so by the terrified subservience of the pathetic Aunt Patience who makes her see women are 'fools . . . shortsighted . . . unwise'. The more spirited Mary tries to be, the more helpless she feels as a woman, and when her uncle says admiringly 'they ought to have made you a boy' she wishes bitterly they had. But what disturbs her most is the feeling that she is becoming attracted to Jem Merlyn, her uncle's brother, who, though not a brute, is a ruffian and as dominant as his brother. Mary, though she has 'no illusions about romance', knows that there is 'something inside her' responding to Jem – 'Jem Merlyn was a man and she was a woman' and that was the way of things.

Mary's despair over her own sexual urges is matched by her consciousness of what Joss can do to her if he wishes. Violence is everywhere – this is above all a violent and turbulent novel both in the brilliant landscape descriptions and in the emotional intensity generated – and she senses it. Joss lays a finger across her mouth, he bends her wrist, he tells her he could have 'had her' the first week she arrived at the inn, his mouth hovers over her, but he says he will resist 'riding away with you to glory' because he has a 'soft spot' for her. More and more Mary becomes aware that sexual attraction is the ruin of women.

Even nastier is the shock for Mary when she discovers, late in the novel, that the seemingly gentle and kind Vicar of Altarnun has in the drawer of his desk hideous caricatures: no man can be trusted. When the vicar forces her out on to the moor, she is 'degraded' by his eyes. Her disgust only pleases him. Everywhere she turns Mary is leered at and treated as being of no account. Men, and what they do to other men – the scene in which an idiot boy is stripped naked and whipped is one of the most powerful in the book – sicken her. And yet, at the end of the story, she cannot resist Jem's invitation to share his life, 'because I must'. She is a woman saved, a woman believing herself to be in love, but a woman beaten, left with no option, capitulating without joy on the basis of hope, a woman following the dictates of heart and body but not mind. It was a deeply pessimistic view of a woman's life.

The novel was reviewed as a Cornish tale of smugglers and villains with great emphasis on the sense of atmosphere. The definite feeling among the critics was that it was all 'jolly good fun' and 'an exciting brew . . . just the thing for a late evening's reading'. It sold very well at once, with Gollancz reprinting on publication.[1] Within three months *Jamaica Inn* had sold, in England, more than all Daphne's first three novels put together and had become her first big commercial success. Naturally, Victor wanted more, as soon as possible, more of the same, and urged her to give him another novel quickly. But she had also signed a contract with him, a month before she signed one for a novel, for another work of non-fiction. This she had put aside when the idea for *Jamaica Inn* came to her, but now she turned to it and suggested she should first write another biography, in the style of *Gerald*, about her grandfather George du Maurier. Victor would much rather have had another novel, but he was wise and sensible enough to encourage his young author to follow her own inclination. So Daphne began researching material for what became *The Du Mauriers*, looking out family letters and searching for birth, death and marriage certificates, but just as she had gathered together enough to make a start, the news she had dreaded came through: Tommy's battalion was posted to Egypt and this time it was no rumour.

For the last three and a half years Daphne had got away with only playing at being an army officer's wife. She performed as few duties as possible and, beyond writing letters to try to better the conditions of those poor wives she had seen in the married quarters, she did not involve herself in the life of the regiment, social or otherwise. But when, early in 1936, it was confirmed that Tommy's battalion was indeed destined for Egypt she realized at once that she would be trapped in the kind of situation she dreaded. Once in a foreign country she would have to live cheek by jowl with the rest of the officers' wives, she would be unable to escape to Cornwall and would become more prominent, especially since Tommy had been promoted and she was now the wife of the commanding officer. She would also have to learn to run another household, with foreign servants, whose language she could not speak, putting her at an even greater disadvantage. There was absolutely nothing she looked forward to about this posting. It was no good friends and family envying her the opportunity to see some other part of the world – if she was going to travel, she wanted to do it on her own and not be transported with a two-year-old child to a way of life she detested the thought of.

But her feelings of dread did not for one moment cause her to consider *not* going with the regiment. It was her duty, the first real test of herself as an army wife. She loved Tommy and, though she suspected she would not be as miserable without him as he would be without her, she too could not have faced a long parting. She duly sailed with Tessa and Margaret, her nanny, in March 1936 on the SS *Cameronia*. At least the voyage was pleasant, with the sea calm, the breezes invigorating and the Captain not only very civilized but a reader of Conrad. Life on board ship was more endurable than she had expected and also more dramatic. A woman who maintained she had not known she was pregnant gave birth one night and Daphne, together with all the other women, was asked by the ship's doctor if she could sew some baby clothes. She couldn't, of course, never having plied a needle in all her twenty-eight years,[2] but she did visit the new mother and tried to be supportive in a vague kind of way. As ever, what ordinary women had to go through, and the fortitude with which they accepted their fate, astonished her. Repeatedly, such events reminded her of how privileged she was and she scolded herself for not always remembering this.

Once in Alexandria all awareness of being lucky left her. She hated it from the moment she arrived. The house the Brownings settled into, 13 Rue Jessop, was thought quite beautiful by the subsequent occupants,[3] but Daphne rated it merely as 'nice' and damned the garden as 'little better than a cat run'. There was an excellent housekeeper called Hassan, so she had none of the domestic worries she had anticipated, but she did not feel comfortable. Hassan would appear each morning to be given his orders and she had no orders to give, simply wishing he would do whatever was necessary. Tommy was extremely busy, eagerly planning manoeuvres in the desert for his troops, and Tessa settled down very happily with Margaret who took to Egypt at once. This left Daphne with plenty of time to herself, but instead of relishing this happy state of affairs it only increased her restlessness. What was the point of having so much free time if she couldn't go for long walks? In Alexandria, quite apart from the heat and dust, she found walking was impossible. There was, she reported to Foy, 'nowhere to walk', and when she tried she exposed herself to 'natives who were doing their toilet and worse'. She swore 'every other person is blind or has a limp or sore' and, though she said defiantly that she knew very well how this judgement made her sound, she was convinced 'the natives are dirty'. She tried to fight what she knew was mere prejudice but failed – 'I can't *help* thinking the natives are *filthy* and never really clean.' She made no attempt to learn to speak the language but at the same time complained bitterly that 'the creatures don't speak English'.

It was not only the natives she despised – she loathed the English out there too. She condemned them in one sweeping generalization as 'horrible Manchester folk'. The place was 'full of gossip' and the main pastimes were cocktail parties and charades – 'it is ghastly'. She described to Angela 'the cocktail party in the mess . . . God knows what it cost, as there were about 350 guests and everyone drank champagne cocktails'. Though commenting that she supposed she would get used to it all 'in about a month', she did no such thing. By the second month her hatred for the whole of Alexandria was more violent than ever. 'Imagine', she wrote to Foy, with an exaggeration not meant to be amusing, 'the sham buildings at Wembley suddenly planted in a very dreary sea-side resort like St Leonards-on-Sea that by some unfortunate chance had been invaded by half-castes . . . it is entirely lacking in charm, much as the outskirts of Southampton lack charm.' Savagely, she sneered at those 'who talk about the glamour of the East'. There was no glamour. Even the seafront reminded her of 'an inferior

Blackpool' (though she had never set foot in Blackpool). Grudgingly, she admitted it was pleasant swimming, and that, once
they had procured a boat, some Sundays spent on it were quite
enjoyable, but these were not to be compared with the bliss of
sailing *Yggy* out of Fowey harbour. The only people who made
social life tolerable at all were John and Karen Prescott (Tommy's
old friend, who had taken him to Fowey, and his wife) and two
other couples, the Deakins and the Agars (who were a Royal Navy
officer and his wife). These six people had no idea Daphne was as
miserable as she was, but then it was difficult to guess. In her
head she might rage and fume and hurl abuse at Egypt, and in her
letters there was some outlet for this, but to the world at large
she presented a perfectly calm and composed front. A little aloof,
perhaps, until one got to know her, but then she was known to
be shy, and known also to be a writer, rather an exotic creature
in that setting. Clearly, she needed to set herself a little apart, be
a little retiring, in order to get on with it, and this was allowed.

What she was getting on with was *The Du Mauriers*, regretting
she had ever started on it. She had asked Victor Gollancz for an
extension of time to write the book before she left England and
now tried to get down to it. It proved harder than she expected.
The temperature in the room where she wrote was over 80°F even
in the morning and by the afternoon, in spite of keeping the
shutters closed, it had climbed to nearly 100°F. Everyone else, she
wrote to her publisher, simply lay about gasping, but she was
doing her best to work. By July, she was afraid her simple family
history was 'developing into a sort of *Forsyte Saga*' and also afraid,
though she did not tell Victor Gollancz this, that it was getting
into a muddle. She had started off 'writing it like *Gerald*, so that
it reads like a novel', but had then become so absorbed in all the
old letters she had found – 'a miracle I came across them' – that
she was afraid she was becoming bogged down. Her instinct was
right. The book is divided into five parts, beginning with the story
of her great-great-grandmother Mary Anne Clarke, mistress of
the Duke of York. All the facts were real, but the dialogue, and
much of the background action, is imagined and this time the
clash between fact and fiction caused her to feel uneasy. In *Gerald*
she had made up nothing, essentially, but in *The Du Mauriers*,

because the characters were not known to her, she sought to bring them alive by inventing situations which were sometimes hard to marry with the facts. It became 'a grind' to write, the weather grew hotter, and she began to feel positively ill, sitting sweating over her typewriter, hour after hour, in the appalling heat of August. The rhythm of the finished book reflects the dogged determination of how it was written – against the grain, with none of the confidence she had felt with Gerald. Finishing it at the beginning of September, she wrote to Gollancz: 'I am pleased to say the du Mauriers have had enough said about them . . . done about 100,000 words . . . I feel it is something of a *tour de force* to have written it in an Egyptian summer.' She couldn't decide how it had turned out – 'too dog-tired to think at all' – but hoped she had produced 'the sort of fat leisurely book that people enjoy reading during winter evenings over their knitting . . . talk of nostalgia, I'm bulging with it'.

When the manuscript had been sent back to London with the Deakins, who were going on leave, Daphne was more than ordinarily exhausted. She was thinner than ever, but could not eat because she felt sick. Now the book was finished, she had no energy, and especially not for the lively three-year-old Tessa, who she reported to Foy was 'rather too much in evidence'. Listlessly, she lay on her bed, longing for England – not only Cornwall, but all of lovely England. 'I had never realised I liked England so much,' she confided in her mother. Her 'longing for Fowey' was 'so intense it is a pain under the heart continually'. She dreamed of Cumberland too, remembering the greenery and rushing streams and still, dark tarns, and even of Oxford Street, which she had always hated, but for which she now had 'a vivid affection . . . the rain, and the jumble of buses'. Great waves of depression swept over her when she woke up, and she told her mother never would she have believed '*mal du pays* could be so bad'. Finding a description of the plant Daphne in a book one day, she was struck by how it applied to herself: 'The Daphne loves its roots in the shade and its head in the sun . . . it is very short-lived in hot dry soils.' Well aware of how all this sounded she vowed, 'If I go on much longer I shall burst into tears of self-pity.' One thing was certain: after this posting was over she was never going to go 'east of Looe, or west of Par again'.

Naturally, Daphne's extreme listlessness, her increasing pallor and her lack of appetite had all been noticed and were causing concern. Margaret, under the pretence that Tessa's prickly heat rash needed examining, asked for the doctor to call and, when he obliged, wondered if he would just cast his eye over Mrs Browning, about whose condition she had her suspicions. These were proved correct: Mrs Browning, the doctor reported, was definitely pregnant. Going into Mrs Browning's room, Margaret found her lying face downwards, sobbing into her pillow. She refused to believe it was true – she did not want another baby and had done everything possible to prevent becoming pregnant. It was treated by her as an unmitigated disaster – 'The worst!' she wrote, dramatically, to Tod, 'another infant on the way!!' The only consolation was that now she had an excuse for going home to England, 'because nothing will induce me to stay here and have it'. She felt so ill, unlike the first time, and dreaded to think that 'because the baby started when I was thoroughly run down it will be a mingy, awful thing with yellow skin'. It would turn out, she was sure, to be another girl and not the son she longed for – 'a fretful, puking daughter with Egyptian colouring, born complete with tarbrush'. She would keep 'a bucket . . . handy for such an eventuality', she joked, gloomily. Tommy, trying to cheer her up by predicting it would be twin boys this time, only made things worse. If by some miracle even one boy emerged, she told her mother, that was the only thing which would 'compensate for this awful blow'. All she could eat was the occasional cream cracker – nothing else would stay down. Clearly, she needed to escape the fearful heat, both for her own sake and the baby's, so a holiday in Cyprus was quickly arranged in mid-September.

This interlude was a great success from the minute she and Tommy and Tessa and Margaret boarded the ship to take them to Cyprus. They stayed in a good hotel up in the mountains and she was invigorated by the sharp air, so different from the dusty heat of Alexandria. She even climbed Mount Olympus in spite of feeling sick, and in the evenings she read Mrs Gaskell. Slowly, she managed to adjust herself to being pregnant again and, if it had not been for the necessity of returning to Alexandria before going to England, she felt she could now cope. But Alexandria was even worse than it had been before, when they returned at the end of the month – 'a nightmare', she vowed to Tod, 'I didn't know it was possible to hate a country with such intensity'. All that kept her going were plans for her return home to 'an English winter, fogs and all'. Told that all the ships might be full of people going back for the coronation of Edward VIII, she was in a panic until Tommy had secured berths for her, Tessa and Margaret. She utterly confused her mother with complicated arrangements about where she would have her second child. She did not want to go into a home – 'I have a grim antipathy for Homes' – but instead instructed Muriel to rent an apartment in Queen Anne's Mansions[4] and to wire in code when she had found out the price. 'SAGDA' was to mean 'terms too high' or 'ADIPB' to read 'anticipate much difficulty'.

By November, with all her plans made, and with the weather cooler, she was much happier. She stopped being sick and was greatly cheered by Victor Gollancz writing to say that he was delighted with *The Du Mauriers* and was going to print 10,000 copies, the same as for *Gerald*, with every anticipation of doing as well with it. At last, well enough to visit Cairo, a long-awaited treat, she found it no more enticing than Alexandria – 'like Hammersmith Broadway . . . and the Bazaar an inferior Burlington Arcade'. She had also seen the Pyramids, which, she wrote to Tod, were 'just like a couple of slag heaps, my dear, on the Great Western Road'. Not only could anyone who wanted it have Egypt, they could have 'the whole Eastern hemisphere', and she swore she had persuaded Tommy to retire if he was ever sent to India.

With a prejudice against a whole country and its people as violent as Daphne's, there was obviously no hope of her ever learning to adapt, and nor did she try to. It was no joke of hers to say she had no intention of enduring another foreign posting – she meant it. After this second baby was born, she planned to return with Tommy to Alexandria, when he in turn had finished the three months' leave he was due to have in May, and see his term there out, but as far as she was concerned there must be no more foreign postings. The thought that this might stand in the way of Tommy's career did not seem to occur to her – she swore that, although Tommy loved his work out there, he hated Egypt too, and that his own health suffered. He had had bouts of stomach trouble and complained of lumbago, and she was convinced that he would not be fit until he was home. Bracing him to bear her departure, which he dreaded, she tried to look ahead to the next happy summer in Fowey. This comforting vision was marred only by the thought of the second baby. Her heart sank when she contemplated managing two (though in fact she had done very little managing of the existing one).

Margaret went to Cairo for a weekend off just before Christmas, leaving Tessa to be looked after by her mother, who found it all 'rather exhausting', though she admitted Tessa was 'very well behaved while nanny was away'. Her little daughter was a mystery to her. Right from the moment of Tessa's birth she seemed to concentrate on stressing how different she was from herself – she was 'all Browning' and 'more like Angela than me'. Even when she was reporting Tessa's cleverness it was only to disapprove and say how she 'disliked precocity in a child'. Any show of independence and her daughter was 'vilely headstrong and dis-obedient', an opinion not shared by her nanny. When Tessa started dancing classes and insisted on a pretty frock to dance in, her mother professed to be horrified by her love of clothes. Looking after her, on the rare occasions when she did so, she was moved to comment to her mother, 'I shall never be a real child lover . . . looking after one is just a grind, I think.' Looking after two did not bear thinking about.

Yet she was not exactly the cold, remote figure these remarks might suggest. Always gentle, always kind, she was, from a young child's point of view, a very attractive mother to have. She had a sense of fun, which small children relished, and an imagination which appealed to them. The distance she felt between herself and Tessa was not shared by Tessa, at that stage. But, unconsciously or not, she was extending the kind of treatment to Tessa which she herself felt her own mother had dispensed, and it had hurt her greatly. Then, she had thought it somehow her mother's fault; now, she acted as though it were Tessa's. There was no Gerald this time to complicate matters – though Tommy loved his daughter, he did not have even remotely the kind of closeness to her which Gerald had once had with Daphne. But over and over in her letters Daphne talked about the three-year-old Tessa as though she were observing a fascinating but strange being who had little to do with her. She was repeating the history of a relationship, copying her own relationship with her mother as it once had been. It was as though she wished to make Tessa suffer as she had suffered, which for a woman of such imagination, sensitivity and self-awareness was extraordinary. But, in fact, because Tessa was temperamentally very different, the damage was not as great. Tessa was emotionally much better able to stand her mother's remoteness than Daphne had been able to accept Muriel's.[5]

Quite deliberately Daphne made plans to separate herself from the new baby even before it was born. She was going to leave both children in England when she returned with Tommy to Egypt the following July. It would, she wrote, 'not be worth carting them out', and they would be much happier with their nanny at home. This was a perfectly sensible decision, one made by many army wives whose husbands served in hot countries, but it was an indication that this time Daphne would not even allow herself to think of being unable to leave a three-month-old baby. She had had enough of intrusive emotional bonds. Her father had attempted to bind her with them and now her husband did the same, or tried to, and she was set against children adding to the constraints she felt. But the reality of parting from Tessa proved harder than she had anticipated, and surprised her.

On 16 January 1937 she sailed for England with Tessa and her nanny. Margaret was going to take Tessa to her own home while Daphne went on alone to Fowey, so she left the ship at Tilbury, leaving Daphne to disembark at Plymouth. Saying goodbye to her daughter, and watching her being taken off by Margaret, distressed Daphne more than she had ever thought possible. It was, she reported to her mother, 'agony', and told her more about herself than she dared admit. Would Tessa be happy? Would Margaret be fit enough to look after her (she had been feeling 'out of sorts' lately)? Instead of feeling relieved by her little daughter's departure she only felt guilty and worried.

Once at Ferryside, the anxiety lifted. Margaret wrote, saying all was well, and being back in Cornwall lifted Daphne's own spirits immediately. She went for her beloved cliff top walks, blessing the rain and fog and luxuriating in the strong, cold winds which made others shiver. She was just so intensely happy to be home and pushed out of her mind the awful reminder that she was not home for good. It did occur to her that she could use the new baby as a reason for not returning to Alexandria in July, but she rejected this dangerous temptation. Tommy was wretched without her and his letters, full of his depression, touched her. She could not desert him and must go back to 'that vile place I hate'. She stayed until March in Fowey, loving every day of it, and observing the publication of *The Du Mauriers* from a distance. In Cornwall she felt remote from the book's reception and, because she thought it pretentious to subscribe to a press-cuttings agency, and even worse to buy extra newspapers or magazines, she was not sure whether the book had been a success. The answer was that critically the book had nothing like the reception of *Gerald* – no reviewer was really enthusiastic – and from the sales' point of view it was a slow starter. But 'Q' liked it, and so did all the family, and Tod and Ferdy, so Daphne felt her efforts had not been wasted. Once the baby was born she would start thinking about another book, but she wrote to Victor Gollancz that 'I don't intend doing any work until August . . . suppose you want a novel . . . I would like to do a funny one about Empire society . . . but on the other hand might go to the opposite extreme and write rather a sinister tale about a woman who marries a widower . . . Psychological and rather macabre.' But first the ordeal of giving birth had to be endured again.

To her relief, it was not so terrible. 'The child literally whizzed out,' she wrote to Tod, after the birth on 2 April. It was another girl, but to her own surprise she found 'I didn't mind nearly so much about it not being a boy. Third time lucky?!' To another friend she confided that since 'the child' had arrived so easily, she could be forgiven both for being a week early and for being a girl. Tommy, who arrived back in England in May, was 'in the seventh heaven' at it being safely over and the baby not the undernourished scrap they had anticipated, but a healthy, pretty baby. It was he who chose the name – Flavia, 'heroine of one of his favourite books, *The Prisoner of Zenda'*. Within days of Flavia's birth her mother had decided she was quieter than Tessa and not as robust. This helped Daphne keep to her original decision to leave both children in England when she returned with Tommy, and she went ahead with arrangements for Margaret to look after them both at Rousham, her mother-in-law's home, where her sister-in-law Grace could act as guardian. The three months of Tommy's leave flew by, but 'like everything one looks forward to enormously', she wrote to Tod, 'hasn't come up to dreams'. It had proved impossible to shut out of her mind the thought of returning to Egypt and she was once more experiencing a mild post-natal depression, not helped by the imminent sale of the Cannon Hall cottages. Her mother and Angela and Jeanne were to live full-time at Ferryside and 'some shilling [disappointing] people from Kensington' were looking round the cottages, while she and Tommy were once more living there.

On 30 July, the Brownings returned to Egypt and Daphne tried to settle at once, in spite of the heat, to writing her new novel, the 'psychological and rather macabre' one. By the end of September she was obliged to report to Victor Gollancz that she was 'ashamed to tell you that progress is slow on the new novel and there is little likelihood of my bringing back a finished MS in December'. Progress had actually been worse than slow – 'the first 15,000 words I tore up in disgust and this literary miscarriage has cast me down rather as I have never done such a thing before and hate going over the ground again'. She tried to blame the weather but knew this was not a good excuse, because of having written *The Du Mauriers* the year before, 'though how they found their way onto my typewriter . . . heaven knows'. Sitting staring at this same typewriter, with the heat making even her fingers perspire and stick to the keys, she experienced a feeling of panic. What if she had lost the ability to write at all? All she had was a provisional title, *Rebecca*, 15,000 words in the waste-paper basket, and her notes. These read: 'very roughly the book will be about the influence of a first wife on a second . . . she is dead before the book opens. Little by little I want to build up the character of the first in the mind of the second . . . until wife 2 is haunted day and night . . . a tragedy is looming very close and *crash! bang!* something happens . . . it's *not* a ghost story.' But she could not at first think what the crash and bang would be, or even the 'something' that happened. Instead, she found herself fantasizing about Cornwall and in particular about Menabilly. It sustained her in the terrible heat to wander in her daydreams through the woods around Menabilly and to hear the sea pounding in her ears. The story took on a hallucinatory quality from the first, long before she had worked out the details of the plot – the unnamed heroine's interior life was what became important.

Meanwhile, struggling to get over her 'literary miscarriage', she was finding this second Egyptian experience had something to recommend it. In November she went with Tommy on a trip down to the Libya border and was mesmerized by the beauty of the desert. Here, at last, she could feel the 'magic of the East' whose existence she had denied. They camped – 'sleeping under an umbrella' – and got up at dawn, with stars still in the vast sky, 'to make a hearty bacon and egg breakfast at sunrise'. She adored it – this was exactly how she wanted to live, far from other people, like nomads. She wrote to Grace that she was now, like Tommy, 'desert mad . . . I didn't know I had it in me'. It gave her an ambition: she wanted to 'cross the Andes with a pack on my shoulder'.

Instead, she returned to Alexandria for another month to try to make some headway with *Rebecca*. Victor Gollancz was chasing her and wanted to announce the book in his next catalogue. She had signed a three-book contract with him and he was eager to see the first fruit. But, though she applied herself diligently, she still found she had not accomplished much. Partly this was because she was not sleeping well and had not the psychic energy she needed to write. After Flavia's birth she had resorted to sleeping pills and wrote to her mother that she always kept 'half a medinol'[6] beside her. Then there was the socializing in which she was obliged to take part. Tommy's battalion was ending its tour of duty in Egypt and there were endless farewell parties, which she hated but could not always avoid. No one who was at these functions knew how much the young, pretty, demure and shy-looking commanding officer's wife inwardly raged at 'the effort of talking . . . I don't know how people stand it'. Nor did they realize the effort any kind of entertaining in her own home caused her. She had servants and needed to do nothing except give orders but this, as ever, was precisely the trouble: she couldn't. Tommy, who liked a well-run house, was exasperated and, she wrote dismally to her mother, 'says even the best servant would go to pieces with me'. Her feelings of inferiority in this respect, and of being intimidated, went straight into the character of the second Mrs de Winter. She herself felt an outcast, an outsider, someone who did not fit in and was aware of it. She began to imagine what it must be like to feel as she did, but to have a social background, and a marital one, which would make those feelings even more acute. More and more her theme came to be not simply one of how jealousy motivates people but how feelings of isolation distort reality.

By the time she and Tommy sailed for home in mid-December, she had completed only a quarter of the novel and wrote to her mother just before leaving that 'I haven't been able to get going properly over here'. She was worried that the reunion with her children and settling down in a new home would further prevent her from working, and Victor was snapping at her heels. This was one of the reasons why she intended to go down to Ferryside for Christmas without the children. Her mother was shocked to be told this – surely, when she had not seen her children for almost five months and would be with them only ten days between landing and coming to Cornwall, *surely* she could not leave them behind, especially Tessa, who would realize what was happening? But Daphne could and would. She was defensive but determined. Tessa, she wrote, was 'just *too young* to join a communal life of grown-ups' and Muriel clearly did not appreciate 'what a handful she would be'. There would be no peace – 'it means meals together and being in the big room all the time, no sort of nursery existence, and you will think me ridiculous perhaps, but I *do* not think it is right until she is 6 or 7 to be taken away to stay like that. You will say she is no trouble, she is advanced for her age, but that is more or less my point . . . I do so *dread* her becoming too pre-cocious and for the next few years want her to lead as quiet and nurseryfied an existence as possible.' She was anxious her mother should not think her 'a brute . . . or unkind' which would make her 'very unhappy'. Muriel, who had had three children, was told that she probably did not realize 'what a strain' Tessa would be. And besides, if she came with them, 'I should get no work done'.

So Tessa and Flavia stayed with their nanny, and Daphne and Tommy had a relaxing time at Ferryside. Angela was about to have her first novel published – *The Perplexed Heart* – and there was that to celebrate as well as Christmas. Progress on *Rebecca* went better, but once more had to be put aside while the Brownings moved into a new house. It was called Greyfriars and was at Church Crookham, near Fleet, in Hampshire, near where Tommy was now stationed. Daphne loved the beautiful old house immediately, but reunited with her children found settling down difficult. Like many writers, she found domestic disruption the hardest thing to handle – she could not concentrate while everything was not orderly and organized, even if she did have servants. She needed to have a set routine, to feel that everything ran smoothly, everything was comfortingly familiar, before she could enjoy the peace of mind she needed to write. Eventually, it came. By the beginning of March she was writing at a tremendous pace and enjoying herself, though she was a little unsure of what she was producing. 'It's a bit on the gloomy side . . .', she wrote to Victor, 'and the psychological side' may not be understood.'

By April she had finished it and sent it to Victor – 'here is the book . . . I've tried to get an atmosphere of suspense . . . the ending is a bit brief and a bit grim.' It was, she warned, certainly too grim 'to be a winner'. Victor gave it to his senior editor, Norman Collins, telling him to read it at once – 'it ought to be looked at for the possibility of turning it into this year's Cronin'. Norman Collins read it in two days and reported back euphorically: 'The new Daphne du Maurier contains everything that the public could want.' Daphne had been wrong: she, and Gollancz, had their winner.

Chapter Nine

The report Norman Collins gave Victor Gollancz on the manuscript of *Rebecca* was a model of its kind. What he had realized straight away was that this novel had a most unusual quality. It was, he wrote, 'sentimental . . . but in a haunting, melancholy way' which captured the reader's attention and sympathy from the very first paragraph. But it was also 'passionate . . . not that there is any sign of physical passion' and, though melodramatic, 'brilliantly creates a sense of atmosphere and suspense'. He gave a summary of the plot, then commented: 'I don't know another author who *imagines* so hard all the time.' The faults of the novel – 'the spelling is quite incredible' – lay in a certain clumsiness in the writing, but he thought this unimportant – there was a power here which he assured Victor would make it 'a really rollicking success', maybe even greater than A. J. Cronin's *The Citadel* of the previous year, which Victor longed to repeat.[1]

Victor himself then read *Rebecca* and shared his editor's conviction. In his own letter to booksellers which he sent out a month after receiving the novel he wrote that he never remembered a book which so obviously contained every single one of the essential qualities of the bestseller – 'it is moving . . . it contains an exquisite love-story . . . it has a brilliantly created atmosphere of suspense'. His first print run was 20,000 copies and he immediately started rolling the kind of publicity at which he was so adept. This thrilled Daphne but also made her nervous. 'I am worried', she wrote to Victor, 'that you and Norman Collins are taking so much trouble over the book, and I only hope it's not an awful flop, because you'll all lose a lot of money.'

Money was very much on her mind. 'God knows,' she wrote to Victor, 'I have no desire to be rich, but my husband possesses nothing in this world but his army pay and . . . I do definitely consider myself the breadwinner.' The army pay of a Lieutenant-Colonel of the Grenadier Guards was £1.17s.0d. a day, which gave some substance to her claim, considering their joint expenses. 'It's a bit grim sometimes,' wrote Daphne, 'when I think in the middle of the night how difficult it would be for us if my mind stopped working.' Victor reminded her that she would be receiving, apart from her £1,000 advance, 20 per cent of all sales in the UK up to 10,000 copies and 25 per cent on sales between 10,000 and 20,000, so that already, with the subscription from booksellers at 15,000 copies before publication and a reprint of 10,000 in hand, she need have no night-time qualms. Whatever else it was going to do, *Rebecca* would make a lot of money, especially since 'film people are already sniffing around'.[2]

The summer of 1938 was the happiest Daphne had ever known. Buoyed up by the accolades for *Rebecca* which came flooding in before publication, and comfortably settled in the charming old house, Greyfriars, she felt well and in control of her life once more. Yet she by no means took it for granted that all those who had praised *Rebecca* were right. Always wary of flattery, and recognizing a kind of copy-cat applause when she heard it, she was not at all sure her novel would make the impact her publisher anticipated. She herself saw it as 'rather grim', even 'unpleasant', a study in jealousy with nothing of the 'exquisite love-story' her publisher claimed it to be. There was more hatred in it than love, in her own opinion, and she had tried very hard to show her unnamed heroine as intimidated, humiliated and even abused throughout most of the story. Never before had she entered the mind of any of her characters to this extent – again and again in the novel she used fantasy to heighten the reader's awareness of the dream-like state in which the second Mrs de Winter lived. She had done this from the beginning of her writing career, but now it dominated her writing, so that what happens in this woman's mind is more important than what actually takes place around her. The book begins with a dream and retains this fantasy element to great effect throughout. There are endless daydreams, some projecting into the past, most concerned with the future, so that the reader is constantly pulled out of the events taking place and drawn into the strange and haunting imagination of the heroine. 'I could imagine' becomes the constant refrain.

The author also worried about whether, behind the obvious excitement of the plot she had so carefully concocted, critics would recognize that she was trying to explore the relationship between a man who was powerful and a woman who was not, just as she had done, in a different way, in *Jamaica Inn* and, to some extent, in everything she had written. She had wanted to write about the balance of power in marriage and not about love. The heroine, after the terrible scene in which she wears the same dress as the dead Rebecca and is angrily ordered to take it off by Maxim, lies on her bed reflecting that there is 'nothing worse, so shaming and degrading, as a marriage that had failed'. It is important to her that no one should guess how humiliated she feels, how threatened her marriage is. And Maxim is a husband who is prone to humiliating her at every turn even when he thinks he is being loving. He treats her, she feels, as he does his dog and she is reduced to begging for his love, any love, 'as my father . . . brother . . . son'. Even when it is revealed that Maxim hated and murdered Rebecca, the heroine still seems subservient to him and has to plead with him to grant her a different status – 'I'll be your friend and companion, a sort of boy,' she cries, in desperation. When put to the test, at the inquest, her contribution is actually to faint. Once more, Daphne had created a man the reader is bound to dislike to the end – harsh, dominant, bad-tempered – and a woman for whom only pity can be felt. But would reviewers notice any of this? She had more misgivings than she cared to admit, except to herself and her publisher.

In the event, the critics, though almost unanimously praising the novel, did not see what she had wanted them to see. Most of them stressed that *Rebecca* was 'unashamed melodrama' and harped on its 'obvious popular appeal' in a way that always sounded faintly derogatory, in the author's ears at least. *The Times*, whose opinion Daphne still rated highest, was rather patronizing, commenting that the 'material is of the humblest . . . nothing in this is beyond the novelette', and yet admitted there was 'an atmosphere of terror which . . . makes it easy to overlook . . . the weaknesses'. Beside that, Daphne did not care so much that the *Sunday Times* rated *Rebecca* 'a grand story' and was positively irritated that it was labelled 'romance in the grand tradition'. One or two reviews pointed out that Miss du Maurier was 'an odd writer . . . hard to pigeon-hole . . . mixing the grossest fantasy with the most admirable transcription of little scenes . . .' That was more what she wanted to hear, but she still craved a different kind of assessment. Frank Swinnerton in the *Observer* almost gave it to her. He, too, stressed *Rebecca*'s popular appeal, but he thought something more should be said of it than that. It was, he commented, 'not a paltry fake, and the fearlessness with which Miss du Maurier works in material so strange . . . is magnificent'. He thought that 'the sniggers of meticulous sophisticates' should be ignored and instead found it commendable that 'a young writer of extraordinary talent should risk absurdity and should unquestionably triumph'. Victor Gollancz put another reprint in hand at once, bringing the number of copies to 45,000 within one month of publication.

Daphne was elated, but more by the money than the praise. 'Could you give me a rough estimate of what I've earned from *Rebecca*?' she wrote to Victor. 'It would help me budgeting expenses for the coming winter.' (The answer was £3,000, less her original advance.) She had been so keen that the book should sell, and so conscious of her debt to her publisher, who had been lavish with expensive advertisements, that she had done something she had always vowed she never would: in August, on publication of *Rebecca*, she was a guest at a Foyle's Literary Lunch. She agreed to let Victor persuade her on condition she did not have to speak, and sat in silence while the other two authors, Margery Allingham and E. V. Lucas, made speeches. She disliked the experience intensely and condemned her fellow authors quite savagely – 'Women shouldn't speak in public unless they are born with the gift, and damn few women are. And the efforts of Miss Allingham and Miss Lucas . . . proved to me I am right!' She thought their speeches embarrassingly bad and the whole occasion an appalling waste of time. Not even to please, or help, Victor, nor to boost her sales, would she ever attend such an event again. It made her miserable to be stared at and she wrote to Foy that authors never should be seen or heard. She herself had no desire to meet other authors, even those contemporary authors she admired at the time, like J. B. Priestley and Graham Greene, and belonging to any kind of literary circle held no attractions for her at all.

Throughout the autumn of 1938 the success of *Rebecca* grew and grew, constantly amazing her. In America, too, where it was published by Doubleday in September, its success was instant, though the reviews were often sarcastic. Comparisons with *Jane Eyre* were even more numerous than they had been in the British press, usually to the detriment of *Rebecca*. But just as Frank Swinnerton had defended the author against the suggestion that she was a mere cheap populizer, so several of the American critics warned against dismissing *Rebecca* as an inferior *Jane Eyre*, pointing out that even if much more crude and less sophisticated in the writing, it had its own real power and a strange passion easily comparable with Charlotte Brontë's. No one, either side of the Atlantic, paid any real attention to the battle between the sexes in *Rebecca*, or saw it as a psychological study in jealousy, as Daphne had hoped. But beside her enormous success this was merely puzzling, and she had no intention of complaining. The money poured in (another reprint brought copies to 60,000 by the end of the year) and she set about husbanding her earnings. She was determined not to be like her father in his rich years – she wanted to put almost everything into the bank and had no plans for spending any of it on luxuries. She was rightly proud to have earned so much, and Tommy, who had no false pride, was equally delighted, though more enthusiastic about some spending. The future looked bright indeed, except for a shadow slowly looming ahead: the approaching threat of a war that Tommy believed was sure to come in the next year.

Whenever she looked back on her childhood Daphne saw very clearly how protected she and her sisters had been, 'three doves in a gilded cage', cosseted by a father who wanted to keep them safe in a predatory world. Breaking out of that cage had hardly resulted in her becoming any less protected. She was still, at the age of thirty-one, insulated from the harshness of an era in which even some of the rich wavered in confidence. In her role as wife of a commanding officer in the Grenadier Guards she was almost

Gerald du Maurier, Daphne's father, 2 years after his marriage, at the height of his fame.

Her mother, Muriel, shortly before she gave up acting on the birth of her third daughter in 1911.

The du Maurier family in the garden of Cannon Hall, Hampstead. Angela and Jeanne sit close to their mother, while Daphne separates herself and grabs her own chair.

ABOVE *The three du Maurier sisters in the conservatory. Daphne again sits slightly apart, scowling at the camera.*

LEFT *Mlle Fernande ('Ferdy') Yvon, who taught Daphne at her French finishing school and became an intimate and influential friend.*

ABOVE *Frederick Browning (known as Tommy to his family) with his sister Grace and mother Nancy.*

LEFT *Geoffrey Millar, Daphne's actor cousin, with whom she had a mild but significant adolescent flirtation.*

Daphne in 1929, when she was having an affair with film director Carol Reed (inset), and writing her first novel, The Loving Spirit.

Daphne rowing herself from Fowey to Ferryside, the house at Bodinnick which the du Mauriers bought in 1926.

RIGHT *Tommy Browning, the immaculate Grenadier Guards officer with whom Daphne fell in love in 1932, and married 3 months later.*

BELOW *Maureen Luschwitz (later Baker-Munton) in 1947.*

BELOW *Daphne holds her first baby, Tessa, in 1933, betraying a certain nervousness in handling her.*

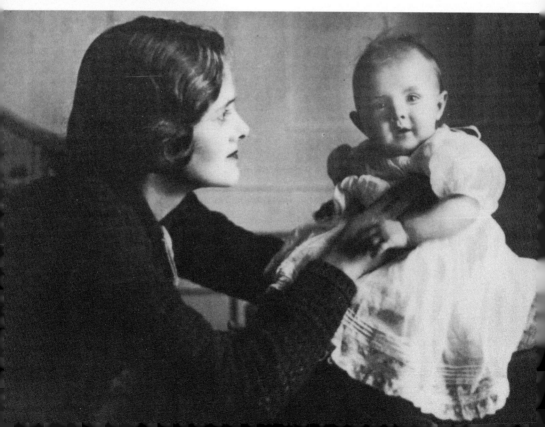

LEFT Henry ('Christopher'), Puxley in whose house Daphne and her children spent part of the war and with whom she became infatuated.

BELOW right to left Œnone Rashleigh, daughter of the heir to Menabilly with whom Daphne became friendly; Foy Quiller-Couch, Daphne's closest friend in Cornwall; Morwenna Rashleigh; Betty Symondson, Foy's cousin; Anne Hanson; Jenny Porter; Jennifer Rashleigh.

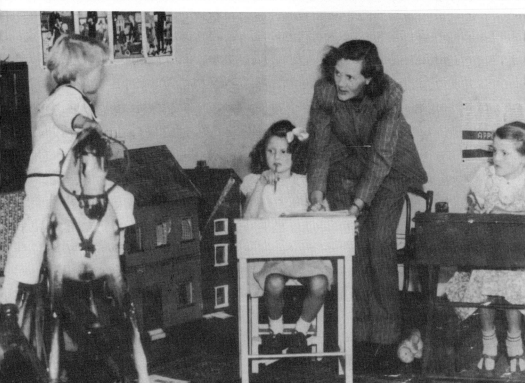

ABOVE *Menabilly, the house Daphne rented for twenty-five years and restored, which was the inspiration for several of her novels.*

BELOW *Daphne teaching her daughters (Flavia, centre, and Tessa) in the nursery at Menabilly during the war. Kits is on the rocking horse.*

as shielded from reality as she had been as a child. But towards the end of 1938 it began to dawn on her, as it did on almost everyone, that war was indeed coming, and when it came no one would be immune. Bombs would not discriminate between privileged and underprivileged, rifle shots would kill officers as well as men, there would be no way in which she could preserve her charmed life intact.

Slowly, because she had never shown much interest in politics, Daphne began to pick up from Tommy what was happening. He could talk of nothing else but 'the wretched lack of preparedness' in the British Army and raged and thundered, wrote his wife to Tod, against the 'incompetent nincompoops' at the War Office, who did not seem to realize this. Only Winston Churchill, according to Tommy, knew how badly equipped the army was and how slack its discipline had become. He himself was writing a new Drill Book for the instruction of the whole army, but he knew it would be too late to have much effect. He was, Daphne wrote to his sister Grace, in a great state about it all, but she confessed she loved him 'stamping . . . and declaring . . . the army is a bloody undisciplined rabble'. But she felt afraid in a way she had never done before. Everything was at risk, everything she had could disappear in a flash.

Grace, who was in hospital having a hysterectomy, received a letter from her of a kind she did not usually write. 'I'm bad at talking face to face,' she confessed, 'a foolish shyness prevents me,' but she wanted to explain what she was feeling at the moment. She had taken to reading the Bible regularly, in a slightly embarrassed way, searching for some kind of comfort in the face of approaching chaos. The Gospel according to St John, bidding everyone to be of good cheer, had appealed to her and made her think about what optimism meant. It was surely a way to conquer fear. 'The only real enemy of every living person', she wrote to Grace, 'is not so much fear of bodily hurt as acute fear of being unhappy. We are afraid of war not for our own selves being bombed, but because people we love might be taken from us and we ourselves made miserable. Therefore the root must be self-pity. We don't want to be lonely. The Stoics conquered grief and pain by a sort of armour of apathy which must have helped to destroy them, therefore apathy is no good. One has just got to be above self-pity and recognise that every individual soul is working out his own particular jigsaw puzzle which is part of a universal jigsaw and that everything will fit into place eventually, it just has to be.' It is to be hoped Grace waited until the effects of the anaesthetic had worn off before attempting to make sense of this confused logic, but what followed was a little clearer. 'If someone you or I love dies tomorrow,' wrote Daphne, 'it's not destiny laid down for them at the toss of a coin, but their own little jigsaw fitting into place and linking up, and because of it your and my little jigsaw comes nearer to completion.' So if Tommy were killed in action this would be part of some master plan and therein lay the comfort.

Unfortunately, it was not enough of a comfort. Daphne struggled to convince herself, tried hard to develop her own philosophy by taking a bit from the Greeks, a bit from the Bible, and by mixing legend with superstition, which is what she ended up doing, but only confused herself. She wished she could share Tommy's deep and very simple religious faith. He believed in God and the triumph of Good over Evil, of Right over Wrong. He would go into battle, as he had done before, trusting in the Lord. She marvelled at this faith but could not share it. Far more to her liking was the idea that the individual must change and put faith in himself. If everyone changed themselves, if each person became unselfish and kind, then the whole course of history would be changed and war averted. In this mood she was highly receptive to the words of her old friend Bunny Austin, then at the height of his fame as a tennis champion, who had become inspired by Frank Buchman's[3] call for a kind of moral rearmament. Bunny explained to her that the 'Oxford Group', as it was first known (later becoming the Moral Rearmament Movement, or MRA) was trying to start a moral revolution by starting one in each individual. He told her he himself was convinced Buchman's ideas represented the best chance of stopping the outbreak of war and that he was going to devote himself wholeheartedly to the movement. Daphne professed herself interested – and so did Tommy – but at that point took her interest no further.

In Fowey that autumn, on holiday enjoying one of Tommy's

leaves, she could hardly bear to think of the beautiful coastline soon perhaps to be bristling with guns, the sea full of destroyers, the beaches infested with mines. Everything in the landscape she loved was threatened. Her feelings of apprehension deepened and the happiness of the summer already seemed remote. Miss Roberts, her old landlady at Nook Cottage, with whom she had kept in close touch (as she did with all friends and servants she had liked), had cancer of the bowel and, visiting her in hospital, Daphne was humbled by this little old lady telling *her* to cheer up, war might never happen. She wrote to Grace saying how ashamed she was of herself, and that she was going to try to be a better person.

But back at Greyfriars she found this hard – her irritation was so easily aroused, and yet she knew she really had nothing to complain about and should make the most of what Tommy warned her was 'the lull before the storm'. The children had colds and Tessa was annoying her by 'joining in the grown-up chatter, as she always does, given half the chance . . . I feel agonised'. She found Tessa, at five years old, 'most alarming', she wrote to Grace, 'she walks so quickly and her voice is the loudest I have ever heard'. As for eighteen-month-old Flavia, she had decided she was neither as pretty nor as quick as Tessa and there was already a disparaging if affectionate note in all her remarks about her. She knew she shouldn't judge her small children so harshly, but confessed to her mother, 'Instead of thinking my children are marvellous I am super-critical.'

Her own intolerance of almost everything dismayed her. Apart from the children's colds she was also exasperated by her husband's stomach trouble. He was having frequent attacks of 'me tum' and also of some sort of colic which she dismissed in letters to Tod as 'only a chill'. Even the ordinary tribulations of life made her exhausted – she told Tod she could hardly cope with the traffic, and after one visit to London when she had spent forty minutes driving herself from Oxford Street to the Strand she had returned home hysterical. If she was so feeble that she could not survive children's colds, husband's chills and heavy traffic, how, she wondered, was she going to survive war? She succumbed to a sore throat and lay in bed feeling 'wretchedly unworthy'.

Bunny Austin, visiting her at this time, in November 1938,

found her more receptive than ever to the MRA beliefs. To his delight, she agreed to sign a letter to the *Sunday Times* and other newspapers already signed by himself, Peter Wood and Prunella Douglas-Hamilton. In this letter the cause of MRA was explained as 'our nation's destiny . . . we must rearm our moral might'. This meant 'casting out fear, hate, pride and self-seeking which divide man from man, and form the root causes of war. It demands that we first admit our own faults before trying to remedy the faults of others.' This was what Daphne herself was trying, and failing, to do, and it seemed to her the MRA cause made perfect sense. So she went, in January 1939, with Bunny to an MRA conference in Eastbourne, staying at the Grand Hotel, and, shielded by Bunny from any attention, she listened carefully to all the speakers and at the end of the week felt genuinely inspired. She decided not only to support MRA but to offer to do something to help.

But first she wanted to complete an adaptation of her own novel *Rebecca* for the stage. She had decided to attempt this because, as she wrote to Victor Gollancz, 'my next book has not come in any definite form yet, not even in my mind', but she wanted some work to do to take her mind off the thought of war and this was the only thing that had presented itself. (The success of *Rebecca* had, she commented, been 'the cause of my present laziness'.) She had also decided that if the newly released film of *Jamaica Inn* was anything to go by, she would be wise to try to adapt her own work for any other medium. She was furious with the film. 'Don't go and see it,' she told Victor, 'it is a wretched affair.' The depiction of the wreckers particularly enraged her – instead of being violent and ugly she thought they had been made into '*Peter Pan* pirates', and the effect was quite the opposite of her intention.

The literary exercise of adapting her own book proved interesting. Once she started examining *Rebecca* she was struck by how difficult it was to keep both atmosphere and suspense without having the heroine's interior monologues and without being able to describe the landscape. Dialogue was not her strong point, and once everything had to take place within the framework of the spoken word she was surprised at how constricted she felt. She tried to introduce more banter between Maxim and his sister, and to heighten the already dramatic episodes, but she felt something had gone out of the story and only hoped the acting would restore it. She finished the script at the beginning of June 1939, not entirely convinced it would ever be produced, and was immediately overcome with domestic problems, which had been there all the time, but which, while writing, she had managed to ignore. The chief of these was the health of Margaret, the children's nanny. Ever since their return from Egypt she had had appalling migraines which incapacitated her for two or three days every month. Clearly, she needed a complete rest, so as soon as the stage adaptation of *Rebecca* was finished, Daphne packed her off home for a holiday. This left her with both children to look after. Tod, who was coming to stay, was warned that she would find herself with both girls climbing on top of her, which was 'very wearing'. So wearing, that Daphne, after less than a week, employed a temporary nursemaid to look after them until Margaret returned. 'I must say,' she wrote to Tod, 'I am not one of those mothers who live for having their brats with them all the time and I sincerely look forward to the time when Flavia and Tessa will be of a decent, companionable age.' Since they were almost six and two there was a long way to go.

It was a relief when Margaret returned, just in time for the move from Fleet to Hythe, in Kent. Tommy was now commanding the Small Arms School at Netheravon, and Hythe was near his headquarters. The new house at Hythe was not as beautiful as Greyfriars but it had a good garden. The change of residence as usual unsettled Daphne, and Tommy was irritated by the temporary disorder. He was working very hard and when he came home wanted peace and quiet and a well-run house. His wife's inability to run it as efficiently as he had always run his battalion resulted in some heated rows. One was over a cook who served poor food, which Daphne maintained was not her fault. Tommy said, of course it wasn't, but it was her job to confront the cook and either get her to improve or dismiss her and find another. This made Daphne miserable – she hated all confrontation and had no faith in her ability to engage staff. She struggled to provide Tommy with the kind of home life he expected and needed, but resented being thought a failure and resented, too, his emphasis on anything as trivial as how a house was run. Ferdy came to stay for a week, which at least kept Tommy from complaining. He tolerated Ferdy (knowing nothing, of course, of her past relationship with Daphne) but Tod infuriated him. At least Daphne never invited Tod and Ferdy together. She never, ever had friends or even relatives staying at the same time. Everyone invited came on their own, not even overlapping by a day. 'It is a fearful thing of mine', she once wrote to Ferdy, 'that I want people to myself. If I don't have them I just lose interest . . .' But she also realized she was different things to different people, and if she had to cope with these differences she became confused as to who she was. So the rule was always one at a time with the result that people could be part of her life for years and yet never meet or know each other.

Once Ferdy had departed, Daphne found herself getting involved in Civil Defence preparations, much to her own amazement. Tommy predicted that war would be declared against Germany at the end of the summer and he was right. The moment it was, Daphne began practising, at the first aid post where she had enrolled, in how to deal with gassed casualties. She described to her mother how ludicrous it all was, trying to undress people while wearing oilskin gloves, and how difficult to keep her face straight. She said she adored her squad – 'Oh, the uniformed harpies who have lain perdu since 1918 and who now come into their own again.' A certain 'Mrs G', the quartermaster's wife, had on 'a large gent's lounge suit plus her cloche hat' and even 'the fair and fluffy wife of the staff sergeant has suddenly become brisk and determined'. At home, she reported to Tod that there was 'an endless rush of generals to stay' and that Tommy seemed to be becoming more important all the time, but she was pleased that she had managed to cope with such guests to Tommy's satisfaction. She passed on his views on the international situation, all of which were gloomy. He was furious because 'for *years* [he] on manoeuvres has urged the army should have aeroplanes to work with them . . . and all the old generals said "Oh nonsense, aeroplanes are no use to troops" . . . so we have *one* squadron only trained'. He frightened her, too, by pointing out that the French would have to be depended on 'because we only have four divisions out there and the Germans have a hundred'. But she herself desperately hoped some agreement would be reached 'before the real slaughter begins'. It seemed to her, confronted with the thought of this slaughter, that more than ever 'the MRA people are right ... We ought to give up trying to make money, trying to be successful, trying to live by the values of the world and get back to simplicity in all things, kindliness and simple faith ... selfishness is the root of all evil.'

In this mood it was irresistible to use the occasion of an American broadcast to campaign for MRA. The American Literary Societies had awarded her a prize for *Rebecca*, and she took the invitation to speak to them as her chance both to thank them and to urge them to 'try to do for the twentieth century what our ancestors did in the sixteenth, when they worked for that glorious Renaissance ... If we writers faithfully dedicate ourselves ... to giving ... the real sincerity and honesty and truth that we feel in our hearts ... there will be ... a new spirit ... and the false values of the early twentieth century will be forgotten.' Flushed with triumph at the success of this broadcast she agreed to let a young Oxford graduate, Garth Lean, Bunny's co-worker, come down to Hythe to discuss an idea Bunny had put to her. This was that she should be provided with some true stories of individuals who had put MRA principles into practice and transformed their lives. Garth took some of these stories to her and they went for a long walk – 'one always had to go for a walk with Daphne' – and discussed how they could be turned into articles which Garth would place in regional newspapers up and down the country. Tommy was at this time on a brief mission to France and she wanted very much to contribute more to the war effort than fooling around at a first aid station, so she agreed. It was fear, which she could no longer philosophize away, that made her decide to do her best.

It also made her decide, as the New Year of 1940 brought disastrous war news every week, to have another baby. 'I somehow felt', she wrote to Tod, 'the time had come for another effort at a son, but I'm quite prepared for another lumping daughter.' But a son, more than ever, was what she craved and, now that Tommy was likely to be in danger, she seized her chance before it was too late. The moment she knew she was pregnant she felt more hopeful and calmer, though she joked to Tod that the birth 'will probably coincide with the invasion and Hitler's march through London. A decree will go out that all children are to be named Adolf.' One thing she was adamant about: no matter how serious the threat of invasion – and in the spring of 1940 it was very real – she would neither leave England herself nor send the children out of the country. People who did so earned her contempt. Many contemporaries were sending their children to America, and she refused to accept the homes offered for Tessa and Flavia. She commented to Tod, that she didn't want to take the risk of sending the children – 'even if they got there safely, what's the odds on seeing them again? And who's to say that prospective hostesses are not going to get fed-up with English kids after a bit and dump 'em in a camp altogether.' She didn't want her children dumped and exposed to neglect, so she resolved to face out the war with them, however terrible.

In May, Tommy relinquished his post at Hythe and became commander of the 128th Hampshire Brigade. The house at Hythe was given up and Daphne went first of all to Fowey with the children. She had just been up to Edinburgh to see *Rebecca* performed and was pleased by how well it was going, in spite of Owen Nares not being 'really right' as Maxim, though she loved Celia Johnson as the second Mrs de Winter. Once in Fowey, theatrical successes seemed a long way off and she was worried about how she could keep the family together with no real home except her mother's at Ferryside. Tommy's brigade was stationed in Hertfordshire, and wanting to be as near as possible she asked his new batman, Johnson, to try to find them a house to rent in the vicinity.

What Johnson found was not a house to rent but a house where the Brownings could, as Daphne told Tod, 'P.G. in a state of great comfort . . . with some perfectly charming people called Puxley, who have a delightful Lutyens house . . . host and hostess most congenial. I breakfast in bed and wander in the garden and go for walks to my heart's content. She copes with WVS and Red Cross and two evacuee children, and is never rattled or tired (40-ish, tall, good-looking, not terribly strong I should say either). He is a LDV [Local Defence Volunteer] but otherwise does nix, wanders about and gardens, plays the piano beautifully, also 40-ish and looks like portraits of the writer Compton Mackenzie when young.' The Puxley house was called Langley End and the children joined their mother there in July. Both girls, now seven and three, soon adored Mrs Puxley, known as 'Paddy', and she became extremely fond of them. She had no children of her own, but was what Daphne referred to as 'naturally maternal'. She took the children for walks, played games with them, brushed their hair and generally acted as a kind of surrogate mother with Daphne's full approval.

This gave her the time to work the newspaper articles she had written for Garth into a small book. The first of these stories had appeared in March 1940 in the *Edinburgh Evening News* headed 'A Mother and her Faith, comforting words by Daphne du Maurier'. Bunny Austin had given her the bare bones of this true-life story via Garth Lean before he went to join Buchman in America. It was about a woman called Mrs Brown, who had two sons in the navy. She hears a voice in her head assuring her that God will look after them, so that when she is told that the boat one son was in has been torpedoed she has no fear. Instead of being distraught, she is calm and in the end news comes to justify her faith: her son has survived. The story itself, however true, was trite, but even more banal were Daphne's introductory paragraphs. Striving for simplicity and sincerity, she succeeded only in sounding sanctimonious, as though her normal style was crippled by the need to be uplifting (though the stories with which Bunny, then Garth, provided her would have needed nothing short of genius to make them palatable and to transform them into an inspirational message for the MRA cause). She put her heart into the job but, for once, was quite unaware of how unsuccessful the results were in literary terms. Of course, they were not meant to be of any literary merit – they were intended as messages of comfort for ordinary people and on those terms the evidence was that they succeeded. People wrote in saying how much the Mrs Brown story had meant to them and the *Edinburgh Evening News* promptly ran some more comforting words from Daphne du Maurier. A huge variety of provincial papers ran Daphne's version of this and other true stories. Garth Lean worked hard at spreading the net until at one time in April 1940 every corner of England was being comforted by Daphne.

She was naturally very pleased to think she was doing something positive, her own little war effort, so when Garth suggested the newspaper articles should be gathered together and made into a small booklet with an introduction by her she was happy to oblige. She wrote to her agent, Curtis Brown: 'I feel strongly that this is quite apart from my literary work, and is more a sort of National Service . . . and I do not wish to receive any money from the sales of such a booklet,' and stressed: 'I do feel this is a chance for getting money for the Red Cross.' She selected ten stories and was eager to accept Garth's tentatively offered editorial suggestions. But Daphne had been unable to work any magic; the stories were competently written, but they did not seem as impressive as they had done as newspaper articles, though her introduction was everything for which a believer in MRA could hope. There was a need, Daphne wrote, to discover once again old fundamental values, 'truth, honesty, selflessness' and a need to 'learn to give' instead of the inevitable 'to get'. The real cause of war was the putting of self first and the refusal to listen to one's inner conscience, 'the Voice within'. If only everyone would listen to this Voice there would, she vowed, be forged 'a chain of steel round this island that no enemy from without can ever break'.

There was no doubting Daphne's absolute sincerity and she saw no element of humbug in what she wrote. She was trying hard to follow her own advice but worried that she was failing. 'I think I must be a rotten receiving set,' she wrote to Garth, 'a valve loose or something – all I get is a "wait and see" signal, and it will arrange itself.' The publication of her booklet, entitled *Come Wind, Come Weather* (from the John Bunyan hymn), seemed to her the best effort she could make and she was keen to do everything possible to help it along, even instructing Garth to 'ginger up Heinemanns' because to them a sixpenny booklet was small fry. She wanted it to reach as many people as possible and so reluctantly conceded that Garth was right to want to put 'author of *Rebecca*' under the title, however embarrassing this felt to her. All the proceeds, she had decided, should go not to the Red Cross but to the Soldiers, Sailors and Air Force Association – 'I would feel rather ashamed if it couldn't make a good bit for them.' The booklet was published in August 1940 and sold very well (the first edition of 340,000 sold out by October and a second edition of 250,000 was printed).

Daphne's mother was one of the first to write and say how she loved it – 'I adored your little book. The stories were so simple. They made me weep,' and Tommy was 'very pleased with it', she told Tod. Victor Gollancz was not. Daphne had written to him, when the booklet was already being printed by Heinemann – 'just a line to tell you Heinemann are bringing out a 6d booklet shortly . . . just a simple morale propaganda affair . . . didn't think it was your line of country.'[4] Victor was most aggrieved and wrote back saying anything of hers was his line of country and would she please remember that. Lord Leverhulme read it and asked her to contribute to a series he was running in his newspaper, and she also had lots of letters from perfect strangers praising the stories. She felt she had provided 'a sort of mid-way signpost among the blind and deaf' even though also feeling she had 'a ghastly cheek to suggest anything to anybody'. The reception of her booklet gave her the greatest satisfaction and encouraged her to try even harder to follow MRA principles.

By the autumn of 1940, she was feeling strangely happy in spite of the war. It had been a summer full of bad news, justifying Tommy's gloomy predictions. The Germans had overrun Denmark, Norway, Holland and Belgium, and then in June France had surrendered. From August to October the Battle of Britain raged and, though the Germans failed to bomb Britain into submission, the whole country was anticipating invasion. But Daphne felt cut off from the realities of war. Her baby was due in November and as usual the state of pregnancy had made her more relaxed and calmer. Deciding it was unfair on the Puxleys to give birth in their house, she had rented another house for three months from the beginning of October – Cloud's Hill, at Offley, not very far from Langley End – and here she waited for her third child, hoping desperately for a son.

PART THREE

The Years Between
1939–1946

Chapter Ten

At Cloud's Hill, Daphne had plenty of time to reflect on the progress she had made in trying to reform herself. She was not pleased with her reflections, confessing in a letter to Garth that when she looked back on her behaviour during Tommy's weekend leaves over the past few months, she saw she had acted 'like a sour old Army wife in an Indian hill station, who has a disapproving eye on all gaiety'. She had found herself jealous of Tommy's response to the adoration of the eight unmarried daughters of a local family – known as the 'Brigade Butterflies', because of their attachment to the whole brigade – even though she knew perfectly well it was harmless. The Brownings both joked about these girls, du Maurier style, mocking them. But there had been one particular Saturday, just before she left Langley End, when she and Tommy had lunched with the family of the 'Butterflies' and she had been horrified at herself. There was 'a lot of tennis afterwards, and poor Tommy thoroughly enjoying himself as a contrast to hard work, and because, of course, I could not play and felt I looked awful with my floppy clothes, I resented his enjoyment and gaiety amongst a troop of pretty girls . . . and was quite snappy and sour and horrid to him in the evening. I was most ashamed of myself and disheartened to think I could get like that . . . the whole incident quite depressed me.'

But that was not the whole story. What also depressed her was that she was beginning to prefer the company of Christopher[1] Puxley to Tommy's. Whenever her husband joined her at Langley End he arrived exhausted and bad-tempered, endlessly cursing the stupidity of everyone at the War Office and saying he had to do every bloody thing himself. He was unable to talk about anything but the war, which he saw, with reason, as going from bad to worse. Invasion was still a strong possibility, and he foresaw 'a big boil-up in the East' as inevitable. Christopher, by contrast, talked about 'music and birds, and islands and things'. He was quiet, gentle, rather languid, whereas Tommy was noisy, energetic and so worried he had forgotten how to smile except when the 'Brigade Butterflies' were around. Christopher made her feel secure, Tommy made her feel threatened. She was ashamed that when Tommy went back to his brigade she was relieved. The house fell quiet once more and the strains of Christopher playing Chopin, 'divinely', wafted through the air. She lay on a sofa, evening after evening, listening to him play and studying him. He was a man who seemed somehow familiar to her, as though she had known him in another life, in different circumstances and company. His real name was Henry and he was two years younger than Tommy. In the First World War he had been in the Royal Navy and fought at the Battle of Jutland where he was wounded. Now he farmed and helped with Civil Defence, but had plenty of time to follow his passion for music and luxurious cars (he had a Bentley and an Alvis, both kept in immaculate condition). Clearly, he was wealthy and had the ease of manner to go with it. His was an ancient Irish family and he had a photograph of himself taken just before he married in 1920, standing before the ruins of Dunboy Castle at Berehaven, the ancestral home in Ireland, which had been burnt down in a fire. The more she got to know him, the more of 'a menace' he became.

Always used to analysing her own emotions, Daphne was a little afraid to look too deeply into her feelings for Christopher Puxley. It was a relief to leave Langley End and move to Cloud's Hill for three months, even though she immediately missed the comfort and company it had afforded her. She did not mind that Tommy's brigade had now moved out of the area, and that he was somewhere near Ramsgate – 'better for him to be out of sight and hearing'. She preferred to be on her own for the birth with a woman doctor in attendance, which greatly pleased her – she did not like male doctors to assist at childbirth.

In the event, the doctor did little assisting. The birth of her third child on 3 November was easy – 'only half an hour and the doctor hadn't time to get her rubber gloves on', she wrote to Tod

– and the happiest. 'I have done it at last . . . a son!' Her air of triumph was blatant – 'For seven years I've waited to see "Mrs Browning, a son" in *The Times*.' He was to be called Christian, the name written on the cupboard doors of the nursery so long ago, after Christian in *The Pilgrim's Progress* (like Flavia his name came from one of his father's favourite books). His given names were Christian Frederick du Maurier, after his father and to keep faith with Gerald. And Gerald was very much part of the euphoria which filled Daphne, not only because this was the grandson he, cheated of a son, had wanted, but because of that long-remembered wish, so disturbing at the time, that one day he would like to come back as her son. Right from the moment of birth she was saying that Christian looked like Gerald, seemed like Gerald, and would undoubtedly grow up to act like Gerald. Tommy, to whom she saw no resemblance in her son whatsoever, amused her by ignoring this prediction and promptly entering his day-old son for his regiment for the year 1960.

Margaret, the children's nanny, who had seen Mrs Browning with Tessa at six weeks old and Flavia at birth, was astonished by her behaviour this time. This baby was treated quite differently. Mrs Browning could hardly bear to have him taken from her arms to be put into his cradle. Far from not wanting to do much for him, she wanted to do everything. The girls noticed too – at seven and three they were aware that their new brother received all the cuddles and kisses which had been rare in their own young lives. But they were drawn into all the adoration and, instead of exhibiting signs of resentment and jealousy, were surprisingly happy to accept that their mother felt towards Christian what she had not seemed able to feel towards them. There was no doubt in the minds of anyone who saw Daphne then that she had at last been given her heart's desire.

But within a month, in spite of her passionate love for her son, Daphne found herself in the grip of a depression worse than those that had followed the births of her daughters. She could not understand it. She had had an easy birth, had been given the son she craved, and yet by the end of November she felt very low. She tried to tell herself it was because of the dark days, and her worry about Tommy who was on the south-east coast, but she knew it was more than that. She felt distressed about herself, about her own worthlessness, and wrote to Garth that, when she turned 'the old searchlight' on herself, she did not like what she saw. There was, about all her letters to Garth, a pious tone, most unlike the tone of any of her other letters, and it was obvious she was telling him what she thought he wanted to hear. Just as, in the company of different people, she automatically adapted her outward behaviour to suit them, so in her letters she adapted her style and sentiments. But, nevertheless, she was genuinely a little ashamed of herself. She had not in any way betrayed Tommy and yet she felt she had been somehow disloyal in thought. When he dashed home to see her he looked so worn and harassed and she felt guilty that this had ever annoyed her. She came to the conclusion that her depression arose from self-pity and that since she had no reason to feel sorry for herself, in fact quite the reverse, she must take herself in hand and conquer it. The only way she knew how was through work – she needed 'the mental exercise to keep me going and it *is* fun, you know, creating a story and incidents and characters . . . and [I] thump away in the world of imagination'.

She found as she lay resting, thinking about how hateful the war was, that her mind flew to the past, to another, quieter age when there were no bombs, and also to Cornwall, where she yearned to be, out on the sea in *Restless*, the sailing ketch which they now had, as well as *Ygdrasil*, with Tommy at the helm. Into her head came a vision of 'storms, and battles, and the sea, and the hulk of a pirate ship lying at anchor in Frenchman's Creek'. There was a pirate, who would try to tempt away a wife who no longer loved her husband. She wrote to Foy that this war was 'beyond me', and she wanted to escape into another world. But in that other world, she knew before she began that she would be struggling with emotions she felt in this troubled one. In her vision, the pirate bore an uncanny resemblance to Christopher Puxley.

In December, just before Christmas, Victor Gollancz came to lunch and was excited to be given an outline of what Daphne's new novel would be about when she had time and strength to write it. She had her suspicions about how he came 'to motor fifty miles out of his way' to drop in on her, and joked to Garth that she would not be surprised 'if he were a really bad spy and ought to be watched'. He was, she observed, 'a long way from being changed or saved' according to MRA principles, to which she herself still adhered. 'I keep finding I am never grateful enough to God,' she told Garth and, though she had taken his advice and now had a notebook in which to write down her thoughts, she found they were all of a practical nature – 'nothing revealing or stupendous'. She concluded 'that, as probably one of my worst faults is vagueness about practical things, and a sort of general inefficiency about anything that does not interest me (forgiven hitherto by my family and excused by myself as "artistic temperament"), this is where I must first check myself'. Her attempts to do so were valiant and also comic – exactly the sort of thing the du Mauriers would traditionally mock. Since Margaret's migraines had returned and Prim, the nursemaid, could not do everything, Daphne had to look after her children in a way she had never done before. She was quite unable to resist the invitation to return to the Puxleys' home at Langley End when her tenancy at Cloud's Hill ended in January 1941.

The moment the Browning entourage settled in again at Langley End, where there were also two other evacuee children, both girls developed measles and Margaret succumbed to a particularly virulent form of influenza; in spite of Prim's help and the support of Paddy Puxley, Daphne wrote to Grace Browning that 'My life is slightly mad . . . after washing out bedpans and coping with the measled ones I rush . . . and minister to Christian . . . and when I have turned him upside down, pinned his nappy on wrong . . . I hurl him into his cot and find Flavia wanting to put on a party frock . . . I chuck her a doll to play with and then rush to the privacy of a room alone and hammer upon my typewriter at *Frenchman's Creek*, my new book, and I am lucky if I get a page written.' (The life of many a woman writer, but not, until then, one within Daphne's experience.) She wrote with what sounds like a most uncharacteristic smugness to Garth: 'I am very grateful for being given the power to deal with all these little domestic worries and I am sure it has been a discipline. I've always shirked responsibility before. Now I find I can bear it. I seem to know the children more through looking after them . . . God is testing one out on those little points.' As well as knowing the children better she was also involving them in her writing for the first time. Tessa and Flavia were thrilled to be told about the story she was engaged on and loved being told each evening where their mother had got to and what was going to happen next.

Halfway through *Frenchman's Creek* progress was halted because Margaret, when she recovered from flu, was, according to Daphne, 'only functioning four days out of seven'. Margaret herself wrote to Garth that she didn't know what she would do 'without Mrs Browning . . . she is a saint living, creating a spirit of peace everywhere she goes and I just live for ten o'clock at night when everything is finished and she sits by my bed and we have our quiet time together, and all the day's worries are smoothed away and there is a most wonderful atmosphere'. Garth responded by sending *Daily Readings* to help in these quiet times and Daphne, writing to thank him, remarked, 'it is awfully hard to go on slowly and be cheerful . . . but I have been so stubborn and selfish'. Now she could no longer enjoy the luxury of being selfish. While Margaret suffered her migraines, Daphne was up twice in the night with Christian and then for good at six in the morning. She was so tired she felt like a zombie and wrote to Tod, 'Having tied napkins on my son day after day for two months there is nothing I would like to do so much as lie on my back in the sun and eat cherries' – the sentiments of every woman in wartime England, as Daphne perfectly well appreciated. It made her feel a certain solidarity with mothers everywhere to share something of the average load and quietened her discontent that she could not get on with her novel. She was reading Angela's third novel, *The Little Less*, at the time, a story with a lesbian theme, which she thought not suitable for Nanny. She had 'a bit of fun' out of the book but came to the conclusion that Angela should write short stories, not novels, because *The Little Less* 'is so much more a series of episodes than a continuous novel'.[2]

There was some satisfaction in leading such a typically hard life, even within the privileged setting of a Lutyens house with servants, and satisfaction, too, in responding to a request that she should further the MRA cause by making a broadcast to America with

Peter Howard.[3] The effort this cost her was considerable. She came to London on 10 March, running the risk of air-raids, and broadcast from an underground shelter.

She then went back to Hertfordshire and collapsed – she had the same influenza, it was thought, which had debilitated her children's nanny. But after a week of high temperatures, the doctor diagnosed a severe chill on the lungs which developed into pneumonia. She was saved – 'it was nearly all over with your old Daph', she wrote to Tod – by the M & B drug.[4] But she was very ill for another month and at the end of it described herself to Garth as 'so fagged . . . rather like someone who has been up all night at a bottle party'.

She also read into her illness an almost spiritual significance. 'I don't know if I told you, but just before getting ill, when Flave and Nanny, and even little Christian, were smitten again with colds, I said to God, "Now, please, let me take it all – all the pain, all the suffering, all the unhappiness, and let the children have no more" – and the day after I woke with a temperature (and the children have been OK since!).' She was feeling 'stunned' and 'unable to feel things, which I think may be part of God's plan, as though, having perhaps been rather pleased with myself for having coped all through the winter with the children and Nanny and all that, God now lets me see what it is like to be unable to cope, to be plunged, as it were, not exactly into depression again, but into a great void'. She lay in bed, weak and lethargic, 'looking at the world through the wrong end of a telescope, the world itself and the people on it being very small and ant-like, and all their activities a little futile'. She vowed that if she were told that Hitler had reached the next county, she would merely yawn. Her mind centred on an island, the island of her dreams ever since J. M. Barrie had inspired her with the notion, an island just surfacing from the sea. She drew a picture of it for Garth, with the sun behind the island and a boat sailing towards it and signed it 'My dream island which will never come at all'.

By the time she was recovered sufficiently to come downstairs it was April and spring had arrived. She was still very weak and frighteningly thin and pale. At the end of each day she was so exhausted that Christopher Puxley had to carry her up to her bedroom, cradling her easily in his arms. But sometimes she stayed in the drawing-room, covered with a rug, and after Margaret had taken the children to bed and Paddy was seeing to the two evacuee children, Christopher would play the piano for her, especially her favourite piece, Chopin's 24th Symphony. It was suddenly warm and the scent of lilac drifted through the open window . . . Margaret, driven to exasperation by the very music Daphne loved, could not always resist coming down from the room used as a nursery, which was directly over the piano, and complaining that the children could not sleep. She sensed, as every adult in the house did, an atmosphere between Mr Puxley and Mrs Browning, whether Mrs Puxley was there or not. On the surface, everything was innocent, a host and friend amusing a guest who had been ill, but under it there was a highly charged intensity.

This atmosphere went into *Frenchman's Creek*, which Daphne resumed writing in May. She wrote quickly, keeping to her vow to make this a purely escapist novel – 'a romance with a big R!' she wrote to Victor. By Whitsun she told him she had done 60,000 words and that it was 'lightish, you know'. But under cover of this 'lightish' tale, with its lyrical descriptions of the Helford river, was something tougher. The heroine was Dona St Columb, a woman of thirty who felt 'a sudden boiling up of resentment against the futility of her life'. Like so many du Maurier heroines, she wishes she had been a man and has even once dressed up as one to take part in an escapade. The pirate, when eventually she meets him, is no ruffian. Jean-Benoit Aubéry is sophisticated, handsome, educated and even artistic.[5] She realizes she is in love, that 'a glow hitherto unknown to her' has spread through her body. There is a great deal of rollicking schoolgirl fantasy in Dona's expedition with the pirates, but the aftermath is deadly serious. She wakens on board the pirate ship naked and asks Aubéry what she can do until her clothes are dry. 'In France,' he replies, '. . . there is only one thing we could do': he unscrews her ruby earring, and we are given to understand that they make love. Dona is happy at last – she has never felt such joy. Yet at the same time, she knows her marriage is not really threatened – 'women are more primitive . . . for a time they wander . . . and play at love . . . but instinct is too strong . . . they must make their nest'. There is never any doubt that Dona will let her pirate go and return to her husband – 'the Lady St Columb will become a gracious matron'.

Daphne finished the novel in early July and wrote to Grace that Victor Gollancz was delighted with it. All that was worrying him was where he would get the paper to print it on. The paper shortage was acute, but he wanted to bring it out the following month 'in case of a blitz in late summer'. With the phenomenal success of *Rebecca* as an indication, he was going to have a first print-run of 50,000 copies this time, but to do so would take some ingenuity, and while he wrestled with the wartime paper problems Daphne struggled with the task of defending her escapist novel to her MRA friends.

Garth was trying to persuade her to do some more stories but, though she promised to think about it, she was beginning to believe he had mistaken ideas about her. It was, she wrote, 'all right for Lord Elton and Herbert Agar to feed the hungry sheep' but for her own part she felt 'you have still . . . got to keep the novelists whose job it is to tell a story and entertain (I don't mean entertain in a vulgar fashion, but to tell a story – you know what I mean). Novelists who try to do moral uplift always go astray, it's not their forte . . . I am all for being ruthless with trashy authors . . . but I still think people like myself may be capable of creating good and interesting stories about the human character without becoming sort of Winston Churchills.' This was very near to admitting she had had enough of writing to suit MRA purposes. She had, after all, made sure Dona did not go off with her pirate, but instead went back to her husband, which she felt should satisfy Garth. But she did not close the door entirely to the idea of contributing in the future to the MRA effort, and she was still in favour of the movement, though 'the brave new world seems distant, Armageddon rather heaven'.

Meanwhile, Tommy was back at Langley End and once more disrupting the happy atmosphere of piano-playing and discussions about fantasy islands. He was more tired than ever and looked strained. Daphne wrote to his sister Grace that 'when this war is over all the men will look 200'. (Except, of course, Christopher Puxley, whom excessive exercise at the piano had not aged.) He told her she was leading 'the cushiest war life of anyone in the country' and she was bound to agree. Now that Nanny was better, except for the occasional migraine, and the children under her care, Daphne lay in the sun, her new novel about to be published, and felt remarkably well. But she was tense when Tommy was there and was glad to go with him on a boat trip up the Ouse, so that she could be with him away from Langley End. It rained all week but they both enjoyed it, and by the time Tommy had to return she was more confused than Dona St Columb had ever been. She knew she loved Tommy and her sense of duty was powerful – her marriage, and the preserving of it, meant everything to her – but she also knew she was infatuated with Christopher and that she was happier with him.

By late autumn this infatuation was causing at least two people at Langley End great concern. Margaret was well aware of what was happening, but was in no position to articulate her alarm. She adored Paddy Puxley – who alone seemed oblivious – was fiercely loyal to Major Browning,[6] and loathed Christopher Puxley. There was a feeling of apprehension in the house, but Daphne either failed to pick it up or ignored it. What, after all, was she doing that was wrong? She was not technically unfaithful. So far, her obsession with Christopher had led only to being embraced and kissed and she felt their closeness was more emotional, even psychic, than physical. She was bewitched, entranced but not passionately consummating their relationship, though she was aware that she felt detached from her husband, which she thought might be nature's way of helping wives survive this war. Even when Tommy was with her she felt remote from his concerns. The trouble was, she didn't understand half the things he talked about, and some of the tasks allotted to him were so secret he couldn't talk about them anyway. But she knew, all the same, how very important Tommy was becoming and what a Herculean task he had just been given in October 1941. The War Office had asked him to undertake the formation of airborne troops who could land by parachute, and at the same time to train infantry troops to land in gliders. Somehow, these two independent formations were to be moulded into what would be known as the 1st Airborne Division, and it was to be ready for action within a year. As commander of these new paratroops Tommy was now raised to the rank of Major-General and a great deal rested on the success of the whole daring venture. It was a test not just of his powers of leadership but of his ability to undertake a prodigious amount of organization, involving training 10,000 men, equipping 800 gliders, and overcoming the formidable problems of getting all of them in the right place at the right time in all kinds of weather conditions. The necessary liaising with the Royal Air Force called for considerable tact, and the studying of maps and photographs involved in all the reconnaissance work for the greatest concentration. It was very little wonder that, carrying a burden like this, he arrived at Langley End for his brief leaves utterly exhausted. He was working a minimum of fourteen hours a day, every day. He explained to his wife that the role of the Airborne Division was potentially crucial, which she accepted. But the very importance of Tommy's work left her feeling peripheral to his life. She knew this was foolish, knew she was vitally important to him, but it frightened her how rapidly a gulf seemed to be opening between them.

From this appointment onwards, Tommy's leaves grew shorter and fewer, and sometimes he did not even take them, though he desperately wanted to, because of all the work to be done. By the spring of 1942, Daphne was more involved than ever with Christopher and still Paddy noticed nothing. But others did and now one of them decided to act. Grace Browning, who visited Langley End from time to time to see her sister-in-law and the children, received a letter from Margaret asking if she could meet her in Hitchin; she had something she wanted to discuss. Margaret cycled to Hitchin to have tea in a café with Miss Browning and confided that she was worried and upset because she suspected something was going on between Mr Puxley and Mrs Browning. Miss Browning, greatly troubled, said that if it *was* true she hoped her brother never found out, because if he did he would never forgive his wife, whom he adored. But before Tommy had a chance to discover what his wife's feelings were for Christopher Puxley, Paddy Puxley at last did so. One day she found her husband and Daphne in each other's arms and was stunned. She merely told Daphne she had thought she was her friend and left the room where she had found them. Her evident distress and the bitterness of her only remark were worse than any violent anger or hatred. There were no scenes, but clearly Daphne could not go on living at Langley End. Everyone was intent on behaving in a civilized manner, and in keeping their various emotions concealed from children and servants, but plans already formed were hastily put forward. Instead of going to Fowey in June, for the summer, Daphne went in April, for good.

In a letter to Garth Lean, Daphne said that after 'many probings and thinkings' she was moving to Fowey 'to sort myself out'. The reasons she gave him, and everyone else, for leaving Langley End were that she felt she and the children were 'becoming a burden' and that she was particularly concerned about 'poor Paddy . . . who is working day in, day out at war work'. If she were out of the way 'things would be easier'. She wished more than ever that she could be 'in a little hut on a little island', but since she could not, Fowey was best. She could not go to Ferryside, which had been requisitioned as a naval headquarters, and did not in any case think it feasible to land on her mother and sisters, so she rented number 8 Readymoney Cove, which had originally been the old stable and coach-house for Pont Neptune House, built for the Rashleighs of Menabilly. It is a large cottage with a pretty garden right on the little beach, but compared to the Lutyens house Daphne had just left it was small – there were a lot of people to fit into a fifth of the space they had previously occupied. But the advantages of being in Fowey once more far outweighed the disadvantages, though settling in proved a little difficult and was not helped by the continual rain. The girls, especially Flavia, pined for Paddy, but their grandmother and aunts were nearby and soon the attractions of living by the seaside, even in wartime, softened their sense of loss. Tessa, aged almost nine, started school at St David's, along the esplanade, which she loved, and a Mrs Hancock, soon known as 'Hanks' (sister of the wife of George Hunkin, the boatman, who had been Tommy's best man), came each day at 2.30 to cook: soon a routine was established and Daphne saw that she could, if she wished, begin another book.

The book she had in mind was a novel about Christopher Puxley's family. This was disappointing news for Garth Lean, who had never given up hoping either for some more stories or a play Daphne had hinted was taking shape about a group of people in a waiting-room all beset by moral dilemmas. But she wrote to him that everything had changed since *Come Wind, Come Weather* – 'I have been through many varied processes of thought.' She looked at some more true stories Garth sent her, but her verdict was 'in all honesty . . . I do not feel that I am qualified to do them'. Most revealing was the reason she gave – 'not being prepared to stick to standards myself, how can I write saying it is the answer?' Instead, she wanted to write what she called 'my saga novel'.

'Start saving paper,' she wrote to Victor Gollancz, adding that her new story was going 'to be endless, full of birth and death, and love and disaster'. The basis for it was the Puxley family history, about which Christopher had told her. He had also supplied her with a dossier of family letters of which she made even more use than she had of the Jane Slade letters in her first novel and the du Maurier ones in the two books about her own family. John Puxley, Christopher's grandfather, became Copper John in her new novel, which she called *Hungry Hill*, and she used some of his letters verbatim at various dramatic points. In a blue exercise book of George du Maurier's, half-filled with his writing, she made lists of 'translations' – real place names from the Puxley history to be converted into invented ones. By August, she was 'working away like one possessed', and felt that this would turn out to be her longest book, 'probably longer than *Gone With the Wind*'. *Hungry Hill* was the first of her novels to be truly historical, depending as the plot did on a real history before her imagination came into play.

Daphne herself saw it as a reaction to *Frenchman's Creek*, about which she was dismissive, endlessly referring to it as 'frivolous'. *Hungry Hill* was to be solid, wide in scope and rooted in reality. It begins with Copper John, the mine owner, and his relationships with his children. The feud between Copper John and a dispossessed Irish family is dramatic, and the first quarter of the story has tremendous momentum. But in the next quarter, as Daphne was obliged to invent a little more, the momentum falters and by Book Three it becomes melodramatic. Soon it disintegrates into a series of births, deaths and improbable unions, wandering far from the original Puxley history. Book Five is sentimental until the epilogue, in which Daphne writes a moving and convincing account of the family home in flames and the return of a descendant of Copper John in modern times.

The work Daphne put into this long novel was prodigious. She finished it in November and then started going through it, making cuts – 'I adore cutting' – before sending it to Victor in December. 'Here you are,' she wrote, 'and the whole damn story is true, by the way, with a few embellishments.' Alarmed, Victor promptly sent it to be read for libel, but when told this, Daphne changed her mind about the truth and said there was nothing to worry about, because 'the story is a blend of fact and fiction, and all the people concerned are dead'.[7] The paper shortage was still acute but, though he urged her to tell no one, Victor said he was going to print 100,000 copies using most of his paper ration and therefore severely restricting the number of other books he could print. This was a tremendous act of faith and acknowledged by her as such – Victor's enthusiasm and wholehearted backing, especially in difficult times, meant a great deal to her. But though she was open with him about the source of her material, she was secretive about it to others, because she did not wish to draw attention to her connection with Christopher Puxley. There she was, writing furiously about his family history, while he was still in love with her and coming down to Fowey to see her. He did not, of course, stay at Readymoney Cove, but at the nearby Fowey Hotel, and she would slip out, taking a picnic with her, to meet him on the cliff top.

They would go to the Watch House, though it meant entering a wartime restricted area. For £5 a year she had rented this tiny stone and slate building perched sixty feet above Watch House Cove between Polruan and Polperro. It had once been a coastguard's hut, and there were steps dug into the cliff leading down from it to the cove. There she and Christopher could be absolutely safe from any possibly prying eyes – the nearest road was a mile away and the only other building visible was the tower of a distant church. Nothing could have been more romantic or made the war seem further away. She and Christopher would lie there, in the little twelve-by-twelve foot room, the door open to the sky, hearing the screeching of the seagulls as they skimmed the waves which crashed endlessly against the foot of the cliff.

Daphne loved the thrill of these secret assignations and stifled feelings of guilt by assuring herself that Christopher was only a friend. How much of a friend and how much of a lover was something about which she liked to confuse her close friends, and she went on doing so all her life. On the one hand, she would say she was in love with Christopher, that his 'spinning' (code for preliminaries to love-making) was 'divine', and, on the other, drop heavy hints that the affair had never been consummated because Christopher was impotent. In her own mind, so long as there was no actual intercourse, there was no betrayal of Tommy. The love-affair she spoke of was not an 'affair' in the sense others used the word, and was therefore, in her opinion, innocent.

Whatever the truth, it was certainly the case that Daphne, like Dona in *Frenchman's Creek*, was allowing herself only to 'wander for a bit'. She always intended to remain anchored to her husband and never encouraged Christopher Puxley to imagine otherwise. But Christopher himself did not receive this cruel message – he went on hoping, went on visiting her and 'spinning' with her, knowing he had broken his wife's heart. The knowledge that she was responsible for this suffering made Daphne feel guilty and miserable and she wrote to Garth Lean that she was 'trying to help someone very dear to me, who is going through the depths of despair. We have prayed together, and I am hoping that it may be a beginning of the first tiny step in a new life – for me too, perhaps.' She told him that she had had a shock, but that 'I always said that a shock is the only way of bringing Daphne to her knees, didn't I?' She went on to describe a book she had been reading which was relevant to 'my despairing one'.

The book was C. S. Lewis's *The Problem of Pain*, published in 1940, as part of a 'Christian Challenge' series. It was what he had to say about human love in the course of his argument on the problem of pain which fascinated Daphne. 'Love is more sensitive than hatred to every blemish in the beloved,' he wrote, '[and] Human Love, as Plato teaches us, is the child of Poverty – of a want, or lack; it is caused by a real or supposed goodness in the beloved which the lover needs and desires.' This made Daphne think that perhaps there was something Tommy could not give her of which she felt the lack, a lack Christopher could supply. If so, perhaps she need not feel guilty and ashamed? But C. S. Lewis also had this to say: 'The emotion of shame has been valued not as an emotion but because of the insight to which it leads.' Shame led her to feel pain for Tommy and for Paddy and even for Christopher, and the final part of this book warned that 'pain provides an opportunity for heroism'. The heroic role for her was to stop seeing Christopher.

It was not one she assumed. She felt too exhausted to be heroic. *Hungry Hill* – 'not a trifling affair after all' – left her drained and she suffered from a kind of completion depression very similar to her post-natal depressions. The fact that Margaret was also depressed and once again incapacitated by migraines made things even worse. Margaret's health was now a permanent worry and had been for a year. Before they left Langley End, Daphne had insisted she should go into hospital for a week to have 'every test under the sun'. The doctors had reported that there was nothing organically wrong, but that Margaret was 'run down and nervey' and needed rest. Anxious to be sympathetic and caring, Daphne had despatched her to Fowey to enjoy a month's recuperation before the rest of the party joined her. This proved beneficial at first, but by late 1942 'Nanny's heads' were appalling and when she succumbed there was chaos. Daphne wrote to Garth that Margaret, even when she didn't have 'a head', was 'weepy and feeling rotten and down in the dumps'. She had tried 'reading from the Bible to her, after finishing Christian at night, and talking quietly and trying to get her to realise that by resigning herself the power *will* come from God. She is so inclined to rely just on *me* talking to her and getting rather sloppy and sentimental about it, which I feel is *absolutely* the wrong end of the stick.' She felt exasperated but swore, 'I *do* want to help her, but I do *not* want to have to sit and hold her hand.'

Her mood crept into what she described to Tod as 'a very cynical short story, called "Happy Christmas" ',[8] about a refugee couple being treated as Mary and Joseph were. Her own Christmas was not happy in spite of the valiant efforts of her mother and Angela to make Ferryside (reclaimed from the Navy) festive. Tommy was not home for it. Instead, he had 'flown to North Africa . . . I hate him going out into it all'. The New Year of 1943 found her depressed and weary of counting her blessings. She knew she was lucky to be so comfortably housed, lucky never to be short of food, lucky not to have been bombed, lucky to have her husband still alive, but she did not feel any happier for all this. The only thing that cheered her up was her son. He was her absolute delight, an enchanting cherub of a child whom, at two, she judged not only intelligent but talented and perfect in every way. She had his destiny all planned out: he was to be a man-about-town and a charmer – 'heaven help any woman who crosses his path in twenty years' time'.

The news, in January, that Tod was in hospital confirmed Daphne's feelings of imminent disaster. She was having an operation, and Daphne begged to be allowed to pay for her to convalesce at a comfortable hotel. She was worried about Tod's fate once she had recovered: her millinery venture had failed and she was surely too old to be a governess. Tod felt the only alternative was to become a companion, and so Daphne, at her bidding, wrote her a glowing reference, describing her as a 'long-standing friend'. She wondered, though, if after the war anyone would be able to employ companions or any other kind of servant – 'we shall all have to live like Australians'. Tod recovered well but still Daphne's sense of foreboding continued.

Then, in the middle of February, she heard that Tommy had been in a glider crash: it had come at last, the phone call she had always dreaded, the knock on the door she had imagined, heralding the end of her run of luck.

Chapter Eleven

Arriving at Netheravon, in Wiltshire, where Tommy had crashed, Daphne was immensely relieved to find that his injuries were restricted to a torn shoulder and a clot on the knee, but she was quickly aware that the psychological damage was more serious. Tommy was furious with himself for landing so badly, and underneath the fury was a nagging worry that, at forty-six, he was too old to lead an Airborne Division. It was nearing the time when this new division would go into action and, after all the exhausting months of preparation and gruelling training, he wanted to be with them, but he felt deathly tired. Daphne's support at this point was vitally important and she did not fail him. Though she had little of the nurse in her, she was good at talking him out of his depression and restoring his confidence in himself. She stayed three weeks with him at Netheravon, then took him back to Fowey to make a full recovery.

It was a strange interlude for both of them. Spending so much time with her husband again, Daphne felt closer to him than she had done since the war began. On leaves, there had barely been time to establish any kind of rapport before he was off again, and at least half the hours spent with him were devoted to much-needed sleep. On the occasions when she had gone to stay with him she told Tod it had been hardly worth it – 'because I didn't see very much of him. He left . . . at 8.30 in the morning and returned at 8 in the evening.' But now, at Readymoney Cove, things were different for a while. They read together and talked and caught again some of the intimacy of their previous companionship. Sometimes they went and picnicked on their boat, *Restless*, laid up for the duration of the war. Their sense of humour had always been remarkably similar and now Daphne sat beside him, she reading *The Times*, Tommy reading his yachting papers, both exchanging titbits of information and mocking the more absurd items they came across. When the end of March came and Tommy had to return to his division, she could hardly bear to contemplate what lay ahead of him. He was going to North Africa and real danger. The air trip he would make was in itself enough to frighten her, never mind what he would face when he arrived.

Once Tommy had gone, she felt restless and bitter. Like most wives left at home she blamed the war for her marital difficulties. If there had been no war she would never have met Christopher Puxley, never have grown apart from her husband. Even those weeks of Tommy's convalescence had not been enough to restore in full the relationship they had once had. Fowey, that year, did little to soothe her. An order was issued that no boats were to be allowed on the river – 'so I shan't even be able to steal away in my small dinghy for an afternoon's peace', she complained to Tod. Pridmouth beach, below Menabilly, was also to be closed to the public, so there would be no walks along the cliffs with the children to picnic there. 'How I loathe all these restrictions,' she told Tod, adding that she thought them quite unnecessary. The censorship of letters was another new thing which enraged her – 'If there is going to be snooping at people's private correspondence in this country then it's simply a start of the Gestapo and we are becoming Nazified.' The war was ruining everything, including the publication of *Hungry Hill*, from which she hoped so much. She was dissatisfied with the appearance of the book – it had a 'queer, unfinished look' about it and the paper was 'awful', not to mention the print, which was tiny. But she knew that for Victor to have kept his promise to print 100,000 copies was such an achievement that it would be churlish to complain.

What she did feel disposed to complain about was taxation. She had made a great deal of money, not just out of *Rebecca* (the huge royalties plus the money from the Hitchcock film) but out of *Frenchman's Creek* which was also being filmed. She should have been rich and yet she was not. 'Would you like to know the facts about present-day taxation?' she asked Tod. 'With selling film rights, etc., I earned last year [1942] £25,000. I thought my fortune was made. I have just heard £22,500 is to be taken in tax![1] So I net altogether £2,500. So that actually my sale of *Frenchman's Creek* has given the government enough to buy a Lancaster bomber! I think I shall go about with a placard saying "I am a benefactress and am winning the war more than any WAAF".' Pride and indignation were about evenly mixed, but they were tinged with fear – she was terrified of getting in a financial mess, as Gerald had done. Her attitude to money revealed, she liked to say, her French peasant mind, but there was little of the peasant about it. She had a very comfortable lifestyle, which she believed to be 'simple', and she wanted to maintain it. Although, on the one hand, she had no interest in accumulating large sums of money, or in buying luxuries, on the other she wanted to hold on to what she had, so that she never need worry about the disappearance of her ability to earn more. Money, as she had recognized before she ever earned any, brought with it independence and power. She wanted above all to feel secure and not to have to depend on her husband as most wives of her age and class were obliged to do. So she had both a casual and yet an intensely attentive interest in what she earned. She had no accountant at that time – her financial affairs were looked after by her solicitor in Fowey and by her agent, Curtis Brown, and she tried to keep track herself of everything she earned and spent.

But she had other worries as well as financial ones. In the spring of 1943, she wrote to Tod, saying her household was driving her mad. Margaret was utterly loyal and immensely hard-working, but quite apart from the dreaded migraines, and now her teeth which needed extracting, she was used to 'ruling the roost' and this was causing trouble. She had had 'a fight with the new cook', who promptly threatened to leave. All three children had colds again and Tessa had poisoned herself, sucking rhododendron leaves – 'What a life!' The 'cushy' time Tommy had rightly accused her of enjoying in the early days at Langley End had gone for good. She could hardly get five minutes on her own, and she found this lack of privacy maddening. To get out of the Ready-money cottage she went visiting more than she felt inclined to, pushing Kits in his pram, a daughter on either side, to see her mother and sisters at Ferryside, or the Quiller-Couches at The Haven, or the Foxes, especially Mary Fox, who lived next door at Pont Neptune Cottage. But apart from her family and very old friends, Daphne made no new contacts. She was a young mother with three sociable children and yet she spurned another young mother who lived in Readymoney Cove. Mrs Beddingfield had two children, Hugh, who played with Tessa, and Elizabeth, who played with Flavia, but Daphne was not interested in making friends. She was never rude or openly unfriendly, but simply kept herself to herself and never had any friends of her own age who had young children as she did. For female company, she depended on her sisters, especially Angela who was a very popular aunt. She saw them regularly, though both of them were working on the land. Jeanne had put aside her Art and had taken on a market garden two miles from Fowey with which Angela helped. The enforced camaraderie enjoyed by women in her situation was not something Daphne wanted (although she enjoyed being part of the Readymoney Cove fire-fighting squad). The idea of swopping tales about minor childhood illnesses, comparing recipes, relating stories of naughtiness – all this was anathema.

Stuck in Readymoney Cove, battling with the domestic arrangements which caused her so much irritation, she longed for distraction to take her mind off the war. *Hungry Hill*, published on 5 May, with as much fanfare as Victor could manage in wartime, ought to have provided it. Daphne, this time, made no pretence of not caring what the critics said – she cared very much. *Hungry Hill*, she hoped, would set her in a different category as a novelist and silence forever dismissive references to *Rebecca* or *Frenchman's Creek*. It therefore came as a shock when *Hungry Hill* was pronounced too long, too shapeless, and too ridiculous; no one, not even those who were kinder, hailed the novel as a great step forward. 'I was quite distressed', she confided in Garth Lean, 'when the critic . . . in *The Observer* implied that my sole intention in writing was to get the book dramatised and screened. If only he could have seen the toil and the midnight oil to give the best I had.' For the first time she allowed herself to believe there was prejudice against her because she was a bestselling author, whereas up to then she had accepted all criticism philosophically and even modestly.

Her disappointment was hard to get over, particularly since

Tommy seemed to be permanently in some danger zone or other. His Staff Air Commodore was killed just before he left for Algiers and she found it difficult to control her anxiety that Tommy would share his fate. 'This sounds like self-pity again,' she wrote to Garth, 'but the war is such a wretched thing.' According to Tommy, it was about to get more wretched still. He was now Airborne Adviser to General Alexander, the Supreme Allied Commander (in Tunisia, Sicily and Italy). This involved co-operating with the American glider pilots and overseeing the individual divisional and brigade airborne formations operating in different places. Daphne became so apprehensive that her fear affected the way she treated her children. Not a mother who normally fussed, she now could not bear them to swing on the iron bars enclosing the beach, and suddenly became a 'Mrs Brown' (code for women who wouldn't let their children do anything). She felt they were at risk in a way she never had done before and, even though Fowey was not a particularly dangerous place to be, she wished she could take them away and hide with them until all the horror was over (though she still, even had it been possible, vowed she would never send them to America and was furious that the Minister for Information had sent his son).

In fact, she was going to have to move in any case because her lease on Readymoney was coming to an end in September. The need to find another house, preferably one which was bigger and more secluded, would become urgent. It was at this point that she heard that Dr Rashleigh might be willing to let her rent Menabilly. Instantly, Daphne seized hold of this possibility and became obsessed with making it a reality at whatever cost.

It was nearly seventeen years since she had first seen Menabilly, but she had been back many times and had been granted permission by Dr Rashleigh to walk in the woods whenever she wished. The house was still as she had glimpsed it in 1926, seeming to her asleep and forlorn, waiting for someone to love it. Suddenly, Dr Rashleigh, who was seventy-one, decided to sell the contents of the house and let it for a peppercorn rent until such time as he himself died and his cousin inherited the estate. But although the rent was minimal, the terms of the suggested lease were tougher than they at first appeared. It would be for twenty years, but during that time the house had to be maintained at the lease-holder's cost. Since it was in poor condition to start with, and needed a new roof immediately, the expense would be considerable, though, of course, for no eventual gain – the heir to Mena-billy expected to live there and he had six surviving children. Never, at any time, could Daphne possibly have had grounds for deluding herself that there was the remotest chance of her eventually buying Menabilly, or of leasing it in perpetuity: the heir, William Stuart Rashleigh, and his large family were very obviously waiting in the wings. Furthermore, Daphne also understood, as she explained to several correspondents, that Menabilly, because it was entailed, never could be sold.[2]

None of this made any difference. Twenty years was a lifetime – by the end of it she would be nearly sixty, Tommy would be nearly seventy, the children would be grown up. Twenty years, in wartime, was quite unreal – nobody could survive if they tried to look ahead twenty years. She wanted the house so badly that, as she wrote to Tod, 'I'd rather be rooked than not have it.' She said she knew she was making her eagerness too apparent, but she could not help it and would agree to any conditions. Everyone thought her 'quite mad', especially Tommy, but it was her money that would restore Menabilly, so the decision was hers. The insanity of taking on such a house in wartime intoxicated her – what a risk, with building materials virtually impossible to get, what a challenge with all the skilled workmen away fighting, what a nightmare with a huge house to run and only one devoted nanny as a permanent help. It was folly and she gloried in it, barely able to conceal her impatience until the lease was signed.

This took time. Dr Rashleigh could not be hurried. He agreed to the lease in June but still had not signed it by August. At his age, in poor health, he could die at any time and the heir take over. Hardly able to bear the suspense, Daphne allowed Christopher Puxley to visit again. The weather, during the week he came down to Fowey, was glorious and she felt happier than she had done for over a year. Writing to Tod, she described Christopher as 'the nicest man I know', adding hastily '(after Tommy!)'. She said everything now seemed 'to be going smoothly' and part of the smoothness was a feeling that she had her infatuation with Christopher under control. She seemed to have come to an understanding with herself: there was a war on, her husband was fighting abroad, and she was tired of examining her conscience. Christopher was kind and good company, and she was fond of him, so why torture herself with guilt? Garth Lean chose that summer to remind her of what he saw as her duty – 'I see your writing . . . as one of the deciding factors in what happens . . . are you writers going to rise to the mission God has laid on them?' He told her straight, '*Hungry Hill* won't feed the hungry sheep who look up and are not fed,' and reminded her, ' . . . your destiny calls you . . . beware of running away from the destiny God has for you.'

The only destiny Daphne felt calling her was Menabilly. The lease had finally been signed in mid-August 1943, and the very week Garth sounded his clarion call the workmen had moved in. The Office of Works had granted a permit for £250 to be spent on essential repairs and once these were done she intended to move in. Tommy came home on a brief leave and she almost wished he hadn't. He looked 'completely shattered' and she reflected to Tod, 'The war just wears these men out – I only wish he was a conscientious objector.' He warned her he might be posted to India soon, and if so, would be unable to snatch leaves with her. Instead of depressing her, this warning came as something of a relief – these leaves were so unsatisfactory, a torture in some ways. She would never have chosen a long separation, but if it had to come she thought she could stand it better than lots of leave-takings. And she would be able to devote herself to Menabilly.

It was a hectic autumn, supervising the work on the house and trying to organize its renovation, and she was glad to have finished a play she had written with great speed in the summer. This was *The Years Between*, which, she frankly admitted, was autobiographical in inspiration.[3] It concerns a woman whose husband, an MP, is believed killed in the war. She has to rebuild her life for herself and her young son, which she does so successfully that she is elected as MP in his place. She also rebuilds her personal life, growing closer to a friend – quiet, gentle, in contrast to her dynamic husband – and is about to announce her engagement to him when the 'dead' husband returns. He had merely been on a secret mission and had been thought dead. She is then faced with the awful truth that in the intervening years she has changed and so has he – he expects to pick up where he left off, but quickly realizes that she has a new life in which he has no part. The husband is bitter, the wife torn, and the war is blamed for everything. In the end the wife stays loyal, just as Dona did in *Frenchman's Creek*. The curtain comes down, the final outcome still unclear, with the husband going off on another mission from which it is implied he really may not return; though the audience is left in no doubt that, if he does, his wife will put him first.

The provisional title was *The Return of the Soldier*, and Daphne certainly saw it as containing a strong message. She described it to Garth Lean as 'rather sad . . . the sort of thing that might happen in a lot of homes' without actually acknowledging to him that it was happening, or something like it, in her own. Plans for the play to go into production that autumn faltered, and while she was waiting she began writing a treatment of *Hungry Hill*, the film rights of which had just been bought.[4]

This work fitted in well with supervising the Menabilly restoration and with teaching her daughters, now aged ten and six. Their school had closed and she was obliged either to send them further afield or to turn governess herself. Once having decided to do this, she applied herself diligently but found it hard. How could she teach Tessa and Flavia when she could hardly spell and her grasp of grammar was by no means certain? But although conscious of her failings she did not let them inhibit her and managed to make her lessons lively and interesting, though restricting them to subjects about which she really did know something and for which she felt enthusiasm. It was easy to share her love of literature, to pass on her French and to go through all the Art History she had learned from Gerald. She had a talent for reading plays aloud to them, and making up her own versions of well-known legends, but, naturally, when it came to subjects like maths very little was taught. In the afternoons, there were long walks, or the routine visits. Whenever she could park the children with her mother and Angela, Daphne would slip off to Menabilly to see what progress had been made. By October the roof had been patched up, the plumbing was working (after a fashion), and she told Tod the house was 'beginning to look quite perky'. The sooner she could move in, she wrote to Garth, the better – Menabilly was 'the nearest thing I can find to a desert island at the moment – the ghosts and bats will keep visitors off'.

On New Year's Eve 1943 she was able to write her first letter from Menabilly to Tod, telling her that in spite of the chaos they had managed to move in for Christmas and, to complete her happiness, Tommy had been there. She described the transform-ation which had taken place[5] – all the ivy trimmed from the windows, which now had new frames, and all the eight rooms that were to be used (a whole wing was shut off) decorated and furnished. The nursery was on the ground floor, at the front, papered in green and white stripes with pink roses, and the walls had large pictures of scenes from *Peter Pan* on them. The library, which was dark panelled, had a new white carpet and heavy tapestry curtains. She was triumphant that she had accomplished so much, by devious means, and for once Tommy had been impressed. He loved Menabilly too, but soon had to leave it to go, as he had expected, to Ceylon. (This was only to be a brief visit to advise South East Asia Command on airborne matters.)

Once he had gone, Daphne was eager to settle into a new routine. The running of the house, with Margaret the only resident help, was going to be hard, but she was determined to adopt a relaxed attitude to housekeeping standards. 'It is my theory', she confided to Tod, 'that endless brushing and dusting is unnecessary and, personally, the only things I like bone-clean are the bath and the lavatory pans. I'd clean a room once a fortnight.' What puzzled her was how untidy her children seemed to be when she felt herself to be naturally tidy. Margaret tidied up after them, but since she was also doing the cooking, she was clearly very over-worked. Mr Burt, the elderly gardener, chopped logs as well as gardening, and his wife, whom the children adored because she was so jolly, came in to help with the cooking now, but not even Daphne could pretend this was sufficient to run a house the size of Menabilly. She hated engaging servants, so it was Margaret and Mr and Mrs Burt who between them organized three teenage girls to come as undermaids. Margaret Rowe, whose family also lived on the estate, was one of these.[6] When she started work at Menabilly she thought the nanny, Margaret Eglesfield, was Mrs Browning, because she seemed to be in charge, and that Mrs Browning herself was a guest.

That first winter at Menabilly, the winter of 1943–44, turned out to be bitterly cold. The open fires and the few electric and paraffin heaters in use were completely inadequate for the large, high-ceilinged rooms and the icy passages, but Daphne had no patience with any moaning – none of these inconveniences mattered when she was 'lucky enough to inhabit this lovely old house and its mellow, peaceful surroundings' she told Tod (who had not yet seen it). Already she felt inspired as she sat in 'my rat-ridden ruin' and kept thinking about a seventeenth-century Cavalier. The reference to rats was no exaggeration – at night, the children lay terrified as rats raced across the ceiling of the nursery. The gaps between all the ceilings and floors were infested with them, but Daphne accepted them as part of the house and tried to make her children think of them as soldiers engaged in fierce battles which she would describe with enthusiasm. All great fun while she was talking, but afterwards, lying with little bags of warmed salt strapped to their ears to ward off the earache brought on by the intense cold, the children's fear returned and they were scared to get up and go along the passage to the lavatory. They hated, too, the way beetles were invariably found in the vast, deep bath which, when filled, turned green – the water came from an old pond and was pumped half a mile to the house through an inefficient filter. Then there were the bats which swooped in and out of the rooms at dusk.[7] No mesh frames had been fitted on the windows, and the bats, like the rats, were regarded by Daphne as belonging to the house: she loved everything about it and longed to start writing a novel about the people who had lived in it.

But first she had to solve the problem of the children's education. From Menabilly, it would have been possible for the children to go to Tywardreath school, on the school bus used by the local children, but Daphne considered this school too 'honky' (common). Any other school would have involved driving and, mysteriously, Daphne no longer drove. She had let her driving lapse since the war began and, though it would have been the easiest thing in the world to take it up again, she made no effort to do so. The isolation of Menabilly was something she relished and wanted to preserve. On the other hand she did not want to go on teaching the children herself, so by February she had found a Miss Richardson to come three times a week. She admitted to Tod that the children did not like their new teacher, three-year-old Kits going so far as to hope Hitler would soon kill her. She was large, with short cropped dark hair, and wore an incongruous hat perched on one side of her head. Being a du Maurier, Daphne could not resist mocking and imitating her, though to Miss Richardson herself she was polite and charming, and she was genuinely grateful to have her, because her presence meant a working routine could be established.

Daphne ate breakfast in bed, had a bath, then wrote from ten in the morning until one o'clock. Kits was allowed in the same room so long as he made no noise – something never permitted to the girls. He played with his lead Red Indian figures, Laughing Thunder and Grey Wolf, content to be near his mother until he was taken off for his mid-morning rest at eleven. At one o'clock Daphne had lunch, on her own, believing children should not eat with adults until they were twelve (when Tessa was four she had stipulated eight as the right age, but when she was eight this was raised to twelve). All three children joined her for coffee afterwards, and then they would go out for a walk. This, for all of them, was a favourite part of the day. They loved to be with their mother, who had no difficulty at all entering into their games and jokes. Half the time she initiated both and could seem no older than they were themselves, relishing all kinds of behaviour which another adult might have labelled silly. Daphne walked quickly, with long strides, and the children ran to keep up. She loved to see them chasing in and out of the shrubs and trees, glorying in the space and freedom, and was filled with a conviction that this was paradise for children – it was exactly what she would have wished for herself as a child. The idea that Menabilly might not be every child's idea of heaven did not occur to her. She expected them to be perfectly happy playing only with each other, though in fact they loved to play with the other children who lived on the estate and those who came up from the village nearby to explore the woods. Their mother did not forbid this but nor did she either encourage or quite approve of it.

She was nevertheless observant enough to see that Miss Richardson would not do forever, especially for Tessa whom she had always judged clever. Reluctant to send her to boarding school, against which she had a great prejudice, she suddenly began to toy with the idea of asking Tod to come and be governess. It was true Tod was nearly sixty, but she was energetic and strong, quite recovered from the illness of a few years ago and working as a companion in Yorkshire. Daphne wrote to her that spring, saying 'it would be great' if she could come and solve the problem of the girls' education. It would also solve a great many other problems – with the utterly dependable Tod there she would be able to get far more writing done. Tod was a friend of more than twenty-five years, tried and tested and never found wanting in Daphne's service. She would not only be able to teach the children, she could supervise the running of the house and be in charge when Margaret had 'one of her heads'. Even more tempting was the prospect of Tod taking over in an emergency – if Margaret was ill there was chaos. Left to do it herself, Daphne couldn't cut a slice of bread without hacking the loaf to shreds and grew bad-tempered with those who wanted more than the bread and dripping with which she was quite satisfied. Unfortunately, Tod could not leave the situation she had just taken, so for the time being Miss Richardson had to be kept on.

Once settled in Menabilly, and writing again, Daphne had thought that she could shut the war out. It proved not so easy. Almost as soon as she moved in there was a tragic incident which impressed upon her that there was no pretending the war did not exist. During 1940–41, when the threat of invasion along the entire South Coast was thought real, mines had been hurriedly laid at the river mouth in the vicinity of Menabilly. In January 1944 it was decided to clear these mines, and during the operation one soldier was killed and another horribly injured. Daphne and every-one in the house heard the explosion and soon a party of soldiers came running up from the beach bearing the injured man on a makeshift stretcher. An ambulance was sent for and until it came Daphne stood, helpless, while the wounded man, bleeding heavily, was given a drink. It was her first sight of what war could do, and even though in her imagination she had visualized far worse, scenes that Tommy had described, scenes she had read about with sickening regularity, she was still shocked and shaken by the reality.

Even her beloved Menabilly was not safe. She felt a return of the overwhelming fear that had gripped her at the start of the war, and this grew when Tommy returned for a week's leave in May, after a bout of influenza, to tell her 'something big' was about to happen in which he would be heavily involved. He had been promoted again, to Lieutenant-General (and was made a CB that year), and was on the verge of being in charge of exactly the kind of dramatic operation for which the Airborne Division had been intended. General Eisenhower and Field Marshal Montgomery were going to attempt to seize the north bridges of the Rhine and enter the Ruhr. The Airborne Division would be asked to capture Eindhoven, Nijmegen and Arnhem, with Tommy going with them as the Allied Commander. Daphne knew none of the details but wrote mournfully to Tod, 'What carnage there is going to be . . . and what will have been achieved? Nothing.' She saw 'poor little Kits', only three, and his generation all doing the same thing as their fathers in twenty years' time, and it made her shudder.

Tommy, preparing for the big operation in September, was on regular sorties to France with his paratroopers. On the wireless commentaries were given on the progress of the gliders on D-Day, 6 June 1944, and she raged at their insensitivity – 'the gliders are going down now . . . there they go . . . into a mass of shell-fire' – as though it were some kind of sport or entertainment. She listened, tense with apprehension, wondering if Tommy was in one of them and whether he would be hit.

He did his best to reassure her though, since his view of the war was for the most part pessimistic, his words were not exactly comforting. Every day he wrote to her,[8] affectionate little notes, of necessity hurried, but keeping her posted. He addressed her teasingly as 'My Own Beloved Mumpty' and always signed off 'God bless 'ee, the bumps, and small Tiny' with a row of kisses for each. Always, he looked ahead to a time when 'this filthy business' would be over and the two of them could once more be out in *Restless* or in *Yggy* – or, better still, a new and bigger boat. That was how he sustained himself: sketches of, and notes about, new boats filled his letters. One paragraph would touch on 'a fearful party' he had just been in and the next expand on plans for a boat. He asked for her reaction – 'What is the answer – do we start building . . . ? . . . personally, I feel that if you can afford the very small amount of pence required we should do so.' The very small amount was £3,000, hence the need for agreement – he certainly did not have that amount himself. The fact that Daphne would be paying for a new boat caused him no embarrassment, and he was a little irritated when she took time to consider. But he was very aware of how much he owed his wife in every way and for their twelfth wedding anniversary, 19 July 1944, wrote her a touching tribute: ' . . . In two days' time we shall have been married twelve years, the last four of which have been a sore trial . . . but we are happy, in that you have your beloved house and family (including a small man) . . . less, however, another man. We have hopes that things will clear up at a not too distant date and that the wear and tear of war will be lightened . . . To say that I have never for one moment regretted marrying you is a mere platitude, because I can't imagine any other state of life except to be married . . . I miss our "routes" . . . and have almost forgotten all our small sayings and doings, but they'll all come back.'

His faith was not shared by his wife. She worried constantly that the resumption of 'routes' (routines), about which he wrote so blithely, might not be as straightforward as he anticipated. For a start, he had no idea that she now had her own 'routes', that she was creating around herself a life in which he had no part, and in which she did not really want him to have a part. She knew this to be cruel, but she could not help it – she *liked* being virtually on her own, with half-days in which, in spite of the children, she could be quite solitary. She liked eating on her own, sleeping on her own and going for long walks on her own. It was not so much that she saw no place for a husband, as that she saw a place which would have to be clearly marked out, and wondered whether he would accept the demarcation line. She had never wanted complete togetherness, even in the first passionate years of her marriage, and now she knew she could not tolerate it. Thinking about the future, as Tommy did all the time, consequently unnerved her: wonderful, of course, but also full of tests – tests she had explored in *The Years Between* (which was now being rehearsed). The biggest test of all would be what would happen if, after the war, Tommy were posted somewhere which would mean her leaving Menabilly. This made her feel, she confessed to Tod, 'on the edge of a precipice . . . it would break my heart to go'. She felt guilty, putting house before husband, but she could not help it. News, in late August 1944, that the 'hazardous show' Tommy had warned her of was about to come off deepened her guilt, and she tried to think more positively of the return of a man who was in danger of not returning at all. On 16 September he wrote saying he was going 'on a doings which ought to give the Germans a proper jolt'. Then there was silence for several days.

When Tommy wrote again, five days later, he was at his most laconic, telling her there had been 'a somewhat hectic battle' and that 'we seem to have done our job . . . the Boche doesn't know whether he's standing on his head or his heels'. It had all been 'fairly hair-raising if you like that sort of thing'. But another letter, posted on 24 September, showed a change of mood. All buoyancy had gone. 'We have had a very tragic time,' he wrote, ' . . . as we have been unable to reach the 1st Division in time to prevent their annihilation . . . we've got a major battle on our hands to keep the corridor open . . . a great success but the whole thing is overshadowed in the North.' He felt 'terrible' about the fate of the 1st Division (at Arnhem). Soon he was feeling still worse. Reports had reached him of the newspapers' coverage of the events at Arnhem and he was very distressed – 'People don't seem to have been told that there was only rather less than a third of the Airborne effort and that the whole thing was 80 per cent successful . . . if it hadn't been for the atrocious weather and sheer bad luck the whole thing would have been 100 per cent successful, which in a war would have been phenomenal.' He was very depressed and Daphne was immediately sensitive to how upset he was, not just at the loss of life at Arnhem, but at the way the campaign had been represented as some kind of wilful waste. When his next leave came up, she agreed to go up to London and spend it with him there, to save him wasting precious time trailing down to Cornwall.

Their last leave together had been in May that year, before D-Day, and she had written afterwards to Tod that 'it was rather heartbreaking'. This time, in October 1944, post-Arnhem, the poignancy was greater. They treated themselves to a weekend at Claridge's and Daphne was bound to confess that in spite of constant assurances that luxury was of no interest to her it was 'by no means to be despised . . . it *was* a joy to ring a bell and have it answered and to eat grouse and peach Melba for supper instead of baked beans on toast'. The only trouble was that Tommy did not have the energy to enjoy this treat. As well as the usual exhaustion he was suffering from a heavy cold and could not sleep. She felt a tenderness and pity for him which surprised her – here was her husband, nearly forty-eight, spending his mature years as he had done his youth, one of that unlucky generation of men caught in two wars. She saw that he was not only fighting the war but living and breathing it, giving himself totally to it. The only good news he had for her was that he had an idea he would not be wearing the Red Beret (the distinctive emblem of the Paratroop Regiment)[9] much longer.

He was right. In December he was appointed Chief of Staff in South East Asia as Lord Mountbatten's right-hand man. This meant, of course, being posted to Ceylon, which he had already briefly visited, on a long-term basis: the separation he had envisaged was inevitable. The news, commented Daphne, was 'depressing . . . because one is bound to get a little out of touch', and she again acknowledged, 'I've brought the subject to the fore in *The Years Between*' (which had opened in Manchester in November and was scheduled to move into the West End of London just as Tommy left). His departure depressed her but, once back at Menabilly, she recovered quickly. Far more worrying was the alarming news that Dr Rashleigh was ill. 'His life hangs by a thread,' she told Tod, and if he died she knew her lease would be null and void unless the heir took it on. She hoped 'the old man will live forever', but knew that at well over seventy there was little chance of his surviving even ten years. Turning her attention to the heir, William Stuart Rashleigh, she told Tod, 'I hope to charm him . . . but he sounds even more tricky than the old doctor and for two pins would step in now, I believe, if he could.'

It was surprising that she was puzzled by this, and it was an indication of how, right from the beginning, Daphne had become possessive about a house she only rented. In spite of the clear stipulations in the lease, she had begun to convince herself that these did not mean what they said. Every month, every week, every day she remained in Menabilly deepened her love for it and her conviction that it was hers by what she called 'right of love'. She had already spent a great deal of money on it, but the money did not matter measured against her emotional investment. As she wrote to Garth Lean, 'It makes me a little ashamed to admit it, but I do believe I love Mena more than people.' And because of this love she was prepared to fight to keep a house in which she had lived only one year, a house legally belonging to someone else.

Chapter Twelve

Dr Rashleigh did not, after all, die. He recovered and the crisis over Menabilly – the first of many – was over. Once Tommy had departed, Daphne started to think seriously about that story revolving round a seventeenth-century Cavalier which she wished to write. Victor Gollancz was very eager that she should produce another novel, though he had agreed to publish *The Years Between* first. In November 1943, he had signed up Daphne for a three-novel contract, after the publication of *Hungry Hill*, offering her a £3,000 advance on each book and a royalty of 25 per cent on market sales – extremely advantageous terms, but then she was his star author and the returns for Gollancz were still vast. Now, he urged her to get on with the first novel due under this contract and she told him she would get down to it in the spring.

She had enjoyed writing *The Years Between* more than she had imagined she would, but she had not enjoyed the team work involved when it was completed, reporting to Tod that sitting in on rehearsals and being required to change lines did not suit her at all, although she was always obliging. Being in Wyndham's, her father's old theatre, where the play opened in London, was a disturbing experience. She felt Gerald's presence all around her and longed for him, she wrote to Tod, 'to be playing Clive Brook's part [the husband], and telling everyone what to do'. She knew he would have been 'so proud of me', and what a thing it would have been 'for him to be in his daughter's play'. The manner in which Clive Brook played the soldier-husband role surprised her – he made the character so sympathetic – whereas Nora Swinburne, as the wife, made her character unattractive. When Daphne finally saw her own play performed she reported to Tod that Nora 'misses the bus every time'. Instead of admiring the wife the audience admired the husband and it seemed to her the whole balance of the play was wrecked. The reviews reflected this. Although the 'quiet realism' of the play was praised, the critics found the husband-wife relationship suspect and particularly felt it was inconsistent with the drift of the play that this couple would stay together. It was summarized by one critic as 'a rather grey play about an awkward customer who is foolish enough to believe that people and things do not change in three or four years'. The best part was reckoned to be not that of the brave wife but the returning husband – 'a strained, disenchanted man'. The only people who really liked the play were Daphne's MRA friends. Garth Lean wrote that it was 'so unusual these days for the lovers not to bolt . . . I was tremendously encouraged by it, most grateful for the lead you have given'.

The play behind her, Daphne began work on *The King's General*. She wanted to base it on the history of Menabilly and the Rashleigh family and was rather hurt that the Rashleighs were not as willing as Christopher Puxley had been to let her consult family papers. This worried her. She wrote to Œnone Rashleigh, daughter of the heir, to whom she had been introduced by Foy Quiller-Couch, asking her, 'Could you tell me quite frankly how your father and the family . . . feel about a Civil War Menabilly novel? If they shrink from the names Menabilly and Rashleigh appearing on the printed page it will be quite easy to give false names for the house and the family, though in a sense that is going to spoil the history. But I should very much dislike to cause offence, so do be utterly candid and tell me.' Œnone, who knew her father was, in fact, opposed to the idea, nevertheless helped Daphne as much as possible. She sent her copies of various family letters from the sixteenth and seventeenth centuries together with a family tree, copious notes on the different family members, and a résumé of local history in so far as it affected the family. A. L. Rowse, who lived nearby, also advised her on which books to consult (he had been introduced to Daphne by the Quiller-Couches two years before and she was greatly impressed, describing him to Tod as 'about to be the leading historian in England'). But although this helped Daphne to get the history straight, what mainly intrigued her in the Menabilly story was the tale of a skeleton being discovered in a bricked-up room by some workmen in the nineteenth century. She spent a long time, before she began the novel, trying to decide who the poor incarcerated man could have been and how he could have been forgotten. Many hours were devoted to 'poking about the three buttresses', she told Œnone, 'with the wild hope of coming across the secret room' found by the workmen and since forgotten.

It surprised Daphne how much she relished the research involved in preparing to write her novel and she was proud of her own application. Though she had often said of herself 'I have the mind of a butterfly', she found she could concentrate when she cared enough, and she cared very much about getting the history of Menabilly right. It took her three months to finish going through 'massive tomes' and make detailed notes, chapter by chapter, on how her story would evolve, but then, poised to start writing, and excited by the challenge, she was plunged once more into domestic drama. Margaret, upon whom the whole household turned, was ill. The migraines seemed to run into one another without respite and, no matter how much she wished to be sympathetic, Daphne could not cope with a nanny-cum-housekeeper who collapsed so regularly. In fact, her whole relationship with Margaret was becoming a burden to her – as well as a burden to Margaret herself – and she was desperate to find a way out which would be fair. Margaret had been with her nearly twelve years and during that time worked hard and devotedly. Daphne had implicit trust in her but had never become in any way close – she let Margaret get on with her job, and was grateful to her, but temperamentally they were very different, and once the move to Menabilly had been undertaken the isolation made these differences more important. Margaret was under much greater stress, running such a big house with the help of three teenage girls who were willing but untrained, and also looking after three energetic children for much of the time. She also found the house itself quite frightening at night, especially when, as happened every time there was a storm, Mrs Browning chose to go out, often not coming back until the early hours of the morning, soaked but exhilarated. So Daphne found herself in the kind of situation she dreaded: she had a servant to whom she owed loyalty, whom she quite frankly wanted to get rid of, and yet, if she did so, she would not only feel brutal but would be left quite unable to manage her household.

The situation worsened daily: Miss Richardson had gallstones and left. Then the doctor, to whom Daphne had sent Margaret, reported, so she told Grace Browning, that 'Nanny has none of her glands working, only has one ovary, has a strepto bug in her system, a faulty left lung, and has had some sort of shock to the nerves . . .' Clearly, problems apart, the poor woman needed a complete rest. Margaret herself wrote to Garth Lean, whom she had met in the Langley End days, saying, 'I have been in the most miserable health . . . and get *the* most devastating fits of depression . . . you know I have been with Mrs Browning twelve years and it has been my life. Now I realise that the children are growing up quickly and perhaps I should have other interests as well . . .' So Margaret, too, realized that change must come. For the time being, Daphne arranged both a holiday and treatment in London, but her mind was running on a more permanent solution: Margaret must be found some other position and Tod must come and take over.

She promptly wrote to Tod once more suggesting the idea, and this time Tod was free to accept. But then, and just as Tod had become excited at the idea and had begun to make arrangements, Daphne decided she could do without her after all. In a twelve-page letter which was a masterpiece of tact she wrote to Tod telling her that she had met a Miss Riley, who was willing to teach the children and seemed 'very suitable'. She could come out every day from St Austell and really 'this would be a better solution'. The ever-obliging Tod bravely hid her disappointment, only to be told a month later that since Miss Riley had thought better of her offer, and had withdrawn it, it would now be all right for Tod to come after all. It was a measure of Tod's complete devotion that she expressed no irritation at this blithe assumption that she would rearrange her plans yet again: she promptly did so. Arrangements were made for her to move to Menabilly in the autumn.

But this did not help Daphne during the writing of *The King's General*. Margaret staggered on after her holiday, supposedly being helped not just by the girls but by Marjorie Johnson, wife of Tommy's batman, who was living in a flat prepared for her in the house. Daphne had not wanted more people to be around her but had seen it was her duty to offer the pregnant Mrs Johnson a billet when her husband went with Tommy, and had hoped it would work out well. It did not. Mrs Johnson had her baby while she was at Menabilly and needed looking after herself. Driven to distraction, Daphne retreated into the seventeenth century and very successfully ignored the chaos around her. She was entirely relaxed about any kind of mishap, and also about the state of the house, just so long as she could go on writing. Tessa's two goats, Freddie and Doris, were allowed to wander wherever they liked, on condition they didn't actually sleep on the beds, and the rabbits and bantams, though meant to be outside, were not unwelcome either. On fine days the children roamed the woods and on wet days explored the shut-off north wing which their mother worried about, because it was unsafe, though she did not make much effort to stop them. Here, all the rooms had heavy shutters, some of the ceilings were collapsed or covered with orange fungi, and ferns grew out of the walls. Tucked away in her room, where even Kits was not allowed to disturb her, Daphne wrote serenely on.

She finished *The King's General* in mid-July 1945 and sent it to Victor, apologizing for its length, and saying, 'I hate to think you may have to turn down four other novels for my awful bloated book.' He was planning a first print-run of 75,000 and she suggested he should print fewer copies, in order to leave enough paper for someone else's book, but Victor was so thrilled to have the novel that he would not hear of it. The war was soon going to be over and the paper situation would rapidly improve, therefore, he said, she must not feel guilty.

The mere mention of the war's ending aroused very mixed feelings in Daphne. Ever since Tommy had gone to the Far East at the end of 1944, she had been trying to prepare him for the difficulties they would face when he returned for good. Tommy couldn't understand what she meant and was merely bewildered. His wife sent him cuttings from magazine articles on the subject of the problems which would arise for married couples after the war, and he simply could not see their relevance to himself and Daphne. 'I quite agree reinstating our routes may be difficult but we *are* much more together than most people and have always been happy to sit on the opposite sides of the fire reading,' he replied to her warning and thought the subject closed. Even when she sent him her play, which he had never seen performed, he saw no message for himself, merely instructing her to insist on its being properly promoted so that there would be more money for boats – now *there* was a topic he did not mind discussing forever.

But Daphne, too, could be obtuse. After VE Day in May 1945, she began to expect Tommy home any minute, and when he failed to appear, acted as though this failure were deliberate on his part and he did not want to return. This was unreasonable because Tommy had told her repeatedly that the chances of his being able to come home as soon as the war in Europe was officially over were slim. On 23 May 1945, he spelled this out very clearly – 'I honestly don't think', he wrote to her, 'that there is going to be much chance of a man getting back soon,' and on 10 June he went further, writing that he was going to be stuck until the war with the Japanese was over, so she was not to 'count on a man coming back at any predictable time'. In spite of this, Daphne persisted in telling all her correspondents that Tommy was 'in no hurry' to return and even, though said jokingly, that he was 'having far too good a time out there'. This was quite untrue and she knew it. In all of Tommy's almost daily letters throughout 1945–46 there was never the slightest suggestion of any enjoyment. On the contrary, his exhaustion and depression were patently obvious. Sometimes he thought he would crack under the pressure – 'I'll blow up one day . . . I am a commander not a staff officer, and one day I'll let fly and tell everyone where to get off.' That was if he had the energy – for his health was troubling him. He felt 'deathly tired', had a return of his old tummy trouble, and had pains both in his left leg, the one he had injured in his air crash, and the muscles of his shoulders. He had to force himself to be 'up to the mark in the office' and was 'without interest' in anything outside it. But, in detailing the stress he endured, he was sensitive to his wife's own problems and wondered in one letter, rather wistfully, 'Whether if I'd been a dud and was commanding a district in England, whether you would have really been pleased or whether you'd have been disappointed seeing all the doings going on without your man in the swim. The funny part is, that apart from the fact that one feels right to be doing the best of which one's capable, I have no desire to do anything more than I have to.'

On his thirteenth wedding anniversary, as was his custom, Tommy wrote a letter to Daphne in which he made his feelings very clear. He summarized the years then told her, 'I've never for one single second regretted accepting your proposal of marriage, though I was a bit scared at the time and was too much of a gentleman to refuse you!!' He went on to pay handsome tribute to what marriage to her had done for him, saying it was thanks to her he was not 'a nervous wreck ... probably a neurotic ... all due to your love and care of a man'. But most poignant of all was the final part in which, with a sweet simplicity, he looked forward to their future – 'You needn't worry about us being able to settle down ... after the war.'

The week the letter was written, Christopher Puxley came to stay at Menabilly (puzzling the teenage helpers by leaving his shoes outside the door of his bedroom each night). He and Daphne and the two younger children – Tessa, thought 'too beady' at twelve, was safely away, staying with Grace – went off to St Ives for a holiday in the Bentley. The children quite liked him but found him very silent on this occasion, even more so than usual, and full of gloom. It was hardly surprising. Daphne, who for the last three years had been trying to get Christopher to accept that this wartime relationship must end when Tommy came home, had to tell him this might be the last time they could really be together.

No sooner was this holiday over than there was another kind of farewell, as another era ended. A group of MRA adherents were to sail to America on a Liberty ship and Garth Lean came down to say goodbye, spending the day with Daphne. He wondered afterwards if there had been 'something you wanted to say but not quite' because she had seemed different. That 'something' he sensed, but which Daphne did not articulate, was her feeling that she was no longer committed to MRA principles, no longer believed the world revolution could begin with each individual starting a revolution within himself or herself. 'Don't put me on a pedestal,' she had already written to him, 'my feet are made of clay.' Now, though she never formally disassociated herself from MRA, and remained a friend to Garth and Bunny, she was disillusioned.

She was also, as always after finishing a novel, tired and depressed. This was how Tod found her when she arrived to live at Menabilly in the flat vacated by Mrs Johnson in October 1945. Tod had spent holidays at Menabilly and was liked by the children, from whom she received a warm welcome. Now slightly plump, with her brown hair turning grey, she appeared to them not so much as a governess but as their mother's oldest friend. She had a rich, cultured accent, which they enjoyed mimicking, and she always looked neat, wearing tweed suits with pastel-coloured blouses and matching cardigans. Her jewellery consisted of two favourite brooches – one moonstone, one a little gold four-leafed clover – and she wore lily of the valley scent. She had brought with her home-made shortbread and a rich fruit cake, which, with the state of the food at Menabilly, were gratefully received ('Your mother', she told the children pityingly, 'could live off the smell of an oil rag').[1]

Life changed as soon as she was settled in. At 9.15 the children went to her flat, knocked, and heard her say 'You may enter.' There would be a delicious smell of bacon and toast, and it felt cosy and comfortable. (Tod found the cold at Menabilly quite unbearable and saw to it that her flat was the warmest place.) The girls took to her at once, which was fortunate since there was open warfare between them at the time, but Kits was not at first won over. He naturally preferred his mother, who so openly adored him and to whom he was so close, and would not, at almost five, readily give his allegiance to any other woman. But eventually even Kits tolerated Tod, and Daphne was left free to correct *The King's General*.

Sheila Bush, who had started working for Victor Gollancz as his secretary, and had taken over from Norman Collins as Daphne's editor with *Hungry Hill*, saw at once that, so far as editing went, there was a great deal to do to this novel. Daphne always acknowledged this perfectly cheerfully – she knew her spelling was atrocious, her paragraphing haphazard, and that she made many a grammatical slip. She had always needed someone to put these minor things right and had been grateful for the tedious work in which it involved her editors. There was never anything of the prima donna about her – on the contrary, she was humble and self-conscious whenever she sent in a manuscript, and always, even when she became a long-established bestselling author, said that she expected to have her typescript sent back with 'See me' written all over it. When it came to general editorial criticisms she was equally receptive and willing to listen to any suggestions for improvement – 'If Norman Collins can think of any alterations . . . to the general story, will you please ask him to let me know?' she had written to Victor when she gave him *Rebecca*. And when Norman did suggest various ways in which she could strengthen the narrative, she proved she meant what she said by giving them careful consideration. With Sheila Bush, she had now begun a working relationship which served her well.

The plot of *The King's General* was the most complex Daphne had yet attempted, because it covered so much real history and yet had interwoven in it an entirely imagined love-story. It begins with an atmospheric monologue, in the style of *Rebecca*, then moves on to a light-hearted, romantic flashback with a feeling of *Frenchman's Creek*, before expanding into a dense saga reminiscent of *Hungry Hill*. The character of the heroine, Honor, is central to everything that happens, and when she is crippled in a melodramatic accident near the beginning of the story of her life (which she is relating), it becomes obvious that this is to be a love-story of a very strange and dark kind. 'You will never see me wed to the man I love,' warns the crippled Honor, '. . . but you will learn how that love never faltered.' She refuses to let Richard Grenvile see her and he marries someone else. Firmly, she schools herself to forget him, but when the Civil War breaks out she is sent for safety to Menabilly, where Richard finds her. There follows a very odd chapter in which Honor and Richard dine together, the first time for fifteen years they have been in each other's company. Richard says he still wants her and Honor makes him inspect her injuries. These are described as 'crumpled limbs that he had once known whole and clean'. Richard does not flinch but 'kissed my ugly twisted legs'. All looks set for reconciliation and a happy outcome, but then Honor decides that, in spite of the tenderness he has shown, Richard has changed – 'suffering and bitterness had turned him hard'. He is cruel and ruthless, 'what my tragedy had made him'. If she lets him come back into her life, 'I must put up with the fever engendered in me which could never more be stilled.' She is a strong woman, but she knows Richard is stronger and that if she lets herself love him she will become his victim – 'First a soldier, second a lover', Richard will never put her first, he will only bring her 'torments'.

The backcloth to this tragic love-story is the Civil War in which Menabilly is invaded by the Roundheads, giving Daphne not only the opportunity for some effective atmospheric descriptions of the sacked house but the chance to bring into play the secret room which so fascinated her. It is Richard's weak and pathetic son who is incarcerated there and dies. But more interesting than all this drama is the way in which Honor's love for Richard develops. All around her she sees women losing men because of the war, and not always because they have been killed or become exiles – 'the aftermath of war . . . another marriage in the melting pot'.

The novel was dedicated to Tommy (knighted in the 1946 New Year's Honours List) – 'To my husband, also a general, but, I trust, a more discreet one' – which he knew, of course, would make people think Richard Grenvile, 'first a soldier, second a lover', this man 'violent from his youth . . . cruel . . . hard', was based on him. Tommy, far from objecting, was amused but hoped 'it will have a nice ending for a change, because you know what I think of your sad endings'. He enjoyed making suggestions by letter, especially about the heroine, who he thought 'ought to be fair, young, innocent and locally adored, but in the end proves a drunkard, sleeps every night with a different gentleman and has committed innumerable murders!' He also had another idea – 'Why not dedicate it to Mountbatten, because he's a big man . . . it would be a good ploy.' More people might buy it, bringing in more money for boats. When the novel was finished, and Daphne expressed the same high hopes she had had for *Hungry Hill*, it was Tommy who gently warned her, 'You want to be careful about being too pleased, because it might be a colossal flop,' though after reading it he, too, was sure of its success, because it was 'most beautifully written and very exciting'. He laughed at the idea of people identifying him as the general in her story, especially 'locals ... who will probably ostracise us, and a good thing that would be'.

The reviews, when the book was published in April 1946, were, or so Daphne thought, patronizing. She did not relish having *The King's General* praised for its 'glorious teenage exuberance', nor for being not 'matter-of-fact historical but romantic historical'. As far as she was concerned, there was plenty of accurate historical fact in it, and none of her painstaking research, all those weeks reading up local history and absorbing the details of the Rashleigh family history, had been acknowledged. Nor did she like being told that her prose style was 'within a few hundred years or so' of the period. But it sold well, and with Tommy fitting out his splendid new boat (in Singapore, where he was now stationed after Ceylon) money was needed.[2] He had told her he expected to be back in the summer and tried to console her for this delay by reminding her that some of the Dutch officers didn't even know if their wives were still alive.

Daphne responded by suggesting they have separate bedrooms when he came home. This threw him and he took a while to reply, especially as he was afflicted with a bad attack of 'me tum' just then. Finally, he wrote: 'I've never answered you about having a little separate room from you. It is very hard to say, as I've now been living on my own practically since 1941 – which is five long years, except for brief periods of being with you. I just don't know ...' But a month later he returned to the topic again and this time he did know – 'I never answered about whether I'd want a separate room from you' (obviously forgetting he had), he began, and then said, 'NO! – I want my routes, but in case it makes you start not sleeping as you fear, I can always creep into the spare room.'

This harping on separate rooms, even if it was out of consideration for his comfort, was not exactly calculated to make a man feel his arrival home was eagerly awaited. By June, a month before his estimated return, Tommy was in a great state of nerves anyway. He knew he had aged and worried about it. He had, he wrote, put on weight – 'You'll find me round as a tub' (though this was a ridiculous exaggeration) – and he now wore reading spectacles. There was much agonizing over what kind of frames to have but he assured her that whatever he chose 'a man will have them carefully designed to suit him'. But about his thinning hair he could do nothing, lamenting that she would find him 'bald as a coot'. It was very touching, his anxiety about his looks and whether she would still find him attractive, but more serious was his confession of how he felt. He was 'worn out' and could hardly get up in the mornings. One day he blacked out, which naturally terrified him. His left leg now hurt when he walked any distance and he feared she would find him 'much changed'. He would be crawling back 'in my fiftieth year which is quite a business when you think of it in cold blood' wanting only 'a quiet life and a complete rest'. This, he was sadly aware, was not the husband and father everyone looked for. 'I worry', he wrote, 'that I'll prove a disappointment to my children . . . I'm not cut out for too much fun and games.' The other big worry was whether he would have to ask his wife to leave Menabilly. He didn't know what his future would be – nobody would tell him, though Mountbatten, who had returned already, had promised to find out. There was a rumour he might become Military Secretary at the War Office, which he liked the idea of, except that it would mean living in London. But whatever happened on his return, he reminded her, 'God is very good to me. Except for this last four years not being properly together we have a great deal to be thankful for.'

His last letters home became more and more excited – 'I'm pretty perky as the thought of routes and you and Yggy and the bumps and all doings is buoying a man up.' He could hardly wait to see her – 'Only ten days left and the last eighteen months will seem like a dream.' But to Daphne, those last eighteen months were not something which she wanted to wipe out. Quite frankly, she had enjoyed them. Tommy's persistent emphasis on their instant return to 'routes' of every kind unnerved her. Life was now quite easy and comfortable with Tod in charge of the children and without Margaret. She had thought long and hard, as she confided in her sister-in-law Grace, about 'the kindest yet wisest thing to do regarding Nanny'. Margaret had had a complete collapse in the spring and Daphne managed to steel herself to have 'quite a talk' with her in which she suggested Margaret should go on an extended holiday (for which Daphne would pay), then think about her future. She also floated the idea that Margaret, who was clever with her needle, should set up as a dressmaker and said she would give her £500 to start. What Daphne wanted to avoid was 'any break in a harsh or abrupt manner', because she was well aware of, and grateful for, Margaret's 'many years of devoted service'. To her relief, Margaret accepted that the time had come to leave – she had been wearing herself out and was not particularly happy at Menabilly, nor was she doing the job for which she was trained. Tessa and Flavia, aged twelve and nine, no longer needed a nanny, and Kits had never been looked after by her in the same way.

So in April 1946 Margaret had left and Daphne felt released from 'the awkwardness of it all'. She had plenty of time to herself and liked her solitary evenings. Tod had been firmly warned that she must not expect to share Daphne's company – 'I *must* have evenings alone . . . a curious little routine of a tray by the fire . . . awful, probably very selfish thing.' Since January, when she had gone to London for the removal of a cyst, she had been trying to look after herself better and part of this attention to her health was indulging her already strong desire for resting in perfect peace. She saw nobody socially except her mother, Angela, and Angela's friend Angela Halliday, sometimes Jeanne (though she was now in St Ives, painting) as well as Foy and Clara Vyvyan, and even they never intruded on her evenings. Now, Tommy would be back and she would have to learn all over again to share her time. When her children had burst in to tell her the war was over she had replied crossly, 'I know it is, now go back to bed,' and a large part of her allegation that Tommy did not want to come home was due to a desire to pretend this was true: if he did not want to hurry back to her, she need not feel guilty about not wanting her peace to be threatened.

There was no pleasure in being honest with herself – it simply made her miserable. If she loved Tommy – and she knew she did – why did she not want him back in her day-to-day life? She was afraid and yet at the same time resentful – she couldn't help her feelings. But when she heard that her husband would land at RAF Northolt on 19 July, she suddenly found herself capable after all of genuine excitement. She made great efforts to look as beautiful as possible for him. Instead of the usual slacks and jumper she wore an elegant suit and blouse, and her blonde hair was sleek and shining after a visit to the hairdresser. She had always, even while living as she did at Menabilly, paid great attention to her face, despite her love for casual clothes, and now she made herself up with great care. When she had completed the transformation she went 'up to London with my heart beating with excitement', putting behind her all doubts and uncertainties about her marriage and 'determined to make a real effort . . . and not seem to be different at all, and give him a great welcome'.[3] All this was because 'I do love him very deeply', and she was not going to let the war spoil that genuine love whatever had happened during it to them both. The fact that 19 July was their fourteenth wedding anniversary seemed to her the best of omens.

At nine o'clock on the evening of 19 July, Daphne stood on the tarmac of the airport. If Tommy had put on a little weight during the last year of the war, she had lost a great deal and was even slimmer at thirty-nine than she had been when she married him. If he had aged, she looked more youthful. All the fresh air and rest in Cornwall during the last year had made her fit and healthy-looking, her skin tanned, her eyes bright. Her face looked softer than it had done, framed by hair she now wore touching her shoulders, slightly waved and parted at one side. She could not have looked more alluring. As she stood there, waiting for the door of the plane to open, she imagined Tommy feeling as she did and a great wave of emotion gripped her – it was all going to be all right after all.

But it was not. From the very moment Tommy came down the steps and strode across to her the great home-coming 'fell flat'. He did not wrap her in his arms, or even hold them out for her. Instead it was 'a peck on the cheek' and that was all. She rationalized this as his dislike of public displays of affection, which she herself hated. He was surrounded by his staff and did not feel free to greet her as he would have done in private. But there was another cause for surprise: behind Tommy was a very beautiful young woman, Maureen Luschwitz, aged twenty-three, who had been his Staff Officer (PA) for the last year, and whom he was now bringing back to England to continue to work for him.

Daphne knew about this but she had not been prepared for
Maureen's beauty. The moment she set eyes on her, she jumped to
the unjustified conclusion that this girl was, or had been, Tommy's
mistress. The fact that he showed no interest in Maureen at all,
merely ordering her to see his luggage through customs and report
for work at an address which meant nothing to her (she had never
been to England before) the next morning, was beside the point.
By the time the two of them had reached the flat in Whitelands
House,[4] where they were to stay, Daphne was wondering bitterly
'why I had bothered to come up to meet him even, he would not
have noticed my absence'.

Their first night together was as different as possible from anything she had imagined. He did not make love to her and though
'this sounds silly and bitter . . . it was all a queer anti-climax'.[5]
This, at any rate, was her given version of what had happened:
she had been spurned, ignored, made to feel unattractive. The
weeks ahead, with Tommy at Menabilly, were ones she dreaded.

Part Four

The Breaking Point
1946–1960

Chapter Thirteen

The next six weeks were among the most tense in Daphne's whole life – now, more than ever, she needed that ability to appear calm and cool and charming, when emotionally she was in turmoil. She felt that she was acting even more than she usually did, forcing herself to smile and say the right things and appear completely happy, because her husband was home at last. They went down to Menabilly and out in *Ygdrasil*, and Tommy seemed 'very pleased, and we rushed about Fowey', but she knew that all this 'on the go' as she described it was in fact moving them 'miles apart in our minds'. At the end of this agonizing six weeks, when he went to London to take up his new posting, which was, as predicted, to be Military Secretary to the Minister for War, he still had not made love to her – 'there was no "Cairo" [sexual intercourse] all the leave'. It seemed there had been no 'Cairo' for several other leaves either, but that 'in the war I thought it was just because his mind was too full of war'. Now, she felt unwanted, 'a dull, grey-haired, nearly-forty wife'. This was 'bad for my morale' and more significant 'it just made me say to myself, "Well, if he doesn't want me, I damn well know someone who does." ' She hated to find herself thinking like this – 'I *don't want* to think like that. I don't want my marriage to break up like so many other people's do' – but could not help herself. She was more hurt than she had ever thought possible, but equally determined that nobody should guess.

It was only to Ferdy that she confessed her misery and bitterness in two long, impassioned letters. Tod, the other person in whom she had been used to confide, was, of course, now living with her so it was to Ferdy, in France, that she chose to unburden herself.[1] But Ferdy was not told about how she herself had appeared reluctant to resume this particular side of her married life – there was no mention of the suggestion she had made that her husband might like a separate room, or that she had been steadily bombarding him with cuttings about the difficulties married couples would experience after the war. The whole tone of her letters was one of outraged distress: Tommy had rejected her, he was unfeeling, he did not find her attractive. She was wretched, the injured wife who had waited so patiently for him to come home, only to find that when he did he was not interested in her.

Clearly, something had gone very wrong, but it is very difficult to decide exactly what this was. Daphne's letters to Ferdy breathe sincerity in every line – this was no performance, no attempt to present herself as the injured party and conceal the truth. Yet it was not the whole truth. Quite apart from the fact that she had given signals to Tommy that *she* might not want to resume 'Cairo' immediately, she fails to admit that she made no attempt to make love to him. His letters right up to the moment he returned are full of love for her, full of impatience to be with her, full of an almost tangible yearning for her. Her letters to him she later burned but, in those that survive to other people, all the references to Tommy contain not one expression of real excitement about the approaching reunion. What they reflect instead is an edge of panic. Yet as she wrote to Ferdy, when the day came she *was* excited and hopeful, and then just as suddenly devastated by being 'rejected'. But, of course, because of her history with Ferdy she knew perfectly well that her account of there being no 'Cairo' would hardly be thought a disaster by her old teacher. It might actually be thought significant in another way: perhaps she was no longer interested in any kind of 'Cairo' herself and was once more struggling with the boy-in-the-box.

This is the point at which hypothesis has to take over, however unsatisfactory: what seems likely to have happened when the two of them were reunited is that Daphne, even if her heart was 'pounding with excitement', seemed distant and tense, because she felt guilty about Puxley and had not been looking forward to Tommy's return; and Tommy, although desperately eager to show his love for Daphne, seemed abrupt and preoccupied with work. They were both nervous and they were both waiting for the other to make the first move, a move which never came. Once at Menabilly, where he was put in a separate, though connecting, bedroom, he waited in vain for a sign from her. It is a sad scenario, and one hard to understand when it is remembered not only how attractive both of them were, but how genuinely they had loved each other. But it was nevertheless a situation many couples found themselves in after the war. What was hardest to do was *talk* about it to each other – there was a shyness, a loss of that ease of communication which comes from always being together, and a feeling between couples that suddenly they were strangers.

The sadness of it permeated Daphne's letters of this period to Ferdy. It occurred to her that Tommy's 'rejection' of her might be thought a kind of poetic justice – 'You might say "serve me right", because of that "someone" I have hinted at in my letters to you, but that someone loves me too well not to know that my marriage must come first with me.' What distressed her was not only the sexual rejection but how much she cared about it. From this point onwards she began to make remarks about sex not really being important, and even indicated she had never really cared for full 'Cairo', but this looks like a deliberate attempt to convince herself as well as others. She certainly did not acknowledge that the reason for the sexual difficulties in her marriage might be that she now found all heterosexual sex abhorrent. What she had enjoyed with Puxley was the 'spinning', not full intercourse. But to Ferdy she gave every indication that far from finding 'Cairo' repulsive she regretted the lack of it greatly. She wrote, 'if Tommy just looks on me as a dull old thing he is fond of . . . the outlook is dreary'. It frightened her to think 'Well, is that side of marriage finished for ever?' Because if it were, if there were to be 'not even "Cairo" to make a bond, there is little but past loyalty and ordinary affection to keep us together at all'. This not only demonstrated how much importance she placed on the sexual side of her marriage, but also that it occurred to her that this was the only way they had been truly together. She had realized 'how very different we are in mind and thought . . . it is worrying because I don't want things to be like that'. She couldn't sleep, and Tommy, in his separate room, could not sleep either. She took sleeping pills regularly now, instead of occasionally, and when she fell into a restless sleep it was to dream of her father. 'I dream so often of my Daddy,' she wrote to Ferdy, with infinite pathos, 'I think he watches over me, from wherever he is.' Dreams of her father at this time, when she was so disturbed about the sexual state of her marriage, cannot help but seem significant.

This was the secret subtext to the story of those six weeks, but even the surface narrative was full of problems. Most of them involved the children. Tommy came home to children aged thirteen, nine and five and a half, whom he hardly knew. He had confessed in some of his letters to Daphne how worried he was, and the reality of resuming his role as father proved every bit as difficult as he had envisaged. Like so many men coming back from six years of wartime army life Tommy had forgotten how to behave in a domestic situation. He shouted and swore, and the children had never experienced this – their mother *never* shouted. Nor had they been subjected to any real discipline. Their mother, although strict about manners, was not in the habit of giving orders. Tommy gave them and expected them to be obeyed, sharpish. If Daphne was angry, the worst that could happen was a tight-lipped silence or her swift, disapproving disappearance, but they now discovered that if their father was angry – and his temper was short – it could be terrifying. Daphne told Ferdy she thought his hectoring manner and unjustified rages were 'the effect of having millions of men under him, it is like Hitler. This sounds absurd, but . . . no one must argue with him.' Nobody dared.

Tommy certainly was not proud of his temper and had no idea how frightening he could be. He desperately wanted to show his love for his children and to have them show their love for him. But he was not only up against the disadvantage of his own unconsciously bullying behaviour, but against a wife who had in no way kept him alive in her children's minds as a loving father. There was no careful preparation for his return, beyond warnings that they must try to keep quiet because he would be tired. On his leaves, there had been no chance for them to establish any kind of rapport. So now, he came home as a virtual stranger, and one of whom all three of them were a little afraid. He tried hard to act as he thought a father should act, making determined efforts to be jolly and play games – bombing the two younger ones in

their bath with soapy sponges, having cushion fights, and inventing a kind of indoor Olympics (known as the Monkey Skin Game)
which had four events in it: boxing, hurdles, long jump and show
jump, all performed before an audience of teddy bears.[2] He could
even be funny, pretending he was walking downhill as he passed
the nursery window, so that his head sank lower and lower. But
just as suddenly he would yell at them for some minor misdemean-
our and all his jollity was forgotten. It was all extremely confusing
for them, and Daphne realized this only too well.

The child who suffered most was the one who had actually had
the best chance of pleasing her father. Tessa, at thirteen, was pretty
and lively, and Tommy was quite charmed by how she had grown
up. But this was the trouble, as Daphne explained to Grace.
Tommy 'treated her as if she was 20, then realised she *is* only 13
and has rather dropped her, if you know what I mean'. She could,
she wrote, 'see it all so well' from both their points of view. Both
father and daughter were disappointed in each other, and the
mother looking on found it 'infinitely pathetic'. In no time at all
Tommy was complaining that Tessa was 'ill-mannered and needed
school which made poor old Tessa get aggressive and awkward'.
Tessa, for her part, was 'hoping for understanding and not getting
it'. She was 'too old to be romped with' and so felt excluded.
Allowed to eat in the evening with her parents, a privilege still
denied to Flavia and Kits, she did not find this the happy time it
should have been. Daphne found it agony to witness how Tommy,
with no knowledge of teenage girls, misjudged Tessa's maturity
at every stage and made her pay the penalty. But however sensitive
her reading of the situation, she did not seem able to act as
mediator between the two of them. More successful was her protection of Kits. Kits was hers and he was going to remain so.
Though in her letters to Ferdy she commented that 'it's awful, his
Greek feeling for me, he can't bear it if I go away, and even if I
go out to lunch from here he's in an awful state', at the same time
she was not really prepared to share him with Tommy. The artistic
side of Kits, strong in any case, was encouraged, and even had his
father tried to forge the kind of bond Daphne had with their son,
it is unlikely it would have developed. As for Flavia, both parents

referred to her as 'old Gumbo' or 'old dopey': her role in life at that time was to play with Kits and keep the peace.

Peace was hard to maintain, not just because of all the strain involved in settling down as a family again, but because that family now included Tod. Daphne had been absolutely honest with Tommy about Tod's coming, knowing she irritated him profoundly, and he had written agreeing to her becoming the children's governess, while expressing the fervent hope that their energy would tire 'old Tod out and keep her quiet'. But when he arrived at Menabilly, Tommy quickly realized there was no hope of that – Tod was a force to be reckoned with and she drove him wild. She incensed him by pontificating on matters about which he knew a great deal and she knew nothing, and he could hardly restrain himself. Sometimes his dislike came out openly. Once, when Tod, who had a sore throat, asked if anyone could suggest how she could treat it, Tommy could not prevent himself from suggesting, 'Cut it.' Tod stalked from the room, and Daphne said Tommy must apologize, which he duly did. But he muttered constantly about her being 'a silly old arse, always belly-aching'. The trouble was that he wanted his wife to himself and he only seemed to manage that when they were on board his wonderful new boat, *Fanny Rosa*, shipped back from Singapore and his pride and joy.

'It quite hurts me', Daphne wrote to Grace, 'to think of the money going on that old hulk. All my precious hoardings from films!' But Tommy was oblivious to the cost or to where the money had come from. *Fanny Rosa* was his reward for surviving the war – 'I do want a nice big ship after all these many years,' he had written, and the cost of £8,000 (without some of the more extravagant fittings) he reckoned as well within his wife's means. She was, after all, to be paid £65,000 for the film rights of *The King's General*, and even after enormous tax there would be 'enough for my boatie'. He despised as faint-hearted Daphne's preference to 'be canny and try and spread it out over ten years to give a feeling of security'. Veteran of the war that he was, Tommy had little respect for such far-sightedness. The knowledge that his wife, as part of her Sunday 'routes', sat entering everything she had spent each week in a little red notebook, he found extraordinary.

So far as her marriage went Daphne was not prepared to look too far into the future at all. 'I feel somehow lost now,' she wrote to Ferdy, but stressed that she must not tell anyone else this. 'I will see how life goes this winter,' she added, and said that she would try to visit Tommy every month in London in the hope things would get better. But they didn't. When she did go up to London after Tommy had started his new job, she reported that he was 'completely absorbed in his work which I know so little about, so that it is difficult for me to take an intelligent interest even in that'. Returning to Menabilly she was more depressed about their relationship than ever and 'felt quite rotten'. The cause was partly physical – she told Ferdy 'that bad anaemia started again and then I had to have a tooth out, and I felt I was looking unattractive and old'.

She had 'a down-feeling' about herself and the next time she went to stay with Tommy 'saw my "someone" [Puxley] and felt that after all I was not such a dreary old fool . . . ' She also saw Carol Reed (married himself since 1943, but already on the edge of divorce) and her old friend Pat Frere (Edgar Wallace's daughter). 'Tommy', she commented, 'was nice and pleased to have me to stay (although there was nothing else), but I have a feeling that he likes his own little flat up there on his own better than he likes this house down here. I think he has a vaguely jealous feeling against this house . . . so he retaliates by having *his* flat and feeling that up there it is *his* show. But I feel that all these separate things make for a kind of barrier, and I wonder how and when we are ever going to share things and be together again.'

Not, certainly, ever, if she were to stay in Cornwall and he were obliged to live most of the time in London, but never at any time did Daphne contemplate giving up Menabilly, nor did Tommy ask her to. Contrary to the impression she gave Ferdy, Tommy did *not* like 'his own little flat' better than he liked Menabilly. He did not like it at all and was always desperate to get down to Menabilly, which he loved, if not with quite the same passion as his wife. His life in the Whitelands House flat was dreary and comfortless, and the travelling backwards and forwards at weekends to his real home exhausting. Except that they saw much more of each other, the new regime was little better than in the war, and the emotional distance between them was bound to grow. Daphne understood this perfectly well, telling Ferdy, 'The sad thing is that looking back now over the years, I realise that the thing that kept our marriage happy was the actual fact that we were together all the time and I somehow adapted myself to his ways. Our minds and thoughts were really poles apart, but I used to squash my thoughts so as to be "in" with him . . . now the less we see of each other the more apart we become.' None the less, she let the unhappy situation continue. Put brutally, there was nothing Tommy could have done – he had to be in London, where his job was – but if Daphne had been prepared to sacrifice Menabilly she could have made a home in or near London for both of them, so that their marriage would have had a better chance of flourishing once more.

But it was not even as cruelly simple a decision as that of giving up the house she adored and a way of life in which she was happy. The deciding factor was her recognition that the damage done was irreparable – just as in *The Years Between* the past could not be reclaimed. Her description of herself as previously keeping 'in' with Tommy falsely suggested he had dominated her. What he had done was fail to be in tune with her mercurial character, and now she realized he never would be. With a feeling of great regret and helplessness she saw that nothing could be done about it. It wasn't that Tommy was not worth sacrificing Menabilly for, but that the sacrifice would be pointless. She would be left with nothing. The effect on her as a writer was as disastrous as the effect on her as a woman. She found it impossible to contemplate writing anything at all – 'I somehow can't get down to thinking about anything or working out a story.' All she could think of was her own secret drama. Her anguish was pent up but to the world at large she presented a smiling face, amazed that she could carry off the pretence of happiness. Tommy did the same. Seen together in Fowey, they were admired as a totally contented couple, and even friends staying with them saw not a hint of strain. Nobody realized how deeply Daphne's self-analysis probed, or was aware that she saw herself with a cast of mind quite different from her husband's. There was no room, she decided, in Tommy's scheme of things, for her own waywardness – he was too correct and controlled, too straightforward altogether. The very quality Daphne had admired most in him – his absolute integrity – now seemed an irritant. Tommy was, in the best sense of the word, a simple man who saw everything in black and white, whereas she was devious, highly complex and employed all kinds of subterfuges and pretences (not all harmless) in her personal relationships. Tommy was always what he seemed, Daphne never.

But nobody guessed. Like the second Mrs de Winter, who had cared so deeply about 'the disgrace of a failed marriage', she preserved intact the façade of contentment. Maureen Luschwitz, Tommy's PA, had come down to Menabilly during that first six weeks and had been enchanted by the Brownings' home life. She liked Daphne as much as she liked Tommy – they seemed to her the ideal couple, both so good-looking and charming and blessed with three lovely children. The curious mixture of formality and casualness which characterized their family life fascinated her as it did most visitors and seemed wholly enviable. On the one hand, meals were at set times, precisely when the gong went, routine was strictly adhered to and exquisite manners were everywhere in evidence. But within this framework there was plenty of scope for a different kind of spirit of a more Bohemian character. Daphne's love of 'jam-a-long' ways prevailed, with clothes and conversation equally relaxed and a good deal of mockery going on. The telling of amusing anecdotes, the spirited mimicking, the sly teasing and uproarious laughter at every kind of pretension, made mealtimes not the staid things one normally found in country houses. Daphne never did a thing in the house except pick flowers and arrange them, but she did not *seem* the sort of woman who did nothing, nor even the sort who depended entirely on servants. It was a very attractive set-up and Maureen, only twenty-three and impressionable, fell under its spell. When Daphne, who appeared to have realized her assumptions about Maureen had been wrong, suggested she might like to act as her part-time secretary as well as working for Tommy, Maureen was delighted to agree and from then onwards was a frequent guest, quickly becoming very involved with the whole family. Never, at that time, did she think of the Brownings as anything but supremely happily married and fortunate.

That first winter of Tommy's return, 1946–47, the winter in which Daphne had told Ferdy that she was going to wait and see what happened, set a pattern which was all too easy to follow without any kind of confrontation between herself and her husband. Nothing 'happened', but there was no resolution of their difficulties. In January, Tommy went on a rapid tour of Europe, so that for some weeks he did not come down to Menabilly. Daphne found this a relief, and not only because she felt freer. It was a viciously hard winter and she dreaded Tommy's complaints about the cold at Menabilly (about the only thing on which he and Tod agreed). The electricity was off for days at a time, the water froze in the pipes and, in spite of wearing all their clothes in bed and heaping covers on top, no one was ever really warm. Tommy was better out of this, though he was experiencing rigours of another kind. Everywhere he went he saw destruction which horrified and depressed him. Berlin was smashed up beyond anything he had expected and he saw with his own eyes the devastation caused by the Allied bombing throughout Germany. Seeing 'the misery of Europe', he wrote to Daphne, made him think of his own future. He was 'keen to get out of the army' but felt compelled to stay in, because 'I feel there is a bit of work for a man to do in this world yet'. When he returned to London he went to church and prayed for guidance as to what he should do. He also went to the House of Commons, seeking another kind of guidance, and came away unable to fathom 'what this government is on about'. Like so many men he had come back from the war to a country in which he was no longer sure he had a place. The new Labour Government bewildered him and he did not think it was because he was not a Labour supporter (he was a Liberal) – but simply that he found those in power unimpressive, especially Attlee, who 'makes me weep . . . he is so pathetic'. To his wife he confessed, 'There is a lot of staleness about everything and probably about myself, which gets me down.' More than ever he longed 'to be at Menabilly for good'.

The mere thought made Daphne tremble. The first time Tommy came home after his tour he complained bitterly about the state of the house and compared it most unfavourably with the house of a friend he had just visited where everything was immaculate. Tod, who was on holiday at the time, was treated to a letter in which Daphne said how depressed this made her feel. When Tommy was not at home nobody gave a damn how chaotic the housekeeping was, but when he was there she was made to feel a failure 'because I can't organise tea for 800' as his friend had been able to do. But she still wanted to try to get closer to Tommy and it was she who suggested they should go abroad for a holiday, just the two of them. She hadn't been abroad, of course, because of the war, for nearly a decade and yearned for some southern sun, if a place not ruined by bombing could be found. Who knew what magic it might work? Tommy, who had had quite enough of abroad, was more interested in some kind of sailing holiday in England, but in the end agreed to go to Switzerland for two weeks in May. Daphne was full of new hope, imagining Tommy relaxed and the two of them rediscovering that easiness between them of the Greyfriars days, to which she now found herself harking back nostalgically in a Gerald fashion.

Although the holiday was enjoyable, it worked no miracle. She and Tommy walked a lot, read and swopped comments as they used to do, but there was none of that coming together, either sexually or spiritually, which she had looked for. This lack of true closeness was still not something ever discussed – both of them had a natural reticence about voicing their intimate feelings and fears, and each waited for some sign from the other which never came. They were friends, they loved each other, but it was no longer possible to imagine they were truly united. She was relieved to be back in Cornwall, on her own with the children.

And still she could not write, though the summer was as wonderful as the winter had been terrible and she felt happier, resigned to what she could see was going to be the way of things with Tommy. These were good times. She and the children would set off every day through the woods down to Pridmouth beach to spend hours swimming and sunbathing. All she wore was 'my sharkskin pants and a red hankie round the bosom' and she took these off to swim naked as she always had done if possible. She loved to get brown and so did Flavia, whereas Tessa and Kits remained stubbornly pale and were teased. Lying on a rock in the little cove they had made their own, Daphne observed her children and was pleased with what she saw. She felt that the 'real companionship' she had looked forward to when the girls were small had perhaps arrived – now that they were fourteen and ten she could talk to them and share confidences with them, and she was altogether more comfortable. She saw how pretty Tessa had grown and was amused by her 'beadiness' about people's love-affairs. When she was on her own with her she found Tessa gratifyingly intelligent and well-read yet still she felt distant from her, as though this could not be her daughter in spite of the striking physical resemblance. It was in Flavia that she was beginning to see something of herself – 'old Gumbo' was not after all so 'dopey' and had a dreaminess and diffidence about her which her mother recognized. Kits, of course, was altogether perfect, as he had always been, and she gloried in him. The thought of him having to go away to prep school was so unbearable she shut it out of her mind firmly.

Another thing she shut out that summer of 1947, as she basked in the sun, was the approaching necessity for her to go to America. She had been shutting out the possibility ever since 1942 when she had first been told that 'an American woman claims that I copied a book of hers when I wrote *Rebecca* (I'd never heard of her or her book, needless to say)'. She had been obliged at the time to go up to London from Cornwall and 'answer a lot of silly, irrelevant questions before the American Consul. One of them was: "How many novels have you read in your life?"! And another: "State on what dates you read them"! Of course the American courts are quite crazy.'[3] The American Consul was very nice and agreed the whole thing was ridiculous. There had been no mention of alleged plagiarism until the Hitchcock film of 1940 had been such a success. It had all started the year before when in the *New York Times* Book Review *Rebecca* was compared to *A Sucesora*, a novel written in Portuguese by Carolina Nabuco. It was not the Nabuco family who sued. Instead, the family of another novelist charged Daphne with plagiarism. The literary executors of one Edwina L. Macdonald sued Daphne du Maurier, her publishers in the USA, Doubleday Doran & Co., Selznick

International Pictures Inc., and David O. Selznick United Artists, on the grounds that *Rebecca* allegedly plagiarized a story first published in October 1924 in *Heall's International Magazine* under the title *I Planned to Murder my Husband*, and which then appeared as a novel called *Blind Windows*, published in 1927. Forty-six 'parallelisms' were submitted as evidence of plagiarism.

Since that visit to the American Consul five years before, Daphne had suppressed her fear that she might actually have to appear in an American court – the prospect was too awful and too unreal to take seriously. But now, to her alarm, she was told the law had moved in its ponderous way and she was required to present herself before a New York judge. She simply could not credit it, but Nelson Doubleday, her American publisher, whom she had already met in London, assured her there was no alternative – she had to come. He tried to make the ordeal as bearable as possible by inviting her to stay at his Oyster Bay house and to bring with her whoever she wished, so that a duty visit might be turned into a pleasant holiday. Daphne was distraught at the prospect and even more so at the mere idea of this absurd case succeeding. She wrote that 'the sword of Damocles' hung over her and that if the case went against her it would be 'bankruptcy for all'. But the Doubleday invitation made her decide to take Flavia, Kits and Tod with her and try, as Nelson Doubleday had suggested, to get something out of the visit. Tessa was to start school at St Mary's, Wantage, before they went, a decision heavily influenced by Grace Browning, who pointed out that her niece really needed better teaching than Tod could provide, and that Tessa wanted to go to boarding school anyway. For a long time she had felt lonely and miserable at Menabilly, reduced to walking on her own or playing with her goats for company. What she craved were girls of her own age and a life away from gloomy, if lovely, Menabilly. This, Daphne found almost perverse, but she had given way.[4]

Preparations for the American trip dominated the autumn, with Daphne in a great state about her wardrobe. Her own 'jam-a-long' clothes would not do, so it was a trip to Harrods to buy 'a pleated silk jacket and skirt, black markings on grey, piped black'. An even bigger problem was the children's clothes. They had virtually none, and the best she could do was get a local dressmaker to run up shorts and shirts that were at least new, for both of them – ten-year-old Flavia dressed exactly like her seven-year-old brother. Apart from the bore of having to kit everyone out, there was the worry over money. The permitted travel allowance in the immediate post-war era was a mere £35, and Daphne did not see how that could possibly enable her to 'go to New York for my stinking lawsuit'. Even if more money could be obtained (which it easily was) she was feeling anxious over her finances. *The King's General* was earning handsomely, quite apart from the film rights,[5] but she envisaged the whole lot disappearing and bitterly regretted letting Tommy indulge himself with *Fanny Rosa*. She had no new book in mind and worried that, if she had dried up completely and lost the *Rebecca* lawsuit, ruin would stare her in the face.

By the time everything was arranged and Daphne, Tod, and the two children embarked from Southampton on the *Queen Mary* in November 1947, Daphne was exhausted and tense. She dreaded having to appear in court, and even the prospect of staying in luxury with the Doubledays did not really attract her – she never felt comfortable in strangers' houses, and though Nelson Doubleday was not exactly a complete stranger, he was not yet a friend, and she had not yet met his wife,[6] who was reputed to be tremendously elegant. Daphne imagined her as being 'like that awful Mrs Simpson', and dreaded meeting her. When she did so, she experienced the greatest sense of shock.

Chapter Fourteen

On the second day of the voyage out on the *Queen Mary*, Ellen Doubleday went to introduce herself to the famous English author who was to be her guest when they arrived in New York. She knocked at the door of cabin B 108 and, when she entered, Daphne stared at her speechless, then sank down on to her bunk, clutching Kits. In a letter she wrote to Ellen six weeks later, when she was back in England, she described how overcome she had been and how she had instantly been transported back twenty years in time until she was 'a boy of eighteen all over again with nervous hands and a beating heart, incurably romantic and wanting to throw a cloak before his lady's feet'. A boy, not a girl, the boy she explained she had 'locked up in a box' long ago when she had accepted that, since she was outwardly a girl, she must face facts and live as a girl. But seeing Ellen, whom she cast immediately in the role of Mary Stuart, and later of Rebecca, the boy sprang once more from the box she had thought sealed forever.

Her feelings of excitement were mixed with ones close to terror. She struggled to compose herself and talk to Ellen – who saw that for some reason she was the cause of consternation but did not understand why – though inwardly Daphne was recognizing that her conscious denial of one part of herself throughout her adult life had been 'one long lie'. She took Ellen back to her childhood, in that letter she finally wrote, and asked her to imagine 'D. du M. as a little girl like Flave, only very shy, always biting her nails. But never being a little girl. Always being a little boy. And growing up with a boy's mind and a boy's heart . . . so that at eighteen this half-breed fell in love, as a boy would, with someone quite twelve years older than himself who was French and had all the understanding in the world, and he loved her in every conceivable way . . .'[1] But Ellen was not for one moment to imagine that this was a confession of lesbianism – '. . . by God and by Christ if anyone should call that sort of love by that unattractive word that begins with "L", I'd tear their guts out.'

In her own mind, she had seen herself as something other – not a lesbian but 'a half-breed', someone internally male and externally female, and she was proud of how she had reconciled these two halves. 'And then the boy realised he had to grow up,' she told Ellen, 'and not be a boy any longer, so he turned into a girl, and not an unattractive one at that, and the boy was locked in a box forever. D. du M. wrote her books, and had young men, and later a husband, and children, and a lover, and life was sometimes lovely and sometimes rather sad, but when she found Menabilly and lived in it alone, she opened up the box sometimes and let the phantom, who was neither girl nor boy but disembodied spirit, dance in the evening when there was no one to see . . .' But then in walked Ellen, on board the *Queen Mary*, and she was overwhelmed with longing for her.

It was a longing she fought fiercely – 'I pushed the boy back into his box again and avoided you on the boat like the plague.' It was inconceivable that she should reveal what she felt about her hostess – it was better that Ellen should think herself disliked than come anywhere near guessing the effect she had had. But once at Barberrys, the Doubledays' house on Oyster Bay, Long Island, Daphne began to see that Ellen was as much in need of her, though in an entirely different way, as she was of Ellen. On the surface so elegant and sophisticated, the perfect hostess who ran a house as Daphne could never have done, Ellen was facing troubles of her own with great bravery. A proud but acutely sensitive woman, she was struggling to deal with her husband's crippling neuritis, and to conceal her distress at the way his violent swings of mood, diagnosed as being alcohol-related, affected her. Daphne, with her intuitive understanding of people, picked this up very quickly. Nelson Doubleday had made as big an impression on her, when she met him in London, as Victor Gollancz had done, and in addition he had another attraction: he was like Gerald. She thought his personality 'so terrific' that it 'just dwarfed' other people's, but at the same time – as with Gerald – she felt instinctively that underneath there was 'a great simplicity and somehow the heart of a child . . .' Impulsive, moody, flamboyant, Nelson fascinated her almost as much as Ellen did and he found her amusing and entertaining. The fact that Daphne was such a favourite with Nelson helped Ellen greatly and made her the most welcome of guests, appreciated by the whole family. Daphne admired, meanwhile, how the incomparable Ellen – 'the Rebecca of Barberrys' – organized everyone superbly and exerted effortless control over every detail of her household to brilliant effect, but she sensed also that here was a woman under strain who was suffering. At night, when the children were asleep, the two women talked to one another, often sitting in each other's rooms, ready for bed, tired after their respective busy days – especially Daphne, who was appearing in court – and gradually they became confidantes. There was a growing sympathy between them, an exchange of emotional tenderness, but nothing else.

For Daphne, this was hard – 'Watching you at Barberrys was very hard to bear.' She loved how Ellen looked, how she moved, how she spoke – 'You looked lovelier every day. It just defeated me.' She was that locked-up boy again and wanted 'to ride out and fight dragons for you . . . or else to conquer new worlds and bring back the Holy Grail'.[2] Instead, she had to go to court and be cross-examined by a prosecution lawyer whom she hated. The case turned on what was fair usage of common themes and on whether she could have read the original story of *Blind Windows*. The prosecution had worked hard, digging out a review of *Blind Windows* in the *Times Literary Supplement* which Daphne admitted she read regularly, and arguing she could have read it there. They even produced copies of Edgar Wallace's novels, which Daphne naturally also agreed she had read, to show they had advertisements for *Blind Windows* in them and would have brought the story to her attention. By the time Daphne was called to the stand she felt she was in an Alice in Wonderland situation, but she managed to answer each question sensibly and carefully. She testified that she had begun thinking of *Rebecca* as early as 1932, but had not started writing it until she was in Egypt for the second time, in the summer of 1937, and had finished it in April 1938 in England. She categorically denied ever having heard of

Blind Windows or its author. It was 'utterly degrading' to have to answer questions about her writing, because this writing was 'absolutely personal'. Talking about it was the most obscene of exposures and she could hardly control her voice. But worse still was the dreadful irony of it all: here she was, on trial for something she had not done, called to answer a charge of which she was completely innocent, when really it seemed to her she should be standing trial for something quite different of which she *was* guilty. 'When I got up on that bloody stand . . . I wasn't just fighting a foolish case for plagiarism, I was fighting all the evil that has ever been, all the cruelty in myself . . . all the rottenness that is in every one of us.'[3] When the prosecution lawyer called her a liar this was 'so very perceptive of him', not for the reason he thought but because 'my life has been one long lie for as far back as I can remember'. She then explained to Ellen what she had meant by this dramatic announcement – she had always been 'pretending to be sweet and good and kind, and in reality none of those things. Merely the person who dances alone in the long room, thumbing her nose at the world.'

The trial and the self-control she was having to exert at Barberrys made her ill. What she did not tell Ellen was what else she thought might come out – that 'I had written *Rebecca* about my feelings of jealousy re him [Tommy] and Jan Ricardo, and I was so terrified of that coming up in the Box and making publicity that I was nearly off my rocker.'[4] She was considered to have acquitted herself magnificently in court and, though the judge deferred his decision, to be going to win her case without doubt.[5] But she was left feeling sick and weak, and took to her bed for several days. Ellen saw that she was looked after perfectly. There were many more talks, a deeper exchange of confidences, but still no overt declaration from Daphne. It was bliss to be so pampered, after the austerity of Menabilly – bliss to have pine essence in her bath, tempting meals brought on trays, and to be cosseted in the luxury of Ellen's home.

Tod and the children revelled in it too. Ellen was as thoughtful about them as she was about Daphne – a wonderful birthday party was organized for Kits, seven years old on 3 November, and Flavia was taken out of her absurd boys' clothes and put into pretty dresses chosen by Ellen. Tod was in her element, delighting not only in the general standard of living at Barberrys, so much to her taste after the deprivations of Menabilly, but most of all in the company. As well as the Doubledays' own family and their young friends – Ellen had two daughters by her first marriage, Madeleine and Ellen (known as 'Pucky'), and a son, Nelson, and a daughter, Neltje, by her second – several famous authors also flocked there. Noël Coward visited while Daphne was staying and they renewed the intermittent friendship they had had ever since Gerald had introduced them. It was all glitter at Barberrys – the food, the wine, the warmth, the conversation, the beautiful people . . .

Back at home Daphne heard the news that Tommy had just been appointed Comptroller and Treasurer to HRH Princess Elizabeth and would be in charge of her household at Clarence House. This was a prestigious appointment but an unexpected one and, though she was proud of her husband, Daphne took time to adjust to what it would mean for her. The first thing she realized was that this would confirm that Tommy's life was mainly in London and hers in Cornwall, which relieved her greatly. She wanted to be alone in 'my rat-ridden ruin', and never more so than on her return from America.

She retreated to bed, huddling under blankets against the bitter cold and unable to eat the awful food 'plonked down by a resentful Hanks'.[6] Yet, although she felt so ill physically, partly with exhaustion and partly because she had some sort of virus, she described herself to Ellen as feeling 'queerly happy and at peace'. She had Ellen to love. Ellen's photograph now stood on a chest of drawers in her bedroom 'where none has ever stood before', a fact noted and commented on not only by Kits but by Tommy. Kits complained it wasn't 'routes' to have a photo there, to which his mother replied that it was now. She lived for Ellen's letters and when they came they sent her into immediate and wild fantasies. She sent Nelson off on a voyage in her mind and Tommy off on another with Princess Elizabeth while the respective children were scattered over the globe so that Ellen and she could be alone at Menabilly. Ellen would come and be Rebecca and transform it and meanwhile, the fantasy retreating, a kiss was sent for Ellen and she was told to wear the red and black dress Daphne loved her most in, and gold clips in her hair.

For Christmas she sent Ellen a very significant present – a little jewelled flag 'given to me by my Daddy when I was about twenty, and I used to wear it jauntily on the lapel of my coat'. Anything and everything given to her by Gerald was infinitely precious, so to bestow such a gift on Ellen was a real mark of love and respect. Fortunately, Ellen appreciated the nature of the gift – sent through the post in the most casual manner and entirely against English law – and was also aware of the value of the diamond, sapphire and ruby flag shaped in the emblem of the Royal Yacht Club. She took to wearing it all the time and cherished it, but in her letter of thanks said she wanted to return it to the du Maurier family on her death and would leave it to Flavia.

Ellen's reaction to Daphne's fantasies about her was to be half amused and half apprehensive. She valued Daphne's friendship deeply, finding her supportive and even wise when she talked to her of her troubles with Nelson, but she was careful, while reciprocating all the affection, to make sure Daphne understood that she herself could give only so much and no more. Ellen had no boy-in-a-box locked up inside her, nor did she wish to have bestowed upon her a boy's love. Taking the greatest care not to wound her new friend, and saying that she felt everyone had the right to love as their passions dictated without any kind of censure, she nevertheless stated quite flatly that if Daphne hoped for more than friendship she would never be able to give it. But she was happy enough to play the fantasy game, asking Daphne to choose who she would like to be if Ellen was to be Mary Stuart – 'I can only see you as Joan of Arc or Boadicea . . . [or] Elizabeth might do for you, in her lonely and ribald moments.'[7] She included all of Daphne's family in her affection, even Tommy, whose courtesy in writing to her to thank her for the care she had taken of his wife had charmed her. She thought Tommy sounded lovely and mentioned that in his letter he had seemed 'so discerning about you . . . a feeling of admiration, love and respect for you'.

This drew forth Daphne's contempt – 'My God, your description of his letter . . . is a hit below the belt. Love, yes, admiration, perhaps . . . but respect?'[8] Tommy knew nothing about her and neither did Ellen, and if they were to know what she had done there would be no respect. 'Do you and Tommy see me as a sort of gallant Mrs Miniver, propping up the White Cliffs of Dover?' Well, she was no such thing. What she deserved, in fact, was penal servitude for 'allowing a man to drink himself to the brink of insanity while his wife lost her youth because of it'. Out came everything about Puxley – though never given his real name, always referred to as John-Henry of Hungry Hill – and her awful guilt. Tommy, she added, knew less about her after fifteen years than Ellen did after five weeks. He was sweet and lovable but she couldn't talk to him. It didn't matter because now she had Ellen – 'Ellen, what have you done to me?'

She had 'a childish feeling' of wanting to send Ellen anything she wrote in the future, as an offering, 'like a child thrusting a bunch of daisies into its mother's hand'. And that was another thing: she found herself wondering what it would be like to be Ellen's daughter, even, at one point, carrying this other fantasy to the extreme lengths of imagining she might be the spirit of a child Ellen had miscarried. The significance of this was not lost on her and she did not pull back from it – 'How distressing if my desire to be with you . . . is merely a subconscious, thwarted longing to have sat on Mummy's lap at the age of two!' She laughed at the idea of 'what fun the psycho boys would have with me' before deciding 'to hell with psychoanalysis'. Yet at the same time she acknowledged to Ellen, as she never had to anyone else, how passionately she had longed for her mother's love and how completely she felt it to have been denied her. 'I don't want to cry pity about my own childhood but never, never did I have a glimmer of understanding from Mummy, never one touch of her hand . . . I can't remember *once* being held by her, feeling her arms round me, sitting on her lap. All I can remember, from the very beginning of time, is someone who looked at me with a sort of disapproving irritation, a queer unexplained hostility.' This resulted, she explained, in her extreme shyness – 'I became tongue-tied with shyness, and absolutely shut myself away, a dreamer of dreams' – and also in her longing for maternal love 'turning towards someone else at the age of eighteen'. The effect had been 'lasting and I think always will last'.[9] Even now, she confided to

Ellen, she had such violently angry dreams about her mother and in them nearly killed her. She advised Ellen to demonstrate her love for her children continually – 'give your whole heart, on an equal basis . . . one must never deny oneself to one's children, ever.' All memories of doing exactly this to Tessa and Flavia when they were young had been wiped out.

The letters between the two women flew backwards and forwards with the greatest regularity, often crossing with each other, so mutual was their need to write. Ellen's were mostly concerned with Nelson's illness, especially after it was finally discovered that he was suffering from lung cancer, and Daphne's with more and more fantasies about them being together either in Italy or alone at Menabilly. But gradually the fantasies gave way to an urge to write about Ellen and, gazing at the photograph in her bedroom, which she said had an hypnotic effect, she began to think of an artist painting Ellen's portrait and how such an artist – male, of course – would feel about her.

At the beginning of February 1948 she decided to write a play called *Mother* to be about a heavily disguised Ellen. 'In a fever of composition,' she wrote, 'I seized a notebook and pencil and began.'[10] Ellen was to tell nobody and she herself would 'be stretched on the rack, and drawn and quartered before I ever admitted such a thing'. She liked writing plays, she told Ellen, because it was so quick, and she indeed completed *Mother* in two weeks – 'almost Noël Coward' in speed. Nobody, she vowed, would ever guess that Stella, the mother of the title, was Ellen – it would be a secret between them. Also secret would be the knowledge that meeting Ellen had caused 'a revolution' in her own inner life. Since finding Ellen, she had become 'queerly light-hearted and free now', when previously she had felt all that was ever to happen in her life had happened and everything was static. Ellen was 'the sledgehammer' which had woken her.

All this made Ellen nervous – 'bursting with pride'[11] that she had inspired a play, on the one hand, but apprehensive about how she would be portrayed and how well Daphne would have disguised her identity. She insisted on being sent the script and was vastly relieved when she had read it. Daphne had done her job well – no one could possibly tell that this play, about a middle-aged woman whose artist son-in-law falls in love with her, was really about the playwright herself and Ellen Doubleday. The character of Stella was, as Daphne had told her, merely what Ellen might have been in an English setting and in a different set of circumstances. But, however deeply buried, there was a subtext to the play which contained Daphne's real thoughts on the nature of sexual love.

In the play, Stella and the son-in-law reach the point of almost going to bed together. The audience is left in doubt as to whether they actually do so, but in the next scene Stella has clearly rejected her son-in-law, who goes to America with her daughter, his wife. Ellen assumed they must have gone to bed, and said she would not have done so; but Daphne was indignant and replied that she had not intended any consummation. It all went to show, she said, that other people's minds were filthier than her own. But what it also went to show, though no one saw it, was that the playwright was as obsessed as she had always been with how much the sexual act mattered. When the son-in-law kisses Stella she says it is impossible for him to love her 'in that way'. This mystifies him – how can there be different ways if they are in love? – but she sticks to her firm belief that right and wrong exist and must be recognized. It is all right for them to kiss, to express love for each other, but the sexual act must be denied them: standards must be maintained. Ellen commented thoughtfully that while she saw very little of herself in the play, she saw a great deal of Daphne.

Daphne was more interested in a paragraph Ellen had cut out of her letter, and speculation as to what it had been about drove her, she wrote, into 'a state of erethism' (abnormal excitement). In the missing paragraph Ellen had said she had feared the play might have the same subject as *The Green Bay Tree*, a play which her husband Nelson had watched with Lady Asquith; halfway through Lady Asquith had proclaimed, 'Why, it's all about buggers!'[12] Ellen never did reveal to Daphne what she had imagined, which was wise – Daphne had lashed out once before at lesbians, alleging that she was certainly not one – 'nobody could be more bored with all the "L" people than I am.' These people, the infamous 'L' people, were nothing to do with what she was – 'I like to think my Jack-in-the-box was, and is, unique.'[13]

It gave her an enormous sense of satisfaction that those who became involved in the production of the play – Irene Hentschel and Binkie Beaumont – seemed to think either that it was about Carol Reed and his first wife, or that it was about Daphne's own mother, and even more satisfaction that 'every actress in London over the age of forty wants to play Stella'. Fay Compton, Peggy Ashcroft and Diana Wynyard were all in competition. She came to London to consult about casting and was taken by Tommy to have tea with Princess Elizabeth and Prince Philip. Ellen was enthralled by the description of the Princess as 'sweet but sort of shy', and Prince Philip as 'a menace' (attractive) except too fair and pale really to attract her seriously. Ellen, alias Rebecca, would have been, Daphne wrote, in her element, and there was even a hint that so, for once, had she been.

The only thing spoiling her new happiness was Christopher Puxley. His wife, she told Ellen, was in New Zealand and she had gone to see him, a furtive meeting which was a great mistake. He now looked like Nye Bevan, fat and fleshy, and swayed on his feet even before he had anything to drink at lunch. Once more she repeated that she had wrecked his life 'more completely than an atom bomb could', but that she had nothing but the most commonplace sympathy and pity left for him. She couldn't see in him any trace of the man she had loved, and refused to allow anyone who had so 'let themselves go' make love to her. Ellen had to understand that and think what she liked.

By now letters were beginning to frustrate Daphne – she wanted to *see* Ellen again, even if it would be a kind of torture. But she also had a genuine and compassionate desire to respond to Ellen's need for support at that time – she wanted to show the woman she loved that her feeling consisted of more than empty words, that she really would do anything to help and sustain her and that she could be solid and dependable however her fantasy letters sounded. Nelson was now extremely ill and had only a fifty-fifty chance of surviving the operation he was about to undergo. Daphne wanted to be at Ellen's side, in the hospital, to go through the bedside vigil with her, while Nelson's fate hung in the balance; and Ellen, for her part, sensing the strength in Daphne, wanted her there. It was a chance for Daphne to be the tender, faithful friend she so badly wanted to be, and for Ellen to acknowledge she had her own needs and was not as composed as she always seemed. So in March 1948, Daphne took the unprecedented step of suggesting to Tommy that they should both fly to America and visit the Doubledays. 'What have you done to me,' she joked to Ellen, 'to make me want to fly three-thousand miles just to look at you for a week?'

The two of them went in June, Tommy highly diverted by Ellen's arranging after the crisis was past (Nelson survived the operation) for Eisenhower to come to dinner. She quite fell for Tommy and he admired all her Rebecca qualities, as Daphne had known he would. But in spite of the thrill of seeing Ellen again, she felt 'very down' once back home. Helping Ellen, and even Nelson himself, had been a new and rare experience for her.[14] She had discovered qualities in herself which pleased and surprised her, qualities of patience and unselfishness which she had struggled to acquire during the war years and felt she had failed to learn. Sitting with the exhausted Ellen while she slept, and watching over her, had moved her deeply.

There was trouble over who should play Stella, with Gertrude Lawrence now replacing Fay Compton as favourite. She wished Ellen herself could star in it, but then decided that would be intolerable because she couldn't bear to see an actor kiss her. Her love for Ellen was greater than ever and what disturbed her was how much love she wanted still to *give*, not to receive. She was, she wrote, the recipient of so much love herself – Tommy's, her children's, even poor old Puxley's – but she was dreadfully aware that 'all I do is take'. To Ellen, she had wanted from the first to give, and now the feeling was all mixed up with wanting to create, as in writing – 'Kissing your hands is like writing a poem.' She worried that Ellen might hate to be told this and begged her that if she saw her as 'just one more Venetian [lesbian] wanting to make a pass' she must say so. If she did, Daphne would throw her into the Hudson River and then herself, because she refused 'to be classed with that gang'.[15]

Ellen, who had only then been told that her husband had not more than a year to live, and was desperately trying to make that time as good for him as she could, tried to explain her own emotional make-up to the passionate Daphne. She said she was shy in all relationships, but that this shyness which afflicted her had nothing to do with disliking 'Venetians' – it was just how she was, reserved and hesitant. Daphne seemed to accept this as a sign, as clear as Ellen was capable of making, that their friendship could continue, even if it was an unbalanced one. But, in fact, it was beginning to change after that visit; it was the arrival of Gertrude Lawrence in Daphne's life which began that subtle change.

Gertrude was, at first, 'that silly bitch Gertie'[16] who, after endless prevarication, had decided to accept the part of Stella. She arrived from her home in America to begin rehearsing at the end of September and immediately Daphne had to take three sleeping pills every night, because watching Gertie play Stella made her 'so jittery'. She hadn't realized, she told Ellen, 'how damned personal the play was' until she watched what Gertie made of Stella-who-was-Ellen. The play had become 'a travesty' because Gertie, instead of being Ellen, was 'a dyed-haired tart clinging to youthfulness', and it made her ill to watch. Gertie was kissing the son-in-law actor all wrong – the two of them were 'in a sort of clinch' and would end up any minute 'having each other's pants off', which made her rage.[17] She went home each night to Whitelands House, where she was staying with Tommy, quite distraught but unable to explain why. She was aware that she hardly spoke to him, though he was 'sweet and kind' and not only set the table and cooked food for them both but made sure there was a hot-water bottle in her bed. She felt like the hard-working husband while Tommy was the caring little wife she had never been. It occurred to her that maybe by having a career from the very beginning of her marriage she had upset the balance of it – it had given her 'a masculine approach to life' which perhaps had done her no good. Ellen, on the other hand, was 'the complete woman I never have been'.

Meanwhile, Tommy was having his own struggle and experiencing a feeling that he was past his best. When he took up his new job as Comptroller of Princess Elizabeth's household he was worried that he would be out of place, an old fogey among eager youth, and unable to keep up the pace demanded, particularly by the energetic young Prince Philip, the Duke of Edinburgh. He had written to his wife in February 1948 that he was 'struggling' in his attempts to organize Clarence House, but it was not a struggle anyone noticed – on the contrary, everything seemed to be done with the greatest of ease. The idea that 'Boy' Browning (which was how he was always known there) was finding his job a struggle and felt exhausted, never entered anyone's head. Nor did anyone find his age a disadvantage – in fact, Prince Philip thought it a positive asset, because Tommy was able to deal with some of the more elderly courtiers, many of whom had served in the army with him. Everyone was impressed by his efficiency and vitality, and his cheerfulness and charm made him immensely popular. Yet every night he was crawling home to the Whitelands House flat with barely the energy to eat, feeling depressed and low.

The flat itself was dismal. It was on the sixth floor of the block, overlooking the King's Road, and nothing had been done to it for a long time. There were three small bedrooms, a sitting-room, a tiny kitchen and a bathroom, but the decor and furnishings were shabby and the general atmosphere comfortless. There were few carpets, the floorboards squeaked, and the whole place smelled faintly of gas. For a man like Tommy, who liked elegance, it was a disappointing place to come home to, especially when Daphne had returned to Menabilly and he was once more on his own. It had not even been broached that Daphne might move permanently to London – already, it had simply become the *modus vivendi* that she lived in Cornwall, with brief trips to London, and he lived in London, travelling to Cornwall at weekends.

One of the first consequences of this was that Tommy became more dependent on alcohol, though never betraying any signs of it in his job. This tendency to drink too much was not new, nor was it unusual in men who had survived the war, especially if they had served in the Far East. He had noted his own increased intake before he returned home, telling Daphne in his letters that he was having 'too many gins in the evenings' and that he intended to cut down, but this proved difficult. He reported with regret that he 'needed his nips in the evening'. Just before he returned home he wrote miserably, 'I'm afraid my capacity for hard liquor has grown considerably ... four strong gins between 7 pm and dinner . . . a couple of glasses of white wine with my dinner . . . two whiskies before bed.' He vowed that when the strain of the war was over and he was no longer living in a hot climate his consumption would drop, but it didn't. Daphne, who was not censorious about such things, noted that he was drinking heavily, but she passed no judgement. She hated the way drink made him belligerent, but felt it was a battle Tommy had to fight himself. He tried, but knew he was not winning. His irritability after he had drunk a fair amount made weekends difficult. He would arrive on Friday night, very late, and spend Saturday pottering about happily in *Fanny Rosa*, but by Sunday afternoon, with the prospect of returning to London in front of him, not even alcohol could cheer him up. His depression at the thought of returning was so visible that Daphne began to call him 'Moper',[18] a name which stuck and was used by the whole family from then on. 'Boy' at Clarence House, alert, smiling, keen, became 'Moper' at Menabilly, lethargic, gloomy, and depressed a lot of the time. When 'Moper' left, Daphne felt a weight lift off the whole household.

Yet strangely enough she was getting on better with Tommy than she had done since his return from the war two years before. Her love for Ellen and her involvement in her play made her happy, and she was accordingly softer and gentler with Tommy. Several times that autumn of 1948 they went out in *Fanny Rosa* and, instead of resenting Tommy's dictatorial manner on board, she enjoyed herself. They sailed to the Fal, with Daphne steering most of the way, and anchored there 'and it was lovely'. She thought he had changed, that he had shed the persona he'd acquired during the war. So beguiling was the spell of the beautiful September weather that she even began to think of having another baby before it was too late; but, she told Ellen, it would be impossible because she was 'too embarrassed' to approach Tommy. She knew it was almost unbelievable but assured Ellen they could not talk about anything intimate.

This was why she had been so shocked when, during one of these pleasant outings on *Fanny Rosa*, Tommy suddenly said to her, 'Duckie, I want to discuss something very serious.' In her head at that moment she had been having a fantasy conversation with Ellen, and she pulled herself out of it with a start – 'Oh God, I thought at once, my conscience pricking me, he's going to ask me why . . . can't I be more affectionate, something too terribly embarrassing, and I got myself all set up for an intimate talk.' But the talk, when it did come from Tommy, who 'looked like a guilty schoolboy', was not in the least intimate, nor, in her opinion, the least serious. He told her he had a huge overdraft and couldn't pay his bills – 'he produced a little crumpled batch of bills from his pocket, and his bank statement.' It was 'so pathetic I could have wept' – but instead she burst out laughing, partly with relief. What if he had wanted to discuss their non-existent sex life? What if he had guessed about Ellen? She told him that she would clear his debts and pay some money into his bank account – 'It was exactly like giving Kits pocket money.' But once more she reflected on the possible damage her financial independence had done her marriage – 'I mean, really, women should not have careers. It's people like me who have careers who really have bitched up the old relationship between men and women. Women ought to be soft and gentle and dependent. Disembodied spirits like myself are all *wrong*.'[19]

But in practice she did not for one moment subscribe to her own belief. She was completely taken up with her play, which had changed its title from *Mother* to *September Tide*, and was going to Oxford for its opening to support the cast. In particular, she was supporting Gertie, for whom this play was 'now or never for herself'. Gertie, from being 'a silly bitch' and 'a dyed-haired tart', was beginning to fascinate her. 'I've broken down quite a few of Gertie's defences,' she told Ellen, 'not that she has many.' The glamour, Daphne had discovered, was hardly even skin-deep and, once past it, Gertie was a mere schoolgirl. She was 'utterly different' from Ellen, a person for whom one could have little respect, whereas Ellen inspired absolute respect – and, Daphne added, if she ever saw anyone not showing Ellen respect, 'I'd kill them.'

But if Gertrude did not inspire respect in the same way as Ellen did, she aroused Daphne's protective instinct. She examined the schedule for the pre-London opening anxiously, concerned that Gertie would be exhausted. 'I'm worried about that journey from

Blackpool to Leeds,' she wrote to Evie Williams, Gertie's secretary, 'because, looking at my Atlas, it seems a cross-country business with changes of train.' Gertie had a sore throat and Daphne wanted her to have a car, door-to-door, but 'knowing managements, I can make a pretty shrewd guess they won't produce one. This is something I would like to do for her ... but can you fix it without her knowing ... say it's the management or ... anyone ... but if she thought it was me she might think it bloody impertinent. But I just can't bear the thought of her hanging about draughty platforms on a wet Sunday ... let me know the cost and I'll send you a furtive cheque.'

Looking after Gertie during the play became an obsession, but Daphne was careful to conceal the extent to which she was trying to make things easy – she didn't want her to think she fussed. Gertie was almost ten years older than she was, but *she* felt the senior. Gertie, she felt, had an air of eternal youth about her, like Gerald, and she saw how the young identified with her. In Oxford, she joined the company for the opening and found herself swept along in the wake of the exuberant star. Kenneth Tynan gave a party for them in Magdalen College (charging ten shillings entry fee to eager undergraduates), and seeing Gertie in action was a revelation. It happened that Guy Symondson, Q's great-nephew, was at Trinity at the time, and after she had been to the party Daphne dropped him a note describing how 'at one stage Gertrude and I were hemmed in by a trio called Richard, Owen and John with a sort of outer ring beyond ... we were all getting ourselves dated up for a night in London – the one called R ... most attractive, said "Let's leave this place, go across to my digs, play soft music and turn lights down low" – Gertie would have gone but I was firm.' She insisted that Gertie must return with her to the Mitre and get some sleep before the next day. When that day dawned, Gertie was 'fresh as a daisy' but Daphne felt worn out and had a cracking headache.

Later, when she had observed Gertie for longer and in different circumstances, she saw that, again just like Gerald, she could suddenly 'turn into Lady Macbeth' and wallow in a depression which it was difficult 'to get her to snap out of'. Her mood-swings were violent and made Daphne feel calm and matronly. Gertie's gaiety she loved – 'gaiety is so damned important . . . the light-hearted tossing of responsibility aside, which is the only thing worth living for'[20] – but she was deeply sympathetic to this other 'down' side. Gertie hated to be alone as much as Daphne loved solitude, but this trait only reminded her all the more of Gerald and she was tolerant of it. Rather harder to accept was Gertie's love of fame, a very un-Gerald-like attribute and, of course, anathema to Daphne herself, but even then, so completely was she under Gertie's spell, she was prepared to be amused by it. When she took Gertie to lunch at the Savoy and the table she had booked was not prominent enough for the star to be noticed, she gracefully arranged for another – anything to keep Gertie happy. What she herself got out of all this was a feeling of exhilaration in Gertie's company – she was so magnetic, so unpredictable, and in her company Daphne felt lifted out of that dreary, stoical state into which she had allowed herself to slip ever since the end of the war.

One day, she walked into Gertie's dressing-room and found her standing there wearing only a bra and girdle. 'You look like the *Vie Parisienne*,' she told her. 'Put some clothes on or I'll smack your bottom.' Gertie was 'delighted' and made a funny face at her – 'talk about a playful kitten!'[21] Immediately, Daphne imagined walking into a room and finding Ellen similarly attired and knew she'd have turned and gone straight out again – 'feeling I'd done something terrible, like unveiling the Madonna'. It came to her in a flash, she told Ellen, that suddenly she could see the truth of something her father had tried to explain, which was 'the difference between the women men marry and the women they don't. God – but it's wonderful! Talk of inspiration, I see it, truly, and squarely . . . there's all the bloody difference . . . it's fundamental. You are the kind men marry. Gertrude is the kind they don't.'[22]

If this was not a clear indication of what was happening, what followed was clearer still. She said she'd like to discuss this difference with a mutual friend of theirs who had a dreary wife. 'To be blatantly vulgar,' she concluded, 'anyone with a spice of imagination would prefer a divan with Gertrude to a double-bed with her.' The comparison was obvious: she herself loved Ellen but there was no question of this love being requited 'in that way'.

But faced with Gertie she was aware of the boy-in-the-box beating furiously on the lid, screaming to be let out. Gertie was the kind men didn't marry but shared a divan with, and Daphne was becoming hopelessly attracted by her. But decades of pretending to be the person she was not had schooled her to control and conceal her emotions so perfectly that there was no danger of anyone guessing, least of all Gertie. Only Ellen, reading between the lines, could sense what might be happening, and she herself was so wretched, with her husband slowly dying, that she hardly had time or energy to notice it. Daphne was concerned for her and for poor Nelson himself and vowed she would now become, in Ellen's time of trouble, 'a kind of clear-thinking brother who holds your hand'. But at the same time Ellen was to remember 'You are the mother I always wanted.'[23]

Meanwhile, Gertie was neither mother nor sister. She was '*La* Lawrence . . . temperamental [who] wants me to dance attendance'. And Daphne danced.

Chapter Fifteen

September Tide ran in London until the beginning of August 1949, giving Daphne ample opportunity to get to know Gertie better and to become as infatuated with her as she was with Ellen, though in a quite different way. If part of the attraction Ellen held for her was to do with wishing she were her daughter (though a daughter who would have liked an intimate relationship of another kind), part of the attraction Gertie exerted was to do with Daphne wanting to be *her* mother. From the moment Gertie had arrived to begin rehearsing the play the previous September, Daphne had fussed and fretted over her health and welfare in a thoroughly maternal way. She worried in her letters to Evie Williams, Gertie's English secretary, about the star being tired, having a cold and not being cosseted enough. She continued to do a great deal of cosseting herself, endlessly arranging cars for Gertie when the management would not, and seeing that all the tributes to stardom Gertie had been used to – flowers in her dressing-room, flowers in her hotel bedroom, champagne after the show – went on being readily available. She saw that, whatever her outward demeanour, Gertie lacked confidence and needed constant reassurance, which it became Daphne's role to give her.

But there was more to Daphne's obsession with Gertrude Lawrence than merely being attracted to her exuberant personality or wanting to take care of her. Watching her play Stella, hearing her speak the lines written for Stella with Ellen in mind, many of them poignant and emotional because of Daphne's feelings for Ellen, was a deeply unsettling experience. Daphne stressed again and again to Ellen how *unlike* her Gertie was, so much so that at first she found it almost offensive that Gertie should attempt, in the guise of Stella, to play Ellen at all. But as rehearsals went on,

Gertie began sometimes to catch the spirit of the part, and then Daphne felt confused and disturbed. A dangerous transition seemed to be taking place – Gertie, on stage, could become Ellen for minutes at a time. Daphne found herself staring at a fantasy love-affair on stage which she had created, and the actress embodying her fantasy became confused with the woman who had inspired the role. Inwardly, Daphne was moved by Gertie on stage while outwardly, off stage, she went on telling Evie Williams she simply wanted to look after her.

It was a role which she assumed at first with some amusement, constantly remarking in her letters to Ellen that she could see right through Gertie. She knew perfectly well that the star gave 'everyone hell' backstage, but 'cooed like a dove' should Daphne come to see her in the play. Then her acting was impeccable, but when the author was not present it disintegrated sometimes into near farce or went over the top into melodramatic tragedy. Daphne decided that Gertie was 'fundamentally lonely' and by no means as happily married as she professed. She also thought Gertie would 'never be adult, which is why I find her so fascinating'. She told Ellen she got 'a lot of fun out of spoiling Gertie' and part of the fun was in allowing herself to be swept along in Gertie's wake and sharing her social life. She let Gertie take her to lunches with Noël Coward and even went with her to Noël's house near Dover to spend the day with him and his friends. She was amazed at how much she enjoyed it all – the endless repartee, the laughter, the whole slightly risqué atmosphere she remembered from her father's day. It was easy to be amusing in return, to sit back and drink and smoke, and swop anecdotes with these lively, clever people, and she now came up from Cornwall to London with remarkable frequency.

This was pleasant for Tommy because, apart from having his wife with him, it meant she was available to accompany him to royal functions. She enjoyed some of these occasions more than she normally cared to admit, describing to Ellen how the sight of the Queen dancing in a crinoline at a ball had been 'quite beautiful', and the whole occasion 'a lovely sight, women in tiaras and glittering gowns'. She herself had 'my little diamond coronet affair pinned on the side of my head and Tommy's Indian Stars across the bosom' and was wearing the kind of dress she never wore – 'off-the-shoulder . . . a sort of dusky pink, with clinging folds' – and knew perfectly well that she looked stunning. Gertie had made her 'borrow the frock from Molyneux', the smart dress designer of the era. The idea of trading on her name and her royal connections to *borrow* a dress to wear at a Buckingham Palace ball had never entered Daphne's head, and she was half appalled at the idea. But the bold Gertie had told her not to be naïve – Molyneux would be glad to oblige, knowing who the dress was for and where it was to be worn – and marched her off to the couturier's herself. She also chose the dress, scorning Daphne's own preference for either a simple white or blue gown which revealed nothing. Once she saw the transformation in her appearance, Daphne appreciated at once what Gertie could do for her, though not, at that stage, as much as Ellen could.

What both women had done for her, apart from enriching her personal life, was to inspire her to write. Almost as soon as *September Tide* was safely launched Daphne was busy writing a new novel which had arisen out of her recent involvement with the theatre and actors. In spite of whirling about with Gertrude and attending social functions with Tommy, she got down to *The Parasites* in February 1949. This was the first book she wrote in a wooden hut which she had had erected in the grounds of Menabilly, well away from the house. The roof of the house was being mended and this caused such loud and constant noise that she found she was distracted. 'It is ideal,' she wrote to Ellen, 'it's at the end of the stretch of grass here, that looks down at the far end at the sea . . . curiously enough, it's just a few yards from the place I've wanted always for my grave.' She shut herself up to write for so many hours a day (six, in three sessions) that she couldn't sleep because she didn't get enough exercise – 'my mind gets too awake . . . I have to resort to red pills which never make me wake up fresh.'[1] Yet *The Parasites* was one of the easiest novels she ever wrote and, unlike all the others, written without any detailed preparation. 'The whole thing', Daphne wrote to her editor at Gollancz, Sheila Bush, 'was rather drawn from the subconscious spread with fiction, and when one lets oneself go like that it's quite often a purge for the author but a headache and nuisance to everyone else.' What she was purging herself of was guilt about what she had allowed to happen in her life.

In the novel she took on the persona of all three main characters, who were created to represent different facets of herself. Maria, Niall and Celia, 'the three people I know myself to have been', are the children of 'those dreadful Delaneys', a stage couple. It is a contemporary story of a theatrical family, full of stage atmosphere and freely admitted to be highly reminiscent of Daphne's own background. Maria is an actress, Niall a popular composer, Celia an artist and they are all accused by Charles, Maria's husband, of living in a world of fantasy and of being parasites. The story is told in a complicated way, alternating between past and present and between first-person narration and third-person description, so that often it is extremely confusing – nothing could have been further removed from Daphne's usual style. But what begins to dominate the novel quite early on is the relationship between Maria and Niall, who are actually stepbrother and sister, and their love for their father, who is closely modelled on Gerald du Maurier. Papa Delaney cries a good deal and says 'You're all going to leave me one by one' and is furious when Maria is kissed. His marriage, Maria observes, may not be as happy as everyone thinks – 'adoring a person doesn't mean you're happy' – and fairly soon his wife is killed off (just as the wife and mother in *The Progress of Julius* is disposed of).

Maria's own marriage to the boringly dutiful Charles is also suspect and here Daphne purged herself of many of those feelings which had already gone into her two plays. Her husband, Maria suspects, only 'loves the idea he once had of me' and doesn't really know 'the closed shell' that is her mind. She thinks he got her character 'wrong from the start' and has never realized 'she's a chameleon'. The 'tragedy of life', she sees, is not that people one loves die but that 'they die to *you*'. She knows she should not have married, nor should she have had children, because she knows too that she hasn't loved them enough. But the thought of giving Charles the divorce he wants angers her – 'the part of an injured wife was one she had never played'. It becomes vitally important that if Charles does divorce her (she has been unfaithful) 'nobody must know that I feel anything, that I mind'. She knows 'he does to me the thing I have done to others' and sees herself as being punished – 'he makes me look a fool . . . it serves me right'. Meanwhile, Niall, whom she really loves, sails out to sea and deliberately sinks his boat, which if, as Daphne claimed, Niall was only a facet of herself, means that a kind of suicide of some part of her takes place.

What is interesting and different about *The Parasites*, apart from the autobiographical element, is its humour. Daphne was certainly not thought of as a witty writer, though in her own life she more often made people laugh than anything else, and relished the absurd, but in this novel she showed she was perfectly capable of satire and even slapstick. There is a scene in which the Delaneys have a country house weekend in which the father behaves insultingly and a farcical situation develops, and here Daphne displays a talent for humorous writing not visible anywhere else in her work. She laughed while writing much of it and enjoyed highlighting the ridiculous. But for du Maurier enthusiasts at the time it was a difficult novel to accept. Where was the mystery, the exciting plot, the feeling for landscape which they had come to expect? Why was it so complicated? Where was the simplicity of style they looked for? She herself agreed 'a lot of that book is a strange mix-up of the things and feelings I went through . . .' and was rather amused by what she described as 'a sort of embarrassment' she felt about it. But in spite of this feeling that *The Parasites* was perhaps more revealing than she had intended, she had no large ambitions for it – the critics this time would not be able to disappoint her in the way they had over *Hungry Hill* and *The King's General*.

This was just as well because the reviews when they came were 'dingy' and she felt she had let Victor down. He had adored the novel and not only printed 100,000 copies, but assured her it was her best book yet 'with a real chance of permanent survival'. His fury with the harshest of the reviews, by John Betjeman, went into a letter marked 'not sent'. He wrote to Betjeman, in defence of Daphne, that never in twenty-seven years of publishing had he ever complained to a reviewer, but his review in the *Daily Herald* was inexcusable. He didn't object to Betjeman's right to say he didn't like *The Parasites* – 'all your colleagues agree with your estimate' – but some facts were wrong. He had picked out 'harmless sentences as dull and obvious' yet his own first paragraph had been 'a piece of intellectual dullness'. It was 'stupid' to suggest Daphne wrote 'to titillate the public and secure sales . . . at this point my gorge rose . . . it is *bloody* rubbish to suggest Daphne senses the public mood and adapts to it accordingly.' With such a publisher as a champion it is no wonder Daphne felt she needed no other defender.

Her own attitude to the critical reception of her books nevertheless hardened from this time onwards. Never again was she going to leave herself vulnerable to scathing reviews and the dejection which came from not living up to high expectations. But more dangerously, a paranoid edge began to creep into her reactions to the way in which her novels were received – she was coming to believe that, as 'Q' had unwisely encouraged her to think, she never would be forgiven for being a bestseller: the critics had it in for her and that was that. This became a protective device in the most obvious way and she clung to it. But as far as *The Parasites* went, she was bound to admit that nobody except her publisher and Gertrude Lawrence really seemed enthusiastic.

During the writing of *The Parasites*, in the spring of 1949, her epistolary friendship with Ellen deepened all the time, and even though they addressed serious matters and profound issues, there was always an underlying humour and even gaiety about their letters. This, more than anything, was what Ellen and all her family appreciated most about Daphne – not just her interest in them and concern for them, but her ability to see humour in almost every situation, often at her own expense, without being heedlessly flippant. She liked to tell Ellen amusing anecdotes about Gertie, such as relating how Gertie had been invited for lunch with George Bernard Shaw and was in a panic as to how she should behave. 'He was a man of routine, she understood, and went to bed every day at two o'clock. "Go upstairs with him," I told her, "and he'll live till 99." Trills of girlish laughter and coos of delight . . .'[2] Then there was the great interest in each other's children she and Ellen had. They swapped concern and stories about them in affectionate, gossipy letters. In a way Gertie was at first like another teenager and Daphne could feel herself being influenced by her. But Gertie knew more than any teenager did. Once, Daphne had corresponded with Ellen about one of Ellen's daughters, to whom she herself also wrote – as she did to all Ellen's family – and had become fascinated by the young girl's reported references to the difference between 'necking' and 'petting'. She wrote that she'd asked Gertie to clear up the mystery, and when Gertie had made the distinction, in a few succinct words, she'd asked which she indulged in herself. Gertie was scornful – 'she said she did not do either, she preferred doing what happened naturally.' Daphne was not disposed to press on with this conversation, but speculated that she 'took this to mean honest-to-God-between-the-sheets, as my Daddy would have called it. Such a good expression, I always think.' Soon after her enlightening chat, a postcard arrived from Gertie:

> Women are like geography:
> From 16 to 22, like Africa – part virgin, part explored.
> From 23 to 35, like Asia – hot and mysterious.
> From 35 to 45, like the USA – high-toned and technical.
> From 46 to 55, like Europe – quite devastated but interesting in places.
> From 60 upwards like Australia – everybody knows about it, but no one wants to go there.

Daphne thought this very funny, and enjoyed pointing out to Ellen that while she was 'in the devastated class', Daphne herself was 'still high-toned and technical'.[3]

But, however high-toned, she had nobody with whom to be technical. She was still obsessed with Ellen, telling her how she dreamed about her almost every night. But by the summer of 1949 she found photographs, telephone calls and letters not enough – she wanted to be with Ellen and proposed, at the end of May, coming to Barberrys for a whole month on her own if Ellen would not come to her. She also knew – 'my radar tells me' – that Ellen was once more in great need of support. Nelson had died in January,[4] which marked the end of a heartbreaking year for her, during which she had strained every nerve to make his last months happy, and also the end of a powerful partnership. Ellen suffered and Daphne, sensing her suffering, wanted not only to write letters of consolation – which she did, letters full of tenderness and touchingly expressed distress for her – but to be with her, able to put her arms round her and shelter her.

In June, Daphne did indeed go to her, in a state of great excitement – 'terribly and deeply happy about coming'. The visit was only a qualified success. 'I suppose I did come and stay a month?' Daphne wrote afterwards. It had all been 'like a dream' and not always a pleasant one. There had been too many people around Ellen, making calls on her time, and Daphne, ever possessive, had not had her to herself enough. What she wanted was to go to Italy with Ellen, just the two of them, maybe to Florence, where she need share her with no one and they could be really alone.

Ellen, although professing eagerness, stalled throughout the rest of the summer, writing that she felt lethargic and didn't think she could make the trip until the winter. This displeased Daphne, though she was perfectly sympathetic towards Ellen's 'battle fatigue' after the hard year she had had, and she became increasingly restless. Gertie had gone back to America, which made Daphne still more frustrated – all the fun she had been having stopped abruptly. Nor did she have any work on hand, because she had finished her new novel, *The Parasites*, before she went to visit Ellen and had no other ideas. Her days were taken up with sunbathing and swimming – she announced she was developing such muscles she would soon look like a Channel swimmer – and trying to be nice to Tommy when he came down to Cornwall. Ellen had ordered her to do so, instructing her to walk straight up to him and give him a big kiss when she landed after her return flight from America. She had been determined to try to follow this advice, since she felt permanently guilty about her husband, but at the airport Kits, wearing his first pair of long trousers, had walked boldly past the barrier and kissed her first. She was so thrilled she forgot about Tommy. 'It shows', she remarked, admiringly, to Ellen, 'how he is going to attack life and women – that's why Daddy had such a good time.'[5]

She tried hard, that summer, to have a good time with her own family, while yearning partly for Ellen and partly for Gertie, without whom she now felt incomplete. There were many times when she appeared to succeed. This was the summer of *South Pacific* and Tommy brought records of the show's songs down to Menabilly. Daphne loved them – she and Kits danced to them while Tommy played his drum and the girls sang. At times like this she felt she had succeeded in creating a happy family, describing to Ellen what fun these sessions were and how hilarious it was to see Kits 'whirling around looking like Nijinsky with his long hair, singing: "I'm in love, I'm in love . . ." '⁶ She was light-hearted and carefree at such moments, and again jogging round the countryside in a trap pulled by Flavia's pony, or on the boat *Fanny Rosa* (so long as Tommy was not being bossy). There were picnics and long walks, and endless hours sitting cross-legged on the lawn, chatting the day away with whoever was there. Prince Philip came down for some sailing and, though she fretted as usual about the responsibility of being hostess, she clearly enjoyed his company and thought the visit 'a terrific crumb' (boast). What everyone saw was a very attractive woman looking younger than her forty-two years, tanned, blonde, always laughing, with her eyes as well as her mouth, someone confident and at ease with herself, in the prime of life.

It was a false picture. Her frustration by the end of August was raging and when Ellen once more put off the trip to Italy, which they had both been planning for a year, she announced that she felt 'suicidal'. It gave her a kind of grim pleasure that no one could possibly guess – 'I am so used to hiding my real feelings.' It was, she wrote to Ellen, 'a hell of a blow, beloved',⁷ but she tried to understand the reasons, and encouraged Ellen to try to explain how she felt. Then Ellen confessed that, apart from the lethargy which had overtaken her after the emotional exhaustion of the last year, she also felt that to go to Italy with Daphne would be 'just running away and escaping'. She thought she should stay at home 'and pick up the pieces', but at the same time was anxious that Daphne should know that if *her* need to get away was urgent, then she would come. In reply, Daphne wrote a spirited send-up of an International Bureau of Advice letter which Ellen and her whole family thought so funny that it changed Ellen's mind. She decided that being with Daphne, receiving from her what she once called 'the oxygen of laughter', would revive her more than anything in the world.

But Daphne had been genuinely angry with Ellen, all the same – 'You will never know the state of rage and fury I have been in for the past fortnight' – and her anger exploded when Ellen was tactless enough to say in one letter that she had felt guilty about not having written sooner. 'Christ, who do you think I am?' wrote back Daphne. 'Do you think I have no pride?'[8] She hated to feel Ellen was in any way patronizing or indulging her, and even more that Ellen was clearly not as desperate to go on holiday with Daphne as Daphne was for her to come. But a promise was finally made that Ellen would come at the end of September, which tided her over the desolation of Kits at last going away to prep school.

She had always accepted that, although it was all right for daughters to be educated at home, sons must follow the traditional path. But she dreaded Kits following it – 'What shall I do without him?' she wrote and then added that she knew she *must* do without him because it wasn't good for a boy to be so dependent on his mother. She had, too, a deep-seated fear that by her excessive adoration of him she might 'turn him into a homo', as she put it, whereas she wanted him to be a ladies' man like Gerald. She relished the thought of him breaking women's hearts in a few years and commented once in a letter to Ferdy that 'he kisses divinely, just like Gerald'. Her love for Kit was so intense that if anything happened to him she was distraught, whereas if anything happened to the girls she was sympathetic but cool and largely unmoved.

The holiday with Ellen, soon after Kits left for West Downs, was a disaster. The two of them met in Paris, then went on to Florence. Instead of bringing them closer, being alone together in a foreign country simply revealed how unalike they were. Daphne liked to walk everywhere, loved hanging out in 'honky' (vulgar) bars, hated shopping and loathed talking to anyone else in the hotels in which they stayed. Ellen, on the other hand, hated walking, liked discreet, sophisticated restaurants, liked to shop and was interested by her fellow guests. But worst of all was Daphne's failure to win Ellen over to any kind of real intimacy. Although Ellen could not have made it plainer that she had not a

'Venetian' feeling in her body, Daphne had always hoped that, when they were truly alone, her love for Ellen would be reciprocated in some tangible form. All she received from Ellen was the endurance of 'one kiss which lasted about forty seconds'.

The interchange of letters after they had parted and Ellen had returned to New York showed a new and bitter Daphne (though, as ever, the bitterness was leavened with humour – there was always a funny side for her). She called these frank letters 'brandy and gin letters', admitting she only had the nerve to write them because she was 'under the influence of a stiff drink'. In one of them, she replied to what she described as two wounding accusations Ellen had made – one, that she lacked perception, and two, that 'I lack humour in your presence'. These were the two qualities in which Daphne most prided herself and which she thought Ellen had valued most in her, and of the two the alleged lack of humour stung most. 'As a matter of fact,' she replied, 'I am shaking with silent laughter most of the time, but you are probably not aware of it. The greatest heaven in the world is when two people can laugh together. We have got near to it at times. Not near enough. Besides, my sense of humour is rather warped. Almost the highest peak was reached when you sat on the side of your bed in Florence, with tears running down your face, saying, "Maybe if I changed my hormones I'd feel different." It was so goddamn funny that when I think about it now, in the middle of the night, I become hysterical.'[9]

In another letter, replying to Ellen's complaint when they parted that she couldn't smoke on board the returning ship because cigarettes were all 'in bond' and therefore unobtainable, Daphne told her quite viciously to 'try loving someone who has been in bond two years and is likely to remain so for another twenty'. She didn't know what this might drive her to – 'What happens to the waters of the Arno that are pent up behind a dam and can't get to the sea they crave?'[10] A madhouse or a monastery was the only solution, though in her darkest moments she fantasized about drinking a whole bottle of brandy and going down to the Place Pigalle to pick up a prostitute then shooting herself afterwards – 'Because I would be so revolted by myself. Being fastidious. Which I am.'[11] As soon as she'd written this letter she followed it with a letter of apology and, by good luck, Ellen got the second letter first. But she was still angry with Daphne and took the chance to reiterate what she had said from the beginning of their friendship: she had nothing against 'Venetians' but she was not so inclined herself and insisted on living her life how she wanted to, without being made to feel guilty because she was thwarting Daphne.

This plunged Daphne into a state of depression, though she accepted Ellen's ultimatum. The 'autumn glooms', which always made her melancholy, were particularly bad that year. It seemed to her that, ever since meeting Ellen, she had become 'more and more what you do not want'. It upset her to think how 'blundering and hopeless' she had been, she who was 'king of advisers and rather good at it' to others. She felt she had made a mess of her relationship with Ellen and become a burden to her. Ellen was swift to deny this and to emphasize that Daphne had been a rock during two of the hardest years of her life, a friend without parallel whom she, and her whole family, valued beyond all others. Some kind of equilibrium was restored but not entirely to Daphne's satisfaction – something had gone out of her feeling for Ellen since their holiday.

She could not help but contrast Ellen's affection for her with the far more urgent and freely expressed need of Gertrude Lawrence. Gertie was writing her 'ecstatic letters' about *The Parasites* – she wanted to play Maria in a stage or film version – and begging her to come and have fun with her in Florida. There was no intellectual exchange of ideas in any correspondence with Gertie, as there was with Ellen, nor even the same intelligent, clever teasing, but Gertie's letters were slapdash and funny and appealing, and when she read them Daphne found herself less lonely.

It was, she realized, a strange kind of loneliness from which she sometimes suffered – not the loneliness which comes from having 'loved but lost' but rather from 'feeling the loneliness of a loved one never known'.[12] She felt there was an experience of loving and being loved that she had never attained, and it had nothing to do with sex. It was to do with being perfectly in tune with someone, which might involve the body, it was true, but was more to do with the fusing of mind and spirit. 'You will say I get this with my husband,' she wrote to Ellen, but she did not. 'I *don't* want a man . . . waiting for me . . . because that would not be the answer . . . nothing is more amusing than to have fun with glamorous or menacing men, but that's a diversion, it's not home . . .' So what was 'home'? It was 'a kind of peace', a peace she recognized, from his letters[13] (which she was at that time reading), that her grandfather George du Maurier had found with his wife and even Gerald with Muriel, in spite of apparent evidence to the contrary; but she had never found it. She felt she had tried, with Tommy, but had failed, and now she had 'gone back to nature'. It was her belief that 'what is strongest in you comes out in the middle years'.[14] She couldn't help wondering if 'other writers, or artists have felt the same, women, I mean'. Mixed up with her theories about reverting to nature was the conviction she had expressed to Ellen before – that in being so career-minded she had somehow gone *against* nature and reaped the consequences. 'I think one has to choose, you know. Either to create after one's fashion, or be a woman and breed. The two don't go together and never will. Maybe there should be a rule against women who work marrying. They can't have it both ways.'[15]

Ellen was rightly worried by Daphne's increasingly distorted view of her life and tried to console and put an alternative, more attractive hypothesis forward. But what saved her friend was what had always saved and rescued her: the very work she saw as fatal to her human relationships. In Florence, Daphne had felt the first faint stirrings of a novel about a woman, a widow like Ellen, who would have many of Ellen's characteristics and even look like her: the point of the novel would be that this woman was the source of great torment to others. She made it plain to Ellen that she was the inspiration for the heroine, just as she had been for Stella in *September Tide*, and this would be another secret between them. 'I may add,' she wrote, 'the woman will be a widow. And I don't want a libel case on my hands.'[16] By the summer of 1950 she was 'brewing hard' about the woman, whom she had decided to call Rachel – 'a cold-blooded bitch' – and by the autumn had the novel all planned out in a notebook. But before she began to write, she paid another visit to New York, in November, this time to see Gertie as well as Ellen – Gertie, who had written 'hectic' letters and longed for her to come down to Florida and bask in the sun with her.

Daphne was well aware – she was *always* well aware – of exactly what she was doing, but so was Ellen. No matter how deep their mutual regard for each other, neither of them could pretend there was anything but a limited future to the development of their friendship. Daphne's need for something else was painfully evident and, though she visited Ellen first, it was to Gertie that she was increasingly drawn. She feared Ellen would be jealous – and if she were, a postcard[17] from Gertie thanking Ellen for 'loaning Daphne to me' did not help – but she could not stop herself. She was drawn to Gertie like 'an alcoholic and must get to the bottle or bust'. In Florida, in the sun, she and Gertie were 'like two silly schoolgirls', playing games in the sea, cavorting on the beach, laughing and shrieking and losing all inhibitions. Gertie, unlike Ellen, was not inhibited about any kind of sex. Never for one moment did Daphne think of her as one of the despised 'L' people; she regarded her as simply able to respond to every kind of love. Later, she was to lay responsibility for what had happened at Ellen's door: if she had never met Ellen she would never have written *September Tide*, and Gertrude Lawrence would never have come into her life. But this train of thought went further: if Ellen had not shut her out – 'if there had been no iron curtain between us' – then she would 'never have left Barberrys, so it was just as well for the Browning family you fenced yourself in'.[18]

She could hardly tear herself away from Gertie to return to the Browning family but, having done so, she plunged herself immediately into the writing of *My Cousin Rachel*. Even though it was bitterly cold, she went to her hut at 10.15 each morning from the middle of January onwards, wrote until 1.15, broke until 3.15 and then continued to 7.15. She had an oil stove and an oil lamp in the flimsy hut, through which the wind whistled all day long, and she wore two sweaters, a sheepskin waistcoat and had a rug over her knees. Every now and again she drank black coffee from a thermos.

Her story was about jealousy and unfounded suspicions, and she told Ferdy it was going to be 'rather sinister and a bit creepy and you will never really know whether the woman is an angel or a devil'. She first wrote a complete draft in pencil in a small red account book. The first few pages, which she wrote out in full, came to her in a rush, then she made notes for another twenty-three chapters, outlining the plot and experimenting with bits of dialogue. These went into the final version almost intact, though expanded, and the new writing was devoted to the interior monologue of the narrator, Philip, the counterpart to the heroine of *Rebecca*. She was excited from the beginning, knowing she had a good plot and that the sense of atmosphere with which she had made her name was powerfully present. This time, she wanted to explore jealousy from the man's angle, and to show how simple it is for a woman to manipulate a man. Technically, Rachel is yet another female victim – after all, she loses her husband, loses Philip and in the end loses her life – but she is really the stronger of the two. Philip is driven almost to madness by her and not for a second does he dominate her.

As usual, Daphne worked hard at concocting a thrilling plot, wanting readers to be in suspense right up to and including the end, but buried in this complicated tale was the same fascination with what jealousy could do to people as there had been in *Rebecca*. The difference is that this time a man is jealous and 'a man's jealousy is like a child's' says Rachel – open, obvious, easily dealt with. He is 'ridiculous . . . like a sulky schoolboy' and so is his interpretation of what making love means. When she lets him make love to her, one night only, after he has presented her not just with the family jewels but with a document making over his estate to her when he dies, he sees this as 'a pledge of love' meaning she will marry him. She sees it as nothing of the sort: it was simply a thank-you and had no other significance. Philip's innocence, his naïvety and his sense of honour seem absurd to her. Implicit in this is her belief that all men are absurd, always making so much of a simple bodily transaction. Whereas Philip wonders 'what can be worse' than infidelity, to Rachel that kind of infidelity is nothing.

By April 1951 Daphne had finished the novel and immediately planned to return to Gertie, who had been writing her 'mournful' letters. She had also sent snaps of the two of them in Florida 'with incriminating things on the back'. She didn't tell Ellen what these were, but reported that Tommy had looked at the snaps and been very silent afterwards. In July, once *My Cousin Rachel* was in production – with Victor Gollancz ecstatic, recognizing that this was 'du Maurier bang on form' and another bestseller assured – she went to America again, this time mainly to see Gertie.

The situation between Ellen and Daphne was now delicate. Ellen was annoyed by Daphne's relish for conspiring and plotting unnecessarily. For example, Daphne wrote, in June, saying she wanted to come to Barberrys without Gertrude, but didn't want to admit this to Gertie. Would Ellen ring her up and say the house was going to be full up and Daphne would have to sleep on a sofa, so it would be better if Gertrude came later . . . ?[19] Ellen knocked this scenario on the head immediately and told Daphne sharply not to start creating dramas. This passion of hers for 'keeping people in compartments' was absurd – there was absolutely no reason why they could not all be together in a perfectly civilized way.[20] If Daphne couldn't bear this and decided not to come at all, then Ellen would be hurt, but she was not going to pander to Daphne's whim. So Daphne was obliged to go to Ellen's with Gertrude and didn't enjoy this situation at all – not that Ellen saw the situation as such. Daphne could not help contrasting Gertie with Ellen, or observing Gertie through Ellen's eyes. In some ways it was a relief to return home.

But once at home, she was discontented. Tommy was 'in a stinking mood' with her and she was horrible to him in return – so horrible that her children had for once taken his part and urged her to be nicer to him. Instead, she consoled herself with a younger man, called Frank Price, whom she had met at Ellen's and then again in Paris. Frank worked for Doubleday, and was charming, clever and fun. He looked, according to Daphne, a bit like Danny Kaye, but also slightly as she imagined ten-year-old Kits would look when grown up. But what had really drawn her closer to Frank, even before her visit to Gertie in Florida, was the discovery that he too was attracted to both sexes – 'We both freely admitted to each other mutual Venetian tendencies.'[21] This made her feel safe and comfortable with Frank and she encouraged him to kiss her 'on the roof of the *Tour d'Argent* in front of all Paris'. She admitted to an alarmed Ellen – alarmed at what this would do to

'Frank's already outsize ego'[22] – that from kissing 'we advanced somewhat further'. But to Ferdy, remembering her reaction over Carol Reed, she wrote that her behaviour with Frank had been 'quite correct' and he was just a 'someone' whom it was 'fun to go around with . . . harmless and intelligent'. Now, back from New York and missing Gertie, she had Frank to stay while Tommy was in London. They 'lay on the sofa until 2 am and kissed' – and she didn't care a bit if Tommy suspected anything – there was 'no harm in it' and she was always careful to behave if the children were around. The thought of Frank boasting and starting gossip did not perturb her – she knew there was gossip about her anyway.

When Frank left, she felt she was 'in a vacuum'. She found herself thinking over the good time she had had with Gertie and the fun with Frank, and wrote to Ellen that she would like to hear an argument, really well put, between two scientists on the merits of 'Cairo' (men and women) versus 'Venice'. She thought that 'Venice' would win for her, because she felt much more confident and assured, as though she were a pilot in an aircraft.[23] It disturbed her to acknowledge this – 'Oh God, I don't know' – and she was back to crying, 'truly, truly I should have been born a boy. Don't you think?' But all the same, preferring 'Venice' to 'Cairo' did not make 'Cairo' necessarily repugnant: she told Ellen, with what reads like a show of bravado, 'I seem to have fun either way.' She then made a veiled allusion to Ellen's possibly having thought, wrongly, that she was interested in another woman, apart from Gertrude. She wanted Ellen to know it was not true. Ellen was irritated that Daphne could imagine it mattered either way and told her to 'get this Venetian chip off your shoulder', while reminding her that she could 'go to Venice with whoever she pleased'[24] with her blessing. Daphne was outraged by this and replied, 'I glory in my Venice, when I am in a Venice mood, and forget about it when I am not. The only chip is the dreary knowledge that there can never be Venice with you.'[25]

Nor was there any with anyone else for the next few months, though these were happy ones on the surface. *My Cousin Rachel*, published in July 1951, was a tremendous success. So far as readers and publishers were concerned, this was the Daphne du Maurier they wanted, bang on form. Victor's first print-run was the largest ever: 125,000 copies – but even that was not enough. This was, in the first year, a bigger run-away bestseller than *Rebecca* had been in a comparable period – *My Cousin Rachel* was reprinting to the tune of 25,000 copies within three months. Even the critics (with the exception of Marghanita Laski, who upbraided the author for her bad grammar) applauded. Daphne had gone off to New York again and wrote defensively to Victor: 'If anyone gives me a good review let me know.' When Victor passed on all the excellent reviews, she was amazed, especially by the *Guardian* – '. . . it is in the same category as *Rebecca* . . . but is an even more consummate piece of story-telling' – but determined to be cautious. 'Many thanks for the reviews,' she wrote, '. . . but I never will be a critic's favourite.' She was not going to let her defences down again.

In her own life she was busy building them up even higher too. She had another meeting with Frank, this time in London, and she derived some curious satisfaction from feeling she had put him in his place. They had had lunch and were walking through Mayfair hand in hand when Daphne suddenly saw Carol Reed. ' "Oh!" I said, "there's Carol. I must go after him." "What do you mean," said Frank, "you can't leave me like this." "I can and I will," I answered, "see you in Paris sometime," and without a backward glance I *ran* about twenty yards . . . after Carol and tapped him on the shoulder. "Daph, darling," he said, and holding hands we walked away together . . . and spent the whole afternoon . . . having a wonderful heart-to-heart. Frank flew back to Paris but on what sort of hard chair I don't know.'[26] Nor, as she made plain to Ellen, did she care. She even encouraged Ellen to tell this story to those in the Doubleday office in New York, because she knew they would relish it. 'I guess it's the first time he's been left flat, standing in the street.'

It was this side of Daphne – the spontaneous, the slightly cruel, the outrageous – which came to the fore that winter while she wrote a new collection of short stories which were a completely new departure. These were strange, morbid stories, in which deep undercurrents of resentment and even hatred revealed far more about Daphne's inner fantasy life than any novel had ever done. ('All those stories have inner significance for problems of that time,' she later wrote.) They included a novella, 'Monte Verita', which completely bewildered Victor Gollancz, who commented: 'I don't understand the slight implication that there is something wrong with sex.' This novella is about a woman, Anna, who is mesmerized by a mysterious sect who live in a secret world in the mountains in Central Europe. She joins them and disappears. The whole point of the story is that in her 'Monte Verita' Anna has found a spiritual happiness she could never find with her husband or any man. Sexual love between a man and a woman no longer means anything to her, and all the young women who became part of her sect are now saved from 'the turmoil of a brief romance turning to humdrum married life'. What disturbed Victor most was that in the first version Anna, once she is safe in her Monte Verita, turns into a *man*. At Victor's insistence, Daphne changed this and Anna remains a woman but, as he had picked up, the general drift of this highly metaphorical story *is* that there is something wrong with sex between men and women – it spoils relationships, it drains energy, it gets in the way of self-fulfilment. Written by a woman who was in the middle of her first love-affair with another woman for twenty years, it seems strikingly significant.

The title story, 'The Apple Tree', seems even more so. It tells of a man who, after his wife has died, notices an apple tree, which has never borne blossom or fruit, suddenly flourishing. He becomes convinced that the tree represents his wife, whom he never really loved because 'she always seemed to put a blight on everything' and because they had lived 'in different worlds . . . their minds not meeting'. All his efforts go into trying to destroy the tree, but in the end, when finally he has hacked it into logs and given it away, he trips over its root and is trapped in the snow. It is very hard to decide quite how Daphne intended this story to be read: is the hatred of the man for his dead wife justified, or does he get his deserts? Or is the whole story meant to damn marriages in which true minds do not meet – as in her own, according to her confession to Ferdy? Later in life, Daphne said that 'The Apple Tree' was based on feelings about Paddy Puxley, but it seems far more convincing that the resentment which fuels it stemmed from her feelings about her own marriage. Whatever the origin of 'The Apple Tree', it was all of a piece with the volume's general theme of sex as trouble, in one way or another, of the sexual urge causing violence and even murder.

Two of the other four stories very forcibly emphasized this and have a distinctly nasty tone to them. 'The Little Photographer' tells of a rich woman on holiday who has everything she wants except a lover (her husband is not with her). She finds herself wanting to have a love-affair, as long as it can be 'a thing of silence' with a stranger, so that it is just sex and nothing more. She sets her sights on a crippled photographer whom she meets while working on a cliff. She asks him, 'Why don't you kiss me?' and he does, which gives her a delicious furtive sense of excitement – 'What she did was without emotion of any sort, her mind and affections quite untouched.' But eventually sex with the photographer becomes a boring ritual. One day she doesn't turn up. He is distraught and says she is his life, he cannot do without her. He tells her she is wicked when she offers him money to go away, and she pushes him over the cliff. Her husband arrives to take her home and she thinks she has got away with both the love-affair (in which there was no love) and the murder, but on the last page it is made clear that she will not do so and will be condemned to a future life of guilt and blackmail.

All the details of the plot in this unpleasant story are incredible, but the atmosphere is convincing. The coldness of the woman, her contempt for the poor photographer, her ruthlessness – all these repel but fascinate. The woman's ideal, 'passion between strangers', sex as something to discard, is ugly but argued with such conviction that the attempt at the end to make her pay some sort of price seems weak. Another story, 'Kiss Me Again, Stranger', has an even more brutal view of sex. A young mechanic picks up a cinema usherette. They go into a cemetery and she tells him to kiss her but that she likes him silent. He feels himself falling in love with her and starts fantasizing about their future together. He leaves her reluctantly and goes home. Next day he reads about the murder of an RAF man and realizes that the murderess was his girl. The plot is totally unbelievable, but once again the atmosphere is not.

After such macabre happenings, the other two stories in this collection come as a relief, although here again, in one of them at least, there are autobiographical connections freely acknowledged by the author. 'The Old Man' is a simply told story which turns out to be a spoof. The old man is described as big and strong. He lives by a lake with his wife but has driven his children away, so he can be alone with her, 'which is what he has always wanted'. In the last three lines it is revealed that the old man is, in fact, a swan. Often, after she had written this story, Daphne would refer to Tommy as 'just like "The Old Man" ' – wanting her to himself, jealous, she believed, of the attention she gave her children, especially Kits. 'But that is not the whole significance of the story,' she commented. 'The real significance is that Moper [Tommy] must not kill his only begotten son but kill the petty jealous *self* which is his hidden nature, and so rise again.' This, she thought, 'is the truth behind Christianity and all the religions'. But the story she liked best, and which 'just came bubbling out', fitted into no pattern. 'The Birds' is a wholly atmospheric story, beautifully paced and unmarred by the intricacies of plot which sometimes spoiled Daphne's original ideas. The tension of birds attacking humans in hordes is sustained throughout. The birds themselves, shuttling on window-sills, pecking at glass panes, swooping in from the sea in millions, are horrifyingly real. ' "The Birds" ', wrote Victor Gollancz, elated, 'is a masterpiece.'[27]

The whole collection thrilled him, but he was firm in telling Daphne that he did not at all like two other stories she added – 'No Motive' and 'Split Second'. She was, he told her, 'one of the few authors . . . with whom I can be frank'. 'No Motive' jarred on him and 'Split Second' was poor. Daphne, as ever, accepted his judgement and dropped these two stories. She told him he really was 'the *only* publisher in the world' even though she was 'a tinge sorry' about 'Split Second'. He was 'dynamic, exuberant, tender, intolerant and the only publisher for me'. Victor responded that she was 'beautiful, adorable, gracious, charming and good'. This was indeed the high-water mark of their relationship as author and publisher. But Victor warned her that even though he loved the stories she must brace herself for shocked reviews – the violence in them would be noted and probably found abhorrent coming from the pen of the 'romantic' writer she was supposed to be. He was, on the whole, right. Nancy Spain in the *Daily Express* in particular was revolted by the stories and attacked the author. Victor replied to her in a storming letter which this time he sent, only to be soundly told off by Nancy Spain in turn. Her review, which he had called 'low-down', was, she wrote, perfectly accurate – the stories were 'all concerned with malformation, hatred, blackmail, cruelty and murder' and he shouldn't object to her saying so. Anyone writing such stories was surely sick.

Daphne's own response was to ask who Nancy Spain was and then to dismiss all the reviewers as 'nearly always indifferent writers who can't make a living from their own books and are forced to make a living through shoddy journalism . . . kicking at writers more successful than themselves is probably the only thrill they ever get'. Victor was, in fact, doing her no favours by encouraging her to take this attitude, so that soon she was no longer able to detect genuine and potentially helpful criticism. But it was a pity this collection did not merit more attention, and that it was 'The Birds' which monopolized any attention it did get, because it was a huge improvement on Daphne's previous short stories of her early years.

Not only were these new stories better written, they also showed a shift in the balance of power between the sexes which she had been working out for some twenty years now in her novels. The women were no longer pathetic and exploited, the men no longer always powerful and dominant. Now, women were often in control and making men suffer. Women had become quite vicious creatures, perfectly capable of tricking, and even killing, men as they had been tricked and killed in the early stories. Daphne's friends and family were rather taken aback at this strain of brutality she displayed, but she was unrepentant and talked cheerfully of 'my macabre tastes' without seeming to fear any significance being read into them. But this collection was highly important: it represented a change not only in Daphne's style but in her subject-matter – her 'macabre tastes' at last were acknowledged and given an outlet, reflecting the confusion of her inner self.

Chapter Sixteen

My Cousin Rachel had been even more rapturously received by Daphne's American publisher than it had been by Victor Gollancz, and she agreed to go over for the publication of the book. This meant, of course, that she could see both Ellen and Gertrude, so as soon as her short stories were finished she began planning her visit. Ellen thought *My Cousin Rachel* 'one of your masterpieces' and announced that she saw Daphne very clearly in Philip, but that in spite of some 'physical and other characteristics I couldn't miss' Rachel herself, to Ellen's relief, was 'like no one'[1] . . . Daphne replied that she was right – 'in the writing of the novel I turned myself so completely into Philip I was beguiled, and she could have poisoned the entire world and I would not have minded.'[2]

But this time Daphne was particularly anxious to see Gertie, who had been sick, and, though all the tests to which she had been subjected had revealed nothing sinister, Daphne was worried, sensing some deep malaise. Richard Aldridge, Gertie's husband, was going to be away in March, so she could stay in their New York apartment. Gertie warned her that Richard was liable to change his plans, in which case they might have no privacy, which would be a strain. Instead of being put off, Daphne began to fantasize about climbing 'fire escapes . . . on the East Side if I want to have any fun'. She had her fun but saw how tired Gertie was – she was starring in *The King and I* and was the toast of New York – and suddenly realized she was also ageing. Gertie had a cold and seemed very low, and all they did was watch 'awful films on TV'. Daphne had to go to a publishers' dinner and, when it came to the time, Gertie 'put on that face' and said it was 'just like Cinderella':[3] Daphne going out and her staying in. She went with Gertie to an acting class she was conducting for students, and was perturbed to observe that the students thought Gertie a bit of a joke. It made her feel tender and protective towards her, though sometimes there would be such a flash of the old, brilliantly cheeky and vital Gertie that she wondered if there was any need. Once, driving through the awful New York traffic after the show, a taxi driver cut in front of their car and screamed at them for obstructing him. Gertie rolled down her window and yelled at him, 'Fuck you, we're in a hit.'⁴ This was so much the showbiz put-down that Daphne dissolved into hysterical giggles and adored Gertie all over again. She went to Cartier's and bought her a heart-shaped brooch.

There followed the usual visit to Barberrys, accompanied by Oriel Malet, a young writer (also over to promote her book, which had just won the John Llewellyn Rhys Prize), whom Daphne had met in London, and liked. She enjoyed Ellen's company as much as ever, but there was a new distance between them, another change in their relationship because of what was happening between Gertie and Daphne.

Once, Daphne had wanted to be alone with Ellen all the time and had resented the other people in her life, but now, enjoying a different kind of relationship with Gertie, she was able to be close to Ellen without needing to have her to herself. This made no difference to the *depth* of their friendship – it had been tried and tested and found solid for too long now to be truly endangered – but only to the way it was conducted. They still confided in each other absolutely, but Daphne was not in such desperate need, nor did Ellen worry now about what she could not give. Both of them realized their friendship was settling down into a less intense phase, one that would endure but never regain the fire of the last few years.

For Ellen there was a new element. She wrote to Daphne, after this visit, that a 'slight touch of romance'⁵ had entered her life. It was nothing serious but it was pleasant and had shown her that she was not quite as dead as she had thought herself – though Daphne was not to 'get in a stew'. Daphne could not resist remarking a little sarcastically, 'So the lady is for burning after all, but, of course, in a perfectly respectable way.'⁶ She wrote that she had never believed for one moment that Ellen, any more than Stella in *September Tide*, was dead 'that way' – she had always known she was 'only deliberately asleep'. What was annoying, and even at one time distressing, was that she herself had never succeeded in waking Ellen up. Now she did not want to. Gertie had satisfied her instead, though she enjoyed speculating as to what might have happened if she had 'dressed up like a man' – maybe her fantasy romance with Ellen could have become a reality. She paid tribute to what her infatuation had done for her literary life: loving Ellen had resulted first in *September Tide* and then in *My Cousin Rachel*, and the disturbing short stories. She felt 'drained of all emotion' except for 'the drag of Gertie pulling in the opposite direction'.[7] In August 1952, after Ellen had paid her a brief visit as part of a European trip, Daphne was moved to reflect on what made people want to make love – 'What makes people get the craving? . . . There never seems an answer. You might say loneliness. But to my mind, drinking and making love are the two most lonely pastimes on earth.'[8] Gertie, too, was lonely and wanted her to go to the Florida Cape again with her, but Daphne, not realizing Gertie would be free, had already arranged to go first to Switzerland, then walking in the Rhône Valley with Clara Vyvyan, her friend for over twenty years.[9]

Clara loved roughing it and was off on a walk down the Rhône with a rucksack on her back. Daphne said she would go with her – it was just the kind of jaunt she loved. Clara had her doubts. She knew perfectly well that Daphne liked comfort whatever she said, but rather against her better judgement agreed she could join her to walk some of the route. In the event, the idea was a success. Daphne joined her for two weeks and adored every minute of it – Clara found her 'indefatigable' and was amused by her habit of finding some 'high niche in the mountains or . . . some mid-stream boulder where she would squat and meditate for hours'. Daphne went off on her own sometimes, exploring, and would return 'in a mood of mountain ecstasy'. The two of them made fires and boiled water in a billy-can, and Clara maintained she 'could feel that Daphne . . . was separated from her everyday-self by a new sense of freedom'. What puzzled her were the two sides to her friend: on the one hand the genuine love, after all, of the simple life, but on the other the contradiction, to Clara, of a rucksack full of 'cosmetics, vanishing creams . . . lotions . . . and also scents'. Daphne's clothes fascinated her too: 'a white jockey cap, socks, mountaineer's boots with yellow laces, linen blouse and a zip linen skirt on top of white cotton shorts'. Swinging along the paths she unzipped the skirt and walked in shorts, then in villages she zipped it back up – 'she was feminine . . . [then] on the yonder side up rolled the skirt and she strode forward like a boy'. It was, wrote Daphne, 'one of the best holidays ever . . . we lived like two tramps . . . never felt so free of ties in my life'. In some ways it was even better than behaving like a schoolgirl with Gertie, because she didn't feel Clara needed anything from her, and she came to the conclusion that the best holidays were always those spent with people with whom one had no emotional ties.

Back at Menabilly, Daphne began yearning to see Gertie, before winter arrived, but then heard she was ill again. This was not at first alarming. She assumed, as most people did, that Gertie was simply exhausted after a gruelling summer in *The King and I*. But Fanny Holtzman, Gertrude's lawyer, wrote to say that Gertrude wanted her to know that she was suffering from something more serious than exhaustion and, though tests had initially shown nothing sinister, there was now the suspicion that she had hepatitis. From Gertrude's collapse, at the end of August, in her dressing-room after a matinée, until she went into a coma on 6 September, Daphne was kept closely informed of her progress. But the end, when it came, was devastatingly sudden. Even though Daphne had not 'liked the sound of something wrong with the liver', and had written to Evie Williams, 'It sounds to me like a tumour,' she had not imagined Gertie to be in such imminent danger. The news that Gertrude, aged only fifty-four, was dead was a shock so severe that it rendered Daphne virtually catatonic. Those who were with her at Menabilly – her husband, her children, Tod, and Maureen – were horribly aware that she was utterly grief-stricken and quite unable to speak or cry. She went to bed and stayed there for several days, not eating or sleeping, simply lying there, staring sightlessly, so bereft and pitiful no one was in any doubt that Gertie had meant everything to her. It was frightening for her family to witness, particularly as none of them knew the exact nature of her love for Gertie. It seemed an unaccountably extreme reaction, not sufficiently explained by the knowledge that Gertie had been Daphne's 'dearest friend'. Only Ellen knew the truth, and it was only to Ellen that she could open her heart.

On 18 September she wrote to Ellen, in extremely simple, direct words, all the more moving for being on the surface unemotional, a kind of testimony to her love for Gertrude. 'You, who know me better than anyone,' she wrote, 'may understand the inner meaning of the story "Kiss Me Again, Stranger"; the lines in it "Go from me, and don't look back, like a person walking in their sleep", were actually said, from the pillow, to me as I left her for the last time about 2 am . . .' She told Ellen she could not talk about 'these things' to anyone but her, 'because in a strange way it's all mixed up with you (not your fault, darling). *But* if there had never been a *September Tide*, I would not have seen her, in fantasy, as doing what I wanted you to do, or started the gay, happy friendship. *But* for the knowledge that you really couldn't be what I wanted you to be, I would never have gone on that Florida weekend; and so become beguiled and bewitched (nothing, except gay flirtation, had ever happened before that). No regrets. It was such fun, and so happy, and so entrancing. Never sordid. I suppose, cold-bloodedly, you could say "Two lonely people getting rid of inhibitions." I don't know. It doesn't matter. The odd thing is, once you have loved a person physically, it makes the strangest bond (I suppose not always, no, sometimes, I think it could mean nothing, like playing tennis). In this case, it meant a lot. I couldn't talk to her, you know, like I can to you, or have the peace, that you give (or the fever either!), but there was so much warmth there and generosity of giving, if you know what I mean, that I cannot imagine it ever being equalled by anyone in the world. I think, if one was Gauguin in the South Seas or loved a native girl, and never even spoke their language, in a way it would be like that. Yet there was a mutual language. Something all mixed up with theatre and writing. Knowing that only that, and "work", were what mattered most.'

To everyone else, Daphne struggled to put her grief into some kind of acceptable form, but it was miserable work. Her only comfort was that, like Gerald, Gertie was not suited to either illness or old age – 'she could not have borne the later years to come, the real enjoyment of her life was over, she was in a sense marking time. I felt this with Daddy and I felt it with her.' To Victor Gollancz, whose wisdom she respected, she wrote: 'I would like . . . a treatise on how to look at loss through death, having been knocked quite off my balance by the sudden death of Gertrude Lawrence, who happened to be my dearest friend . . . what philosophy? How to cope with loss and the emptiness of waking up in the morning and thinking what now? (I have no business to think this with a dear husband and children, but I think you, with your intuition, understand the somewhat erratic schizo personality that is mine . . .).'[10] To those around her, who did not know the truth, it seemed an exaggerated response to the death of a woman to whom she had been a close friend for only four years, but her family saw the misery in her face and were frightened by it. The 'state of numb emptiness' continued for the next few weeks and she had to stop thinking of the good times she and Gertie had planned to have again in Florida, because 'it just leads to suicidal thoughts'.

During this time, when she was openly mourning Gertie, Daphne constantly equated the loss with the loss of her father. It was not that Gertie had meant to her what Gerald had meant, but that both of them symbolized all she loved most about life – both had that Peter Pan spirit she envied and marvelled at, and the death of both of them was a reminder that it must finally die. 'She never grew up,' she wrote of Gertie, as she had written of Gerald, and that was it precisely. She put all her feelings about Gertie's immense vitality into an obituary for *The Times*, 'which they hadn't the nerve or decency to print. I'd love to know why. I shan't ask.' The only person she could talk with about Gertie was Noël Coward (he himself had added a note to the official obituary), who was 'very hard hit', but she felt he would get over Gertie's death more quickly than she would herself, 'living down here, gloomy autumn weather, etc., and no work on hand . . . I'll have to pull myself together somehow.'

It was unfortunate that there was a certain pressing urgency to pull herself together at the end of that awful month following Gertie's death: she was invited to Balmoral and had agreed she must go. When Princess Elizabeth became Queen, in February 1952, Tommy had become Treasurer to the Duke of Edinburgh, and she knew it was her duty to accompany him, though she dreaded the prospect. Fortunately, Tommy hurt his arm sailing and since this meant he would be unable to shoot they did not go. Instead, Daphne went on her own to Venice, where she was the guest of Ronald Armstrong, who had been British Consul at Geneva for twenty years and was now retired.

This was an unusual friendship which had begun some years previously after Ronald Armstrong had written her a fan letter. A correspondence developed and she and Tommy were invited to visit him, which they had briefly done on one of their rare holidays together. He became known as 'Penfriend' and Daphne would imitate him endlessly and hold entire imaginary conversations with him out loud. He was sixty-two when she joined him in Venice (to her forty-five) and 'a perfect dear'. He gave her what she needed – good company – without expecting anything in return. It rained, but she wrote that she had never had 'such a delightful cultivated companion and with a sense of humour that can only be compared to Daddy's'. She was well aware that Penfriend flattered her, but saw no harm in this, commenting in a letter to Flavia, 'it is too late in life'. Penfriend was 'a bit old . . . I mean, it is no good for menace, but now and again his eyes twinkle which is vaguely stimulating'. Considering Penfriend was homosexual, and she knew he was, it was an odd stimulation, but it amused her, made her feel happier, to flirt with men *especially* if there was no future to it. If they were elderly, if they were homosexual, then so much the better.

Once back at Menabilly, with all the children away at boarding school and Tommy back in London, she knew that the pulling herself together she had to do was now truly upon her. 'I have felt this strange restlessness for about a year now,' she wrote to Victor Gollancz, 'I wonder if it is the change of life? But isn't forty-five a bit young?' Like so many women, she was taken by surprise at how middle age and the onset of the menopause affected her looks. With her phobia about fat, and her dislike of all ugliness, she was dismayed by the increasing lines on her face and the thickening of her waist, which she found, to her horror, measured

29 inches, after a lifetime of being as slim as a reed.[11] Some photographs taken for publicity purposes in the early fifties clearly showed the change in her physique – 'I look aged with a kind of humped back, which is irritating' – and she was moved to comment: 'I look and feel my age ... what I mean is, I find myself really not bothering very much any more ... some sort of loss of energy.' She realized only too well that, although the basic change in her appearance was one she could not help, there was also a deliberate side to what was happening and she was defiant about it, caught between not wanting to care and yet caring very much.

Her hair annoyed her, never 'seeming to be right', and she was irritated that this bothered her. After the short bob of her adolescent years and then the shingle of her twenties she had worn it loose, quite long, gently waved and framing her face very attractively. Before her first trip to America in 1947 she had it cut and permed. The result was not flattering, both the shorter length and the rigidity of the perm making her face look square and less delicate, and her jaw harder. She still made herself up carefully, even for windswept walks on the Gribbin, but the make-up was more of a half-hearted disguise than an enhancement of her features. The way she dressed changed too. Ever since she had come to live in Cornwall she had worn trousers, but as the forties gave way to the fifties, the style of trousers changed – from looking graceful in the loosely cut slacks of the earlier decade she began to look rather military in the straight-legged new shapes which tended to emphasize the increased weight on her hips. Large, ornate belts became a feature of her wardrobe and, though often very beautiful in themselves, looked rather awkward. She settled down into what was almost a uniform of no-nonsense casual dressing, though even now all the colours of shirts and jumpers and trousers were carefully chosen and co-ordinated – casual was never to mean scruffy or untidy. Far from 'not bothering any more', she simply made the decision to accept the changes in herself and adapt to them.

Tommy, meanwhile, had begun to make a new life for himself in London, and that life included friendships with women as well as following interests, such as ballet, which his wife had never shared. There were plenty of people at this time who warned

In the afternoons, when she'd finished her morning's writing, Daphne liked to take her children, Kits, Flavia and Tessa, for walks through the Menabilly woods.

RIGHT *Ellen Doubleday (wife of Daphne's American publisher) who was the inspiration for September Tide and My Cousin Rachel.*

BELOW *Daphne, c.1949, working in the garden hut she had had erected in the grounds of Menabilly. (Note the dictionary, of which she was in frequent need.)*

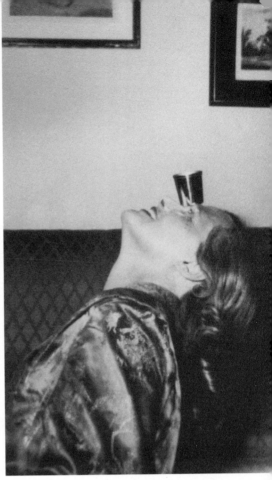

ABOVE LEFT *Gertrude Lawrence, whose talent for enjoyment endeared her to Daphne – she relaxed with her as she did with no one else.*

ABOVE RIGHT *Daphne at a Doubleday party in America, entering into the spirit of things.*

LEFT *Daphne with Frank Price, who worked for Doubleday, and with whom she had a strange friendship.*

RIGHT *Daphne looking apprehensive on board* Jeanne d'Arc *in 1959 with her husband who tended to be dictatorial when sailing.*

BELOW *Daphne and Tommy walking down the lawn at Menabilly.*

ABOVE OPPOSITE *Kits at the wheel of his first car with his mother (who in 1939 gave up driving for almost 30 years).*

BELOW OPPOSITE *Daphne with Tessa on her left and Flavia.*

RIGHT *Olive White, Miss Eire 1961, who married Kits Browning (inset with her a few years later) in 1964.*

BELOW *Daphne playing cricket with her grandson Rupert outside Menabilly. As a child she had loved to play, when she pretended to be 'Eric Avon'.*

ABOVE *Daphne in 1946, walking up from Pridmouth beach with her children.*

BELOW *The same scene, 30 years on, with Kits and his family: from left to right Freddie, Olive holding Grace, Ned and Robbie.*

RIGHT *Daphne on the rocks below Kilmarth in the '70s, wearing the clothes and cap which became almost a uniform.*

BELOW *Daphne 3 years before her death, suddenly fragile and wistful.*

Daphne that if she left Tommy on his own in London the inevitable would happen: he was bound to turn to someone else and have an affair. This infuriated her, and anyone issuing such Cassandra-like warnings got very short shrift indeed. Her defence was given in career terms: her career was not only as important to her as Tommy's was to him, but right from the beginning of their marriage it had been financially far, far more lucrative. With perfect truth she could argue that her income made their way of life possible, and that should her writing stop they would soon be in trouble in spite of those past earnings she had tried to salt away. To write she had to have peace, and to have peace she had to be at Menabilly. She was convinced that if she had moved to London she would not have been able to write a word. Whether this would have happened there was no means of knowing – 'peace', after all, had been found by her in the past outside the confines of Menabilly and she had also written well in decidedly non-peaceful circumstances – but it was how she felt. She also felt extremely angry and contemptuous that anyone should imagine she had so little pride that she could bring herself to go and live in London to keep an eye on a possibly erring husband. What Tommy did was his business. She assumed they had an understanding, even if arrived at without discussion, which had caused her a good deal of misery initially, but was now accepted: she had her life, he had his, they each loved the other even if not in 'that way' any more, and that was that.

But her own life was changing just as Tommy's was. As his became less lonely, with the new friends he was making and the socializing which was part of his job, Daphne's became more lonely. This word had not been used by her before, but now, in letters, she would describe herself as 'a bit lonely' with all three children at school. She was left with only Tod, and found herself missing her daughters as well as Kits. She had by then begun to enjoy their companionship and was fascinated by Tessa's boyfriends. She had always seemed distressingly remote from Tessa, but no longer – she was pleased that even if the two of them were not exactly close they had a free and easy relationship of which she was quite proud. What she had never wanted to have was the relationship she had had with Muriel as a teenager, particularly where sexual matters were concerned, so she had set herself to be as frank and approachable as possible. When Tessa, who was now at a finishing school in Oxford, had her first real boyfriend, Ken Spence (who happened to be a godson of her father's), Daphne was delighted for her and tried to be as helpful as possible. Tessa was advised to 'keep it all light and gay' and on no account to 'get too menaced' (attracted), because at her age 'you will probably meet dozens of young men all equally menacing at first sight'. She was anxious to invite Ken to Menabilly, though only if Tessa wished, and when her daughter confessed that she was attracted to him Daphne hastened to assure her that she 'understood about that weak-at-the-knees feeling'. The important thing was to have fun, but 'don't Go Too Far!' It pleased her, in view of her own past relationship with her mother, that Tessa could confide in her and that she could share her feelings – 'imagine the old woman to me!' – and she very earnestly tried to warn Tessa about how boys reacted. 'Remember . . .' she wrote, 'this is very medical, that young men have little or no control over their nods [du Maurier code for penis] and a really good kiss can send their nods rocketing so that the poor boys really don't know what is happening to them and get in a great state. This places a great responsibility on the girl . . .' It was 'bliss to be able to say these things', especially when she remembered her own mother's 'cold, awful, suspicious look at me after . . . having been out late in Carol's Lagonda . . . her sniff and her tight mouth . . . it drove one to deceit'. She wanted to be sure that her children were never driven to the kind of subterfuges she had had to employ.

To Ken himself she wrote the kind of letters her own mother had been quite incapable of writing to Carol – warm, witty, friendly letters without a hint of disapproval. As Tessa became keener on Ken, and Ken wanted to marry her, Daphne handled this situation very well. She said she would adore them to marry one day – '[I'll] get in a crinoline and have a reception in the long room with the Bishop of Truro present' – but that, since Tessa was only eighteen and Ken still up at Oxford, an actual marriage now might be foolish. Long engagements were 'surely dreary . . . you are 21, she is 18, and you both fall for each other, bang, which is bliss . . . but . . . the whole business of being attracted by anyone is so terribly like measles . . . you might just be infectious for a few months'. While appreciating how they felt, she thought they should both try to be 'as free as possible', though 'I could not have a son-in-law I could love better than you . . . wiping the budding tears from my sentimental eyes (I really am rather sentimental at heart, under a well-trained brittle exterior . . .)'. When Ken duly came to Menabilly, Daphne could not have been more friendly or easy, and after a year or so, when Tessa was growing less interested in Ken, to his distress, she was sympathetic and advised him that it 'always pays dividends never to let on' that one had 'a wretched jealous feeling' about one's rival.

But when none of her children were at home, she felt low and depressed. She knew that the only way to get over Gertie's death and cure the restlessness was to work – 'without work I am utterly lost' – but no idea for a book had arisen. The only thing to do was manufacture one, so she consulted Victor on whether he thought a book about her ancestor Mary Anne Clarke, mistress of the Duke of York, in the style of *The Du Mauriers* would be acceptable. Originally, she had promised to write *Mary Anne* as a play for Gertie to star in, but now, with Gertie dead, the idea was unthinkable and she wanted to turn it into a biography. Victor said he would prefer it as a novel (*The Du Mauriers* had not, of course, done well commercially, compared to the phenomenal sales of the novels). This gave Daphne something to be going on with and she spent the winter of 1952 researching material and employing assistants in London to send her information she needed which was in the British Museum and the Public Record Office. But her mind was not entirely occupied, as it usually was when writing a novel, and she found herself with plenty of empty hours to reflect on what she thought about death. In spite of not being religious she decided she did believe there was some kind of after-life and also some meaning to life itself. She believed, too, that 'things are meant'. She often felt she was in training for something 'meant' that would happen to her and wondered if it was getting nearer.

The long, wet November days were dreary and suited to a kind of morbid introspection. She went for walks with her dog, getting soaked as she made her way through the woods, dark and forbidding in the gloom of rain and fading light, and stood on Pridmouth beach wrapped in mist, watching the winter sea boil and rage, and listening to the hoot of the fog horns. After weeks of this she began to feel dragged down by the weather itself, and the first words of discontent with Cornwall appeared in her letters. She still loved it, and adored Menabilly, but she wished that in the winter she was 'in a studio in Paris'. Everything was suddenly 'shilling [disappointing] here' – the rain, the dullness, Tod 'with her face, I don't know why', and the awful suppers – 'I scrape some bits of ham, going bad, and eat it with the fag end of a stilton all heaped on a tray and listening to *Any Questions*.' It was a dismal routine and *Mary Anne* was giving her little true satisfaction, though she liked looking at all the old documents she had gathered together.

She started writing in January 1953, but almost immediately had influenza, and by the time she felt well enough to continue it was March. Even then, she reported to Victor and Sheila that she was 'plodding ahead . . . not very fast' and that this was going to be a book 'written with the head not the heart'. The difficulty she was having, the lack of flow, was, she thought, due to 'not writing in the first person after so long'. By April she had only completed a few chapters and was feeling panic-stricken – something had happened to her style and she didn't know what it was. She read over one chapter 'and it was like blank verse . . . supposing my whole style is beginning to alter . . . like a lush painter turning abstract'. Her sentences seemed to her 'short, almost harsh' and still she could not seem to make real progress. 'How frightful', she joked, 'if I am going to turn into a writer like James Joyce, who, I once read, could only write half a page a day and then had to be dressed entirely in white or he couldn't concentrate at all.'

It was hard to keep on writing when she had so little faith in what she was producing – 'you'll have to be ruthless', she warned Victor, ' . . . don't pass what is doubtful' – but if she stopped she felt she would have 'nothing at all to be interested in'. This was not quite true: she had Tessa's approaching marriage. Tessa had fallen out of love with Ken, only to fall in love with Peter de Zulueta,[12] 'a Welsh Guardsman', as Daphne described him. By the spring of 1953 Tessa wanted to marry Peter, even though she was only nineteen and, her parents felt, much too young. Daphne had always promised herself that she would not interfere in her children's romances, but there was something about Peter – 'something I cannot define' – which 'makes me wary'. She also noted that Peter was a hard drinker, even though he held his drink very well. However, Tommy had him checked out, and since the report on him from his superior officers was complimentary there were no grounds for objecting to the marriage. She set herself to like Peter and overcome her intuitive feeling of suspicion and succeeded admirably. She wrote friendly, cheerful letters to him, just as she had done to Ken Spence (with whom she remained friends), making jokes about the grandeur of her daughter's London wedding plans. If she had had her way, the wedding would have been in Fowey, with the service 'at St Monica's by the Gas Works and the reception at the Odd Spot Café'. But, though she thought Tessa too young and the wedding too grand, she loved the idea of new blood coming into the family and rather surprised people by expressing delight at the thought of grandchildren soon.

The wedding was fixed for March the following year, but meanwhile Daphne wanted *Mary Anne* out of the way. She finally finished it at the end of September 1953 and sent it to Victor, dreading his verdict. This time Victor was not as frank as he had once boasted he always could be with her. He wrote to Sheila saying the novel was muddled and would have to be clarified and that lots of quite substantial cuts would be needed, but to Daphne he expressed great enthusiasm and made light of the faults, as any sensible publisher would. To Doubleday, with whom he was hoping to publish simultaneously, he wrote that 'Sheila spent several intensive weeks at work, then I stepped in and had a go'. Daphne was not as happy with his 'go' as she let Victor think, writing furiously that 'Victor did his thing of ringing up and wanting to alter words . . . stupid things . . . who cares . . . it was just like a master teaching grammar on the end of a telephone and showing up one's work to be corrected'. Nor did she like Sheila changing some French words she had used into English, and suggesting cuts in places she thought did not need them. But neither Victor nor Sheila knew that they were offending her – to both of them she had written letters positively ordering them to be critical and saying how she depended on their help. The real trouble was that she didn't like the novel anyway. 'The whole thing', she wrote, 'is lacking in human interest and reads like a newspaper report.' The only consolation was that 'it is definitely not romantic – I'm done with romance forever (no pigment left!)'.

Once all the corrections had been made, Victor was suddenly immensely pleased with the book and thought it would outsell *Rebecca*. It was the only time he seriously miscalculated, ignoring Daphne's own instinct. The first print-run for *Mary Anne* was 135,000 copies, the largest he ever printed for any of Daphne's books and the only one which took years to sell out. It came out in June 1954. She went up to London to have lunch with Victor and was philosophical about the indifferent reviews, feeling she had deserved no better for once, while he raged. She took the opportunity to please Tommy by accompanying him to a state banquet which she rather enjoyed, because it all looked so magnificent. The only 'wain' (embarrassing) part was shaking hands with the Queen and the Duke of Edinburgh – 'The Dook giggled when he saw me, do you suppose he thinks I am funny? Of course he only knows me in trousers, being jam-a-long at Mena. He shook hands and muttered "Have you only just made it?" as though I'd only dashed that second from Mena, changing in the passage on the way.' Back home she retired to bed exhausted as usual and read a book called *How People Go Mad*.

Chapter Seventeen

She felt 'strange' and could not quite account for it by telling herself she'd written one book she hadn't liked much and had no ideas for a new one. 'You know my old thing of wanting to test myself,' she wrote to Flavia, who was now at St Mary's. 'Well, it still holds good.' She wanted to keep in training for whatever test was coming and went off for another holiday with Clara Vyvyan.[1] This time it was Greece, mostly by bus, 'the greatest fun but terribly exhausting'. She had 'a fearful urge' to consult the Delphic oracle, but when she did there was no answer, though she noted that the words above the temple door said 'Know Thyself'. The best moment was 'a day on the top of the Pindus mountains' where the two women lit a fire and cast wild flowers on it as a sacrifice to Zeus. They spent one night in a log cabin with a goatherd and Greek lorry driver sleeping below and had bread and cheese when they rose at dawn. The lorry driver shared his cigarettes with Daphne and she sat and watched the goatherd cut his hair – 'it was *absolute* life, so utterly different from anything one ever does . . . it's like being someone else in a new world'. She returned with her head full of 'old temples and gods and hymns to Apollo' – but she also returned with a temperature and stayed in bed again, surrounding herself with books on Greek religion and on psychology, which was beginning to fascinate her more and more. She still felt 'strange' and wondered once again if this was merely because she was menopausal, or still the continuing sense of misery she felt at the loss of Gertie. She wrote to Ellen that she felt 'permanently restless' and that she wanted to try to understand her own personality in a more profound way than she had ever attempted before. 'My education has been neglected,' she confessed to Victor Gollancz. 'Can't you start a school

275

for training your novelists?'² What she most wanted to discover was why, for so long now, she had had this feeling that she was to be tested – 'interesting why this wanting to test oneself is such a basic thing. To prove what?' She felt if she could answer this question she might be able to sort herself out before her whole life became 'one big anticlimax'.

The psychoanalysts whose work Daphne studied that winter of 1954 were Jung and Adler, and it was to Flavia that she passed on her new wisdom. At one stage, before Flavia joined her sister at St Mary's, and after Kits had gone to West Downs, the two of them had been alone together, except for Tod, and Daphne had felt comfortable with her second daughter, observing she had 'so much about her' which had not been visible while she was overshadowed by both Tessa and Kits. She even went so far as to bracket Flavia with herself in a quite significant way – 'Moper [Tommy] and Tess are pathetic. You and I are not. Boo [Kits] sometimes is, but not very.'³ But, if neither she nor Flavia could be described by that dreaded word 'pathetic', Daphne saw them both as struggling with some deep contradiction within themselves, and this brought her to Jung.

One aspect of Jung's thinking which appealed to her was that she thought his theories seemed to be grounded in biology. He believed that psychological changes, like physical developments, were genetically determined and just as unstoppable. Grandparents thus exerted as great an influence as parents over how an individual matured, and this was very attractive to Daphne with her great interest in family history. But what she identified with most closely in Jung was his explanation that each person has dual aspects within him- or herself, their No. 1 and No. 2 self. She wrote to the seventeen-year-old Flavia that she had always been able to feel within herself two quite separate personalities – 'When I get madly boyish No. 2 is in charge, and then, after a bit, the situation is reversed.' The point was that, as Jung directed, one had to make friends with No. 2 and say 'now don't get carried away . . . No. 2 can come to the surface and be helpful'. She explained that when she was writing she felt all No. 2 – 'he certainly has a lot to do with my writing' – but when she was not, No. 2 caused trouble. The kind of trouble was outlined as

'. . . one makes up one's mind what one thinks of another person and takes no notice of their real character but treats them how one imagines they are, and then one pretends to be the sort of person that one thinks they would like one to be, so the whole thing is one ghastly sort of dressing-up, and that part of one is watching all the time and thinking "Oh, that was a good remark", as if one was watching oneself in a play. It is fearful but I know I am always doing it.' Even though this was expressed in such a breathless stream-of-consciousness style – a style she often employed in her letter-writing when she was trying to be particularly honest – Daphne had actually weighed her words carefully. Clearly, she did not want to tell Flavia about the boy-in-the-box, and this was as near as she could get. Whenever she was in the company of people she did not know, she went on to say, she found herself 'talking sort of eagerly, with a smile, you know how I am when I'm awkward'.

But sometimes her No. 2 came into its own and she felt 'a power thing'. Once, after attending a literary party with Victor Gollancz, a very rare occasion indeed, she related to Flavia how exhilarated she had felt because 'in a minute I had men surrounding me, drinking glasses of champagne, and I was being witty . . . such power, and I couldn't care less about any of them, but was amused – that is the secret'. The same weekend as this party she had dinner with a man who was helping her with her *Mary Anne* research, Derek Whiteley, and found that, as she was saying goodbye to him, 'I went and kissed him full on the lips . . . and now I have had a letter . . . saying that I am a darling and a goddess . . . such power!' When she got back to Menabilly after this flurry of social activity, she put on the record of 'Kiss Me Again, Stranger' (the same title as her own short story) and played it 'over and over then I sang it at the top of my voice in the dark in the empty house, going up to bed, don't you see my point, with no one to hear'.

In view of the letter to Ellen, written after Gertrude Lawrence's death, about the immense significance of 'Kiss Me Again, Stranger', it was a point that Flavia, knowing nothing of the true relationship between her mother and Gertrude Lawrence, could not possibly have grasped; but what is plain enough is that Daphne was trying hard to explain the tremendous contradictions she knew existed in her own personality. She felt she was suffering 'the torments of hell, because I felt no one I had ever loved was real (except the family). In other words, the tribe, the original social group, were real, nobody else.' Sometimes this made her feel on the edge of madness. On another outing to London she took Kits to see Cinerama and suddenly felt sick. The manager gave her a cup of tea in his office – 'it was such a waine [embarrassment] and I didn't know what to say and heard with surprise my voice talking to the man . . . then I suddenly thought, supposing my next words don't make sense, like Turkish . . . [I] got in rather a panic, it's an awful feeling.' It upset her, this consciousness she had had all her life, that she was always pretending to be someone else unless she was completely alone – and these days she was becoming aware that even when alone she did not always stop pretending. 'The thing is, why must I always pretend to be someone else . . . it is what Jung calls "compensation" and "fantasy".' The answer, in the light of her letters to Ellen Doubleday, was that she had struggled her whole life to deny her 'Venetian tendencies', even to the extent of furiously rejecting that there was anything 'Venetian' about them. She wanted Jung's reassurance that her intense frustration was a result of the difficulty she had in reconciling the two sides of her personality, a difficulty which everyone must have. The idea that her inner anguish – and it was anguish, however bright and smiling her outward demeanour – was due to confusion over her sexual identity was one she simply would not acknowledge. She did not want this to be true, nor to admit to herself that, with the death of Gertrude Lawrence, there had died the only person with whom she had truly been able to be herself, No. 1 and No. 2 dissolved into that 'half-breed' she insisted she was.

To Flavia, she was determined to explain the problem of aligning her No. 1 and No. 2 as something to do with her writing self being different from her real-life self. It was all to do with the imagination. 'I am afraid', she told Flavia, 'that like me you will always find that what you *pretend* is more fun than what really happens. The people I write about in books are more real to me than the people I meet and I try and make people that I meet be as exciting as the people in books, but they never are, so one is always aware of a feeling of anticlimax.' The previous year, in September 1953, when the visit to Balmoral, which had been postponed the year before, could no longer be avoided, she had suffered worst of all from this feeling that in order to function at all she had to suppress her No. 2. She had hated every minute of the week at Balmoral, writing afterwards: 'it was desperately wain . . . I felt as if I were sitting on the edge of a chair all the time, not sure what I should do, and even though the present royals are young, one can't help remembering their august rank all the time and being nervous about it.' The only part she liked was being out on the moors, but then the thought of the evenings 'in full regalia' hung over her. She found the Duke of Edinburgh, whom, of course, she knew better, because Tommy had brought him to Menabilly twice, much more approachable than the Queen – 'much easier to talk to . . . I suppose it is because he has knocked about so much'. She was relieved simply to get through the week without disaster and return to Menabilly, where she collapsed, feeling deathly tired. It was 'such a relief to be home and not bobbing up and down to royals'. What she needed was a different kind of holiday, but there was no Gertie to fly off to and she was not tempted to go to America at all if she was not there.

Her sense of frustration grew stronger during the winter of 1954–55 until it reached such a pitch that all she could think about was some kind of escape. Tommy, when he was down in Cornwall for weekends, was annoying her to death – 'I can hear him shuffling about . . . so pathetic' – with his constant complaints not only about the cold but about the fact that they did not own Menabilly and 'had no legal right to breathe here'. She couldn't sleep, took more sleeping pills than usual, and next day wrote off to an estate agent's asking how much they wanted for Jethou, an island off Jersey, which she had seen advertised. Tessa's first baby was due in February and Daphne wished 'it would arrive early so I can escape'. To her astonishment, Tessa had asked her if she would be with her when the baby was born – '*in the room* while she is actually having it!'[4] This touched as well as slightly shocking her and she saw it as further proof that she had a better relationship with Tessa than her own mother had had with her – 'I can imagine nothing I should have hated more than having my own mother present.' It was her chance to respond to Tessa's need and she resolved to do her best, conscious that although things had improved between her and her older daughter they were still not close. She went up to London when the birth was due and sat by the telephone waiting for 'the call that would say "Tess has gone into labour" – such an awful word'. Marie-Thérèse, her first grand-child, was born on 15 February 1955 and Daphne was full of sympathy for Tessa, who 'looked white and washed out – who wouldn't be . . . the baby was 8½ lbs as against *my* babies of 6½'. The baby was 'a pet, but not a scrap like any of us . . . dark hair, broad nose'.

Before she returned to Cornwall, she had seen enough of Tessa as a mother to be struck by the memory of how different she herself had been with her first-born. For a start, Tessa did not seem at all disappointed because her baby was a girl – in fact, the reverse. She was genuinely thrilled to have a daughter, which Daphne thought extraordinary. Then there was the ease with which Tessa breastfed Marie-Thérèse. Watching her, and feeling unexpectedly moved by the sight, Daphne recalled what a disap-pointment it had been to her when she had failed with Tessa – 'Sister Rhead was so contemptuous too, whisking the baby off to a good go of Cow & Gate while I fell back limp on my pillow'. With her new readings in psychology she wondered if she had subconsciously blamed Tessa for this failure as well as for being a girl and whether this had governed her whole critical, remote attitude to her. It made her feel a little sad to think she had perhaps not been such a good mother to her girls, though she hoped that once they had grown up she had done better. Tessa had married and become a mother far too young in Daphne's opinion, but she judged that she had now found her vocation and was relieved.

Flavia, at that period, worried her more. She had always thought her not as able as Tessa, but now she was in her last year at school she began encouraging her to 'do something with art'. This 'something' became a year in Paris[5] with the young writer Oriel Malet, with whom Daphne had spent such a happy time at the Doubledays' home in America. Oriel was the kind of independent-spirited person to whom Daphne was instinctively drawn. She had the same sense of humour, was well-read, loved France, which she knew well, and had become one of the few regular visitors to Menabilly, all the more unusual because of her youth. Daphne thought she might become a friend of Tessa's, but it was to Flavia that she was more drawn, and now Daphne proposed they should both go and live in the Doubleday flat in Paris and attend art classes. The mere thought of Flavia there aroused such happy memories that she felt quite cheered up and she wondered why on earth she did not buy or rent a studio there for herself – it would be 'bliss' and get her away from the gloom of Menabilly in winter.

When Flavia eventually returned and announced that she wanted to do a shorthand and typing course, then try for acting school, her mother was rather irritated and suggested, 'You could always go on with the painting and drawing lessons at that Slade School which is supposed to be good.' The fact that Flavia would first have to be accepted by 'that Slade School', which, since it was so prestigious, might prove a problem, did not seem to register with her, but in any case she had another suggestion – 'I suppose you wouldn't go and study under some great psycho person?' No, Flavia would not. Nor did she want to return to Menabilly, a decision which made Tod say, 'I told you so.' Daphne was annoyed that Tod should ever think she expected Flavia to return there. She never at any time forced her children to do anything, just as she had never been forced. But though she exerted no direct influence, this did not mean she had no interest in their futures – on the contrary, she was passionately interested in their lives.

Especially, of course, in Kits' life. She never had any worry about how Kits was turning out, even when it might have been thought there was cause for a qualm or two. He was at Eton now – the sight of him in his tails was, his mother confessed, far more thrilling than Tessa beautiful in her wedding dress – and his extravagance in her opinion was prodigious – 'Kits is awful . . . he keeps writing for money . . . obviously has no idea of rationing himself. I shall have to be firm next half, but how?' In fact, she had no intention of even trying to be firm – it was her pleasure to overindulge her son, and since he never displayed any unpleasant effects from being so spoiled, she saw no harm being done. Kits was no scholar but this did not trouble her in the least – she preferred him to be the sports-mad fanatic he was, to be fun and full of life, and to remind her of Gerald. He was the 'real lad' she wanted and her ambitions for him were modest. Sometimes she thought he might be an actor, since he was a brilliant mimic, and sometimes a photographer. Whatever he did she would be pleased, so long as he remained his happy self, and, of course, financially, she had already made sure that he and his sisters would come into trusts from her books, which would give them all a substantial start in adult life. That this might not necessarily be good for any of them never troubled her, though it troubled Tommy, particularly where Kits was concerned.

But there were far more serious matters to bother Tommy than his son's attitude to money (which was not in any case so different from his own). In May 1955 he went into a nursing home 'to be checked up on'. Daphne approved of this – 'there he can be fussed and waited on'. Every weekend that he came down to Menabilly she thought he was 'like an old man of ninety' and, though she was sorry for the pain that lumbago caused him, she thought he made too much of it. He complained permanently of exhaustion (still not apparent to a single person at Buckingham Palace, though his cousin Brian Johnston had noticed his fatigue).[6] That spring, Daphne frequently and scathingly described him as 'pathetic', and even considered that 'he might easily go mad. I'm sure he bottles things up and doesn't know his feelings.' This was of course true, but whereas once Tommy had been able to unburden himself to her, now they were emotionally so far apart he could not. She interpreted his depression and tiredness to her children as not merely pathetic but, worse still, 'wain'. All she wanted to do was get away from him – 'to be somewhere but I don't know where'. She was tired of 'his bright moods turning savage' and she was trying 'to screw up my courage and speak about the moods . . . I am damned if I am going to sit through those awful evenings . . . where no one dares utter'. The complaints about the state of the house had reached intolerable levels and she was furious with him for harping on, when, as she wrote to Flavia, 'I *know* all the carpets and curtains are shabby, I *know* the food is deadly, but if I once seriously began to worry about it I should go mad'.

The only thing to do was to go on holiday as often as possible and hope another book would be sparked off. It was bliss to go to Blackpool with Kits – the mere idea of him choosing 'a honky weekend' in such a place made her laugh and she adored all the silly delights of the seaside with him. Then she and Tessa had a wonderful time in St Paul de Vence, where Tessa impressed her by being such a good organizer. No book came from either break, but this did not detract from the pleasure. Writing to Victor Gollancz, who, as ever, was eager for another novel to be on the horizon, she reminded him that 'everything I write comes from some sort of emotional inner life and the ordinary emotions are absolutely stagnant in me these days, so the unconscious has just got to work on its own, I can't do anything about that'. To another friend she once explained further – 'The difficulty is writing comes from within. A character or an idea has to grow like a seed and take possession . . . it's something to do with one's own development and passage through life.' Her own passage seemed suddenly to be stationary, and for the first time she began to express the fear that 'my creative powers may be drying up'. The thought of this was unbearable, not only because she would then feel there was 'no purpose in life' but because her No. 2 persona would have no outlet.

When, by the autumn of 1955, she still felt no seed for a book within her, the prospect of another winter without work so terrified her that she decided she would have to resort to another *Mary Anne* sort of book. This was the last thing she wanted to do, since writing *Mary Anne* had proved such a labour and the result far from satisfactory, but she thought if she researched her French ancestors perhaps a genuine idea would come to her. Anyhow, it was all she could think of and she made plans to tour the Loir-et-Cher area where the du Mauriers' glass-blowing ancestors had lived. This time she was taking as her companions her sister Jeanne and Jeanne's friend, Noël Welch. She did not see Jeanne as regularly as she had once done, because she and Noël had bought a house on Dartmoor and, since Daphne did not drive, the distance, though not so great, meant there was not the ease of contact there had been when Jeanne lived at Ferryside with her mother and Angela. In fact, Jeanne, though her mother's 'ewe lamb', had moved away emotionally as well as physically from her family, and Daphne was well aware of this. She wasn't at all sure how holidaying with Jeanne and Noël would work – 'I do not know what sort of travelling companion Jeanne is, though she is my sister! She is bringing Noël too!' – but since she regarded herself as 'equable' she was optimistic that it would all work out. The other two women did all the driving (Daphne had by then allowed her driving skills to lapse for so long, she had come to believe she had never driven at all) and they all got on perfectly well. It was interesting, she thought, to see how well Jeanne and Noël suited each other, and she was rather intrigued by the harmony between them, though she expressed no opinion on the nature of their relationship. Her sister's career surprised her – Jeanne had gone off to paint at St Ives after the war, where she had met the artist Dod Proctor, who took her to Africa. Her painting had developed greatly after that, and now she was living with Noël, entirely happy with her horses and gardening, producing excellent work. Noël wrote poetry and was clever and lively, and Daphne enjoyed the company of both of them, though not in the thoroughly easy way she enjoyed Clara Vyvyan's.

The great thing about this particular holiday, though, was that a seed was actually planted after all – an idea for a novel sprang into Daphne's head, and the relief and excitement were overwhelming. Instead of an historical novel she was suddenly inspired to write a contemporary novel about a man who takes on the life of his double. It came to her in the middle of a square in a small French town, when she saw a man who she thought looked exactly like someone she knew getting out of a car. The possibilities of such a common mistake came to her instantly: what if a person looked so like another he could exchange lives with him? She began making notes at once, even before she returned home, and felt a great surge of adrenalin at the thought of beginning to write again.

She started in October, reporting to an excited Victor that the new novel 'combines touches of *Rebecca* and *My Cousin Rachel* with flashes of *The Parasites*', but once she had reached halfway 'my labour pains are agony, the main trouble being that of deciding what happens to the other man (not the replacement, who is the narrator, and who takes over – that fires ahead clearly), but I simply must make what is a fantastically impossible story read with complete conviction. Unless the whole thing fits like a jigsaw it won't come off. Creation boils within.' It continued to boil for another six months, during which there were two unavoidable interruptions – the first to be with Tessa when her son Paul was born, in April 1956, and the second an attack of German measles when she was within sight of the end. When she did finish it, she was utterly exhausted – 'I feel I have aged ten years,' she wrote to Foy. 'I've been through all the things my poor wretched narrator has gone through in fancy.' But what was more significant was that she had come to believe that *The Scapegoat* was 'my story and it is Moper's also. We are both doubles. So is everyone. Every one of us has his, or her, dark side. Which is to overcome the other? This is the purpose of the book . . . and it ends . . . with the problem unsolved except that the suggestion . . . was that the two sides of that man's nature had to fuse together to give birth to a third, well-balanced: Know Thyself.' She went off to stay on Dartmoor with Noël and Jeanne to recuperate, not quite sure what she had produced but knowing that, unlike *Mary Anne*, *The Scapegoat* pleased her. She had, she wrote, 'tried to put into words something rather deeper than I have up to date', and to her editor, Sheila Bush, she repeated this – 'it is written at a much deeper level (conceited?!)'.[8]

This makes *The Scapegoat* an interesting novel to study for that 'something rather deeper', and almost immediately it is apparent what Daphne meant. The man she chose to be the narrator is a man who is looking 'for the courage to go on living'. He is depressed, feels his life has passed too swiftly and his only pleasure is to lose himself in fantasy. All he has ever done with his life is 'to watch people', and he has always felt 'an alien . . . too diffident, too conscious of my own reserve'. But inside himself he knows there is another person – 'who clamoured for release, the man within', the other self he was 'so used to denying expression'. The novel becomes not so much the story of two men swopping lives, with all the excitements of plot which result, as the story of *one* man releasing his inner self and experiencing 'the sensation that I myself did not matter any more'. He suddenly has a mission in life: 'to heal', and the family into which he has been brought needs a great variety of healing. He finds himself responding to the love he receives from his double's daughter, and from one of his mistresses, and even to the participation in the lives of all the others. The whole experience is an exercise in what Daphne would herself have liked to do – to release *her* 'man within', her troublesome No. 2. The fact that this released inner self *was* a man helped her to express thoughts and feelings about herself which would otherwise have been impossible. The scenes between the male narrator and his wife and his mistress are further examples, as in *September Tide* and *My Cousin Rachel*, of Daphne identifying with her male character so completely that she was able to believe he was herself in a way no one could ever guess.

But at another level, she had invented a complicated and bizarre story, full of thrills, which included death, drugs, dark deeds hinted at and business dealings incredibly protracted and involved. Her 'fantastically impossible story' does not read with that absolute conviction she wanted after all, particularly at the end when she had trouble getting the double back, but the portrait of the narrator is so strong that this is unimportant. She did not, in any case, want it to be read 'as a fast-moving thriller', but as a psychological study which just happened to be set in the context of a thriller. Unfortunately, this was one occasion when her publisher disappointed her. Victor wrote to Sheila: 'I have been enthusiastic enough not to worry her . . . but cannot control my tone of voice and I think she realises I have pretty grave reservations – (1) Too long. (2) The combined Assurance and Marriage Settlement motives don't quite work out. (3) Signatures not credible. (4) Child in well unsatisfactory.' Daphne had indeed realized all this and was anxious to take on board these criticisms while feeling that Victor had missed the point – all the things he had mentioned, with the exception of the length, were to do with the plot and it made her impatient that he should think they mattered so much. On the other hand, because they didn't really matter, she was perfectly happy to try to straighten them out and also to cut, as directed by both Sheila and Victor. Never at any time did she think of telling them, as many an author with her sales figures did (and still does), that she liked her novel as it was and if they did not she would try elsewhere. She didn't seem to realize that the fortunes of Gollancz rested firmly on the money they had made from her and that the merest suggestion that she might go elsewhere would have been disastrous for the firm. Instead, she wrote to Victor *apologizing* for 'all the hard work' she was causing Sheila, who was going through the manuscript marking suggested cuts – 'I feel so guilty'. At least Sheila appreciated the modesty of such a reaction, writing to Victor that Daphne had been 'angelic . . . about all the millions of points raised with her (it seemed like millions)', though she herself had found working on *The Scapegoat* 'the very d—l . . . so many changes and bits of rewriting'.

The novel was not to be published until April 1957, but simply finishing it (in the previous June) had had a rejuvenating effect on Daphne. Her spirits were higher than they had been for years and she knew it was all to do with 'giving No. 2 something useful to do'. Nobody needed to underline the significance of this for her – she knew perfectly well how clearly it showed the supreme importance of writing in her life. Nothing could take its place. She could tolerate only a few months without writing before being plagued by her discontented No. 2 which had no other outlet. But none of this was obvious to her family and friends who, though knowing how lost she was without writing (she told them so), never fathomed quite how aimless and unsettled her fallow periods were becoming. On the surface, she could seem happy and busy, especially in the summer with a steady stream of visitors coming to Menabilly for their holidays – Tessa and Peter with their two children; Flavia and her fiancé Alastair Tower (a Captain in the Coldstream Guards whom she had met through her brother-in-law); Kits and friends from school; Maureen, Tommy's PA and now a great friend of the whole family, and Monty Baker-Munton, whom she had married the previous year;[9] Ferdy; Ronald Armstrong; Oriel Malet – all these were regulars, and then there were people who came perhaps once or twice for a weekend, like Brian Johnston and his family, Carol Reed, the Prescotts, the Agars, the Deakins, and other friends who were passing through Cornwall. Far from living a reclusive life, she felt at times as though she were 'running a holiday camp'. Tommy, too, had his guests, and sometimes these would be interesting people like

Margot Fonteyn – 'the little ballerina was sweet and no trouble' – or even royalty. Prince Philip had stayed again, rather amazed to be told not to worry if he heard crashes in the night – it was only the old wing falling down. To all these visitors Daphne and Tommy seemed the perfect couple, acting as foils for each other's wit, calling each other 'duck' with such affection, both charming, especially to members of the opposite sex. There was always a lot of laughter, and the idea that Daphne had within her this demanding other self which was placated only by writing was impossible to guess at.

The Christmas of 1956, with *The Scapegoat* corrections finished, was especially happy. Now that the family circle had extended itself – Flavia had married Alastair in July, another smart London wedding – gatherings were even more convivial than they had usually been at this time of year, and Daphne loved it. Her mother and Angela came for Christmas Day itself, and Tod, of course, was there too, so it was a full house. Tommy acted as butler, Tessa and Flavia as maids, Kits was the pantry boy and 'it was like the house in the past with a full strength staff!' Watching them all, she felt proud and happy and, when the New Year arrived, was not at all daunted to realize she was going to be fifty in May. There was a certain relief, she decided, in reaching such an age and 'not to have to bother about emotions any more'. Or, come to that, clothes – 'so stupid to care too much'. She had decided she looked best in blue shirts and slim trousers and she refused to 'feel hopeless any more looking at dresses'. But she knew, at the same time, how dangerous it might be to become totally fixed in her attitudes and get to the stage of not caring about anything at all – 'I must not become detached and so be unsympathetic to other people's troubles'.

Of those sitting round that Christmas table the one who had the most troubles was Tommy. Part of his problem was familiar: he was drinking too much and in spite of desperate attempts to reduce his intake he had not succeeded. Attacks of the 'liver complaints' with which his wife had so little sympathy were more frequent and his left leg, which had begun to trouble him during the war, was making exercise difficult. For some years now he had been going into a nursing home from time to time 'to be overhauled', but any improvement was always temporary. Daphne knew all this, but what she did not know was how serious his emotional problems were becoming. There was a young woman (nicknamed 'Sixpence' by her) who worked in a shop in Fowey, whom he now took sailing. This half amused Daphne but also earned her contempt, though she retaliated merely by mercilessly mocking both him and the girl. In London, however, Tommy was having an affair with a woman about whom his wife knew nothing. Daphne did not want, and never had wanted, to know what he did in London – that was his life, just as Cornwall was hers. She could cut off London without difficulty. But Tommy, a far less complex person who lacked his wife's emotional strength, could not. He was running two lives and he hated it. The strain of pretending everything was fine, coupled with a tiredness that had been draining his reserves of energy for nearly a decade, was bringing him close to breaking point and he did not know if he could carry on. How much he knew of his wife's own problems it is impossible to guess. Small indications she reported – such as his unease over the snaps Gertrude sent and his puzzlement over her time in Paris with Frank Price – suggest Tommy may have divined rather more than he acknowledged about his wife's sexual nature. But if he had, still nothing was said, by either of them. As she had written to Ellen, any intimate talk was taboo.

Unaware of Tommy's misery, Daphne looked forward to the publication of *The Scapegoat*, believing that this, the year of her silver wedding anniversary, was going to be a good one. She wrote to Victor, asking him if he could cut down on pre-publication publicity – 'it irritates the brutes sharpening their biros'. She very much wanted not only to avoid annoying the reviewers, but also to 'break new ground' with this novel – 'I don't believe I ought to go on just resting on sales and faithful fans'. She wanted to attract a new readership and so felt 'softly, softly would be the best approach'. She had her own ideas about getting various eminent authors to read the novel and give quotes for the publicity handouts – an entirely new venture for her and quite contrary to her usual reticence where promotion was concerned. She suggested that, since it was set in France, Victor should send it to André

Maurois, whom she had met in Paris and discovered was a fan of hers. Victor promptly did so, and a very flattering quote came back. Then she began to worry about reviewers, wishing there were some way in which Victor could get J. B. Priestley to review it. She did not want women reviewers – 'women are inclined to be jealous of other women'.

In fact, when the reviews appeared, several were by women and were excellent – 'Nancy Spain, my old enemy, did me proud'. She was elated to have the novel, into which she had put so much, praised – with particularly good notices in the *Spectator* and the *Daily Telegraph* – but was not so carried away that she did not wonder whether 'perhaps they all felt sorry for me for a change'. The sales, on the other hand, were in du Maurier terms, though in no one else's, disappointing, according to Victor (he'd printed 100,000 copies), but Daphne was philosophical about this, saying 'surely the days of great sales are over'. What was more exciting was the tremendous film interest there had been, even before the novel came out.[10] A Hollywood studio wanted to buy it as a vehicle for Cary Grant, but she herself planned to form a company with Alec Guinness to enable him to take the double part. She had great expectations of how brilliant a film it could be in the right hands, which she believed to be Alec Guinness's hands.

Then, with great suddenness, Tommy collapsed at the beginning of July 1957, just before his twenty-fifth wedding anniversary. He was hospitalized but it quickly became apparent that, although there were things physically wrong with him, the main trouble was emotional stress – he had had a nervous breakdown. Upset by this news, but not as yet really understanding its cause, Daphne acted swiftly and compassionately. She went up to London at once to see her husband, who was under the care of Lord Evans, and found him sadly changed – thin, worn-looking, and visibly distressed. It was still not clear to her what all this was about until she received a telephone call from the woman with whom Tommy was having an affair – a call in which the woman voiced her anxiety over Tommy's health and her feeling that his breakdown was the result of his running two lives. The shock for Daphne was profound. It had simply never entered her head that Tommy could be having a serious love-affair, and she could hardly cope with the blow not only to her pride but to other feelings. She loved him and thought he loved her, in spite of the collapse of the physical side of their marriage, and that he should care for another woman to the extent of breaking down because of it seemed to her incomprehensible. But she rose to the sad occasion magnificently: Tommy was ill and for the time being that was all that mattered. She must help him get better before anything was resolved, and that is precisely what she set herself to do.

Everyone except the close family and Maureen and Monty Baker-Munton was told that Tommy was suffering from nervous exhaustion. Lord Evans, reported Daphne, had said the blood was going too slowly through his system, including his brain, and he needed 'pills to thin his blood'. His collapse, in Lord Evans' opinion, was due to 'personality deterioration', which in turn was due to an alcohol-damaged liver plus arterial trouble. If he stopped drinking and took more rest it would help, but only if the psychological basis of his illness was tackled would he really recover. Daphne, hearing this verdict, was struck by the notion that this was the test for which she had been somehow preparing herself all her adult life. 'I feel', she wrote, ' . . . like a soldier who is out of line to pick up strength, or perhaps a battleship having a refit . . . it's queer . . . but once one has been given the courage to face up to a difficulty the battle is half won.'[11] It made her laugh to remember she had once thought she had to get into training for anything as trivial as 'some sort of climbing expedition . . . or a journey of exploration', when now it was obvious 'that what I was meant to get fit for was this present crisis'. She saw it as a battle, but one she and Tommy had to fight together. Her own measure of guilt was bravely acknowledged – 'I have got to put my passion for solitude and my own company behind me, and thank goodness I had put emotions for other people (except my family) away for good some years ago, so I can now concentrate on doing what is right and best for everyone.'

What had first of all to be decided was whether she and Tommy would stay married, or whether there was any question of an official separation and possible divorce. This was quickly resolved: of course they would stay together. Not for a moment did Daphne contemplate leaving Tommy, nor did he wish to part from her.

As soon as he was well enough to leave hospital, she took him down to Menabilly and there, in the August sunshine, he pottered about and grew stronger. Meanwhile, Daphne reflected on her own past love-affair, the only one in her married life, or at least the only one with a man. 'I had a love-affair with a man in the war . . . which dragged on for six years. We were set to end it when Moper came back from the Far East. When Moper showed no interest in me . . . the temptation to go on again was only too easy. Furtive meetings, futile and wretched for us both. Making poison and somehow spoiling the remnants of the friendship. So we cut the knot and . . . he lives . . . with the wife who knew and forgave him. I had an impulse to write to her yesterday. The first time in fifteen years. I wonder if she will understand.' What she wanted Paddy Puxley to understand was that she herself now knew the depth and brutality of the shock she, too, had just received. But was she going to be able to forgive as Paddy had forgiven? This troubled her and drove her to examine the meaning of the marriage vows.

'For richer, for poorer,' she wrote, 'doesn't mean whether you can afford TV or buy a car, but whether the person you marry grows in personality and character or falls away; and for better or worse means whether you can measure up to happiness and joy, or suffering and failure; in sickness and in health means not just cherishing someone who may get pneumonia, but someone who gets sick with longing for someone else.' The fact that this crisis happened in her silver wedding anniversary year was ironic – 'twenty-five years, of which too many have been misspent through both our faults'. She remembered how, standing in church while Flavia and Alastair were married the summer before, and again when Maureen married Monty Baker-Munton, she had 'felt pretty ashamed and shit-like that I'd broken my own word' when she heard the marriage vows repeated. But she could not help feeling disgusted that during those same ceremonies, while she was feeling guilty about a love-affair some twelve years before, Tommy had been standing there knowing he was actually breaking his vows at that very time. 'I don't believe', she wrote, 'I could have gone to . . . Flavia's wedding if I'd been living or even having a wild affair with someone else.' At the end of this letter, written rather surprisingly to Tessa's former boyfriend, Ken Spence, she told him to 'keep it . . . to produce and show to myself or any of the people concerned if crisis comes again'. It was in the nature of a declaration and she wanted it preserved. She also wrote an extraordinary letter which was in the nature of a confession to Maureen Baker-Munton. In this she fantasized that 'Sixpence', the girl Tommy was interested in who lived in Fowey, 'is the second Mrs de W and I – in Moper's dark mind – can be the symbol of Rebecca. The cottage on the beach could be my hut. Rebecca's lovers could be my books. Mrs Danvers, devoted, could be Tod, the old devotee.' Having invented this scenario, she then imagined that 'Moper, in a blind rage, [could] shoot me as Maxim shot Rebecca, and put my body in *Yggie* [*sic*], and take *Yggie* out to sea, and then the old tragedy be re-enacted, and when he married, as he would in time, some younger "Sixpence", be haunted by my ghost.' Even then she was not finished – '*Or*, the present "Sixpence", a symbol of Jan, be taken out to sea and killed because what has happened is that some old ghost of Jan is resurrected . . . just as Rebecca's body was discovered in the boat and brought to the surface. The evil in us comes to the surface.' What she actually claimed might happen was 'something berserk might snap, with that revolver, and that . . . gun, and the arrows. I am not talking madly. I know.' In other words, she thought Tommy might kill her.

It was a letter written with great passion, one which she said was 'a witness of my belief', and which she instructed Maureen to preserve a copy of 'for future family reference'. She also said in it that she had written to Tommy 'a great, long letter . . . saying how to blame I had been for so much of his unhappiness during the past years, and [I] came clean about the Puxley man, and then tried to explain . . . my obsessions – you can only call them that – for poor old Ellen D and Gertrude'. These obsessions, she had told Tommy, 'were all part of a nervous breakdown going on *inside myself*, partly to do with my muddled troubles, and writing, and a fear of facing reality'. Her distress was painfully evident in these outpourings, but so was her determination, in the rest of the letter, that this crisis should be surmounted 'and everyone will be the better and the more understanding for the blow-up of the boiler'.[12]

When Tommy was well enough he returned to London and work in September. Daphne knew this would be the testing time for him and enlisted the help of Ken Spence. Ken became a kind of go-between, visiting the other woman (always referred to in code as 'Covent Garden') and reporting back to Daphne what she was feeling about the situation. Daphne thanked him, but realized that only Tommy could decide if he was going to see 'Covent Garden' again. He did, eventually, with his wife's knowledge. She reported to Ken that Tommy had said 'Covent Garden' had invited him to dinner and that although he did not want to go he felt he should. 'So I said "Why not go for a drink instead?" . . . he looked relieved and said, "Yes." He went and when he came back said, "Well, I seem to be all right. The only thing was she was rather hurt you hadn't let me stay to dinner." ' This naturally enraged Daphne – 'I ask myself, did he, man-like, go to her and say "Daphne won't let me stay for dinner," thus putting the blame of his own not-wishing-to-stay on me; or did he really *want* to stay and yet tell me in the morning this was not the case? Or did she say reproachfully, "Aren't you going to stay to dinner?" I would say the answer was a mélange of all three.' When her rage had subsided the conclusion she drew from this episode was that Tommy was 'a moral coward, and he will be inclined to let this thing drag on to save his face. It will do no good to either, because they will be living on something that is past. Let him take her to dinner at a restaurant if he likes, or drop in for a drink now and again, but to take up the cosy routine . . . is only clinging to something that no longer has any meaning . . . when a person has a tumour, the surgeon doesn't cut out half, he removes the lot.'

But there was more than one 'tumour'. The young woman in Fowey, code-named 'Sixpence', was still attractive to Tommy. By chance, Daphne overheard him arranging to meet 'Sixpence' in church. Daphne herself never went to church, but she related to Tessa how she promptly 'crammed on clothes . . . and spoilt it by going to church myself. No sign of her.' That evening, she was determined to have it out with Tommy and asked him point-blank what his feelings for 'Sixpence' really were. He told her, or so she said, that they were as strong as ever but he knew they had no future. Next day, he was extremely contrite. He went sailing but she knew he 'only enjoys it when the bitch is there'. Her contempt was growing and so was her sense of humiliation. The absurdity of 'Sixpence' and 'Covent Garden' causing such havoc struck her forcibly and instead of feeling distraught she slowly began to feel triumphant. She actually asked 'Covent Garden' to meet her in the forecourt of the British Museum, so that she could size her up and hear her point of view, and felt proud that she had not given way to tears. *She* had not collapsed, but had behaved with dignity and had been civilized and sensible. But it was at a price: as the winter began, she once more felt on the verge of madness – a very controlled madness, but one not to be ignored. Tommy's breaking point was over, but she wondered if hers was yet to come, in spite of all her efforts. From the evidence of her letter to Maureen, it was surely already taking place.

Chapter Eighteen

No sooner was Tommy back at Buckingham Palace (though wondering how long he could go on with his job, since he still felt exhausted at the end of each day) then Daphne's mother died, aged eighty. This had a greater effect on Daphne than she had imagined it would: in her depressed state it was bound to affect her more severely. For the last few years Muriel du Maurier had been steadily deteriorating (she suffered from arteriosclerosis), so her death came as no surprise, but Daphne had never witnessed anyone's death before and she was shocked by the sight of her mother 'hanging on to life by a thread . . . she looks so lost . . . if this is a natural death for an old person the bomb would be more merciful'.[1] The pathos of old age moved her and she declared herself strongly against the 'inhumanity' of putting old people in homes. Muriel had been cared for by Angela, but she had spent occasional spells at Menabilly, looked after by a nurse.[2] Now, watching her die, Daphne wrote to Foy that she wished it were over.

When it was, on 27 November, she wrote to Foy, 'I could not but be thankful . . . but I do wish her last years had not been such a burden for her.' Standing at her mother's bedside after she had gone into a coma she had 'put down my face to touch hers. The face had gone completely spiritual – all the congested, suffering look was absent – and she suddenly turned her head slowly and with eyes closed and still in the deep coma, kissed me twice and then turned her head back on the pillow'. The moment Muriel died, Daphne felt there was a spiritual transformation in her face and had the 'strange psychic experience' of feeling 'a great reunion was going on somewhere between the parents'. It seemed that her mother had been 'completely purged of all her many years of suffering and indeed of the earlier years of trial and difficulty, and things that had not been right inside herself'. The 'years of suffering' were a reference to the last ten years of her mother's life, with her slow mental as well as physical deterioration so upsetting to witness, and the 'earlier years of trial and difficulty' were those in which, Daphne now concluded, Muriel had tolerated Gerald's affairs while suffering more than had been apparent at the time. But to refer to 'things that had not been right inside herself' was deeply enigmatic. It may have been a reference to Muriel not being able to love Daphne as she wished, but it may also have been to do with Muriel's own attitude to sex. In either case, her mother was 'purged' of all that had been less than loving in their relationship, and because of this Daphne seemed to be saying that she herself felt liberated.

She went to her mother's cremation service in Cornwall, then she and Angela took the ashes up to Hampstead and scattered them where Gerald was buried. She was 'sad, but not wretchedly sad, because now they are both together'. Leaving the churchyard she could not prevent herself from wishing she were there too, but it was not, she maintained, because of any suicidal urge, or even 'a gloomy view', but arose from 'a sort of longing I have always had for what is beyond'. It was the residue of her childhood identification with Peter Pan – dying was still 'an awfully big adventure' and it intrigued rather than frightened her.

Returning to Menabilly on one of those dreary late autumn days she hated, there seemed precious little adventure in her earthly life and instead a great deal that was prosaic and dull. Not even the thought of another family gathering at Christmas cheered her – too much had happened in the past six months. Her silver wedding year had, she remarked, turned out to be 'a bit of a frost'. She knew she was going through the menopause – 'no curse since March' – and thought Tommy was having his own change of life – 'I think men have the change far worse than *we* do and make a fearful fuss when they don't feel a hundred per cent and think they are breaking up . . . '[3] (In retrospect, she saw Gerald's depressions, those puzzling feelings of worthlessness around the age of fifty, as part of the male menopause.) The only thing that cheered her was thinking of 'my beautiful boy . . . seventeen, and the naughtiest thing on earth for sense of humour – my Dad all over again'. Otherwise, everything was 'gloom and doom', and if she didn't start writing soon she would become 'demented'.

She was actually, at the beginning of 1958, a little unbalanced anyway. She began imagining that all kinds of plots were surrounding her – that Tommy was being spied on by Russians who were out to get the Royal Family, and other, similar delusions. Half the time she laughed at herself, knowing she was being absurd, but then she would suddenly decide her fantasies were rooted in reality and become agitated. Far too intelligent and self-aware not to realize the significance of these paranoid tendencies, she knew she was fighting against her own breakdown, and that her only salvation was to write. She began to write some short stories, a series all to do with breaking points of one sort or another and revealing with frightening clarity how near the edge she had been. Later, when they were finished, she wrote to Tessa that writing them had got 'my own pottiness' out of her system and that they had been her way of showing she was 'not all that tough' during the crisis with Tommy.

The most significant of all the stories from this point of view was 'The Blue Lenses', a tale in which a woman who has had an eye operation sees everyone who comes near her as having the head of an animal which denotes their character – only she herself still has a human head. She decides they are all conspiring against her – her husband, who has a vulture's head, is plotting with a nurse, who has a snake's. She is aware of a new power in herself to tell truth from falsehood and escapes from the hospital where everyone is lying to her. Eventually, when it is discovered she has been experiencing hallucinations due to pressure on an optic nerve, which is then corrected, everyone looks normal again, but she sees to her horror that now *she* is the only one with an animal's head: she is a deer, and her eyes are the meek and timid ones of a doe. As an allegory of Daphne's state of mind this story was painfully clear – she felt betrayed, exploited and, worst of all, fooled. She had acted well, had helped her husband and stood by him, drawing back from ugly scenes and recriminations because she saw how he suffered too, and because, as to almost all women of that era, the preservation of her marriage was so important to her and divorce deeply shameful. But after the crisis was over, and especially when she heard Tommy making assignations with 'Sixpence', or expressing regret that he could not have dinner with 'Covent Garden', she could not help feeling she had been party to her own humiliation – she was meek and submissive, like the doe. In suppressing her own grief and sense of outrage she wondered if she had injured herself more than she knew.

Another story, 'The Chamois', was extremely relevant to the past crisis and even more confessional in nature. A woman goes with her husband to Greece where he wants to hunt chamois. She tells us she is going to be 'very frank about my husband', who now repels her as much as he attracts her still. What had brought them together originally was a 'communion of the flesh', but after they had been married a while she realized there was 'in reality a chasm' between them and she 'despised the bridge we had made across it'. Everyone else thinks they are happily married, so perfect is their pretence, but each of them knows the truth. They travel to the remote area where the chamois are hunted and the story turns to the husband's cowardice. It seems he has always had a fear of heights which, if he is to hunt the chamois, must be overcome. While he sleeps, she is beset by her own fear: of man (or more precisely, sexuality). She dreams she has touched the hair of the goatherd who is their guide – 'it rose . . . like a black crest' – a man she both fears and yet is excited by. These two fears unite husband and wife and they go off stalking the chamois together. The husband shoots and 'destroyed the thing that frightened me', not the goatherd but the chamois. The goatherd simply disappears.

'The Chamois' was the story which Daphne told Victor Gollancz 'intrigues me most'. It intrigued her because, although she had written it, she was not quite sure what to make of her own symbolism. Still heavily influenced by what she called 'my psycho books', she was always telling her children to 'watch your dreams', and in this case she was watching her own with some alarm. She had always had a fear of something wild in her own nature which she kept tightly controlled, and in her dreams this wildness seemed to take over, often sexually – 'I had a dream in which I was in bed with a fearfully attractive honky [vulgar] young man that I absolutely despised, who got up to nim [urinate] in a pot, and I was so put off and yet at the same time wanted to wax [make love] although I wasn't in the least menaced [attracted] . . . I think it must mean that there is a complete division somewhere between waxing and ordinary liking, the one is not dependent on the other.' Her sexual needs were labelled 'abhorrent' – needs for which she had found no outlet, with the significant exception of her affair with Gertrude Lawrence, except in her writing.

When she had finished 'The Chamois', which she wrote 'at top speed', she wrote to Victor that it was 'the most subtle story I have yet done and *pray* you will see the point of it'. Sadly, Victor did not, though he thought it a very good story, but then he knew nothing about Daphne's personal life. He told her he thought she had 'laid it on too thick' and asked, puzzled, 'is the goatherd really the chamois?'

Beside these two startling stories the others seem ordinary, even those involving murder and death. 'The Alibi' is about a man who wants to escape his humdrum life. Like the narrator of *The Scapegoat*, he really wants to escape from himself and seeks anonymity to find out if he can. His involvement in two deaths for which he is wrongly blamed somehow achieves this, even though the story ends with him under arrest. In 'Ganymede', a homosexual tries to escape his own nature and fails. He goes to Venice and cannot resist a boy he sees there. The death of the boy in a terrible accident solves nothing: the man returns home and it is obvious that the same thing will overtake him again – there is no escape from himself. The backgrounds for these stories noticeably came from holiday locations – Venice, Greece – or London and not from Cornwall, but the tension holding them together came from within herself. The violence, suspicion, hatred and despair fuelling them came from her own 'pottiness' and the writing of the stories was certainly to a very great extent a kind of therapy.

But there was another strand in this collection which was emerging as important in Daphne's writing, and that was her interest in the supernatural. 'The Pool' has a mystical quality to it and is more concerned with the inevitable sadness of growing up than with any macabre happenings. It concerns a girl, unable to sleep, who goes out into the garden during the night. A woman standing by a wicket-gate lets her into a secret world beside the pool.

Another night she runs into the pool, only to wake up and discover she has started to menstruate. Her sorrow is overwhelming, because now the hidden world is out of her reach forever – very much Daphne's own feelings about the onset of puberty. The J. M. Barrie undertones to 'The Pool' were obvious – secret woods, secret worlds where only children were allowed – but Daphne based it on an experience of her own. She had slept out in the Menabilly garden several nights that summer and had woken once with a conviction that someone was there – not a real person, but not a ghost. She sensed all around her another time and another world – it was thrilling but also distressing, and afterwards she went into the house and slept. When she woke up, she found she was menstruating after months of not doing so and of believing she was through the menopause. The whole atmosphere of 'The Pool' was an attempt to recapture what she felt had been a psychic experience.

'The Lordly Ones' and 'The Archduchess' were also tinged with the supernatural, as is the last story, 'The Menace', where the past seems to have powers of rejuvenation. A film star of the silent era finds that when 'the feelies' come in he has no magnetism – his rating is Force G. Every effort is made to increase it by stimulating him with well-tried 'cures' like pretty girls, but it remains low. Then he meets an old friend, they reminisce the night away, and in the morning his rating is Force A. This one sits oddly in the collection, only just earning its place because of the prospect of the actor reaching breaking point, but it is light and witty and relieves some of the gloom of the others. Two more stories Victor turned down as 'quite out of key with the rest' and Daphne accepted his judgement.[4]

Heavy warnings went out to all her family and friends before *The Breaking Point* appeared about how macabre the stories might be found, but she defended them on the grounds that they reflected her view of the world. Her optimism about human nature, so strong during the years she supported MRA, was deserting her and she had had several discussions with Victor Gollancz on how hopeless everything seemed. He sent her his pamphlet on capital punishment, which provoked the response that it was no good forgiving a murderer and saying 'sin no more . . . a murderer should be told "restore life thou hast taken away" '. Her ideas on how this could be done were original but bizarre – 'Teddy boys who batter people to death should be made orderlies in cancer wards . . . and as to the raping type of murderer, I think he should be trained as a midwife (no, darling, I am serious) he would be shattered if . . . he watched new life come into the labour ward.'5 Another of Victor's pamphlets, on the nuclear bomb, brought forth the comment, 'I don't believe any great anti-H-Bomb crusade will bring the answer'. She herself didn't think the planet would be annihilated – 'something will be invented to neutralise the bomb'. The exploration of outer space greatly excited her and she thought this might in some way bring the world to its senses.

Where she parted company with Victor, and revealed her own pessimism, was in her opinion of his socialism. He tried but failed to convince her that socialism was a force wholly for good and that she should support it. To his vision of everyone enjoying a good standard of living, she replied that 'some natures are *not* improved by good living – think of all the well-fed Americans and how preying [greedy] they can be . . . you believe Man is essentially good, but I don't know. I wonder. Often . . . my heart goes out to a stranger, some little unknown woman at a cash desk . . . (I) am utterly moved and love the human race. Then *volte face* . . . a swarm of very noisy smelly people come crashing through a field to the woods here in bluebell time, dragging bluebells from the roots in a careless almost brutal fashion, all yelling . . . and then they strew the beach, once so white and lovely, with sandwich papers, cartons, corn-plasters, contraceptives, and all these are our well-fed millions.'6 She was not a Tory but inclined towards a vague humanitarian, if élitist, liberalism and was always more attracted to the individual politician than to his politics. Tommy influenced her far more heavily in political matters than did Victor. She quoted his opinions often in her letters and had the greatest respect for his superior knowledge. He had fought two wars to defend his country and she was ever mindful that this gave him, and all his generation, the right to expect what they had fought for to be preserved. If Tommy despaired, as he did in the fifties, of 'the general slackness' with which the country was run, then so did she.

Both of them, of course, were firm royalists, Daphne no less than her husband, in spite of hating her week at Balmoral and loathing almost all social occasions connected with the Palace. The Queen had the power to make her cry – 'I blush to say I piped an eye' – when she made a speech and Daphne could be quite overcome when she thought of what a burden being Queen was – 'yet Tommy says she is well able'. She was proud of his position in the royal household and knew how much it meant to him. This made her sympathetic to the dilemma he faced after his breakdown: if he carried on, feeling as he did, still so worn out, then he might crack up completely. He was sixty-two the year after his collapse and it was time to retire (though no one at Buckingham Palace, least of all Prince Philip, suggested it). The prospect of Tommy's retirement loomed over Daphne during the next year and caused her great agony of mind. If Tommy retired and lived at Menabilly full-time, she felt she would not be able to stand his constant presence, nor would she be able to write, but on the other hand she saw that, if he did not retire, he would push himself to the brink and there would be another, perhaps worse, crisis.

In the summer of 1958, when nothing had yet been decided, they went on holiday abroad together for the first time for several years. Without Tommy being aware of it, Daphne had written to Prince Philip to say she thought her husband ought to retire, but that his sense of duty was so strong that the suggestion would have to come from Prince Philip himself. Prince Philip replied that he did not want to lose Boy, but suggested that a break might be a good thing, after which decisions could be made.

The holiday was in the nature of a test, to see what state Tommy was really in a year after his breakdown. The two of them were to drive through France to watch the filming of *The Scapegoat*, and Daphne approached the trip with strong misgivings – 'I hope Moper won't be his usual millstone . . . on the drink he feels ill, off the drink he feels ill.' If he was 'ill' on their holiday she vowed she was going 'to bung him in a French nursing home'. He was not indisposed but neither of them enjoyed themselves very much. Daphne was furious with what she saw happening to her novel – 'not one word of mine in the screenplay and the whole story changed. I think it will be a flop . . .' Tommy was depressed the entire time and when they got back to Menabilly she called in the local doctor to look at him. She had become convinced his condition was 'largely inherited' and made worse by 'all that fatal going up to London'. The local doctor, with the inspiring name of Martin Luther, impressed her greatly. 'He does understand Moper,' she wrote, and 'I have never known a doctor more sensible . . . who really understands him and frankly that takes some doing.' She herself thought that Tommy was 'a semi-mental case, but not certifiable', and, even if he became so, 'I could not bear him to go into a mental home'. There was no question of that. Dr Luther was confident, according to Daphne, that he would be able 'to steady Moper sufficiently to go through the handover at the Palace without making a balls of it'. The idea was to build up his physical strength and keep 'nervous strain and fatigue to a minimum . . . if he is not worried, guilty, etc., the future should hold no fears'.[7]

Not for him, perhaps, but for her the future was once more full of fears. By the autumn of 1958 she had faced up to the fact that Tommy must retire and come to live at Menabilly full-time. At the ages of fifty-two and sixty-two, after twenty-seven years of marriage, they would be together every day in a way they had never been in their lives, and she dreaded it more than any wife facing her husband's retirement has ever done. One thing was certain: Tommy and Tod could not live in the same house permanently. If Tod were in residence not only would the atmosphere be terrible but Daphne would be piggy-in-the-middle. The time had come for Tod to leave and this was cause for further worry – where would she go, how could it be arranged? Daphne had no desire to hurt Tod, but clearly Tommy must, in the circumstances, come first. In the event, arrangements for Kits' future solved the problem. Kits left Eton in the summer of 1958, with plans for a career in films on the directing side. Daphne bought him a camera and projector and he made his first film around Fowey with both his parents taking part (Tommy had to pretend to shoot Tod in the film, greatly to his satisfaction). Daphne loved all this, though seeing clearly 'ambition oversteps possibility', and, recognizing her son's enthusiasm as genuine, arranged for him to go to Cuba to work with Carol Reed – as a sort of odd-job boy to gain experience – for the shooting of *Our Man in Havana*. On his return he needed to be in London, if he were to find work, so Tod was sent with him to live at Whitelands House as a kind of housekeeper. All was now set, in the summer of 1959, for Tommy to hand over to his successor at Buckingham Palace.

Leaving the service of Prince Philip caused Tommy immense distress. In a letter to his godson Ken Spence, Tessa's former boyfriend, he confessed that 'the fact of saying farewell to him . . . probably affected me much more than I expected . . . may you never feel the same sort of hell I am going through at the moment. And it is all one's own fault and can be blamed on no one.' In his misery, and suffering terribly from the recognition of his own weaknesses, he was also well aware of how his poor health and state of mind affected his wife. 'What really worries me', he wrote, 'is the unhappy effect it must have on Daphne, but she is as usual being wonderful though I must be a sore trial to her.' His depression and feeling of worthlessness were profound – 'I am suffering from a violent reaction after retiring,' he wrote a month later, 'and don't seem to be much use to myself or anyone at the moment. I dare say this phase will pass, at least I hope so, as it gives one an inferiority complex and one wonders what one is doing in this life at all.' His 'tum', not surprisingly, had started to play up again, and he commented that 'it affects one's nerves', still not willing to acknowledge that it might be the other way round.

It was early summer before Tommy took up full-time residence at Menabilly, and Daphne knew the real test would not come until the autumn glooms, which she so dreaded, descended. Then, on the dark, rainy days, the full impact of never being able to be on her own would hit her, and she knew she must be prepared. So far as she could see, there were only two stratagems available to her: to be so absorbed in work she would hardly notice Tommy's presence, or to get away from him as often as possible. Neither alternative was easy. To become lost in a book she had first to think of one, and to think of one she had to have the right atmosphere – while she felt so anxious and unsettled no ideas would come to her. Nor was leaving Tommy simple. He was not well and needed her, if not to nurse him, to bolster his confidence.

Whatever her attitude to his retirement, she was concerned for him and dutiful – whenever she left Menabilly someone else had to take her place, which involved the kind of arrangements she found a nightmare. Sometimes she would be presented with an unavoidable reason for leaving him, which even he could understand and put up with – as when she went to be near Flavia, in August 1959, during the birth of her son Rupert – but even then 'I had to dash back as Tommy had one of his depression patches as soon as I went . . .' To justify her absence in the long winter months she needed a project and so, if possible, did Tommy.

The project she decided to embark on was the kind of book she had never attempted before – a straightforward, properly researched biography of Branwell Brontë. She had always loved the Brontës ever since at the age of twelve she read *Wuthering Heights* – 'it's the most extraordinary book, miserable and very highly strung . . . it left me sleepless' – and in 1955 had been pleased to be asked by Macdonald to write the introduction to a reissue of the novel in their classics series. She had taken the task very seriously, using it as an opportunity to go to Haworth and visit the parsonage and the Brontë Museum with Flavia and Oriel Malet. The three of them stayed at the Brontë Guest House ('main meal at 6.30 pm and no alcohol!') and had long walks across the moors, thinking themselves into the lives of the three sisters and becoming quite swept away by the atmosphere of the parsonage, especially the nursery, which Daphne found 'very happy . . . why do people pretend it is gloomy?' When she got back, she read all the juvenilia of the Brontës, published in the Shakespeare Head edition, and was struck by the amount of work done by the ill-fated Branwell. She began to believe he had not been given due credit. Two years later, she wrote to John Alexander Symington, one of the two editors of the Shakespeare Head edition, politely asking him if he thought 'a thorough and complete transcription' of Branwell's works would help to establish him as every bit as talented as his sisters. She was, she wrote, 'fascinated by Branwell and I cannot understand why modern Brontë research has neglected him'.[8] Symington responded enthusiastically and was only too willing to help in any way he could. Daphne bought the full Shakespeare Head edition from him together with a complete set of the transactions of the Brontë Society, and decided 'Yes, I would like to do a book on Branwell.' She did not, however, want it to be like either *The Du Mauriers* or *Mary Anne* – this was to be a serious, scholarly affair, something 'worthwhile' and offering both new material and new insights. But then came Tommy's breakdown, and the short stories which arose out of it. The Branwell Brontë project was relegated once more to 'a hobby for the winter evenings', even though she had been to the British Museum – on the occasion of her meeting with 'Covent Garden' – to study the Brontë manuscripts in the Ashley Library. Her ambition was 'to track down every MS of Branwell's known to exist . . . and to have them photostated and then transcribed'. Once Tommy was installed at Menabilly, she saw that Branwell would provide her with a reason for trips both to Yorkshire and to the British Museum. The irony of wanting to go to London frequently now did not escape her.

The thought of working on this biography put her 'on my mettle' and gave her the opportunity to test herself in a way she had, in fact, always wanted to do. There was a good deal of the scholar *manqué* in Daphne, in spite of her frequent claims to have a butterfly mind. As it was, she was prepared to teach herself by trial and error with the help and generous guidance of Symington, to whom she wrote eager and lively letters, unafraid to show her ignorance and modestly demonstrating her already considerable knowledge. But then, in June 1959, Daphne experienced that shock, well known to would-be biographers who learn that some-one else is also working on the book they plan to do. In this case the other writer was a formidable rival. Winifred Gérin, whose biography of Anne Brontë had appeared that spring, to general acclaim, had begun research on Branwell. Daphne was appalled – she felt that Branwell was 'hers', but she had noticed the reverential reviews for Miss Gérin's previous book, and realized she was a power to be reckoned with.

The reckoning did not take her long. The truth was, she both needed to do the Branwell book and was genuinely fascinated by the project, but there was more than that to consider. She actually relished the thought of a rival and quickly built up the contest with Winifred Gérin into a major issue. She wrote to her, 'a long, friendly letter, wishing her success and saying she is far better placed . . . than I . . . to do a full biography . . . and that I could possibly still do some sort of study or portrait . . .' But to Symington she admitted, 'I don't think . . . we can dismiss the thought of her proposed biography so easily.' She had had 'a success *d'estime*' with Anne, and any forthcoming book of hers will be watched for with 'interest and sympathy'. These were precisely the qualities Daphne felt would be lacking in critics of her own book – 'My novels are what is known as popular and sell very well, but I am *not* a critic's favourite, indeed I am generally dismissed with a sneer as a bestseller and not reviewed at all, so . . . I would come off second-best, I have no illusions to that!' This representation of her critical reputation was exaggerated – *The Scapegoat* and *The Breaking Point* had just had excellent reviews – but it showed her need to be taken seriously. Branwell, she hoped, was going to change this, in spite of 'the critics' favourite', Winifred Gérin (who replied with 'a very nice letter' to Daphne's own, wishing her luck in turn).

During the next six months Daphne strained every nerve to do 'a proper job' on Branwell, cutting no corners and applying herself assiduously to reading the transcripts she had had made of every Branwell manuscript. She passionately wanted to go to Haworth again and spend time looking at manuscripts in the Brontë Museum, but Tommy's ill health kept holding her back. 'I have been in constant attendance on my husband,' she wrote to Symington, telling him, 'I feel rather like Charlotte Brontë when nursing the Rev. Brontë and finding it difficult to get on with *Villette*.' Jealously, she thought often of Winifred Gérin – 'I feel Miss Gérin must be working away at high pressure' – and imagined her, unimpeded, visiting the Brontë Museum and going through the very manuscripts she herself wanted to study. Whenever she had a sudden good idea, such as getting hold of 'the rate books of Little Ouseborn, Yorks. . . . to try and find out who was living in the district in 1748' (to identify an acquaintance of Branwell's who worked as a tutor) she would instruct Symington – 'Don't tell Miss G!' It caused her great anguish every time she heard from someone she had contacted, in her search for Brontë papers or memorabilia, to find 'Miss Gérin visited them a month ago! Infuriating.' She half wanted 'Miss Gérin and I to clash on the doorstep' and when she finally began writing, in the New Year of 1960, she was frantic to 'beat Miss Gérin and be out first'. Victor Gollancz did not help, telling her that if Gérin came out first her own book would be killed. She became obsessed with the need to 'beat her'. Tessa, who accompanied her mother on the second visit to Haworth, which she had finally made just before starting to write, found her full of the kind of paranoid imaginings which had afflicted her after Tommy's breakdown. All that was determined and stubborn and competitive in her was coming to the fore in her desire to win the race with her rival.

In one way, she did. Her book, *The Infernal World of Branwell Brontë*, came out in October 1960, eight months ahead of Winifred Gérin's biography. Victor showed caution, printing 8,000 copies (very generous, even then, for a biography of that sort), far fewer copies than he had ever printed of any du Maurier book (except for the plays). Daphne, while saying to Victor and to others that she quite understood and, of course, she realized 'poor Branwell will only have a moderate sale as he isn't everyone's cup of tea', in fact resented what she considered Victor's lack of enthusiasm. Quite unfairly, she even commented before publication that she was 'more and more bored by the thought of how Victor Gollancz will wreck it'.

As usual, neither Victor nor her editor, Sheila, knew how strongly she felt about the suggestions they made and which she appeared only too ready to incorporate. There were no battles – she simply got on with tightening the narrative and making the cuts recommended – because she lacked the confidence to stick up for her own work. Her great terror was to appear a prima donna, and she had a very real inferiority complex about her own grasp of grammar and syntax, always believing her publisher and editor to be right. In the case of Branwell, she certainly presented them with problems. The diligence of her research showed – this was undoubtedly, in that respect, 'the proper job' she had wanted – and so did her empathy with Branwell, whom she portrayed more sympathetically than anyone ever had done, but her style worked against these excellent qualities. Writing the book, Daphne had found it 'heavy going' and wrote of 'ploughing ahead'. It was, she judged a little gloomily, 'good for the brain', but what it was not good for was a smooth read. She produced a biography in which material from documentary sources was mixed in the most awkward fashion with entirely imaginary suppositions, greatly to its detriment. She frequently suggested that Branwell 'might have felt' quite specious emotions and that he 'may have thought' things nobody could possibly know. This kind of guesswork ruined some of her sharper interpretations, such as her discussion of how Branwell behaved towards Mrs Robinson (his employer's wife, with whom he may or may not have had an affair). Daphne defends him convincingly from any impropriety, arguing her case well, but then, after commenting that 'all is hearsay, gossip and surmise' except for the facts she has given, she promptly indulges in all three.

She could not hope to rival Miss Gérin's clarity and elegance of language but, matched for research and psychological insight, Daphne's biography is every bit as good as the later one. Luckily, the pick of the critics realized how solid her research was and enjoyed the emergence of Branwell as a newly fascinating character. L. P. Hartley reviewed it well in the *New Statesman*, which was balm to Daphne's soul, and so did Muriel Spark in the *Daily Telegraph*. But she was disappointed by how little general attention the book received, though writing to Victor she admitted it was her own fault 'if I don't get publicity through refusing interviews, etc.'.

The main thing, she assured herself, was that she had enjoyed doing the book and it had seen her through the first winter with Tommy. This had gone better than she had expected, not just because she was absorbed in Branwell but because Tommy himself had been absorbed in writing a little history of the Queen's life when she was Princess Elizabeth, while he was Comptroller of her household. The Clarence House archives had been sent down to Menabilly and he had worked all winter producing his account (upon which he was complimented). In addition, he had taken on the job of County Controller of Civil Defence in Cornwall, not full-time but 'as boss of the whole thing'. This got him out of the house occasionally, to his wife's relief. Yet in spite of these interests she felt he was steadily growing dependent on her and she could not stand it. She did not see how she could ever write a novel again, locked into a situation which threatened to cut off her creative powers. *Branwell* was all very well as a challenge, but hopeless for the release of 'No. 2' in her nature.

PART FIVE

Death of the Writer
1960–1989

Chapter Nineteen

Once *Branwell* had been completed, Daphne's imagination lay fallow. In the past, this had never agitated her, but now, in her fifties, it always did. She worried about it in a way she had never done, not only because without writing she felt empty and restless, but because she was even more anxious about money than she had always been. In 1956, assessing her own career and earning-power, she had written to Victor Gollancz: 'Nowadays the majority of my readers really date back to the *Jamaica Inn*, *Rebecca* and *Frenchman's Creek* days, over fifteen years back.' She saw herself as out of fashion and was resigned to 'quite a long cycle until perhaps I am around sixty instead of fifty, when suddenly it will become fashionable to be an ageing figure'. This being so, she envisaged a frightening drop in her income and from then on was always preparing for it. When she had finished the stories for *The Breaking Point* she sent them to the USA, before letting Victor see them, hoping for lucrative magazine publications for them first, because 'with declining sales in future years I think I should watch this market and not let any good offer pass'. It was no good either Victor or even her accountant, Richard Pegler,[1] saying she was being ridiculous and should have no financial worries – she felt that she did, writing in the most exaggerated terms to a friend from Cannon Hall days that because of the trusts she had made for her children – 'the sum entirely for them . . . poor me, never been able to touch a penny'[2] – she did not have the money people imagined. She pointed out that on the money not put in trust she was taxed at 19s. 6d. in the pound and that, as she did not want to live abroad, there was nothing that could be done about it. Victor tried valiantly to reassure her, telling her he saw 'not a trace of falling off' in either her creative ability or earning-power, and that, in any case, her backlist sales guaranteed her a very healthy income, but she could not be consoled. 'The blunt fact is,' she replied, 'my best creative work has been done. I might come out, now and again, with some sort of flash-in-the-pan book . . . but that *steady flow* of the years 1934–1954 has gone forever. Twenty years was a good innings . . .' She scrutinized her sales figures and saw 'even for firm favourites like *Rebecca*' there was 'a steady decline . . . it's as though they were making their last gasp . . .' Figures for her last novel, *The Scapegoat*, 'barely exist, which is a sinister pointer to the future'. (Far from barely existing, *The Scapegoat* had sold 80,000 copies by then.)

It was all absurd, but the agitation was genuine – she was the breadwinner and if she did not bring fresh bread in all the time she envisaged ruin staring her in the face. She saw all her money going to the children (and a very great deal did so), to the taxman (again, true) and into Tommy's yachts, his car and the never-ending upkeep of Menabilly. In the circumstances, her great need was to plunge into another novel and for it to be a success in the old style; instead, she took on the task of completing *Castle Dor*, one of Sir Arthur Quiller-Couch's unfinished novels.[3] Foy, her great friend, suggested it and, because she longed to be working on something and was honoured by the suggestion, she agreed. In many ways, though she did it well, and it gave her a real interest at a low point, it was a mistake. She worried terribly about how well she was doing it – 'it would be awful if they . . . said I had ruined his beautiful style'. It also tired her when she was feeling 'rather off'.

On her fifty-third birthday she had taken a good look at herself and was depressed by how 'haggard' she looked as well as 'fearfully lined and, of course, the old hair, which I don't touch up,[4] is a real pepper-and-salt, and more salt than pepper'. She told herself 'who cares . . . I really could not be bothered to struggle to look a few years younger . . . having had a good innings'. Then, in August, she went into hospital for a dental operation and wondered if her good health had had its innings too. Belonging to BUPA suddenly seemed vital – 'You pay £10 a year and it's a damned good investment.' Struggling to match 'Q's fine English when she got home was not the best way to lift her spirits.

But what really put the idea of writing, or happiness, out of her mind that year was the death of Dr Rashleigh and the desire of his heir to live at Menabilly. The heir was not William Stuart Rashleigh, who had died unexpectedly in 1957, but his son Philip, then thirty-three, who had been badly wounded in the last stages of the war and to whom the peace and seclusion of Menabilly were every bit as attractive as to Daphne herself. When Philip became the heir, and before Dr Rashleigh himself died, Daphne had approached Philip's sister, Œnone Rashleigh, who lived nearby and with whom she had kept in touch since the days of *The King's General*, to ask if she thought 'Philip would let us go on leasing the house when Cousin John goes? Or, if death duties were crippling I believe . . . we might be able to buy, but I expect . . . it would be awful for Philip to let it go from the family.' At the same time she began negotiations with Dr Rashleigh himself to extend her lease, and these continued intermittently for the next two years until in November 1960 he agreed to an extension of twenty-three years on condition Daphne took on the care of all the woods on the estate. She also, before he died, began negotiating for the lease of Kilmarth, the dower house of Menabilly, half a mile away.

Daphne was triumphant – 'safe for another twenty-three years!' – but her triumph turned out to be hollow when, on Dr Rashleigh's death, she was informed that the lease to which he had agreed had not actually been signed. This was 'agony' and she was furious with her lawyer. The question was whether Philip Rashleigh would feel 'bound by his conscience' to honour his dead cousin's agreement. Her own conscience was quite untroubled. She did not for one moment think she might be making life miserable for a man whose desire to live in the house he had inherited matched her own – it seemed to her impossible either for him to want the house as much as she did or to be as entitled to it, whatever the legal position. Menabilly was hers by that 'act of creation' in which she had come to believe long ago. 'If I had not taken it in 1943 it would have been a ruin,' she wrote, with justification. She had lavished money – £30,000 for the roof alone – as well as love and care on the house, and locally there was strong support and sympathy for her position. But Philip Rashleigh was also deserving of sympathy – he and his family had waited a long time for Menabilly to be theirs and had never concealed their intention to return. When Daphne realized Philip was every bit as determined as she was she became quite frantic and had her lawyer in London take soundings from eminent barristers as to the feasibility of contesting Philip Rashleigh's claim. The verdict was unequivocal: she had absolutely no hope of winning any case she brought.

This plunged her into despair – the intensity of her emotion over Menabilly increased every day and was not the slightest bit exaggerated. Yet in December 1952, she had written to Ellen Doubleday that 'the terrible thing is, darling, a confession I have made to no one, but in many ways I have exhausted Menabilly. I know it is my home but it is as though I have squeezed it dry . . .' Faced with the loss of Menabilly, this was now forgotten. In a marvellous reversal of the usual values she wrote that 'houses are not like marriages . . . one cannot just walk out and leave them'. She also seemed to forget that for some time now she had longed to get away from Cornwall and that this gave her the chance to do so. She had twice sent off for details about islands for sale – one in the Channel Islands, one off the coast of north-west Scotland – and yearned to have a studio in Paris, but none of these other options now had any meaning, even though she knew that should Philip Rashleigh relent, she would end up pouring yet more money into a house she could never own. It was impossible for anyone to suggest the time had surely come to surrender Menabilly gracefully and to *buy* another house which would be hers forever and which she could leave to her children. The thought was intolerable – there simply was no other house like Menabilly. At this time in her life, the prospect of having it taken away from her was like a death-knell.

Daphne was a formidable adversary, possessing as she did great determination, considerable cunning and a strong sense of moral superiority. Anxious not to antagonize Philip Rashleigh by exploiting local support, she was not above using it subtly. The *Daily Express* ran a story that she was to be 'evicted' and, though she worried about the effect this would have on Philip Rashleigh, she was not sorry that such an emotive word had been used.

Meanwhile, there was no direct news from him. She heard Dr Rashleigh had left a quarter of a million pounds and that the management of the Menabilly estate had been passed to a firm in Exeter. It was some small comfort that their representative, when he called, seemed 'sympathetic to our cause'. The language she used in her letters during this Menabilly crisis was full of such crusading words: Philip Rashleigh was 'my opponent', 'our adversary', and they were both engaged in 'this battle', 'this contest' and even 'this awful warfare'.

Her mind fragmented, if not seriously disordered, by all this trouble, and *Castle Dor* completed, she announced dramatically that she could not possibly write anything at all 'while my fate is in the balance'. But, of course, when she did not write, and when she could not escape on short holidays with her children, she was more aware of Tommy's troubles, which exasperated her. His drinking had increased and he was resorting to 'silly tricks', like hiding bottles of sherry in the bathroom which had once belonged to Tod. She wrote to their old friends (from Egypt days) the Agars, in the spring of 1961, that 'there is really nothing wrong with Boy', though he had had 'a poor patch at Easter'. But in May, she had to call in Dr Luther, who had him admitted to Fowey hospital for observation. Her patience was running out fast. It was a 'wretched' state of affairs and there was 'no reason for it these days – I swear I don't nag'. It angered her that Tommy, 'when there are so many people really ill with awful cancers, etc.', seemed intent on 'deliberately' making himself ill. Even the cost of his stay in a private room irritated her – '£20 for five days!' – and she added this to her by now running anxiety about the escalating cost of living. Kits had his own flat in Whitelands House with Tod to cook for and look after him – 'it is the most fearful extravagant arrangement. Two flats going for two people! We'll have to stop it next year . . .'⁵ But, before next year came, she felt she must be 'putting something into the kitty' and the only way to do that was to write something likely to be more financially rewarding than either *Castle Dor* or *Branwell Brontë*. A novel was called for but, living under threat of expulsion from Menabilly, she could not think of one.

All her life Daphne had liked her days to be structured, to have her 'routes'. Stability was as important to her writing as inspiration, so it was not until August 1961, when she heard that Philip Rashleigh would give her another seven years, that she was able to contemplate starting a new book. Before she did so, she had her only serious difference with Victor Gollancz and, predictably, it was about money. Her phobia about having come to the end of her real earning-power, and her conviction that her royalties would not be sufficient to live on for the rest of her life, led her to want a paperback deal for her books.

Previously, she had thought paperbacks 'honky', but when she saw literary and reputable authors concluding lucrative deals with paperback firms, she changed her mind. By the spring of 1961 she was writing to Victor that 'the urgency seems to me to get old titles ... into paperback *before* my popularity wanes altogether'. Victor was appalled at the idea and, far from seeing any urgency, saw very good reasons for keeping her books in print in hardback only – as, of course, he was bound to. He had, he told her, 75,000 copies of various books of hers in stock and could not see how he would ever sell these if they went into paperback. But, for once, Daphne was adamant and wrote that since she was 'no longer star quality', and was feeling 'played out ... tired and restricted', she must take her chance while it was there.

Penguin were offering to print a million copies of her books in return for a seven-year licence, for which they would pay an advance of £20,000 against a royalty of 7½ per cent. Even this maddened Victor who, if he had to concede defeat, knew he could get more from Pan. But Daphne disliked the look of Pan books – 'I hate the cheap, vulgar look of Pan' – and was determined to go to Penguin, and to clinch the deal while they were still keen. She reminded Victor once more that her literary future was uncertain – 'I don't want ... to moan ... but more and more it looks as if any work I achieve will have to be of a dilettante nature, a hobby ... rather than the mainspring of my whole existence.' Victor tried one last effort, reminding her rather sharply how hard he had worked for her 'ever since Curtis Brown brought me *Gerald* ... because he said I was the best publisher in England to lift you out of your sales situation with your previous publisher'. He reminisced about how he had 'burned the midnight oil' in his efforts and pointed out she had had in Sheila Bush 'an editorial collaborator whose quality cannot possibly be exaggerated. Take the case of the Brontë book: I cannot think that you fail to recognise the enormous contribution Sheila made by no less than three months' devoted work on the MS . . .' It was an unkind point to make, since Daphne had always fulsomely acknowledged Sheila's help, but also unwise – Victor made it sound as though, without Sheila, she could not manage, which was both insulting and untrue. Sheila's help, though valuable, and highly rated by Daphne herself, was of the kind any good editor could give, and good editors, though not thick on the ground, could always be found.

In any case, it made no difference. Daphne went to Penguin and was pleased. Victor swore he would not agree to the proposed division of the paperback advance (which, at that time, was usually split fifty-fifty between hardback publisher and author, but was now to be 60 per cent to Daphne and 40 per cent to Gollancz) – 'I am quite determined to stick to 50/50 even if it means losing Daphne' – but in the end he capitulated. There was a new tension between author and publisher and the only way to dissipate it was for a new novel to unite them. This, Daphne decided, would have to be a historical novel about her French ancestors, the novel she had been about to write when the idea for *The Scapegoat* occurred to her. Tommy told her he was sure people were sick of hearing about her family history, and, though she agreed he might be right, she could think of nothing else. The only problem was getting to France to research it – 'hope for this looks bleak . . . Tommy is in a down patch . . . the girls, married, shrug off responsibility, otherwise I could be replaced now and again'. Kits, of course, was not thought to have any such responsibility – he was free as air, providing his mother with endless interest in pursuit of his career as a television film director. He was working for Associated Rediffusion and had just earned his union card, which made her 'tremendously pleased . . . he loves every minute of it'. She had very firm ideas on mothers who tried to keep adored sons tied to their apron strings, and also some bizarre ones, writing that she was sure 'it drives them to buggery'. The merest notion of her son being homosexual was one that terrified her, and at every sign of his heterosexuality she was immensely relieved. Kits, with his career, his flat in London, his fast car, and now an apartment in Suffolk (which he rented after he came into his trust at twenty-one), was leading exactly the kind of life she wanted him to lead and he must not be interrupted.

Nevertheless, if she did not use her children as stand-ins to look after Tommy, she did not see how she could leave him for more than a weekend. The only bright spot in this difficult situation was that she now had a young woman housekeeping at Menabilly, who was proving very dependable. Ever since 1943, the house had been run by a succession of local girls, some better than others, like Gladys Powell, who stayed ten years. Tommy had always been extremely critical of these arrangements, though not of the girls themselves. After the war, he had been all for 'getting a couple in' to run the place, but Daphne hated that idea. Tod, of course, had helped to run the house, but once Tommy retired, and Gladys had married and left to have a baby, the need for some kind of permanent housekeeper was urgent. It was Tod who, before she left, approached Esther Rowe and asked her if she would like to come and work in the house. Esther was married to a docker, Henry Rowe (whose sister Margaret had been a maid at Menabilly in the war years), and lived in Mrs Viall's old cottage on the Menabilly estate. She was twenty-eight and had a small boy, Ralph, which made it difficult for her to get the secretarial work for which she had been trained. She was reluctant to become a general help but, with little prospect of any other job, she agreed to give it a try. She was young, pretty and vivacious – the three qualities both her employers liked most to see. She brought some gaiety into what was by then rather a sad and silent house, and Tommy in particular responded to this, however depressed he was. Daphne often commented that the presence of cheerful younger people lifted his spirits and she was grateful for Esther's. Her letters began to mention 'my nice young Esther', and with Esther in charge, though with Mrs Burt still coming in to cook, there seemed at least a possibility of getting away to France. Once the summer holidays were over, she planned to get started, but before that she had her role as grandmother to fulfil.

By the summer of 1961, there were three grandchildren: Marie-

Thérèse, aged six; Paul, aged five; and Rupert, Flavia's son, aged two. Daphne was a proud grandmother but brought to the role the same prejudice she had as a mother: she adored the boys and was harder on the girl. She was as much fun to be with as she had been when her own children were small, but she had exactly the same expectations – that someone else should have the day-to-day care of them. In changed times, the arrangements were not always to her liking. None of her grandchildren ever stayed at Menabilly without a nanny or an *au pair* girl to care for them, though in her opinion none of these young women were ever a patch on the old-style nannies. She was also sharply critical, reporting to Tessa on one occasion how horrified she had been to hear the *au pair* call Marie-Thérèse (known as 'Pooch') 'a dirty little girl' because she had wet her knickers; and her indignation was great when she observed Paul had been kept 'on the lavatory an hour *solid*'. She didn't, of course, think of interfering, or of taking over herself, nor did she appear to have any memories of leaving Tessa and Flavia as small children without having the faintest idea how they were being treated. It was ironic, too, that she should instruct Tessa not to leave her children again for a long time, after they had stayed at Menabilly without her for two weeks, because they might miss her. Pooch, she reported, had cried for Tessa and, in her grandmother's opinion, needed her – 'I said, "You want your mummy, don't you?"' Paul she adored, referring to him as 'a tiny seducer' and confessing she stole into his room furtively to kiss him when he was asleep.

But for all her pride and interest in her grandchildren she was hard on them in a way that, as small children, they never suspected. Her ideas on how children should behave were very firm and if they did not comply she complained (though never to them). A child, in her opinion, should, above all, be imaginative and love games of make-believe; a child should want to be outside all the time; a child should enjoy being read to; a child should be polite, respect elders and be as quiet as possible inside the house; a child should smile, be visibly happy and never, ever, want to grow up. When her grandchildren did not conform to this pattern she was dismayed, especially by the lack of imagination and the noise. The noise children made inside the house, crashing about, was always a great strain. Both she and Tommy often had to leave the room, united in their horror at the modern child's behaviour.

Sometimes she thought her life was swallowed up by every role except that of writer. She was a grandmother and wife these days with nothing at all for her 'No. 2' persona to do. But once the autumn started she began on *The Glass Blowers*, deciding to forgo the trip to France. Instead, she employed researchers there who sent her copies of certificates and documents she needed and she plunged into what she told Victor was going to be a French Revolution novel only roughly based on the exploits of the du Mauriers, but 'don't expect a suspense story of the French Revolution with heads falling at the guillotine'. It was to be a novel in which the Revolution was seen from the provincial angle, showing how it changed the lives of families 'just as world wars changed ours'. Almost as soon as she started she was in trouble – it was *Mary Anne* all over again – and she was referring to the novel as 'one big tell-him' (boring). Six years earlier, before *The Scapegoat*, she had felt she could recapture the atmosphere and mood of those times, but now it eluded her. The marriage certificate of her great-great-grandparents, dated 1747, which she had found 'so touching', failed to ignite her enthusiasm for their story and she became more and more anxious as she tried to weave a narrative round the miscellaneous facts she had collected. Her notes – copious, as for all her novels except *The Parasites* – included for the first time 'possible alternatives' for story lines. Part One, which related the origins of the du Mauriers, she found she managed well enough, but in Part Two, where she described actual historical events, like the storming of the Bastille, she knew she was becoming lost. When she had finished, she was deeply sceptical about how successful she had been and tried to prepare Victor – 'I can't pretend this is a *Rachel* or a *King's General* or an emotional hey-ho novel,' she wrote, and said she realized 'therefore it will not be a popular cup of tea'. Rather lamely, she added that he might find it 'pretty gripping in parts'.

By the time Victor had read two-thirds he announced, to her astonishment, that he was enthralled and had 'not the smallest doubt' this was her best work yet. (It was surely a giveaway, in view of their recent argument, that he also said that 'technically' it was her best and consequently 'Sheila will have very little to do . . . only minor copy editing'.)

The relief for Daphne was enormous and this news, coupled with the new Menabilly lease, made her feel more relaxed than she had done for some time. This was fortunate because in July 1962 a visit from the Queen and Prince Philip hung over her and required all her attention. She was in fact pleased about this royal visit because 'it makes poor Tommy so happy', and she was determined not to let him down. He organized their end of the visit himself, in his element, conducting it like a military manoeuvre, and writing to his old friends the Prescotts (who were invited for the occasion) that 'Daphne is in a bit of a tizzy about it all'. She was, but not in such a tizzy that she could not see the absurdity of the preparations and of her own panic. Making herself sound like some little suburban housewife, she wrote to Buckingham Palace, asking if she had to wear a hat, and also whether gloves should be worn. A lady-in-waiting replied that, of course, since this was tea in her own house, neither were required. Next to cause her agitation was her dress. She knew she must wear a dress but had only three and swore she could not get into any of them. Once that problem had been solved the state of Menabilly caused her agonies. The cleanliness of the house had never been high on her list of priorities, but other people had different ideas. Mr Burt, the gardener, now eighty-one, took it upon himself to 'wash down the Long Room mantelpiece with Jeyes Fluid!!' and Esther insisted that the whole house should be 'scrubbed and better scrubbed' even though the Queen would only see the one room. At least, Daphne hoped she would only see one room – if Her Majesty were to visit the bathroom, she felt she should take down 'the lewd prints of *Mary Anne* in bed with [the Queen's] great-great-uncle the Duke of York'. Her own contribution was to fill twenty-six vases with flowers, then declare that she was exhausted.

After all the fuss, she enjoyed the occasion – 'it *was* rather splendid to see the big Rolls drive slowly to the front door bearing the Royal Standard and the Queen, a radiant figure in white, seated within'. That was the best part – she thought 'the young Queen looked *stunning*' – but she was surprised to find the whole

hour and a half went quickly and pleasantly. The only disappointment, though Daphne could well sympathize, was that the Queen
was 'not much interested in the enormous spread I had prepared'.
Her sister Angela was a great help, chatting with aplomb to Her
Majesty, and so were the Prescotts. There were fourteen altogether
for tea (Esther fed the entourage) and the only mishap was 'old
Sir Edward Bolitho spilling his tea', but he was forgiven because
he was 'the only one to munch and enjoy a split with cream'. The
visit marked the beginning of a better period for Tommy and
therefore for Daphne too – they seemed to have found a way of
living together which, if not entirely harmonious, was less strained
than it had been for the first three years of his retirement. He
was, Daphne wrote soon after this happy day, 'in rattling form'.

Part of the reason for the rattling form was that he was having
another new boat built, and in the meantime he had bought an
18-foot dinghy named *Echo*. *Fanny Rosa*, the boat brought back
from Singapore, had been replaced by *Jeanne d'Arc*, another
expensive and beautiful boat, and now 'Yggy III' was to replace
Jeanne d'Arc. The building and equipping of it – only the best, as
usual – fully occupied Tommy's thoughts and the cost, in what
his wife regarded as newly straitened times, did not worry him in
the least. 'I expect I shall have a rough and tumble with Richard
Pegler to cough up the money,' he commented cheerfully (Pegler
being Daphne's accountant). With his wife he knew there would
be no rough and tumble over money any more than there was
when she was indulging Kits. Her husband could have his boats
and her son make films without ever needing to beg or even
persuade her to make the money available. She was always generous to them in spite of the permanent worry about her own
solvency. But in 1963, with the publication of *The Glass Blowers*,
she was watching sales anxiously and seeing it as something of a
test case. If *The Glass Blowers* 'sank' she saw the future as looking
grim. The news that Victor had printed 'only' 40,000 copies (and
another 20,000 which were not bound) dismayed her even though
he patiently explained to her the new facts of publishing in the
sixties and pointed out, perfectly truthfully, that 40,000 for a first
print-run was six times more than any other author on his list
enjoyed.

Victor knew, of course, how depressed Daphne was feeling about her own abilities and also about her general status. In spite of her tremendous success, she believed herself to be pigeon-holed as second-rate and, for all her modesty, was hurt by this. He knew the last thing she wanted was recognition in the sense of public attention – what he saw she needed was more respect. He had hoped this would be forthcoming when he heard that the *Times Literary Supplement* was to do a big piece on Daphne's work and he wrote with some excitement to tell her about it. Daphne hoped this appraisal would not be written by Marghanita Laski, whom she loathed, or any woman. When the piece finally appeared it was unsigned, in the manner of the times, but she felt it had been written by a man. The essay was long and serious which gratified her. It began, 'All literature of great popularity is worth examining even if the results prove of psychological or sociological rather than literary interest . . .' and went on to conclude that 'two of Daphne du Maurier's novels *are* of literary interest . . . and . . . form part of an interesting stream of English language fiction'. The two esteemed novels were *Rebecca* and *The Scapegoat*. *Rebecca* was said to be in the tradition of 'daemonic novels', beginning with Milton, which amused Daphne greatly. She was less amused by the verdict that 'Miss du Maurier's historical sense is execrable . . . she has as little sense of the language of her chosen periods as of the probable behaviour, attitudes and outlooks of the people who lived in them.' All her historical novels were attacked, especially *The King's General*. But in spite of this stinging rebuke, the writer of the piece very firmly advised that Miss du Maurier's contribution should not be underrated and that Ronald Bryden, who had written a dismissive piece in the *Spectator* earlier in the year, was quite wrong to have done so.

Victor was upset by the *TLS*'s judgement and Tommy furious, maintaining that only 'a silly arse' could have written it, but Daphne herself was remarkably philosophical. 'It is supposed to be a crumb [boast] to get that centre page,' she wrote to Foy, 'so I must meekly bow my head.' What puzzled her more than her own lack of critical success was why some other writers were so extravagantly praised. It seemed to her that they were often no better than herself – Iris Murdoch, for example, whose success totally mystified her – or Ivy Compton-Burnett, whose novels she found unreadable. She was from now on 'off novels . . . they all seem to be about common young men and women in the Midlands having furious rows'. These she found distasteful – 'perhaps I am a snob in my middle-years'. Critics these days were a 'horrid, young, *honky* breed' who lashed out at anyone like herself who was 'old-fashioned enough to like telling stories'. She couldn't 'bear reality, or at least contemporary reality' in fiction and only liked novels, if she liked any at all, set in the past, or classics. Her reading, once wide, was becoming narrow, restricted to biographies, collections of letters, and still 'my psycho books'. She felt cut off, as indeed she was, from the fiction of her own time and resigned herself to being out of step, just as she had predicted to Victor.

The reviews for *The Glass Blowers*, in the spring of 1963, were not bad but nor were they either extensive or good, and Victor had no need yet to bind up those extra 20,000 copies. He was a little concerned about how Daphne would react, but there was another, far more important matter on her mind at that time and the fate of *The Glass Blowers* for the moment passed her by. Kits was 'working up to get engaged' and she was in a state of great excitement at the prospect of his intended being brought to Menabilly. He had gone to Dublin the previous autumn, to work on Carol Reed's *The Running Man*, and while shooting the film had met one of the models used in a crowd scene. This was nineteen-year-old Olive White, daughter of a plumber, who had been 'Miss Eire 1961'.

At first, Daphne did not take this romance seriously – Kits had brought girls home before and she had seen at once 'he was not really menaced' (attracted). But by the spring of 1963 there was every sign of her son being very menaced indeed since he was rushing backwards and forwards to Dublin at every opportunity. This caused both his parents great concern. He was only twenty-two, very far from properly established in his chosen career, and even though – thanks to Daphne's generous trust – he had money of his own, what she thought of as his extravagance still worried her. Nor was what he told them about Olive reassuring, especially in a year when 'model' meant Christine Keeler. So the bringing of Olive to Menabilly in the summer was an event surpassing the royal visit of the previous year and caused Daphne twice the agitation. She desperately wanted to like and be liked by this girl who seemed to have stolen Kits' heart, and was nervous almost to the point of hysteria before her arrival. The twenty-six vases of flowers were filled once more and the customary panic about clothes gone through. She felt in *awe* of Olive's title, 'Miss Eire', and Maureen Baker-Munton, who was staying at the time, had to point out, with a certain exasperation, that her own title of Lady Browning and her fame as an author were far more likely to intimidate Olive. Daphne could not see this at all.

The moment she saw Olive she relaxed. Olive was beautiful and beauty was always a magic password to her approval. Beauty on its own would not have been enough, but in Olive's case it was combined with a naturalness of manner which Daphne found beguiling. All ideas about what a working-class Irish girl might be like were banished by Olive's perfect poise, her cheerfulness, her natural grace and unaffectedness. She seemed to Daphne 'classless' and that fascinated her. She felt Olive could mix with anyone, being, unlike Daphne herself, perfectly at ease without needing to pretend, and she marvelled at the possession of this enviable quality. Tommy, who shared his wife's veneration for appearances, was equally approving. He prided himself on being able to sum people up just as astutely as his wife could and wrote to Tessa that 'I would say at once she could no more be a Miss Keeler than my left foot.' He thought Olive 'very sweet' and best of all 'completely unspoilt'. His only criticism, after the closest of scrutinies, was that her hair was dyed, bleached he thought, and she wore a touch too much make-up for a young woman. Daphne voiced no criticisms at all: she was dazzled by her son and his girl as the perfect couple – both young, tall, slim, blond, beautiful, cheerful, fun . . .

Nevertheless she was against their getting married, though, as with her daughters, she neither said so in strong terms nor positively interfered. 'My wicked Kits', she wrote, with relish, 'is having a whale of an affair with a girl in Dublin and I'm terrified of him tying the knot – he's only 22 . . . and in the film world . . . it would be madness . . . if only he can keep it on the affair level!'

When it became obvious that Kits was determined to marry and didn't want to keep it on this level, she was puzzled and reflected, 'Why do young people today wish to marry so early?' Men in particular, she thought, should be around thirty before they married. All that summer the delicious speculation continued: would Kits tire of Olive, would the affair fizzle out? Tommy thought Olive 'obviously very much in love with Kits', but found Kits himself 'very cagey' at least when he was at Menabilly with her. Daphne was more intrigued by why Olive was attracted to Kits at all – 'I would have thought she would go for an older sophisticated man of 40.' But she had more faith in Kits' own passion for Olive than his father had and was sure he would marry her. 'I must say,' she commented, 'if they do ring the bells I could not feel ashamed of the addition . . .' On the other hand, she worried that Kits might not be up to Olive, 'but he is so like my Daddy, no doubt he can weather any onslaught and survive . . . when one remembers as a child how much affection he needed, it is hardly surprising he enjoys the mature variety'. If he did marry Olive, Daphne knew she could let him go, with some sadness but without a struggle, and of that she was proud.

In October 1963, soon after Kits and Olive became officially engaged – 'a wedding is threatened for January' – Daphne and Tommy went for a short holiday together to Kits' flat in Aldeburgh. Daphne had been using visits to Suffolk as an escape ever since Kits had rented his apartment there two years earlier and she loved it, finding the light and the skies quite different from Cornwall and appreciating the change. It always struck her as extraordinary to see what kind of life her son led there – 'he knows all the old ladies and invites them to sherry' – and she marvelled at his ability to do his own shopping, 'ordering meat at the butcher's as though he had been doing it all his life'. Tommy's family had come from the region and on this holiday they did a little research, driving to old churchyards and looking up parish records and finding Browning gravestones. The weather was beautiful, fine autumn days with plenty of sun, and the two of them walked along the beach and pottered along the river. In the evenings they read and Daphne even went so far as to do some cooking – she announced that she had discovered 'if one buys good steak and chucks in a few herbs and a bit of butter and grills it, it comes out quite frenchified'. Travelling home, they stopped off to visit the Baker-Muntons, who were struck by how content they both seemed, addressing each other affectionately in the old manner as 'duck'.

Two months later, Tommy was found in 'an unfit state to drive'. As a result of his unfit state two people were in hospital. He was served with a charge to appear at Truro Magistrates Court, where he pleaded guilty to driving while under the influence of alcohol.

Chapter Twenty

Tommy made no attempt to plead any kind of mitigation or justification: he was bitterly and rightly ashamed and overwhelmed with remorse. When his family tried to console him – though it was difficult to find any basis for consolation, beyond a general compassion, for anyone so clearly at fault – he rejected their comfort. He wrote to Tessa, thanking her for her 'sweet letter' of support, that the worst part was the hurt he had done to other people and his sense of humiliation. It was 'one of those things, at my age, I ought to have known how to avoid like the plague'. He explained that he had 'not been drinking at all lately, but I had to go for a Civil Defence meeting and being weak-minded about that sort of thing, had a few whiskies with the result I felt like hell'. But he had got into his car, while knowing he shouldn't, and 'hadn't a leg to stand on' when he caused the accident injuring two others but not himself. The superintendent who had to book him 'nearly passed out' with embarrassment and it was all terrible. He felt, he added, 'such a fool'.

Daphne's reaction, as ever in times of crisis, was to accept what had happened as quickly as possible without wasting time on recriminations. She tried to get Tommy to adopt this attitude, and to calm down, but he couldn't. His remorse at first surprised her with its violence – 'he suffers most terribly' – and then, as it went on and on, it began to irritate her. She felt the lengths he went to in his guilt and self-laceration were exaggerated and even a touch ridiculous. She wrote to Foy that he was 'treating his crime as if he were Profumo and has resigned from every club and organization he has ever joined; if it were fifty years ago he would be leaving for darkest Africa under an assumed name'. This she thought absurd, and said 'it makes the clubs he resigns from feel more embarrassed than he does'. Equally silly, in her opinion, were Tommy's plans to keep a low profile – 'He says that in future we must go to the boat . . . from the steps at Station Hill . . . and I can see so many difficulties getting to and fro that it would almost be simpler to end our days as Mr and Mrs Brown on the Continent.' However dreadful the situation, and she certainly did not underestimate the harm done to the other motorists – she could not help seeing some grim humour in her husband's melo-dramatic reaction. He could see none himself, and she became exasperated, expecting from him a more resolute outlook. She had been expecting some such incident and so was to a certain extent prepared, though when he hadn't returned home she was 'dotty with anxiety', and when the police phoned almost fainted until she was assured he was alive and nobody else killed. 'I have lived for a long time', she confessed to the Agars, 'in the absolute dread that something of this sort would happen, for although he is supposed to be TT . . . he does have a nip now and again.'[1] But once he was home, and she heard that the people he had injured would recover, the agony for her was over. For Tommy it seemed just to be beginning, and Daphne was depressed by the prospect of him slipping back into the deep misery from which he had only recently hauled himself. Here was another crisis and she could hardly bear the aftermath.

What particularly annoyed her was that she suspected his remorse was more about 'loss of face' than anything else and she found it embarrassing that anyone should care so much what others thought. '*Why*', she wrote to Foy, 'must he mind so much?' It had been the same, on a lesser scale, when he failed to get elected to the local council – 'for him to take it seriously and be poorly because of it . . .' She despised him for not being able to accept the blow (or, in this more serious case, the blame) and then rise above it, as she felt she would have done in similar circumstances. She licked her wounds in private whereas Tommy leaned on her and exhausted her with his emotional need. They were right back again to the tortured relationship of 1957 and this time she was not so disposed to be stoical. One of the first things that occurred to her after the court appearance was that he would now say they could not go to Kits' wedding – 'What price the wedding trip now, I ask myself?' Even the logistics of getting to Dublin would probably be too much for him and he would say he was not up to travelling. If so, she was determined to go on her own.

In the event, Tommy's sense of duty and family loyalty overcame his reluctance to be seen in public, even on the other side of the Irish Sea, and they both went to the wedding in January 1964, though Daphne described him as leaving Menabilly 'looking as if he were going to the salt mines in Siberia' – she wanted to burst out laughing at the mere sight of his face. Once they arrived in Dublin, where they had a suite at the Gresham Hotel ('couldn't have been bettered at the Savoy'), they went to meet Olive's family whom Daphne liked at once, describing her parents as 'thoroughly pleasant, honest-to-God respectable'. The Whites' home was the kind of eye-opener to her that the married quarters of the Aldershot barracks had been – she could hardly credit how small the house was and how cramped – 'the little front room crammed with sisters and relatives . . . and upstairs in the front bedroom, which the bride shared with her sisters (one bed) . . . were all the wedding presents spread out, and the bridal gown and the bridesmaids' dresses hanging on a single curtain rail. It was a most touching scene . . .'

The wedding itself was a sensation and she revelled in every minute of it. 'The crowd at the scene of the church', she reported, 'might have been that which greeted the Pope in Jerusalem,' and what tickled her was that all this excitement was for *Olive*, not for Kits, 'being an ex-Miss Ireland Beauty Queen'. None of the large Browning and du Maurier contingent had ever seen anything like it and several, not anticipating the crush, arrived too late to get through it into the church to witness the 'simple and sincere service held in the Presbytery (Kits not being a Catholic)'. When the newly married couple emerged, the cheering throng rushed forward with shouts of 'God bless them' and to Daphne's delight the priest jumped on a wall and ordered them to part to let the couple through – 'I thought of the raised eyebrows of Parson Coe of Fowey church'. The reception, at the Gresham, surpassed any other such event she had ever attended. The meal was 'a test of endurance . . . I gave up at the turkey (having already eaten soup, fish and chicken pie)'. But the moment she loved best was when, after the usual speeches, 'the priest suddenly said "Well, I won't be giving you a sermon and I've earned me five pounds, so how would it be if I led you in a song?" and he burst into a rollicking ditty, something like a sea shanty . . . and the gist going something like this:

> She's the girl I do adore,
> But before I tread the holy ground
> I'll have a drink once more, once more,
> Ah, I'll have a drink once more.'

The spontaneity of it all appealed to her and it was the only time in her life that she felt a social occasion was 'over all too soon'.

The crowd was still waiting patiently outside the hotel when it was time to leave, and as Olive and Kits got into the car to go to the airport Daphne heard one woman remark, 'Ah, she'll never want for nothing no more,' which, she commented, still laughing about this hours later, 'knowing Kits and his extravagant ways, I am led to wonder'. The honeymoon alone was exotic – no mooring in Frenchman's Creek in a little boat for Kits, but instead 'he was off to California, Mexico and Jamaica'. Tommy, surrounded by so much flowing alcohol, looked 'grimmer than when he stood guard at King George v's funeral' half the time, but she knew she'd smiled almost constantly for twenty-four hours and hadn't 'laughed so much for years'.

Once back in Menabilly, the laughing stopped abruptly. The January rain fell every day and, though she reminded herself that she could be 'living in a back street in Manchester, so what the hell', Daphne was almost as pulled down as Tommy. She watched him with misgivings, wondering if he was going to have another nervous breakdown – 'he seems so jumpy . . . as if he were boiling up for something'. He himself wrote to Tessa that he didn't know what was wrong with him but he felt like cutting his throat. *Echo* was proving too hard for him to sail on his own and he was thinking of facing facts and switching to a motor-boat. The only thing that would get her through the winter, Daphne felt once again, was to start on a new book, even though she didn't feel like it and would have to exert every bit of willpower at her disposal to rise above Tommy's depression and get on with it. The book she had in mind was a novel set in Italy and had arisen quite naturally, which made it all the more annoying that she now felt disinclined to work on it. Somehow, she felt she had missed the tide, though in the autumn, before Tommy's accident, she had been all set to go.

The germ for *The Flight of the Falcon* was sown on a visit to Urbino with Kits, and on another holiday with Tessa during which she had seen an old woman asleep in the doorway of a church and had put some money into her hand. She intended it to appear to be a thriller but, in fact, to be an allegory. But when, after Kits' wedding, she began to write she found it hardest to capture what had always come most easily: the atmosphere. She sat writing, wearing an extra jumper and fur-lined boots, and stared out at the rain falling in sheets from a sky dark at three o'clock in the afternoon, and she could not bring the warmth and sun of Italy into her narrative however hard she tried. It was rather like, she wrote to one friend, someone sitting in Urbino in the summer heat trying to conjure up Fowey from guidebooks. She had plenty of those – 'I am surrounded by maps and picture postcards of my city Urbino, but it's not like having a real glimpse . . . so I have to go carefully.' She employed Joan Saunders, of Writers and Speakers Research in Fulham, to find out all kinds of details she felt would help, and pored over the newspapers, magazines and pamphlets duly sent to her together with information on university life there. Then she set out to concoct a modern story, which would be exciting and frightening, as counterpoint to the legend of the Falcon, a German story which had as its theme 'the stripping of the proud, the violation of the haughty and the humiliation of the slanderer'. The allegorical meaning was to do with the Jungian idea of psychological predestination which had fascinated her for so long. She wanted to identify 'that link with the past' in which lost childhoods are part of one continuous pattern until the whole of life is seen as 'an unending journey'.

It was a tall order and she knew it, but she no longer wanted only to entertain with straightforward stories. She wanted to communicate her own theories about life, but to do it in such a way that nobody would guess she was writing about her own emotional experiences. Any kind of realistic novel was out of the question – far too 'waine' (embarrassing) – and hence the allegory.

When she had finished it, at the end of May 1964, she told Victor Gollancz it was 'good holiday fare' but that it did not have 'the depth of characterisation of *The Scapegoat*'. Victor, when he had read it, did not quite know what to make of it and thought it would need to be drastically cut. Meanwhile, in keeping with her declared determination to earn as much as she could 'now I am on the slide', Daphne had sent the novel to America to see if anyone would buy it for serialization before publication. It was 'such a relief' when *Good Housekeeping* offered $100,000 – but at a price. In a staggeringly critical and detailed letter *Good Housekeeping* requested all kinds of changes, including 'the strengthening' of one character throughout the novel and the writing of a completely new ending. Any author loathes this kind of substantial rewriting, but for $100,000 Daphne was quite prepared to oblige, and did so. Victor was in a panic about it all – Sheila and he both thought the original ending better – but the changes went ahead, with the first version retained in the British publication.

Daphne had wanted the novel to be published in December, an unusual time to publish a novel, especially by a 'big' author, but Victor persuaded her that January would be better. She was sure the critics would either 'spit on it' or else 'be silly'. True to her new interest in such things, she had her own ideas about prepublication quotes: this time she wanted him to try Kingsley Amis – 'I know you may smile and say "Nonsense, not for you", but . . . the thing is I did a sci-fi story for him . . . and he was enthusiastic.' Victor replied that Kingsley was 'unpredictable', but he would sound him out tactfully. Otherwise, all she wanted to be sure of was that she didn't 'clash with irritating big write-ups like Iris Murdoch or Nancy Mitford'. She didn't, but nor did she get big write-ups herself. No one spotted the allegorical significance so far as she could see, and this made her even more contemptuous of the critics than she already tended to be. Unlike the disappointing reception of certain other novels – such as *Hungry Hill* – the less than enthusiastic response for this one did not disturb her. On the contrary, the American serialization rights and the fact that the Literary Guild took the novel when Doubleday published it made her consider it quite a triumph. She also felt that in some way she had scored over reviewers because they had indeed 'missed the point'. So did almost everyone she knew who read it, but that made her more amused than depressed – it was quite a new experience to be thought obscure.

By the time *The Flight of the Falcon* came out, Tommy's ill health was driving everything else from her mind. This time 'ill health' was not a euphemism either for alcohol-related problems or psychological ones. Tommy was in obvious agony from pain in his left leg and instead of being able to enjoy sailing in the newly launched 'Yggy III' he hardly had the strength to go out in her at all. By July he was 'feeling like hell' and Daphne reported that the trouble was 'lack of circulation in the left leg'. The only exercise he could manage without pain was wandering slowly down the long lawn in front of Menabilly, his left leg dragging a little, looking at the flowers and deciding he liked best 'the mass of daisies and buttercups which in their simple jollity and freshness outdo all the more sophisticated flowers'. Soon, even this walk proved too much for him and by August he was 'laid up with a swollen foot'.

Both Tommy and Daphne had absolute faith in Dr Luther and refused to listen to their children's advice to get a second opinion. In September, with Tommy now virtually immobile and in great distress, it was finally decided he should go into Plymouth hospital for what Daphne described as 'a lombar symtorhectomy, which I can't spell'.[2] The operation 'didn't come off'. Tommy himself wrote that he just had to face up to the fact that he would have 'a pretty useless left leg for the rest of my days'. He was obliged to use a wheelchair and was told that 'short of . . . amputation there is no radical cure'. The sight of her once athletic, proud, strong husband in his wheelchair made Daphne feel 'constricted about the heart', but what astonished her and brought her nearer to tears was that in the face of very real physical suffering and disability Tommy showed such bravery. He seemed, she thought, 'to have got some inner strength'. He himself explained in a letter to Tessa, 'I have no grumbles as I have been blessed throughout my life with so many of God's gifts that the loss of the use of a leg is a small thing' – this from a man who loathed inactivity, who had been a champion sportsman, lived for sailing and hated to be dependent. What upset him most was that 'poor Daphne has had a trying time'.

But it was a trying time she could cope with 'so long as he is cheerful'. Then, she said, she could face anything. What she couldn't bear were tears, depression, whole days without speaking, sulks and silences, groans of despair, and worst of all diatribes of remorse or self-pity. Tommy's heroic acceptance of his fate this time touched and moved her and she tried her hardest to help him. Not once did she mention feeling restless and resentful because she could not write, and even the prospect of another winter trapped in Menabilly, getting on each other's nerves, did not appal her in the way it had in previous autumns. Instead, she concentrated on their good fortune in having Esther running the house, and being able to afford any material comfort they needed. One of these was adequate heating. Menabilly had always been bitterly cold, but Daphne had never even thought of installing central heating, which seemed to her positively decadent as well as prohibitively expensive – far better to put on another jumper, wrap a scarf round one's neck, pull a fur hat over one's ears and wear two pairs of socks inside fur-lined boots. But now, in view of Tommy's plight, storage heaters were installed – central heating was still going too far – and both of them were ecstatic, in a thoroughly childlike way, at the warmth this spread.

Another blessing was television. Daphne had begun to be a devotee of this medium in 1956, when she first had a television installed, and now that Tommy was obliged to sit still for long periods it became more important than ever – it was another 'routes', usually indulged in from seven till eleven in the evening. Tommy liked *Grandstand*, anything to do with sport and programmes like *The Brains Trust*, whereas Daphne loved anything with fast car chases and thrillers. There was no more settling down either side of the fire and reading – now it was on with the television and anyone staying in the house was simply assumed to want to watch too. If they didn't want to, they could 'lump it', Daphne said cheerfully, and always warned friends before they came that this would be the case. All memories of being irritated that her grandchildren 'do nothing but watch that wretched TV' were forgotten and she was quite amused and proud of her own addiction to 'honky' programmes. Anyone telephoning during them was ignored and she often instructed friends 'don't telephone after seven as I shall be watching TV'. It made her interested in trying to adapt her own work for television, or have it adapted, and also in Kits' plans for TV films. She spent the winter doing 'nothing but scribble a draft script for a film about Yeats' which she hoped Kits would make.

Somehow the two of them staggered through until Christmas and then the family, when they came to stay, saw at once that something would have to be done. There was their father, in obvious agony half the time, and their mother being stoical. As soon as the holiday was over, Tommy was finally persuaded by them to go to London to see a specialist. In the first week in January 1965 he was admitted to the Lindo wing of St Mary's, Paddington, where his left foot was amputated. Daphne stayed at the Great Western Hotel next door and never left his side, except to go and visit Kits, who was living comparatively near, for an hour each day. She hated the hospital atmosphere, however kind the doctors and nurses, and when Tommy said he thought he would never get better until he was home, she quite agreed. But he was sixty-eight years old and had just had major surgery, so the alien environment had to be endured for a little longer. Sitting with him most of the day and evening she was struck by how wretchedly thin he had become and how drawn and weary his face. 'Life has been hell,' she wrote to a friend, '. . . I don't know if I am coming or going.' Her own weariness and distress were as nothing compared to the 'hideous pain' her 'poor Moper' had endured. He was worrying about never being able to sail again, in spite of now having a motor-boat, and not being able to drive. She assured him they would be able to adapt a car to his needs and had a friend search out a three-litre coupé, a green Rover, which could be duly altered.

Three weeks after the operation they went home together by train, travelling in a closed carriage with a nurse in attendance. It was a journey as different as possible from any other they had ever made across the Tamar Bridge – there was no whoop of joy this time or tossing of caps as they entered Cornwall. Instead, Tommy was sedated to help him stand the journey, and Daphne sat silent in the darkened carriage, listening to the sudden rackety noise as the train trundled on to Brunel's bridge. The rain lashed against the windows and when they arrived at Par the afternoon was as dark as night. It was a sad home-coming, but there was relief, too, in being once more in Menabilly. Tommy continued to be brave but it was too much to expect. The ordeal of being fitted with an artificial limb hung over him and he was 'very depressed', wrote Daphne, '. . . and now feeling the psychological effect of the second operation'. At the end of February, he was taken to Plymouth to have the first fitting for his artificial foot, but she could not go with him because she was feeling 'very much under the weather'. She thought it was 'my usual spring bug', but it turned out to be jaundice, and Tommy worried about catching it – 'I've had quite enough illness and bed to last me a long time'. She stayed in her room, in bed, and he stayed in his.

They were both in a desperate plight. Daphne vomited repeatedly and had hardly the strength to lift her head from the pillow, while Tommy struggled to drag himself around, feeling wretched in every way. They were well looked after by Esther and two nurses, but neither seemed to be recovering. Neither ate nor slept much. Daphne wondered if she would ever walk again through the Menabilly woods to Pridmouth beach and in her mind's eye saw the stormy sea and wished she could feel the spray on her cheeks – then, she might feel better. Thinking of Tommy, in an even worse state than she was, was an additional torment. On 10 March, he managed to scrawl a letter to his sister Grace telling her he had contracted bronchitis on top of everything else and commented sadly that 'it would really be more dignified to fade quietly out'. He felt completely finished and even scribbling a few lines was too much – 'it's quite amazing how tired one gets just writing'. During the day, his mind seemed to wander and at night he alarmed the nurses by trying to sleepwalk. Daphne, when told this, remembered how his mother had become confused like this just before she died, and she had 'an awful apprehension' something was going to happen.

On Saturday night, 13 March, feeling a little better than she had done for three weeks, she got up and went through to Tommy's room to say goodnight. He told her he dreaded the night because he could not sleep, and seemed particularly restless, but she was weak and tired herself and could only soothe his brow and promise him the nurse would give him a sleeping pill. In the early hours of the next morning she was wakened by the nurse, who said she was alarmed at General Browning's condition and had rung for the doctor. Daphne went to him and saw at once that his face had changed. She bent over him and could not hear any breathing. The nurse tried to resuscitate him, but he was dead.

All three children came at once and afterwards she marvelled at how each of them had surprised her by demonstrating the very qualities she had not realized they possessed. Tessa seemed so tender and emotional, and it was with her that she wept; Flavia was calm and efficient, and she felt she could leave her to organize everything; and Kits, always appearing to live for the moment, just as she wanted him to, and to be flippant and full of life, was suddenly serious and talked immediately of preserving his father's belongings. And in her staff, too, she knew she was fortunate – 'My good Esther,' she wrote, ' . . . and her husband and the Burts, it is rare these days to have people so devoted, like in the old days on an estate, sparing themselves nothing.' To everyone's surprise, she ordered a post-mortem, which showed 'the clot entered his heart, also the arteries everywhere were poor, he could not have had many months ahead'. His sister Grace was given the fullest description of what she felt had happened and of her own state of mind. It was her firm belief, Daphne wrote, that 'these things get handed down . . . I swear it is handed down . . . we are born with the particles in the blood that will finally predispose us to disease. I think this will be medically proved this century. More and more I go "off" the twentieth century "put everything down to psychology" thesis, and back to probably what the Greeks may have believed, chemistry is all important.' Already, she had decided Tommy's 'bad bouts of gloom' and 'his tum throughout his life', also his 'urge to drink', were all due to 'physical and chemical' reasons – 'a deficiency of some sort'.

There was no grand funeral because Tommy 'loathed memorial services, funerals, and the lowering into tombs'. He never discussed death 'though he was a Christian and did not fear it'. Once, when she had urged him to say how he would like his mortal remains dealt with, he had said he would like a Viking's funeral. This appealed to her and she was tempted to have his body put into 'Yggy III' and sent, all aflame, out to sea, but 'I just can't cope'. Instead, there was a very private cremation, which she did not attend, just as she had not attended her father's funeral – 'I can't face it' – and later she took the casket of ashes and scattered them round 'Yggy I', 'at the end of the lawn, by my Hut, where the daffodils grow, and where latterly he used to sit in the sun, and it was a lovely day . . . and peaceful, and the dogs came too and cocked, which he would have approved of and laughed at, and it was all perfectly happy and somehow "routes" '.

But 'routes' had been changed forever, and she knew it. 'We have been so much together latterly,' she wrote, 'since the retirement, that everything had become geared to him.' She saw with frightening clarity 'the thing of empty rooms, etc., etc., months ahead that in one moment have become without point'. What shocked her most was *how* shocked she found she was. Over and over in her novels and stories she had written death scenes, often with great zest, and yet nothing in her imagination had prepared her for the reality. No other death had affected her like this, not even her father's or Gertrude Lawrence's. The death of a parent, however young, seemed to her 'in the natural order of things' in the way that the death of a husband did not, and she had not witnessed Gertie's death, so that it went on seeming unbelievable. She felt now that she knew 'what suffering means', and what she was suffering from was not only distress at the death itself but from guilt. Throughout the vicissitudes of her married life, and in spite of the breakdown of one side of it, she had always known she loved Tommy even when she appeared to despise him, or to be unbearably irritated by him. Now he was dead, a sense of waste as well as grief overwhelmed her – she could not bear to remember what a mess both of them had made of so many of their years together. 'I have got to try and forget the last days,' she wrote, 'because the sense of loss is terrible.' So was the sense of guilt, and the only way to deal with that was to concentrate on the good and happy times they had had. 'I want my memories to go back to the time when he was well and strong,' she wrote to Foy, 'and I think they will.'

They did, with great and rather startling rapidity. Daphne exerted all the tremendous willpower of which she was capable in wiping out the pain and difficulties she had experienced in her marriage and bringing to the fore the happiness which Tommy had once brought her. She was soon seeing him in her mind only as the handsome guardsman who had swept her off her feet, and banishing forever the bad-tempered, complaining husband who shuffled around the house looking pathetic. She saw him even now in some heavenly yachting harbour waiting for her in *Yggy* and saying 'Come on, duck, jump in, whatever kept you?', and the thought made her smile and feel cheered. She didn't want to be like Queen Victoria, and refused to wear all black – if she did, Tommy would 'peer down from Heaven', ask what on earth she had got on and say, 'she must be mad'.[3] This belief that he *was* somewhere waiting for her was the greatest possible comfort, but she found she couldn't make any plans. 'One's job is over, and one has to begin anew,' she wrote, 'but how?'

Chapter Twenty-one

The tributes paid to her husband on his death were very important to Daphne. She wanted his qualities both recognized and appreciated, and was not a widow who pushed aside condolences. Maureen Baker-Munton, who came down to help her with the shoals of letters which poured in, and who replied to many of them on Daphne's behalf, was impressed by how carefully Daphne attended to the expressions of sympathy and by how many she replied to personally. But at the same time she was capable of seeing how absurdly inappropriate some of the letters were and, as after her father's death, was not so grief-stricken that the farcical side of it all could not amuse her. One letter began: 'I once met your husband forty years ago in the Post Office,' she told Grace Browning, and another: 'I must warn you that it won't get better as the months pass, but worse.' She could hear 'Tommy saying sourly, "Why doesn't the bloody woman go and cut her throat?" '

But most of the letters touched her and were a real comfort – 'Such tributes! I feel like Lady Churchill.' It mattered very much that a telegram had arrived from the Queen and another from Prince Philip, as well as several more from other members of the Royal Family. It mattered almost as much that those who had served with Tommy in the war and knew his worth as a soldier should write and say so – General Eisenhower and General Montgomery in particular. Some of the letters from ordinary soldiers impressed her greatly – she liked to think Tommy had been popular – and occasionally someone would catch the spirit of him with phrases like 'He had the heart of a child' and 'A true knight, in the oldest sense'. The formal obituaries were all read and noted for length, prominence and tone, with comments scribbled across them. One newspaper headed its obituary with 'Boy was a Giant', and across it she wrote, 'All these eulogies won't bring him back. RIP.' No, but they did console her, and her pride in Tommy's achievements helped to sustain her.

Some of the letters surprised her with their warmth or perception. Paddy Puxley wrote, a kind letter from a kind woman whose life she sometimes thought she had ruined. And Philip Rashleigh, whom she had been determined to think of as cold and unfeeling, wrote movingly of how he had met her husband in 1945 and had been amazed by his 'broad smile and most enlivening handshake and his very friendly welcome to a junior officer'. This sort of recognition of Tommy's worth was important to her, but so was the realization of what his death would mean to her. Ellen Doubleday wrote that although Daphne had always been 'a lonely soul' she had had Tommy coming and going. Now, truly alone, adjusting would be hard. Ellen, of course, knew because she had had to adjust herself after her own husband's death. She remembered how swiftly Daphne had responded to her need at the time, and was anxious to offer the same support to her friend now. But Daphne wanted to be by herself for the moment. The distinction between being lonely and alone was subtle and was causing her some difficulty. It was true, she had indeed always been a lonely soul, but she had liked it and had always resented the interruption of her solitary life. Scheming to get more time on her own had been one of the main preoccupations of her adult life and she knew she had resented bitterly those who thwarted this desire. But now she very quickly saw that what Ellen had said was true: there *was* a difference between being a lonely soul and being alone. She felt curiously adrift and wrote of being 'suspended in time', of feeling 'weightless' and also 'not really here'. Some of this was due to shock, and some to the after-effects of jaundice, but there was also a slight feeling of fear. She had been married for nearly thirty-three years, and whatever the circumstances of that marriage, it had been a partnership. Now, it was over and she had to adjust to the change.

All her thoughts about widowhood were clear and sensible.[1] One acquaintance wrote to her that she knew how she felt, because when her own husband died she had realized that 'I was always his puppet, and now he is not pulling the strings any more I am still'. This seemed to Daphne a horrifying admission and one she would never think of making. She had never been a puppet and she was certainly not now 'still'. She knew her life was not over and that grief had not made her feeble or apathetic. But she was shaken and knew that a period of stability was vitally necessary. People who urged her to go away at once for a long holiday annoyed her intensely, and she regretted having urged a holiday on Ellen after Nelson died. 'At the moment,' she wrote to Ellen, a month after Tommy's death, 'I am neither physically nor emotionally ready for a trip anywhere . . . I tire easily and would not enjoy travelling anymore than you wanted to go anywhere after Nelson died. My God, how you stuck me in Paris and Florence passes my belief. All I could think of was wanting to kiss your hands, and not only your hands. If anyone tried that on me I'd murder them! (But then that was always the case with me).'

Those who advised moving right away from her home annoyed her even more. Both bits of advice she felt instinctively were quite wrong. Her surroundings soothed her, she liked to walk where Tommy had walked and to sit where they had sat together. She felt his presence and had no desire to flee from it. It was precious. As for holidays, those would come, but not until she had more energy to organize them. She did not want to be among strangers, who could not understand, and therefore be obliged to make an effort for their sake. She was, she wrote to Foy, two months later, 'settling to the emptiness . . . it does not seem so overpowering now the summer weather has come. I come and go about the house quite cheerfully and everything is "routes" after all. What folly it is when people up sticks at once when bereaved and take themselves to a different milieu. I wonder what they hope to find.'

What she hoped to find herself, eventually, was a greater freedom for her 'No. 2'. In a questionnaire[2] she had answered two years before, she had written beside 'What are your unfulfilled ambitions?' – 'I would like to have climbed mountains and travelled a lot in remote places.' Now there was no reason why she could not do both. Another freedom she wanted for herself was to be more of a grandmother. The grandchildren could come and make as much noise as they liked without her having to worry that this would annoy Tommy. This was something of a delusion – the noise had annoyed her as much as him – but she sincerely felt that her role as matriarch would now be more fulfilling. The fact that Kits and Olive were expecting their first child three months after Tommy's death went a long way towards making the immediate future brighter. When Kits rang to announce the birth of Frederick Kevin du Maurier Browning in June, she was overjoyed. She didn't feel up to travelling to see the baby, but Kits drove down with him and she paid him the highest compliment possible: he was just like Tommy. The beginning of a new generation of Brownings just as Tommy died seemed to her wonderfully significant, a passing of one life into another, a reminder that Jung's biological continuity was what she believed in and must hold on to. She felt that Olive (now nicknamed 'Hacker') was a good mother and a good wife and her son was secure. All she worried about was his future prosperity – 'Olive will soon be serving teas,' she joked.

Then suddenly, just as she was announcing 'I have adapted myself better than I had expected,' an old anxiety resurfaced. There were four and a half years of her lease on Menabilly still to run and she had paid a deposit on the lease of Kilmarth, the dower house of Menabilly, but now Philip Rashleigh suggested to her that since the Kilmarth tenants had left, and it was empty, perhaps she would like to give up Menabilly and take up residence there herself, leaving him free to move into Menabilly. What Daphne herself wanted was a renewal of the Menabilly lease for fifteen years and permission to build a dower house in its grounds at the end of that. At first, Philip Rashleigh appeared to agree to the renewal of the lease if she gave up Kilmarth, but then it turned out this was not his intention at all: he wanted her to move into Kilmarth. Daphne asked him to come and discuss the whole matter, and gave a dramatic account of what transpired. 'I said . . . "You do want to come to live here, don't you?" Stiffly, he replied, "In the course of time, yes" (why not say "I can't wait. It's my life" as I would have done).' She said she had then tried to discuss Kilmarth but he had said he was not prepared to discuss it. This enraged her – 'This abrupt stiff-necked pomposity of his attitude so confounded me that there was nothing to be done.' It was then suggested to her that the Menabilly lease could be renewed for seven years if she paid for the demolition of the wing which had been falling down for ages. She felt 'further conversation was obviously as hopeless as when the Russians sat round the table at UNO vetoing every proposal. I even said to Philip, "This is being just like Vietnam or something," – not a flicker of a smile in response.' She took him to the door, 'longing to plant a kick in his posterior'.[3]

Once again, she had a corner to fight and there was the same relish for battle, but with a difference. She was afraid she would end up with neither Menabilly nor Kilmarth, and this made her more cautious than the description she gave of the scene makes her sound. She also had a lever this time – the Kilmarth lease – and was determined to keep calm and use it. Since this might mean she would have to live at Kilmarth, she therefore had to consider the possibility seriously. During the earlier crisis over Menabilly in 1960–61 she had never allowed herself to think of living anywhere else – it was 'a fight to the death' – but now, especially in her changed circumstances as a widow, she was obliged to. There was considerable pressure on her from both family and friends to take Kilmarth. It was a much smaller house (though still large), much lighter and brighter and easier to look after than Menabilly, which at some point she would have to leave anyway. The lawyers for both sides met but the matter was still not resolved by the end of the summer – first she would think she was secure at Menabilly only to hear she was not, and this naturally played havoc with her already fragile emotional state. Whatever the rights and wrongs of the Rashleigh case, prevarication was certainly very evident.

But the summer of 1965 was surprisingly happy all the same. Tessa came with her children, now ten and nine, and Flavia with her son, aged six. The Zulueta family were going through a bad time that year, with Peter de Zulueta's drinking now so serious that Tessa was not optimistic about how long she could make her marriage survive. Both Pooch and Paul were seriously affected by this situation and arrived needing every bit of support and love a grandmother could lavish on them. Going to Menabilly, for Christmas and in August, were visits of tremendous importance to them, but invariably never quite came up to expectations.

Daphne's intentions as a grandmother were the very best – she felt for the children and wanted to make them happy and cherish them – but what she was able to offer in the way of emotional sustenance was very little. She greeted them, not with a hug but a peck on the cheek, because that was her way, and though she was gentle and kind, taking them for walks and telling them the names of flowers, she kept her distance and was critical. Pooch, unfortunately, was at that stage fat and plain, which her grandmother did not like at all. Nor did she like 'the Zulus' for being what she thought of as difficult and spoiled. For all her imaginative powers, and her own experience as a moody young girl, she did not seem able to put herself in Pooch's position. Instead, she put herself in Tessa's and was indignant at the way she was treated by her children – which was to say in a free and easy manner, in the modern way of which Daphne did not approve. There was no nonsense about children not eating with adults until they were twelve in the Zulueta household, nor any restrictions on roaring and shouting. The Zulus were 'savages' and she preferred Rupert, Flavia's son, who was a model of propriety, 'the most delightful thing in children I have ever struck'. He behaved impeccably – 'not one grizzle, not one whine, not one faint whimper and no loud shouts either'. But even Rupert watched too much television in her opinion, and she was driven, in spite of her own addiction to television, to comment: 'I think modern children have no imagination. It is all distraction or "What can we do now?" ' This in particular was unforgivable – to ask, on a wet day, 'What can I do now?' when outside there were the Menabilly woods to play in, was beyond her comprehension. But she tried to suggest things, controlling her irritation, and some of the suggestions were rich, coming from her. 'How about trying out the Saturday evening meal on your own?' she once encouraged Pooch, and gave her a recipe for 'a really nourishing soup . . . bits of onion . . . bits of cabbage . . . drop of sherry'.

Filling her days like this was not, of course, going to be enough when the dreaded winter came, but she had no hopes of getting down to any writing. Once, her fallow periods had been intervals during which she felt quite happy, knowing they were necessary, but now they terrified her. 'My imagination . . . is completely

fallow,' she wrote to Victor Gollancz, and though she acknowledged 'emotional shock is bound to do this', she wondered if
perhaps it had not done more – perhaps it had dried her imagination up for good. The only way to test this was the time-
honoured one of trying a holiday in the hope of stimulating it. So
in September she went to Venice with her sister Jeanne. Leaving
Menabilly took even more effort than it had always done and she
recognized something superstitious in her reluctance. She had a
feeling common to the recently bereaved, the dread of returning
and finding the presence of the dead person has evaporated in
their absence. But she managed to go, and enjoyed the two weeks,
though she was depressed to realize afterwards that she had no
burning idea for a new book to carry her through the winter.

At this point, John Sargent at Doubleday came up with the idea
that Daphne should write a book on Cornwall, part history and
part travel, which would be illustrated with photographs. The
moment she realized Kits could take these photographs Daphne
was extremely keen on the idea. Kits, by then, had become a
freelance TV director and a photographer and he and his mother
had formed a company – Du Maurier Productions – to make films.
Kits had already made one film, the one about Yeats, for which
his mother had written the script, and she thought it very good
indeed. The Doubleday suggestion was an ideal project for both
of them. It could be spread over several months during which Kits
would come down and drive his mother round Cornwall while
she researched the book.

It was the kind of book Daphne had never attempted before,
but it appealed to her instantly. She loved Cornwall and, though
she had absorbed a great deal of its history and had explored the
county extensively, she welcomed the opportunity to learn more.
The student in her responded to the background reading that
would be necessary, and her imagination leapt at the chance to
describe Cornwall in such a way that others would share her
devotion. But best of all was the thought of spending so much
time with her son, just the two of them working together. There
could be no better antidote to the sadness following Tommy's
death and in addition no better way to relive some of the happiest
memories she had of him which 'might rid the system of sadness

perhaps'. It was no good 'turning into a hump-backed dowager like Queen Victoria', but in spite of starting to read for the new book there were many bad moments that winter. The worst time was Christmas. Always a big festival in both the du Maurier and Browning calendars, especially with Tommy's birthday on 20 December, when she had always decorated a small tree just for him, she could hardly face the prospect. The children insisted she must come to one of them, which she did not want to do, but finally agreed she would. She shared her time between Flavia and Kits and quite enjoyed it, though she was never entirely comfortable in anyone else's home, not even her children's. 'Routes' were so hard to follow when not at Menabilly and other people's got in the way. But the house Kits had just bought amused her tremendously – she described to Foy how Tithe Barn (near Taplow) was the sort of house which 'if passing in a car on a journey one would tap the glass to the chauffeur and say "Would you draw in here and we will stop for lunch?"' It was, she swore, like 'a road-side timbered steak house' and it made her laugh just to see it. Coming back to Menabilly was bleak, especially since in spite of travelling first-class she had to stand in the corridor of the train – 'What happens to old people who travel? It's like prisoners of war going to concentration camps, and the corridors freezing.'

The rain that January got her down more than it had ever done and she felt in danger of succumbing to real depression. She had to walk her dog – Moray, another West Highland terrier – and so went out and walked, but the evenings were long. She did not like to watch television until after seven and, once it was dark at around five, was left with two hours 'to fill in . . . passage-wandering'. Everything seemed to irritate her and she feared she was becoming old and grumpy. Even Esther going to a hunt ball somehow exasperated her and she commented to Foy that times had certainly changed if *anyone* could now go. She could find nothing to read – 'I find myself so choosy about what I read and books get more and more lurid . . .' – and even *The Times* was letting her down – 'It is not so good as it once was, I think in a tiresome endeavour to be what is called "with it" – a phrase I detest.'

In this mood, the negotiations with Doubleday, which had

preceded any mention of the book on Cornwall to Gollancz, led her into further trouble. She had failed to consult her agent, and Spencer Curtis Brown, discovering a contract had been made between Du Maurier Productions and Doubleday for world rights, was livid: 'It is not at all a favourable contract . . . next time you feel an urge to sign a contract you should pause for thirty seconds and put it into an envelope to me first.' He realized that 'this letter sounds like an uncle writing to an inexperienced niece', but felt she deserved it. Daphne accepted this rebuke as she accepted all rebukes – humbly, apologizing for her foolishness, and saying she hadn't thought it mattered, because the Cornwall book wouldn't have a big sale.

While all this was sorted out, and while she waited for the weather to improve so that she and Kits could start researching, Daphne began to seek the company she needed. 'I get very sad when left to my own thoughts,' she wrote, 'and ordinary chatter does not help, but intelligent conversation does . . .' But where was she to get this 'intelligent conversation' from, when she so resolutely cut herself off from all likely sources? She still limited herself to the occasional company of those local friends she had always had – Clara Vyvyan, Foy Quiller-Couch,[4] Mary Fox, A. L. Rowse – and of her sisters and Noël Welch, but this by no means prevented life sometimes becoming tedious. So she turned to friendships conducted in letters, to talking on paper, as many a writer does, rather than take on the burden of new face-to-face relationships. She had always been good about replying to fans (so long as there was a stamped addressed envelope enclosed), but now she began to develop some of these correspondences into real friendships. If a fan caught her fancy, and especially if that fan were young, she was capable of writing with real warmth and interest. Perhaps the fan who best succeeded in capturing her attention and then affection was a young man called Michael Thornton, who first wrote to her as a schoolboy of seventeen, because he loved *The King's General.* After the exchange of a few letters, Daphne let him visit Menabilly, and by the time she faced her first winter as a widow she had started treating him as a real friend. Nor did she simply want to use him as the recipient of her thoughts and comments but, on the contrary, showed avid interest in his career and problems and was tremendously sympathetic. She enjoyed getting his letters and replying to them: a small gap in her day was plugged – she had her 'intelligent conversation' through the post.

There were others with whom, from this point onwards, she established real contact even though she never met them. Many an aspiring writer who had timidly sent a story for her comment was amazed to receive proper criticism and advice. But, though devoting a couple of hours most days to this kind of communication helped her to feel busy – 'I hate to be idle' – it could not provide enough stimulation. It was hard for her to admit she was not as self-sufficient as she had always thought, and harder still to do something about it.

What she did, once the spring of 1966 had arrived, was to plan her first adventurous holiday since Tommy's death. It was not really so very adventurous. She had been tempted for a long time by the idea of going on a Hellenic cruise and sent for the Swan brochure. She yearned so much for the sun and, having loved her short trip to Greece with Clara Vyvyan, she now booked berths for herself and Tessa on the SS *Ankhara*. The minute she had done so, panic set in. She would have to meet new people and it would be embarrassing – she dreaded it, and asked Tessa to write to the Swan people emphasizing that her mother was very shy and did not want to be known. She was also fussed about tipping – 'Do ask . . . if one *tips*, and who . . . so embarrassing if one does the wrong thing. I would think one's cabin steward or stewardess would qualify if no one else.' By March, when Kits had begun to drive her round Cornwall, she was regretting the whole thing and told an old friend, also going on the cruise, to 'look out for an apprehensive grey-haired woman in a black and white coat, tottering along the platform at Victoria'.[5] She wrote to Foy that she couldn't think why she had taken tickets, when she looked at the rhododendrons just coming into bloom. It even seemed dangerous to leave when nothing had yet been resolved about her wretched lease – she had absurd visions of returning to find she had been turned out – and she left for London feeling 'low and depressed'.

Never in her life did a depression lift as quickly. Her letter to Foy after she returned home from the cruise could not have been more different – in her enthusiasm for the holiday she hardly knew where to start. 'Tessa was wonderful,' she wrote, 'so friendly with everyone, and had I been alone I know I should have hidden in our cabin, but she dragged me from my shell and it was really the right thing to do.' Even so, the dragging had taken some doing. The whole ship knew Daphne du Maurier was on board and curiosity ran high, but it was two days before she appeared from her cabin and, even then, she was shepherded and protected by the attentive Tessa. Only when she realized her privacy was being respected did she begin to relax and gradually become interested in the others on board.

It was unusual for her to take to new people immediately, but she took to Sir John and Lady Wolfenden at once and was quite excited at the thought of having made friends with them. Sir John was one of the lecturers on the SS *Ankhara* and Daphne responded eagerly to what she liked to think of as the 'university atmosphere' of the ship. It was exhilarating to sit and listen to such a clever man and afterwards to discuss what had been said, and to find her own tentative ideas well received. And there was another side to life on board ship which she relished. Dancing the evenings away with Sir John, she felt younger than she had done for years. He was not an especially skilled dancer, but not since she danced with Frank Price, more than a decade ago, had she felt such a sense of release. Then, of course, there were the visits on shore to places in Greece she had always wanted to see – 'Delos was the highlight' – and the pleasure of feeling the sun at last (though, in fact, the weather was not as warm as she had hoped, and she had to buy 'a shepherd's short white cloak to cope with it'). She returned to Menabilly feeling rejuvenated, and in her first letter to the Wolfendens told them that they had rescued her from apathy. When Ellen Doubleday came to stay in May, she was pleased to find her so buoyant: with Kits coming regularly to take his mother off to research their Cornish book, her morale was still high.

Her spirits were maintained throughout the summer which followed – a wonderfully hot summer in Cornwall, so that she could swim every day right up to the end of September. She was determined to change her ways and make sure she kept up her new friendship without depending, as she usually did, on the

friends themselves making the running. She invited the Wolfendens to Menabilly, and when she went up to London – 'the hermit
is coming for five days' – was anxious to take them out to dinner.
In one letter she enclosed a clever, satirical ode to Sir John, who
responded in kind, and there was a touching eagerness in her
efforts to show how much she appreciated the warmth both Wolfendens had extended towards her. Not even the still unresolved
question of the lease spoiled the summer, though she was beginning to see that she might have to move into Kilmarth. Even more
surprisingly, she was getting out and about much more, because
she had learned to drive again and was triumphant about it. Once
Tommy had died, she could see that unless she wanted to be
entirely dependent on taxis, or wanted to be quite cut off, she
would have to drive again: with Kits' help she began taking lessons. He had found for her a small automatic car to which she
became greatly attached and in February that year she had taken
her test in a state of intense nervousness. She thought the examiner
'an old buffer in a squashed hat and mac' who did not respond to
any of her polite conversation. 'This little car is called a DAF,'
she told him, but he answered crossly, 'I know, I've seen heaps
of them,' but he had passed her none the less. She could now
zoom off to Par to do bits of shopping, or go to visit Angela, or
even, very occasionally, drive bravely to Dartmoor to see Jeanne
and Noël. Her independence excited her – an independence she
could have had at any time in the previous twenty-five years.

That was becoming the real question: how far did she want to
take this new independence and sociability? She saw very clearly
that she had to choose. If she wished, there was nothing to prevent
her slamming down the portcullis and never letting anyone past
it except her family. She no longer wanted to be as solitary as she
had once been, not because she had suddenly changed her nature,
but because she feared what would happen, or might already have
happened, to her writing. She was almost sixty and saw her late
middle age as a time when stimulus would have to be more deliberately sought out. People, not only places, were needed after all to
work the magic, and becoming a recluse would be fatal. She still
wanted long periods of solitude, but she wanted to be sure she
could end them when she willed.

Here her three children played a vital role. There was in her attitude to her daughters as adults the same detachment as there had been when they were children. She was passionately interested in their lives and very fond of them, but not emotionally involved. As children they had found this a source of some sadness, but in many ways it was a great advantage to them now they were grown up. Nobody wants a mother who is possessive, who tries to run one's adult life as she has run one's childhood. Daphne kept in regular touch, welcomed them for holidays at Menabilly with their families, treated them to other trips with her alone, and was exceedingly generous with financial help (quite apart from their trusts). She asked very little in return and never tried to exert any kind of pressure because she had the power which money gave her. Her critical nature made her hard on them if she thought they were doing something of which she did not approve, but she was surprisingly sympathetic to most of their problems, except one. Both daughters, Tessa in particular, were discovering that their marriages were not a success; and towards the idea of divorce their mother was hostile. She felt that she herself had made her marriage endure and so should they, failing entirely to appreciate that the circumstances were quite different and that not everyone would think she had been right to cling to her own marriage. In spite of this area of profound disagreement, the company of Tessa and Flavia was precious to her now – she relied on them in the sense of being able to talk to them with absolute freedom, and, for a widow who had no intimate female friends of her own age, this was a great relief. She could mock and joke with them and had no need to pretend as she did with everyone else – there need be no façade. They knew, as no one else did, how violently she could express herself, how full of controlled rage she could be while seeming sweet and charming.

With Kits, of course, she was even freer. His mind and hers, she wrote, were the same in so many ways and never more so than over their book on Cornwall. His marriage had made no difference to this rapport, but what is fascinating is the way in which she had been able to let him go, just as she had always said she was determined to. She approved of Olive, seeing her as a stabilizing influence on Kits, and even as the stronger partner, and instead of resenting this she was relieved. She never tried to come between them or initiated any kind of contest for his affections. 'My children', she wrote that summer to Victor Gollancz, 'make wonderful companions, all three of them – I am so lucky.' That was what she most wanted, amusing companionship upon which she could rely, kindred spirits with whom she could truly relax. No friend, of however long standing, quite gave her that. But at the same time she did not want their companionship to turn into any kind of dominance. One of the first things she said after Tommy's death was that she could see 'I shall have to be careful my children do not take over my life', in particular that they did not 'try to push a companion on me, a sort of younger Tod'.[6] She was absolutely emphatic that she wanted to go on living alone and, if possible, at Menabilly, however often her children pointed out its remoteness, its size and its general unsuitability, in their eyes, for a widow to spend her old age in.

But there was no chance of that. Philip Rashleigh had finally made up his mind: he wanted to move into Menabilly when the lease expired in another two years and had agreed that Daphne could have Kilmarth for life. She was forced to capitulate, or lose Kilmarth too – 'My landlord has dealt his blow . . . I must take it as a challenge . . . it is a bit like the breakdown of a marriage without the finality of death or even the disturbance of divorce.' She would move to Kilmarth, though she was horrified at the state it was in and by how much money she would yet again have to spend restoring a house she would never own. She anticipated she would have to spend 'a fortune' on essential building work, and then that her children would 'bully me into getting new curtains' and, even more outrageous, 'central heating which is bad for catarrh'. It annoyed her that so many people kept stressing how much better off she would be in Kilmarth because it was not as big, was so much lighter and had better views than Menabilly, standing as it did high up on the cliff overlooking the sea. Even the lack of extensive grounds was presented to her as an advantage when to her it was a terrible drawback – where would she walk, except up and down an incredibly steep cliff to a beach which was not a patch on Pridmouth? Nobody seemed to realize that for her Kilmarth lacked the most seductive of Menabilly's charms: its sense of mystery, its secrecy. Kilmarth was just a handsome house, lacking excitement. Nor could it ever become part of her in the same way as Menabilly had done. She would leave behind ghosts – her younger, happier self and Tommy. Hating all change as she did, she feared, too, the destruction of her 'routes'. The wrench was one she could hardly bear to contemplate and she was frightened by the prospect of what giving up Menabilly would do to her.

Chapter Twenty-two

In August 1966, Daphne finished writing the book about Cornwall, to be called *Vanishing Cornwall* (after she had rejected the suggestion 'Romantic Cornwall', declaring that she hated the word). She was pleased with the book and felt she had been quite outspoken in her acid comments about tourism. When Victor and Sheila both suggested 'some anti-tourism stuff' should be cut, she was indignant, though as usual gave way to their judgement. But what really annoyed her sufficiently to record her displeasure was the news that although she sent the book to Gollancz at the end of August, they said they could not publish it until the following year. She could see no reason for this – every book she wrote seemed to take longer to publish and she wished she was back in the days when, if she delivered a manuscript one month, it was published the next. At least, she thought, the book should come out in the spring of 1967, ready for the holiday trade. But no – it was to be July, and she was furious. As usual the storming letters about this were not written to either Victor or Sheila, who simply received mild enquiries as to the reason for the delay.

It was some consolation that when the book did appear it was well reviewed, Kits' photographs as well as Daphne's prose receiving praise, and that it became a bestseller even though Gollancz had published what Daphne thought of as an 'absurdly low' number of copies – 7,500 (perfectly good for a travel book). Victor himself died that year, in February, and everyone at Gollancz was nervous about how Daphne would react, especially his daughter Livia, who took over as head of the publishing house. She had no need to worry – loyalty was everything to Daphne, and though some authors considered their loyalty belonged only to Victor himself and left, she never thought of it. She valued

Sheila immensely – 'she knows my ways' – and as ever loathed the idea of change. But it was true that with Victor gone – and she mourned his death greatly – she had lost both a mentor and a powerful influence on herself. For thirty-three years she had abided by his judgement in literary matters and only when money came into the dispute did she overrule him. Now, there was no one at Gollancz, not even Sheila, who could give her the same guidance and if necessary save her from herself. She was too valuable for anyone to risk upsetting, not a healthy position for any author to be in.

The plan of *Vanishing Cornwall* on the whole pleased the critics, who enjoyed the mixture of history, description of landscape and evocation of atmosphere together with Daphne's personal reminiscing. The prologue, in which she described her holidays as a child in Cornwall and then her memories of learning to love it as an adult, was particularly liked and much preferred to the account of Cornwall's origins. There is a lot of historical background and a good deal of retelling of legends in the first part of the book, before any attempt is made to grapple with the Cornish character. Daphne felt on strong ground here, though the Cornishmen among the reviewers felt that she had failed to capture their real character. However, even the Cornishmen liked her 'affectionate summoning of the Cornish *world*' – 'place' was her strength. The *Sunday Times* could not fault the evocation of 'scenery and the changing weather', and the *Observer* thought she had captured 'the special essence of the place'. All in all, not even Daphne, with her paranoid view of critics, could maintain that the book had not been generously received.

She was glad about this, assuring friends that she was about 'to land in the bankruptcy courts'. Kilmarth was financially draining and she claimed to have spent £8,000 on Kits' project of making *Vanishing Cornwall* into a film, which meant 'my own finances are low'.[1] Curtis Brown, her agents, were requested to tell her how many copies of all her books had been sold to date, so that she could see if she was 'sliding towards ruin', which threw them into something of a panic. It was, they replied, 'a really enormous labour' to calculate, and there was no need, because they could assure her that she was still making large amounts of money from royalties on *Rebecca* alone. In addition, she was receiving, from Doubleday in America, £30,000 every year, under an agreement whereby they held her accumulated royalties there and released only this sum, so that the tax to be paid on her whole income in England would not be prohibitive. Knowing all this made no difference – she was worried about money even more than she had been since her letter to Victor in 1956, when she first began to be anxious that she was finished as a high earner. Unfortunately, the bank manager in St Austell chose this moment to write and make some mild enquiries about her overdraft.[2] She was furious – and interpreted the enquiry as 'insulting' and also inexplicable, because she couldn't understand why she had an overdraft anyway. Her accountant, Richard Pegler, had just been obliged to retire, owing to ill health, and she was even more worried than usual about her financial affairs.

Her only comfort was that she could feel 'another novel grow-ing' after she returned from a second Swan Hellenic cruise (as good as the first) in the spring of 1967. She wasn't sure if the idea would continue to grow, but it was sparked off by her now regular visits to Kilmarth to see what needed to be done. The history of the house interested her, as did the history of the area in which it stood. A Mr Thomas of the Old Cornwall Society lent her a 'glorious full-scale tithe map of Tywardreath' and she became fascinated by a priory which had stood there in the fourteenth century. Throughout the summer and autumn she explored Kil-marth itself and at the same time read up on its past occupants from the fourteenth century onwards. She was most intrigued 'by a young woman called Isolda who married Sir Oliver Carminow' and also by a recent tenant of Kilmarth, Professor Singer. Some bottles containing animal embryos were found in the basement and she suddenly saw how she could interweave two stories – the old and the new – connecting them by means of some kind of time-travelling. She thought she might 'switch in time to the fourteenth century in a *Scapegoat*ish kind of way'. This was exactly the kind of story she loved to concoct, and once she had thought of a device whereby the connection could be made – her hero taking an experimental drug – she was excited by the tremendous possi-bilities. She could combine historical fact with psychological study, and that was going 'to give me a lot of fun'. It would, she thought, produce something 'unusual . . . and a bit frightening'.

She did not start to write until after Christmas – all the de Zulueta family were there except Peter (whose alcoholism had made him seriously ill, and over whom she thought it 'better to draw a veil'). Privately, she was prepared to confess to the Wolfendens that Tessa had 'a sometimes difficult home life', but that she was sure her daughter, who had 'loads of courage and guts', would 'keep her particular flag flying'. The grandchildren were 'dear', but she was bewildered by their 'lack of initiative to entertain themselves'. Her own brood, she wrote, never needed to be entertained – all of them had always been perfectly happy, 'Tess with her nose in a book . . . Kits and Flave playing imaginary games and never at a loss'. She had not the slightest idea of how wretched Tessa had once been, lonely to the point of gloomily contemplating suicide and reduced to playing with her goats, nor how displaced Flavia had felt when for years she was obliged to play with Kits and be 'old dopey'. The past was always a happy place for Daphne, childhood enchanted. Pooch and Paul de Zulueta were spoiling her romanticized vision; Freddie Browning, aged two, by contrast, and Robert, born just before Christmas, were still babies and she adored them, and of course Rupert Tower, Flavia's son, continued to please her with his quietness. But thoughts of modern children were in her mind when she started writing her new novel, as well as thoughts of Isolda and of Professor Singer's experiments.

Once she did start to write, she had that feeling of exhilaration she had not experienced since *The Scapegoat*. Again, she had a male narrator, Dick, who agrees to take an experimental time drug which plunges him back into the fourteenth century around Kilmarth, the house where he lives. He never knows at which precise point in time he will arrive when he travels back to the past, which makes the fourteenth-century drama constantly exciting. But the contemporary story has its own appeal. Dick, a rather unlikeable fellow, true to du Maurier form, is married to an American, who has two sons by a previous marriage. They arrive at Kilmarth for a holiday, interrupting his time-travelling, to his extreme annoyance. This gave Daphne the chance to write caustically about marriage and children. Dick doesn't really like either his wife or any of the female sex – women have 'one-track minds and to their narrow view everything male, be it man, dog, fish or slug, pursued but a single course and that the dreary road to copulation'. The only exception to this contempt is Isolda, the woman in the fourteenth century, whose life he has been studying whenever he takes the drug. With her lover, she has 'the kind of relationship that I myself would never know' – blessed, a full communion of spirit and soul as well as passionate. Her husband does not have this closeness with her – 'he has women wherever he goes, but his pride would never brook a faithless wife'. The further the story develops, the more complex Dick becomes, an ultimately sad and wistful figure, disillusioned with his own times, wanting to retreat into the past, yet coming to believe 'there was no past, no present, no future. Everything living is part of a whole.'

So completely did Daphne become immersed in *The House on the Strand* – 'I got so hooked on the story I actually woke up one day with nausea and dizziness' – that she could hardly bear to leave it for more than a few hours. When Dick says he feels that the people he loves in the past are himself, he voices Daphne's own sense of unity – she was 'being more truly myself' through Dick, her creation, just as he is through the fourteenth-century characters. She did not feel she was *pretending* to be him but that she *was* him. His fever – 'if you get bitten by the past it is like a fever in the blood' – was hers, and when his wife and stepsons arrive to drag him away from using the experimental drug, she felt as he did when her own family arrived for holidays. It became a race to finish the novel before August, and she just made it, writing to Livia Gollancz on the 7th that she thought it was 'unusual, moves fairly fast, and would come under the suspense category'. She specifically requested that Sheila should come down and work through the editing with her, since she had such trust in her, and in September Sheila duly arrived. Daphne took her to all the places mentioned in the novel and Sheila saw only too clearly how alive was the story in her mind.

The summer of 1968 was a happy one. Kits and Olive and their family came to visit and she revelled in 'the Browning boys'. Freddie was 'bliss' – and she would have liked to keep him forever 'even if I take to my bed in exhaustion'. It appalled her, though, to see Kits changing nappies or giving the baby his bottle – she felt quite faint wondering what Tommy would have said. Once everyone had gone she missed them all and, in spite of the pleasure she drew from knowing she had a good novel coming out the next year, she began to dread the approaching move to Kilmarth. Every time she walked down the lawn and through the woods to the beach she was thinking that soon she would never do this again, and the thought seemed cruel and unbelievable. She kept hoping that Philip Rashleigh would change his mind at the last minute, but there was no basis for this fantasy: she had to be out by September 1969.

Fighting the beginning of depression, after such a happy summer, she was suddenly shocked by a real tragedy which occurred that autumn. On 21 October, Esther's thirty-eighth birthday, her husband Henry died, aged only thirty-six. He was ill a mere three weeks, with what turned out to be a virulent infective hepatitis, and everyone, especially Esther, was quite unprepared for his death. Daphne was stunned and immediately cancelled a visit from the Wolfendens saying she could not bear to see anyone for several weeks. Her sympathy for Esther and for Ralph, her son, was deep but she found it hard to convey. It was mostly a silent sympathy, in which she tried to be considerate and kind, without any overt gestures of comfort. But she was more affected and felt for her 'lovely young Esther' more than Esther was able to know. Henry's death set her off into wondering, as she had not done for a long time, what she really thought about death. She did not believe in reincarnation nor in 'any idea of heaven', but she saw Tommy so often in her mind's eye that she believed there was 'something'. When Henry Rowe died, the idea that death was natural and only a stage, a transition, suddenly seemed false. Henry's death was *not* natural, nor had his time come, as she felt both Gerald's and Gertrude's had done.

It was very disturbing and saddened her last Christmas at Menabilly. It was sad, in any case, since neither her children nor her grandchildren were there. Both daughters were off on winter sports holidays (she kept hearing about avalanches and worrying), and Kits could not come because Olive had had an operation on her throat and both children had been in a car crash which had left Freddie with a fractured leg. So she was 'solitary, alas' with only Angela to join her on Christmas Day. She found she could not bring herself to decorate the house, though she had flowers everywhere. But then she missed the glory of the Christmas tree, and remembered how Tommy had taken charge of the decorations and how beautiful the long room had looked. She felt nostalgic and sentimental, and was further pulled down by Tessa's divorce from Peter having come through that autumn. Everything seemed in the process of being destroyed, and leaving Menabilly was all part of that destruction.

Every day in the New Year she went to inspect progress on the building work at Kilmarth and was shocked by the expense of everything. The builder, who she was amused to discover seemed shyer than herself – 'he backs into the bushes when I approach' – seemed constantly to uncover new jobs which needed to be done, and then there were all the fittings and furnishings, half of which she swore she did not want, to be paid for. But she was getting some pleasure out of the chaos. She had given orders that a small cellar in the basement was to be made into a chapel – 'for my little Catholic Browning grandsons to say their prayers' – and for separate quarters to be made at the back of the house so that the older grandchildren could be there and make as much noise as they wished. By April, she could see how convenient the new arrangement was going to be, and also how full of sunshine the rooms could be on a good day compared to the gloom of darker Menabilly. When she stood in what was to be her bedroom, at the front of the house, she could see the sea all the way across St Austell Bay and out to the open ocean, and she thought how much Tommy would have loved the view. Her memories of him were by now sanctified – she saw him in her mind's eye forever happy and energetic, and she had even forgiven him for putting his work before her. The previous summer she had been invited to open the new barracks at Aldershot, named the Browning Barracks after him, and had found it one of the proudest moments of her life when three parachutists dropped from the air and presented her with a bronze statuette of a paratrooper. All memory of hating the army and thinking army life pointless had left her.

So, very nearly, had the memory of her infatuation with Christopher Puxley. On a holiday with Kits and Olive to Ireland she visited the old home of the Puxley family, which she had used in *Hungry Hill*, and afterwards found herself wanting to write to him. It was a short, friendly, unemotional letter, which none the less betrayed some anxiety that she had injured him more than she had thought, and asked that only happy memories should remain. It was essential to her, that year, as she prepared to uproot herself from Menabilly, that the past should be tidied up – Tommy was the love of her life, their marriage had been happy, Christopher was only an aberration, and Gertrude Lawrence not acknowledged, except to Ellen, as ever having been her lover. Whenever she thought of Tommy now, she saw the familiar picture of him waiting for her and went towards him eagerly, knowing they would recapture their early married days. These were very much in her mind because, every evening when she got back from Kilmarth, she was in the process of sorting her possessions. She found many of her own letters to Tommy and suddenly decided to burn them, but she kept the photographs and sometimes, one of them capturing her attention, she would be taken by surprise. A snap of Tessa, aged two, in her pram made her pause – 'she does look so sweet' – and wonder why she had not been as enchanted by her at the time. Some of the letters she found did not belong to her – there was a packet containing Tommy's father's love-letters to his mother and these quite upset her. She felt they were so highly personal that they too should be burned, as she had burned her own, but she could not bring herself to do it and sent them to Grace to dispose of. 'This is always the crux,' she observed, 'what descendants should read and what not.' Knowing how she had valued certain du Maurier family letters, and how glad she was to have been given such insight into her ancestors through them, she could not wholly advocate the destruction of all biographical material. It was up to the next generation, she felt, to make its own decision.

A bigger problem than the letters were the boxes of objects belonging to other people and all the odd bits of furniture which had been stored for years in the closed wing of Menabilly, known as 'The King's Road'.[3] 'All this junk', as Daphne referred to it, had to go. She gaily invited family and friends to come and take their pick, informing them that 'half the stuff is white with mould'. Mould or not, some of it belonged to elderly relatives, for whom she had stored it, and who still valued it in spite of never having claimed it. Her children were rather annoyed at her cavalier approach to the disposal of certain valuable items, but all she wanted was to be rid of them. She was determined to be as ruthless and matter-of-fact as possible, but was more disturbed by the endless reminders of the past involved in clearing out Menabilly than she realized. She spent hours and hours on the task and felt both physical and emotional energy draining away.

Deciding that she ought to have a break 'before the final push', she agreed to attend a Royal Academy dinner in London, because 'it is such an honour and . . . the family say I must accept'.[4] Very quickly she wished she had not done so. She had no evening dress, 'have not worn one for fifteen years', and to her dismay the invitation said 'Decorations'. Did this mean gloves? Or worse – 'if it means a tiara, I am sunk'. Assured that no tiara was necessary, she went up for the dinner, feeling distraught at the mess she had left behind. She was so overcome with exhaustion, the heat of the room and a kind of claustrophobia induced by sitting with so many people, that she fainted. This was a warning to her and, though she felt perfectly well afterwards, she tried to take things easier when she returned home.

The move to Kilmarth was finally made at the end of June 1969, when she suddenly got into her car and drove there to spend the first night, not having made any conscious decision to do so. It had become a kind of game, this moving, stretching over two years and played only when she felt like it. Theoretically this had made it easier but, in another sense, it had increased the strain – she felt permanently as though she were teasing herself and could not quite let go. Once she was actually in residence at Kilmarth, which she knew she had for life, she found it 'a very welcoming house', open-faced and cheerful, but, though she managed to con-trol 'the ache for my old home', she could not prevent herself from feeling disorientated. She tried to establish the same 'routes', but, even though she had her meals at the same time, walked her dog at the same time, read her newspaper at the same time and went to bed at the same time, nothing *seemed* the same. She felt she had been 'reshuffled' and could not settle down. None of the new carpets and curtains gave her much pleasure, because all she could think of was the cost – 'I am now so broke, having paid for the new drawing-room carpet, that I may have to hire myself out as a daily help . . . but I should prove "unsatisfactory".'⁵ She felt as if a nice house had 'been lent to me by friends' and that soon she would be returning home. But returning even to walk in the Menabilly grounds upset her – Menabilly seemed 'as remote as Cannon Hall', and she could hardly bear to glimpse it through the trees knowing it was no longer hers. She dealt with this pain by keeping away and restricting herself to her new walk, across the field beside Kilmarth and down the steep cliff to the tiny beach, which was not nearly so satisfactory. She named the hill 'thrombosis hill' and she wondered how long she would be able to manage it.

By July, the month *The House on the Strand* was published, she still felt strange in Kilmarth. It was 'not a creepy house' but she felt shivery, even though 'I do like it very much'. The trouble was that Menabilly haunted her and, when she was down in the little chapel at Kilmarth, she found herself not so much praying as communing with the old house. 'It is just like saying good-bye to someone one knows is going to die,' she wrote to Foy. 'I know this is fanciful, but anyway die as far as I am concerned. And I find myself missing it now in the way one misses anyone who has died and whom one loved, but the process of time will adapt one.'

In the very month of her move to Kilmarth, before the Royal Academy dinner, she had been made a Dame of the British Empire in the June Honour's List.⁶ It was, she wrote, 'wasted on me', and she joked that she would much prefer to have had Menabilly conferred on her ('and Philip Rashleigh sent to the tower'). Her great worry was the scope for mockery – 'Dame Daphne sounds like something out of a pantomime'. She, a great mocker herself, could just hear the wisecracks and shuddered. The mere idea of herself as a Dame was 'ludicrous . . . I don't feel a scrap like one'. She felt she lacked not just the necessary gravitas but also, as more than one teasing friend pointed out, the clothes. Michael Thornton commented that he was sure she would 'wear the title like a dufflecoat', and another friend told her, 'Now you've *got* to wear a dress – Dames don't wear pants, I'm sure.' The congratulations flowed in and there was no doubt at all that, however ambivalent her feelings about the honour itself, she was proud and delighted and touched by the reactions of her family and friends. She laughed most at her cousin Nico Davies' description of reading the news – 'Swallowed my egg the wrong way . . . I had managed to control myself through Bobby Charlton, Basil d'Oliveira, Arthur Askey and Co. . . . then hoorah . . . how rapturously pink Uncle Gerald and all would have been.' This, of course, was what made even the prospect of mockery worthwhile – the certainty of her father's and her husband's pride in her, had they been alive. As Alec Guinness commented, 'How your father would have rejoiced in it.' And, as Lord Mountbatten assured her, 'How thrilled and proud Boy would have been.' Nevertheless, she thought of pleading illness for the investiture, until her children insisted it would be a great day for the older grandchildren. So she went through with it, though she slipped out quietly afterwards to avoid the attention of the press. Sir John Wolfenden wrote a poem about it which summed up her feelings and made her laugh:

> So there it is, the girl's a Dame,
> The so-called accolade of Fame
> Is hers. But what on earth's her name?
>
> Is she Dame D du M? But no.
> Is she Dame Daphne Browning? No.
> Or Browning DBE? Not so.
>
> I don't know how you'll work it out.
> Here is a thing without a doubt
> Some folk will make a fuss about.
>
> Dear Daphne by whatever name
> They call you in the honours game
> To us who love you, stay the same.

But there was no question of her changing – she never used the title. Her family were far more excited by it than she was, though it did cheer her up and make her feel less neglected by her peers. Convinced as she was that critics were prejudiced against her, and that the literary world had never given her her due, this official honour was an acknowledgement that she had worked hard. She was especially pleased that the honour had been awarded during a Labour government – Harold Wilson[7] had been 'my pin-up boy' ever since the early sixties, and she had astonished a coach-load of other Swan Hellenic people by shouting 'Hurrah!' when his election victory was announced during one of their outings in Greece. This was certainly no indication that she had thought through, and approved, of Labour policies, but rather an example of her liking to be different from her die-hard Tory friends, plus a genuine attraction to Harold Wilson himself, who she was convinced seemed honest and straightforward and had a sense of humour.

But any real interest in political issues was still not her style.[8] She cared about many controversial issues in Cornwall, but did not see that this obliged her to do the things she hated, such as attending meetings or making speeches. There were those who took it upon themselves to lecture her on her 'duty' to Cornwall in offensively self-righteous letters. One man told her that since she had made such a lot of money out of writing about Cornwall, she had an obligation to become its financial benefactor. This rightly incensed her. She had taken nothing from Cornwall in any material sense and had given a great deal to it. Tourism is an industry in Cornwall upon which many people depend and her books had brought many thousands of visitors flocking to the county. Though she made no large bequest to silence her critics, she contributed steadily and widely to a huge variety of charities and organizations concerned with helping Cornish people or preserving the Cornish countryside. Always, she requested anonymity after her experience in 1936, when she gave various *Jamaica Inn* rights to the Lantivet Bay Fund[9] and wrote to her mother that she was 'so embarrassed' by the publicity. Her annual contributions mounted with every year and were widely spread – from the South West Cornwall Society for the Mentally Handicapped to the Bodmin Countryside Group – until in all she supported sixteen particularly Cornish causes as well as national ones. The sums were small, but they were steady. It would have perhaps been more politic to buy a tract of land, or a house, and give it to Cornwall in her name, as many others did – to have du Maurier fields as there are Allday fields in Fowey – but her failure to make this gesture was never a sign that she did not care about Cornwall, or that she was mean.

Privately she also kept up a stream of concerned letters to local councils about litter on the beaches and illegal parking. She had no desire to keep away from these beaches those who, like her, loved them, but she could not bear to see any place of outstanding beauty ruined. The Town Clerk at St Austell grew used to her letters of protest and always took notice. But though she cared about preservation, she had no interest in innovation – she looked backwards rather than forwards and was more concerned with stemming tides than initiating change. An invitation to join the Cornish Nationalist Party was therefore exactly in tune with her thinking, and she accepted at once, greatly amused, after a warning that she would never attend any meetings 'because I am a recluse'. She wrote to Foy that she was thinking of wearing the Party's black kilt and quite fancied 'blowing up bridges' should the need arise. The whole idea appealed to her sense of the ridiculous, but there was also a real belief in what the Cornish Nationalists were about. So long as she could maintain her low profile and not be asked to do anything more strenuous than write for their journal, she was happy and proud to think she belonged to a 'rebel' organization.

The rebel in her was still strong, though she knew it was only in spirit and not in her actions that she had been rebellious. At the end of this decade she was beginning to be depressed that she had 'never really broken out', except in her books. Now she felt she never would, and yet the desire to do so had not quite died. She gave a rare radio interview in 1969 to Wilfred De'Ath, a friend of Kits, and talked to him of the things she would like to have done – travelling, climbing, archaeology. When he asked if she were afraid of drying up creatively (which, of course, she was) she said she accepted that her powers were declining, that she could no longer 'churn books out', and tried to reconcile herself philosophically to this. But, in fact, the start of the 1970s looked 'stale and anti-climax' after the excitement of writing *The House on the Strand* (critically received with great enthusiasm) and the move to Kilmarth, together with the fuss of being made a Dame. She wrote to the Wolfendens that 'my batteries are flagging' and 'my muse is absent, ideas will not come out . . .' Even worse, she was 'rather pushed for money' and was trying 'to keep my actual living expenses down to £4,500 a year'.

She began, at the end of the sixties, to be bolder in her dissatisfaction over the sales of her books. Victor was dead and she felt freer to complain to Gollancz that she kept hearing 'from fans and friends that it's impossible to buy any hardback *Rebecca* nowadays'. John Bush (Sheila's husband, now managing director of Gollancz) replied that *Rebecca* was still selling 2,000 hardback copies a year after thirty years and was in plentiful supply. Her agent came in for the same complaints and Spencer Curtis Brown handed her over to Graham Watson, 'an expert on saving authors money on tax'. What she wanted from now on was 'more spending money for myself' and to improve her earnings as much as she could before it was too late. She had forgotten her previous dislike of paperback firms, other than Penguin, and, when their licence expired, was prepared to consider other companies who would pay more.

Graham Watson urged her to stay with Penguin and tried to calm her anxiety about money, assuring her, 'If at any point . . . you need a substantial financial payment, it can easily be achieved.' She was not convinced. Her old age was just round the corner, and she was concerned that she would not be able to support it. Despite being sent encouraging lists of all the royalties her past books were still bringing in, she saw only the outgoings, which, instead of decreasing, seemed to increase. Her children were grown up, but she had grandchildren whose educational future she wished to finance; and she had just taken on responsibility for her Aunt Billie, whom she planned to move from Golders Green to Cornwall, to live not far from her in a bungalow with full-time help. Then there was Cousin Dora, to whom she did not owe as much, but who was family and needed help. In looking after these relations she was not simply acting with kindness but making a statement about how old people should be treated. She believed more firmly than ever that to put the old in institutions was monstrous: since she herself was tough and planned to live to a great age, she was doing as she wished to be done by (except that she would be able, she hoped, to pay for her own independence).

The year, and the decade, ended with feelings of 'nothing to look forward to'. Esther, who lived next door in a separate cottage, sprained her foot and then Ralph, her son, had to have a dental operation, so Daphne was managing on her own. As she sat in bed reading *The Mayor of Casterbridge*, a drip started coming through the ceiling. Soon the drip became a persistent thin stream and she was reminded of being in *Yggy* with Tommy, when leaks always seemed to happen above her head and not his. The builder would have to come and fix the roof: more expense. Pulling her bed into the middle of the room, she vowed she would get herself to the sunshine as soon as possible and find something to write.

Chapter Twenty-three

In January 1970 Tessa was remarried – to David Montgomery, son of Field Marshal Montgomery, whom she had known for about a year – and Daphne was prepared to forget her disapproval of her divorce. 'I was sorry when her first marriage came to grief,' she wrote to Montgomery, ' . . . but we cannot arrange our children's lives for them.' But her marriage put Tessa out of the running as a holiday companion, and Daphne turned to Kits and Olive, who agreed readily to join her in Crete in April. The choice of hotel was left to Kits, 'whose tastes are somewhat fanciful like my father's', and he picked out the Minos Beach Hotel. She hoped it would not be 'jet set . . . clothes always being a problem where I am concerned'. It was not jet set and Crete was her idea of perfection – 'I would be happy to live and die there'. She loved the sun, the scenery and swimming, as well as enjoying it all in the company of her son and daughter-in-law. The three of them played the kind of games she had played with Carol Reed and then with her own children, scrutinizing people sitting in bars and restaurants and making up histories for them as well as mimicking them. Kits, the brilliant mimic, had her in hysterics, and she loved his undiminished sense of fun. The three of them made an interesting trio and Daphne was well aware of this. She liked the attention her beautiful daughter-in-law and handsome son attracted, and being the mother-figure appealed to her. It 'made a bit of a life for Bing [herself], just watching everyone'.

Back at Kilmarth, she began a short-story collection, but was aware that she was having to force herself to do so. She knew that if she stopped writing she had nothing to put in its place and that she could no longer afford to wait until the spirit genuinely moved her – she had to keep in practice. Whatever anyone thought of her books, whether they were scorned or sold in their millions, was irrelevant: what mattered was the *act* of writing. Beside this, nothing else compared. Her interest in her children and grand-children was intense but it was not enough to sustain her without writing. So she set to and began working out ideas inspired by recent holidays. She had a story already written six years before in response to a request from Kingsley Amis, who was hoping to edit a collection of stories on a vaguely science fiction theme. She had been touchingly thrilled that a younger writer who was so successful should ask her to contribute, and even more delighted when he liked the story so much he sent her a telegram saying so. Her confidence in her own abilities was always so low that praise from such a source pleased her out of all proportion (and this exchange was the reason she had previously suggested sending books to Kingsley Amis for quotes). The story was 'The Break-through', and it had never appeared. 'It covers me with confusion', an embarrassed Kingsley Amis had written when she enquired, after a year, what had happened to his proposed collection to have to admit that 'the SF series has totally broken down because of lack of support from writers . . .' He returned the story, 'which I admire very much', with 'great regret and chagrin'.

'The Breakthrough' was written before *The House on the Strand* and was in some ways a rehearsal for the novel. The story deals with experimental work in a laboratory in Suffolk and the idea that when people die there must be an untapped source of energy. A scientist prepares to release such energy from a young man, who will die of leukaemia, into the mind of a retarded child. 'The Breakthrough' is skilfully worked and has an atmosphere of chilling menace about it which Daphne greatly liked. Menace of one sort or another, more sinister than macabre this time, was to be the theme of the volume. 'Don't Look Now'[1] (the phrase she often used herself, before launching into an entertaining fantasy about someone she was observing) was set in Venice. The plot turns on psychic twins (Daphne had seen elderly twins at Torcello) and a small girl who turns out to be a dwarf (again, she really had been surprised by such a mistake herself). The whole story evokes Venice at its most mysterious and depends for its success on the power of hallucination, mistaken identities and, of course, the revelation that the girl is a male dwarf and a murderer. These two stories, one written so much earlier and one very quickly after her holiday, caused her no trouble, but the others were more difficult.

'Not After Midnight' demonstrated how her liking for an intricate plot could lead her into complications which made her writing tortuous. It centred on an American she had seen in a bar who was 'the spit of Silenos' and this gave her the idea for a story revolving round the search by a drunken American and his wife for ancient remains. Drawn into it all is an unsuspecting homosexual teacher who has come to paint and who, in the end, becomes a victim. Long before she had finished this not very successful story, Daphne was taking the unusual step of ringing up her children and asking how on earth she could end it. 'The Way of the Cross', on the other hand, though not easy to write, worked out so well that it turned into a story long enough to be a novella. The idea behind it – a party of seven on a trip to Jerusalem from a cruise ship – was inspired by the Swan Hellenic tours. Each character is a type, but as the story develops each becomes a distinct individual and all of them, as they follow the Via Dolorosa, experience their own personal humiliation. In the end, they have all met the fate they most dread and only a small boy, grandson of one of the pilgrims, is left inviolate. Daphne was tempted, at one stage, to try turning it into a novel, but was worried that she could not maintain the tension.

Tension featured heavily in another story, 'A Borderline Case', by far the most biographically revealing (this collection, unlike *The Breaking Point* and *The Apple Tree*, was not rooted in personal emotional experience with the exception of this story, but in general observation). 'A Borderline Case' had something of a history to it. Maj.-Gen. Eric Dorman-Smith,[2] 'Chink', Tommy's great friend, whom Daphne had first met in 1932 and been 'menaced' [attracted] by (as he was by her), had become involved with the IRA. While on holiday once in Ireland with Kits and Olive, Daphne had tried but failed to find him. In 1968, however, she had sent *Vanishing Cornwall* to his old address and it reached him. He replied, thanking her and sent her a poem as a tribute – 'For Daphne, In Gratitude: Beauty Remembered' – saying that the memory of her beauty still had 'the power to disturb my pen'.

In 1969, Chink died, and she felt free to write a story about a character, ex-British Army, who works for the IRA: a girl is searching for the man who has been her father's friend. The feelings expressed by the girl echo those expressed by Daphne herself when Gerald died, and so the advice 'only by hating can you purge away love' takes on some obvious significance. The girl finds the man, makes love with him, and only after she has returned home realizes he was actually her real father. All this, wrote Daphne, was 'purely imaginary'.

Nowhere else in her work does Daphne have a daughter make love with her father, even though incestuous relationships are touched on, and nowhere else is the anguish of the father- daughter attraction so strongly described. But then incest interested her and she had begun to admit this openly, though in a way that was confusing and caused misunderstanding. In the 1969 radio interview with Wilfred De'Ath she had told him she thought people looked for partners who 'resemble their family . . . the boy looks for someone like his mother or sister . . . the girl for someone like her father or brother . . . the whole thing is incestuous'. She thought 'cleaving to family' of vital importance but 'not when young': parents cleaving to children was 'disastrous', and possessive parents 'dreadful'. Yet 'A Borderline Case' was not intended to be any kind of affirmation that incest was natural. What was natural, in her opinion, was the desire for closeness between family members because they were part of the same whole. She did not condone incest, but she did think that *not* being able to give free rein to incestuous feelings was some kind of tragedy. Everything she wrote, in both her letters and her fiction, indicated a very strong desire on her part, at one point, to enjoy with her father such a relationship which she considered quite normal and which she grew out of as most girls do. But she could not dismiss either the memory of her own feelings or, more importantly, the strength of Gerald's own feelings towards her. This was what she meant by 'the tragedy of incest': that at a certain stage in growing up incestuous desires were normal but they could never be fulfilled, and therein lay the tragedy. Incest itself she found repugnant.

The publication of these stories, entitled *Not After Midnight*, in July 1971, coincided with the first television interview Daphne ever gave. She had written to Liz Calder, in charge of publicity at Gollancz, that she wanted 'no interviews please . . . I'll do a tape for the Australian broadcast but anything else is *out!*' Though not, it seemed, if it would give 'my lad a leg up'. For Kits, to help his career, she was prepared to do what she had never done before, to expose herself to the kind of publicity she both dreaded and disapproved of. Kits' film of *Vanishing Cornwall* had been a great success, running for six weeks at the Curzon Cinema in Mayfair as the second feature, and she now agreed to do a programme if the BBC would show Kits' film later in the summer. 'The bargain was struck,' she wrote to her old friend Bunny Austin, adding that she sincerely hoped giving the lad a leg up would not result in 'a leg down for the distinguished Dame'. In fact, to her own great surprise, she found she enjoyed being part of a television team – 'in a moment it was as though we were a little group working with and for each other . . . it really did open my eyes'. She realized that what she had suspected for some time now was true: solitary by nature she might be, but the company of others could stimulate and amuse her and please her important 'No. 2' self. 'It made me think of the relationship that can exist with an army platoon,' she wrote. Nor did nervousness trouble her as much as she had thought it might, or 'worries about seeming a fool'. It helped that Kits' friend Wilfred De'Ath was the interviewer and, though she was putting on a great act, this was not obvious to viewers. To them she appeared charming and relaxed and most of all amazingly fit and athletic, as she strode across the cliff top, leaving De'Ath, some thirty years her junior, visibly panting. The only real drawback was that she ended up quite exhausted and in need of another holiday.

The programme was shown on BBC 2 on 31 August and Kits' film the following Friday. The bargain had been kept, but she was annoyed that 'they have cut down Kits' film . . . to make it fit into half an hour which will ruin it. You can't have the last word with the BBC – they think they know best.' It was a great success, though critics thought De'Ath had let her off very lightly indeed, and brought her many admiring letters from fans and friends. Beverley Nichols wrote to her that she had been enchanting and would get many offers of marriage. What she did get were letters from admirers asking for her photograph and exclaiming over 'my beauty at the advanced age of sixty-four ... all due to having my teeth fixed ... hurrah for aids to beauty'. One letter, from 'a bachelor of forty', who sent a snap of himself leaning against a white Rolls-Royce, said she had seemed 'bewitchingly naughty ... and delightfully refreshing'. This man also said he never took cream in his coffee – a reference to the story she had told in the television interview about how she and her sisters had always thought men who did so were effeminate. She was very amused by this letter and rather unwisely wrote back 'suggesting we form a black coffee brigade together'. Her correspondent thought it 'a magnificent idea' and admired her 'sexy handwriting'. He was, he said, 'willing if you are'. His next letter, written on Cats Protection League paper, was from 'a nearby tavern on Par beach' and requested an assignation on the cliff. She had the sense to realize she had let the joke go too far and did not reply, but the incident demonstrated to her how potentially vulnerable she was, living where she did. Esther was next door, but she was alone in the house most of the day and all night, and on her walks she was very easy to spot and track for anyone who wished to do either.[3]

This had never troubled her, even at Menabilly, which was much more hidden away, but now it began to, just a little. One day two men 'came round the door asking if I would vote for them to go off on some Youth Travel Association ... order a case of wine or take out a subscription'. She refused, but promptly phoned a neighbour to warn her to 'be on your guard'. When Esther was on holiday – and she was noticeably reluctant for Esther to go on holiday – Daphne found herself thinking 'if I fainted I wouldn't be found for days later'. Once, when a storm brought a tree down on to the telephone wires and her car was out of action at the same time, she realized how cut off she was. But this did not encourage her to think about moving 'somewhere more suitable to my years'. On the contrary, she was adamant that she would never move, never go to live with her children and never have anyone living with her. Fending for herself was something she was quite determined to do, though she admitted that when Esther was away she found 'swabbing floors, emptying dustbins and cooking' exhausting. 'Don't you wish,' she joked to Foy, 'we still had slaves?!'

The television interview marked the beginning of a new attitude towards her own privacy. She still wished to retain it, and would certainly never play the publicity game to the extent of attending literary lunches or book-signing sessions or going on tour, but she was more receptive to requests for interviews. Journalists began to be tolerated, and those who came were agreeably surprised to find how affable and lively she could be, not at all the cold, remote, aloof, reclusive person of her public image. Afterwards she would comment how worn out she was, 'completely drained', when the interviewer could have sworn she had been at ease and enjoying herself: it was always an effort, always a performance, and when she came 'off stage', the more convincingly casual she had been, the greater the fatigue. But the seventies were the decade when she finally began to understand how much publishing had changed and how much certain types of publicity could help to sell books, which she very much wanted to do. Playing the game a little made her more open about her expectations too. The Gollancz traveller[4] for Cornwall, who had always found her the most modest and undemanding of authors, began to notice signs of discontent about the sales and marketing of her books. Penguin annoyed her even more than Gollancz and she finally decided, against all advice, to move to Pan, even though Giles Gordon, who handled the negotiations on behalf of Gollancz, warned her rather cunningly that Pan would treat her 'as a bestselling romantic novelist of the Georgette Heyer, Mary Stewart variety' when her books were 'more serious than that . . . [you] are now a prescribed author for English literature exams'. But the switch to Pan was about money, not ego. The Penguin licence on seven of her novels would run out in October 1972 and they were offering £15,000 for the renewal as against Pan's £75,000. Under pressure, Penguin went up to £30,000, but the lure of the larger amount was too great to resist.

The publicity she did in 1971 prepared her for doing even more – 'perhaps' – for the new novel she was writing. She might have in her, she thought, 'one last hit', and she wanted to make the most of it. For the first time since she had written *The Parasites* in 1949 she had an idea for 'a funny novel . . . mocking everything'. Wit and humour were not associated with her writing and it struck her as odd that she, who was always ready to laugh and loved making and hearing jokes, and adored amusing anecdotes, had never let this side of herself find expression in the books. She now wanted to have a stab at 'a mock-up of what this country may be like in the mid-seventies'. She started *Rule Britannia* in January 1972 and 'worked like blazes', commenting that she had 'never cracked so hard on a book in my life, not even in my young days'.[5] By mid-February she was writing to her granddaughter that this new novel was 'very funny, at least I think so . . . it takes the mickey out of everything, including us as a family'. The heroine is a grandmother-figure, based on Gladys Cooper, who takes in various maladjusted boys and looks after them, helped by a housekeeper and by her granddaughter. The plot revolves round the unification of Britain and America and the arrival of the American fleet. The locals (it is set in Cornwall) resist Americanization. The grandmother is an energetic, unconventional character and great play is made of her eccentricity.

Daphne was quite convinced she had pulled off a fast and funny piece of satire and showed none of the usual diffidence about her work. She was also quite proud at the thought that it might cause some offence in America – 'perhaps one could call it controversial?' – and that it was 'disturbing . . . good, I like to disturb people'.[6] She thought it would be 'popular autumn reading' and was pleased Gollancz showed faith with a first print-run of 50,000 – 10,000 more than for her last novel, though still nowhere near the great days of automatic runs of 100,000 and more. It was therefore a shock to her when the reception of the novel was a chastening affair. Not only were the reviews unenthusiastic – or 'mixed', as Daphne described them – but there was an air of embarrassment about them on both sides of the Atlantic. Nobody wanted to savage Dame Daphne du Maurier, but there was a general consensus that, at best, this new novel was pedestrian and, at worst, it was plain silly. At Gollancz, there were those who had known this was true, but nobody dared say so – Daphne was still the star in their firmament and they were afraid she might go elsewhere.

It took her old friend Frank Price to speak out. He wrote her a storming letter saying he did not like *Rule Britannia* one little bit. The basic premise was ridiculous, the jokes feeble, the characterization hopeless and the dialogue limp. He wondered why Gollancz had not saved her from herself – 'or do your editors just take your manuscripts and say: "It's Daphne du Maurier" '. If he didn't esteem and love her so much 'I would just have lied to you and said it was marvellous'. Others did just that. Nowhere did she express any doubt as to the merits of *Rule Britannia*, the last and the poorest novel she ever wrote. It was making money – Pan had included it in their deal and boosted their offer accordingly by £25,000 – and anyway it had only been 'a bit of fun', not to be ranked with *The Scapegoat* or any of the others where she had been attempting to write something deeper.

She was buoyant in 1972 and very happy with Kilmarth. 'There is no other house within miles that would've been any good,' she wrote to Ken Spence, 'and I should have hated to go elsewhere in Cornwall.' She was even able to become friends with Veronica Rashleigh, who had just married Philip, and to visit Menabilly at her invitation without being overcome with emotion and bitterness. The advantages of Kilmarth, with its separate quarters for the grandchildren, were overwhelming, especially since the Browning boys now numbered three after the birth of Ned in 1970. She observed Kits as a father and simply could not credit how he had grown into this unlikely role – 'Kits, such a flippity as a small boy, literally lives for his brood – no spoiling, stern but devoted, and has just ticked off Freddie for a poor half-term report!!'' She loved to see him playing cricket with his sons and giving them the kind of fathering he had never been able to enjoy himself. He still reminded her of Gerald but less strongly, and she reminded herself that genes were not everything, that not all of a person's characteristics could be traced to an ancestor – they always had something individual too.

Tessa she had no worries about now. She was happily remarried and the only thing that disturbed her mother was wondering whether Tessa, whom she had always considered dominant, was now dominated by David. All wives thought to be 'bossed about' were suspect in her opinion, but this belief ran side by side with a fairly conventional and conservative attitude to marriage. Flavia became divorced from Alastair Tower in 1972, which exasperated Daphne even more than Tessa's divorce had done, though as ever she kept very quiet about her disapproval to Flavia herself. She thought Flavia should have weathered whatever storm there was, and confessed she did not understand the need for divorce in this case, just because 'Alastair may have been a bit silly'. Tommy, too, had been 'a bit silly in 1957 or whenever it was', but she had not divorced him. Flavia, she felt, would drift and she worried about her and about the effect on Rupert.

All three children had regular 'routes' phone calls – as did Tod, Oriel Malet, the Baker-Muntons, and a few others – so that she never felt cut off from them, even if she did not see as much of them as she would have wished. There were murmurs in a few letters that apart from the summer holidays 'they don't often come otherwise'. Fantasies that her grandchildren would come on their own, now some of them were old enough, did not materialize, and she found this hard to understand – *she* would have leapt, when she was the age Pooch, Paul and Rupert now were (seventeen, sixteen and thirteen), at the chance to spend time with a grandmother who lived in Cornwall in a house like Kilmarth. Yet when Pooch had asked if she and some friends could come and camp, the reply had been quite uncompromising – 'Sorry, it's out . . . the farmer is dead against it . . . and No to camping in the Kilmarth garden . . . it would mean everyone trooping in to nim or pal or shelter when it rained.'[8] She wanted them to come on her terms, which, although perfectly understandable and common in grandparents, meant there was always an element of formality in any arrangements to visit her and this made for a less harmonious and affectionate relationship than she would have liked. She had so loved staying in the tiny Golders Green house with her own maternal grandmother that she could not see why her own grandchildren did not want to stay with her. But at the same time she 'thanked heaven for sons, daughters and grandchildren. We may not see them often but we know they are there and when I talk to them on my telephone they are all so loving and sweet.'[9]

When her family did come, in strict rotation, she was appalled by their appetites. The days of cooks who did all the provisioning were long since over, and she had had to learn to do it herself. Esther cooked the midday meal but Daphne did the ordering from the shops, and when the family came her daughters or daughter-in-law cooked the evening meal. She was aghast at how 'a whole leg of lamb . . . was stripped bare at one sitting', when she had intended it to serve six for Monday as well as Sunday lunch with 'still something left for sandwiches'. She had a very small appetite herself and could never believe in the heartiness of others'. Often she remarked in letters that she had just dined handsomely off 'some scraps of meat meant for the dog' or even 'a piece of cheese with mould on it', but she understood, luckily, that her family could not be expected to do the same. When her estimation of how much they would eat fell woefully short of reality she was reduced to desperate stratagems like 'sending Esther out to get some frozen sausages from the Par beach café' to eke out inadequate supplies. But she was touchingly proud of herself for being able to assume what she thought of as these heavy domestic responsibilities after an upbringing in which nothing had been expected of her – the world had changed and she felt she was managing to change with it.

What had not changed was her attitude to friendships, in spite of the warning she had given to herself not to become too shut off from people. Many overtures were made to her, as she seemed in the seventies to become more visible (after appearing on television and agreeing to various magazine interviews), but she rejected most of them and still required those new people in whom she did feel interested to come to her. One of them was Colin Wilson, who lived not far away, and who had interested her since Victor Gollancz sent her *The Outsider* in 1956. She recorded being 'immensely impressed' and when she had seen 'the boy on TV I was struck by his good sense and deep feeling'. When Colin Wilson came to live not far from her in Cornwall, for once she could not resist the chance to meet someone who intrigued her, especially since he admired her stories in *The Breaking Point*, writing 'you really have a most weird imagination' and telling her that at her best she was 'equal to Edgar Allan Poe'. He came to visit and she liked him enough to let a sort of friendship develop, and was encouraged by his advice to 'give far more rein to your streak of weirdness'. But she would not visit him, any more than she would visit A. L. Rowse, and rejected invitations made by another neighbour, Raleigh Trevelyan, to come and meet other writers she admired, such as John le Carré (whose novels she loved).

She had her 'routes' and she could not bring herself to break them. Slowly, they were becoming not simply a way of keeping her life tidy and organized, but a way of life in themselves from which she could not possibly deviate, in case everything should crumble. 'I have felt', she wrote to Foy, at the end of 1972, ' . . . one of the reasons I have a dog is that I have something to get up for, to take him walking.' 'Routes' had to be adhered to or she 'might not want to get up'. Her writing 'routes' were the most precious of all and she clung to them with increasing determination and anxiety. After *Rule Britannia* she turned to another biography, but not of the Branwell Brontë sort – she was more interested now in trying a straightforward historical approach rather than 'delving deep into psychology'. This time, her subject was much further back in the past and far less well known. She had always had an interest in Francis Bacon and his brother Anthony, ever since reading Spedding's *Life and Letters* twenty years before, and now she wanted to do a book about them both. The fact that this would involve real research pleased her, as did the suspicion that no other writer (or reader) was much interested in the Bacons. It would be a challenge both to find out more about them and to make their lives as fascinating as she felt they were. She thought with relish of the 'boxes and boxes of documents' she would have to sift through.

She began work early in 1973 and by her birthday in May was 'having a lot of fun' reading transcripts of documents sent to her from Lambeth Palace library. This research 'never tires me', she wrote, deciding once again that she should have been a scholar, since she derived such immense satisfaction from 'finding things out and establishing the truth'. One truth she seemed on the edge of establishing was that Anthony had been on a homosexual charge in France from which Henry iv had extricated him: a researcher she employed did indeed turn up proof, which gave her a truly scholarly thrill. So did going to France 'on the Bacon trail' with

Kits and Olive.[10] They flew to Bordeaux, rented a car and combined visits to places where Anthony Bacon had lived with a tour of the Côte d'Azur. In Cannes they stayed in Carol Reed's flat – 'delightful, though the entrance was like one to a dingy back room for an abortion' – and when they visited St Paul de Vence, where she and Tommy had once stayed, she was 'peeping back into the past'. She even thought she saw a man like Tommy and felt '*Scapegoat*ish', as though she might not be herself or in her own time. This made her wonder if another novel might materialize, but it didn't.

She returned to face the winter and the writing of the book about the Bacons, which she had decided to call *Golden Lads*. This proved far tougher than she had imagined and was not helped by the sudden depression that came over her, not merely because of 'my usual autumn glooms' but because she heard that Christopher Puxley had died. At the end of August, his sister had written to tell Daphne that he was desperately ill with cancer – 'if you want to see him and feel like making the journey I could put you up, but you may prefer to remember him as he was.' It was all 'pretty ghastly', wrote his sister, and he would see no one except Daphne, if she chose to come. The prospect was so awful – 'his face is drawn and yellow and his eyes sunken' – and it was so many years since she had had any real contact with him, that Daphne chose to write to him instead. When he died, she could not pretend to be overwhelmed by grief, but she was saddened and wanted 'to hurry back into the past' more than ever.

Everything in the present simply seemed gloomy. Cousin Dora, who like Aunt Billie was looked after in her own new home for which Daphne paid, was reported to be incontinent and never stopped complaining, and Aunt Billie herself was fading fast. It was a struggle for Daphne to fix her mind on writing and she became confused by her own filing system, constantly being unable to find what she knew was there and yet needing to be precise. The weather was dreadful that winter and her dog, who was old, found it harder going than she did battling across the field next to Kilmarth, which was 'so thick with mud it is like the Somme'.

The death of Cousin Dora in January 1974 upset her – 'I hate it when old people are on their way' – and the news that there was to be an election annoyed her. She had lost faith in her pin-up boy, Harold Wilson, and was in favour of Edward Heath. She wrote to her old friend Karen Prescott (who had been in Egypt with her when her husband John served with Boy) that when she saw 'these left-wing types and miners and so on, I'm quite relieved Boy and John are not by our side, because they would have apoplexy with rage . . . I can hear Boy stamping and saying "Shoot the bloody lot".' The country was 'in a mess . . . what a world we live in'. All she approved of 'in this permissive age' was that women could wear trousers wherever and whenever they wished. She knew she should cheer herself up by going off on holiday to Greece or somewhere warm, but had not the energy, and none of her family were available to go with her. Olive was expecting her fourth child in June, which ruled out her and Kits, and the girls were abroad. 'I have no holiday plans,' she wrote, '. . . I don't feel drawn.'

By the autumn she still had not been away and the summer had not lifted her mood as it usually did. The birth of Grace in June 1974 was the only pleasant thing that happened. The weather was cold and wet and Daphne hardly swam at all. She had to make a colossal effort to have some sort of holiday before winter set in. This was a repeat performance of the year before, flying to Bordeaux with Kits and Olive but this time driving north to Brittany. It was not as successful as the previous holiday, even though she travelled some of the routes Anthony Bacon had taken and felt nearer to him. She could not shake off the melancholic mood which seemed to have come over her – quite unlike her usual fits of depression. She confided to her holiday notebook that she felt 'mouldy' and that she was 'missing my routes', however much she had wanted to escape from them. She felt homesick and was glad to fly home and do a tour with her researcher, Joan Saunders, of Twickenham, where the Bacons had lived. Even finishing *Golden Lads* did not improve her spirits.

Aunt Billie, aged ninety-three, died on 31 October and the sense of gloom deepened. Daphne's dog would either die soon or would have to be put down and she did not know if she had the energy to train another – though life without a dog would be insupportable.

Gollancz told her that they could not publish *Golden Lads* until September 1975, very nearly a year ahead, and she was sure, in spite of assurances to the contrary, that this must mean they did not really like it and 'only want romances from me'. Then a letter from her agent threw her into a panic: he wrote to say the Inland Revenue might, she reported, 'get onto the Doubleday lolly' which had been kept in the USA for her and out of which she had been paid an annual sum, low enough not to affect her tax position in England. She was sure 'they' would make her bring the whole lot over and 'to my dismay it will probably come under the hatchet of the wealth tax'. She had been warned long ago by her accountant that if ever 'my ill-gotten gains lying fallow in the US' were brought over as a lump sum they would be liable to 75 per cent tax. She had visions of bankruptcy, poorhouses and beggary, and it was no good her agent telling her that her income was 'steady at £100,000 a year', as it had been for the last three years.[11] She confided in her new son-in-law's father, Field Marshal Montgomery, that 'I have made a lot of money in my time, and not being a spendthrift by nature, made most of it over in family trusts. This has brought them [her children] security, which I intended, but has also taken the edge off initiative and the necessity of standing on their own feet.' Tax, she was sure, would rob her of what she had kept for herself and she must keep on writing books 'to refill the empty coffers'. Unfortunately, the only book she could think of was another on the Bacons, this time on Francis alone. It gave her a bitter sense of satisfaction that nobody could accuse her of doing this for money.

Chapter Twenty-four

Hubert Browning, Tommy's cousin, who lived in New Zealand and with whom Daphne had always kept up a sporadic correspondence, had no doubt what the basic trouble was when, at the end of 1975, Daphne wrote saying she was having a bad year. 'It is time you got out,' he told her. 'It becomes more and more of an effort as one gets older but it does a world of good.' Daphne, who was only sixty-eight that year, and still in excellent health, though a little short of breath when she climbed 'thrombosis hill' too quickly, knew he was right. She knew the melancholic feeling might disperse if she went away to the sun, but a dreadful inertia paralysed her. She was 'plodding through' her second Bacon book, weary of her 'routes' and yet unable to alter them, and she was not as cheered by some good reviews of *Golden Lads* as she would once have been. It was flattering to have 'real historians' like A. L. Rowse and Hugh Trevor-Roper praise her research but nobody had been as interested in the book as she had hoped. She knew it wasn't selling well and that her own refusal to be interviewed on television programmes like *The Book Programme* had not helped. 'I watch it,' she said, 'and take such a dislike to my fellow authors preening their feathers and banging on about themselves.' She didn't want to 'bang on' but she did want Gollancz and Doubleday to try harder than she thought they were doing; Frank Price fanned the flames.

He wrote praising *Golden Lads* – 'excellent . . . the best thing you've written since *Gerald*' – but telling her that in his biased opinion Doubleday had done nothing to promote it – 'only one ad in the *New York Times* and a very small thing in the *New Yorker*'. He knew that 'you will say nothing but perhaps Kits could go to Curtis Brown . . . and raise double-hell'. He encouraged her to believe that neither her agent nor her publishers were trying as hard as they had once done. This was exactly what she suspected, but she could not bring herself to have any kind of confrontation beyond the usual letters to Gollancz saying *Golden Lads* appeared to be unobtainable in the Fowey branch of W. H. Smith. Her common sense told her that publishers want to sell as many copies of their books as possible, but she could not shake off the suspicion that she was stuck with her image as the writer of so-called romantic novels and neither publisher nor public would let her change. It drove her mad when 'proof after proof' of romantic novels arrived with pleas for her endorsement, and everyone remained obsessed with *Rebecca* and *Frenchman's Creek*, novels she had written over thirty years ago. She was tired of it all, and especially of *Rebecca*. Never a month went by without someone informing her they were writing a sequel to *Rebecca* or asking her detailed questions about it which she could not answer.[1] The most popular question was why the heroine had no name, which even Agatha Christie (with whom she enjoyed a short correspondence, though always refusing to meet her) wished to know. She seemed to spend more and more time on this kind of correspondence and it had a not unexpected effect on her. Thinking back to the writing of *Rebecca* made her dwell on the story of her own life, and an idea she had toyed with for more than a decade began to take hold of her. In 1977 she would be seventy and, as several people had pointed out, this would surely be the right time for an autobiography. Once her second Bacon book, *The Winding Stair*, was at the printer's she had 'nothing much to hand' and so she decided to explore the possibility of a memoir.

The long room in Kilmarth was bitterly cold that winter of 1975–76, in spite of the fire and the electric storage heater, but she sat down with 'wool socks over fur-lined boots' and began looking through her childhood diaries 'with a view to sorting out a book of memories for my 70th birthday'. It might 'be the yawn of all time', but she couldn't think of anything else to write and her publishers were ecstatic at the thought. She sat huddled over the fire with three sweaters on, reading what she had written all those years ago, and felt worse rather than better. Half of it she thought 'utterly wain' (embarrassing) and the other half 'a big tell-him' (boring). She couldn't think how she was going to make it into anything and she was distracted with worry over Tessa, who was in San Salvador, 'right next to that earthquake country', and, worse still, over Kits, who was in Libya making a film, and might be 'kidnapped by that dreadful man Gaddafi'. She decided all she could write would be a memoir up to the year of her marriage and that she would only be able to do it if she concentrated on her development as a writer – that would give it the justification she felt was needed. Her views on autobiography were clear – 'few people really want to be frank about themselves or their ex-lovers and this is where one is bound to have a lot of glossing over . . . the whole business is fraught with difficulties.'[2] Even apart from these difficulties, 'frankly, I don't consider my life of any interest. I don't mean it was boring to *me*, but it would bore other people. Because it was largely uneventful . . .'

Just as she was beginning to write, in the spring of 1976, and feeling what she described as 'strange . . . with the stirring up of all those memories', a worry which had been at the back of her mind for the last two years suddenly surfaced and caused her intense anxiety. This was the proposed filming of *A Bridge Too Far*, the book written by Cornelius Ryan about the Battle of Arnhem. In 1967, only two years after Tommy's death, a researcher employed by Ryan had written to her asking for her help. He wanted to interview her 'extensively' about General Browning's part in Arnhem and to go through all his papers. In order to do this, he announced, he would come to Cornwall and spend as long as necessary with her, which naturally alarmed Daphne, who wrote back immediately saying the researcher would be wasting his time because she had no information or papers. But the researcher was dogged. Any little thing would help, he replied, 'for example, if anything unusual happened to your family [that day of the Arnhem battle] . . . a birth, a death, a letter, or even the fact that the local butcher managed to put aside an extra chop for you during that weekend'. The absurdity of this request made Daphne laugh out loud at first, but later she became quite angry at his presumption and replied that she had nothing more to say.

When the book came out in 1974, she was sent a copy. She read it, with some trepidation, and was relieved to find nothing offensive about Tommy in it. She thought he was treated fairly, and rather liked the description of him as 'lithe, immaculately turned out . . . [with] the appearance of a restless hawk'. Her main concerns, that Tommy's reputation should not be damaged, and his memory not tarnished, were satisfied. But when she heard that Richard Attenborough was going to film the book she was instantly suspicious. She knew about films. Her own experience had taught her that all kinds of liberties could be taken in the name of dramatic necessity or to suit actors. She wrote to Attenborough asking to see the script when it was ready. He replied that she need have no worries, because he wanted to pay proper respect to everyone concerned. Then it was announced that Dirk Bogarde was to play Tommy and she was convinced he would depict her husband as effete and mincing. Attenborough defended Bogarde, pointing out that he had been an intelligence officer in the army and was able to portray General Browning authentically. In mid-March he sent her a shooting script together with a note saying he would be only too happy to discuss it with her.

Daphne studied this script with the greatest care and realized at once that Tommy was cast as a minor character and that he came out of it with no credit at all. She was furious and extremely upset. Her anger made her determined to challenge Attenborough strongly: she wrote to him saying her husband had been made the fall-guy of the whole Arnhem disaster. In the years since Tommy's death, she had had plenty of time to reflect on how much of himself he had given in the war. The memory of his total dedication, to the point of exhaustion, and of what that had done to their marriage, made her outraged by his role in this film. Confrontation was something she loathed, but she felt she had a duty to protect his honour. The notes she sent Attenborough were detailed. She pointed out that, in the original briefing, Tommy had said to Montgomery, 'We might be going a bridge too far, sir,' and yet there was no mention in the script of this warning, which had, of course, proved to be justified. Why had it been omitted? It was, she argued, crucial, because it established that Tommy had always had his doubts about the operation and that he had been overruled. This fact was clear in the book, but now it had disappeared. Even worse was a scene in the script in which Tommy was seen to dismiss clear photographic evidence that the Germans still had tanks in the Arnhem area. She was sure he would not have done this, and she demanded proof. More insidious was the constant harping in the script on her husband's appearance – it made him sound like a dandy who shrank from dirty work. It was true, she said, that he had always been superbly turned out, but *not* true that this indicated he was some kind of playboy. There were lines in the script such as 'Boy liked to live well'. What, she asked, was this meant to mean? 'Boy couldn't have cared less how he lived. Nor is there any attempt to show his descent in a glider . . . the flak all around and Boy disregarding it. The suggestion is . . . he never heard a shot fired and lived in comfort in his caravan.'

Faced with this formidable onslaught, Attenborough was sensibly silent for a while and then wrote back to say he believed he had now dealt with her objections. He had spoken to Dirk Bogarde, who agreed that Boy's concern for his men must be shown and due attention paid to all her other points. But, as Daphne quickly discovered, there was still to be no scene with her husband saying they might be going 'a bridge too far'. Attenborough's defence was that the words had been spoken to Montgomery and a decision had been taken 'right at the beginning not to show any of the puppet masters – Roosevelt, Churchill or Montgomery'. He promised, though, to try to fit the line in at the end (which he did – Bogarde as Browning murmurs, 'I always thought we went a bridge too far'). This did not mollify Daphne in the least, but there was little else she could do. While she was writing her own autobiography she brooded on what the film would be like and the resentment grew. It was extraordinary that none of this anguish affected her writing – the whole tone of her memoir was determinedly light and the result a slim volume highly artificial in tone.

As with so many autobiographies, what was most significant was what was left out. The deep unhappiness of her adolescent years, so strongly evident in her letters to Tod, is hardly touched on and the conflict with her father is never allowed to appear as disturbing as it had been. The nearest she comes to describing the intensity of her emotion towards Gerald is to confess 'the agony of fear . . . never experienced before or since' when he wanted to go on the Cannon Hall roof in an air-raid. About her relationship with her mother she manages to be more frank, able to confess that it was difficult and that this had something to do with her father's adoration of her, his favourite daughter. She is also frank about Cousin Geoffrey and his sexual impact, though she is reticent about Carol Reed (Carol himself had just died, but Pempie Reed, his second wife, was still alive, and Daphne was worried about hurting her). Rather unwisely, she once more tried to develop her theories about family relationships and incest – she explains herself badly and gives the impression, in jokes about the du Mauriers being like the Borgias, that there was something sinister going on in the family. Her writing career she tracks with accuracy, but fails to show the tremendous effort that went into it, or to identify the themes in her early work of which she was by then well aware. Her love for Cornwall comes across powerfully and the memoir ends on a suitably happy note with her romantic wedding.

The effect of writing the memoir, entitled *Growing Pains*, was catastrophic. Almost as soon as it was finished, Daphne knew it had been a mistake and bitterly regretted allowing herself to be drawn back into the past. The book was a performance and successfully concealed the turmoil behind it. She had a terrible sense that everything that mattered was gone, and she had seriously depressed herself with memories of what she now thought of as her golden years. All the gaiety she remembered contrasted horribly with the dreariness of her present life, and she yearned to be back in the past she had evoked, with everything still before her. She had always thought she did not mind ageing, so long as her health remained good, but suddenly she did mind. Reviewing her own early life, she could not understand why, when she had been so fortunate and successful, she now felt so low and miserable. And this time a holiday did not help.

She went, in September, with Kits and Olive to Scotland in search of another set of ancestors. The three of them flew to Inverness, then hired a car and drove first to Culloden and then across to Ullapool. Kits was as entertaining as ever, endlessly

imitating all the different Scottish accents, the scenery was magnificent, the weather good, but she went on feeling 'out of sorts'
and was not her usual good company. All the old familiar games
of guessing the life histories of strangers palled, the food was never
to her liking, and she found being driven tiring.

Back in Cornwall, at the end of a scorching hot summer, she
felt the holiday had done her no good. Wandering on Par beach
she found herself hating 'all the honks' and was reminded of a
quote of Francis Bacon's as she tried not to show her disgust –
'Every man of superior intelligence when in contact with inferiors
wears a mask.' She knew she had worn a mask most of her life
and now found it slipping. She had always been pleasant and even-
tempered while inside she had often felt vicious and full of rage,
and she had never allowed her real feelings to emerge except in
her work. But now she could hardly be bothered to contain her
resentment of one sort and another. She was fed up with the
world and felt it was 'returning to tribal days', all the blessings of
civilization threatened. 'I am so depressed . . . I think the state of
the world and this country in particular is appalling. It just can't
be my advancing years . . .' Not only politics but the state of the
arts enraged her – 'that frightful Dane who wants to make a film
about the sex-life of Christ – someone should put a bomb under
him . . . Vanessa Redgrave will volunteer to play Mary
Magdalene.' Young people, of whom she had always been in
favour, now, in the mass, were condemned – 'so many of the
young today simply want to break people's windows and knock
down old women': they should all be in the army, which was why
'cuts in the armed forces fill me with gloom'.

Her discontent and distress were very evident to her family and
friends and they all prayed, as she did herself, that an idea for a
book would rescue her. She talked freely of how she longed 'to
get cracking on something else, but my imagination is not what
it was and I can't think of another Francis Bacon to inspire me'.
She went into the winter with nothing whatsoever to write and
no work to do except correcting proofs of *Growing Pains*, which
depressed her even more. Her sister Angela's memoir had just
appeared – *It's Only the Sister* – and she knew it was infinitely
better than her own – funnier, more honest and much more enter-

taining. For the first time she not only felt her age but did not feel well. She was found to have gallstones. The doctor put her on a low-fat diet and, though this made her feel better, she lost a stone in weight which made her feel cold. Then Ellen Doubleday, to whom she had sent a copy of her memoir (which Ellen thought 'divine'), wrote to break the news that she had an inoperable tumour in her throat and was to have cobalt treatment. She felt even more depressed and sad and, though she longed to help Ellen, too low herself to think of going to see her. She hated how 'scraggy and lined' she looked and dreaded the second television interview she had agreed to, for her seventieth birthday and the publication of her autobiography. Her reason for agreeing was the same as before: Kits was to direct, 'a crumb for him'. Cliff Michelmore would do the interviewing, and the filming would be spread over five days so that it would not become too exhausting.

The experience lifted her temporarily out of her deep depression and proved a welcome diversion. Seeing Kits in charge gave her tremendous pleasure and she enjoyed being part of a team again. She was at her most attractive in this filmed interview – apparently quite relaxed, witty, laughing often with her throaty, seductive laugh, and engaging with Cliff Michelmore in a way she had not done with Wilfred De'Ath. The mask was firmly in place and no viewer could possibly guess what lay behind it. The response this time was one she needed. She was never taken in by flattery, but it was heartening to receive so much praise and she relished it. Some of the letters were from unusual sources and gave her a new interest: a man in Parkhurst prison wrote to her and the two of them began a long and satisfying correspondence covering a huge variety of topics. Daphne told him it was a case of 'one prisoner writing to another' but, of course, her prison was of her own making. She had no desire to go on holiday and stayed put at Kilmarth.

Once the excitement of her seventieth birthday and the TV film were over, she was left vulnerable to the depression she had been trying to shake off, and the release of *A Bridge Too Far* could not have come at a worse time. Reports of how Tommy was portrayed confirmed her worst fears and made her ill with fury. She refused to see the film but, relying on the judgement of people she trusted, tried frantically to have it condemned as unjust.

For weeks she was obsessed with this mission and would accept no reassurances either that the film was not as bad as she had been led to believe or that it did not matter. Jim Orr[3] wrote from Buckingham Palace, in reply to her request for support, that he was disgusted Boy had been so cruelly treated, but that she was foolish to let it upset her – 'Cheer up, my dear, you know it is not true . . . Boy would have laughed it off as tripe. You must do the same.' She could not, nor did she think she ought to. She wrote to Lord Mountbatten asking him to boycott the première, but he wrote back saying he could not do so, because it was for a charity he supported. When he had seen the film, he wrote again saying, 'Candidly . . . I could find nothing really detrimental to Boy.' He did not think Bogarde was 'ideal', but 'nobody could think Boy's magnificent reputation tarnished'. The plain truth, he told her, was that, however she felt, Arnhem *was* thought to have been a disaster and blame must accrue to those in charge, of whom Boy was one. Daphne regarded Mountbatten's attitude as a betrayal and none of the letters condemning the depiction of Tommy quite made up for it. Many of these were from men who had served with him and told of their own distress at the film version of the Arnhem events: these touched her, and she could not stop brooding over 'that bloody film'. It entirely dominated her thoughts and, coupled with the misery she was feeling because she had nothing to write, tipped her over into a state of near breakdown, akin to her emotional state after the crisis of 1957. She found she could not even 'write English any more', so distracted were her thoughts, and said that all she was fit for was 'playing football with my two West Highland pups', Mac and Ken.

Even more frightening was the fact that she felt her memory was going. She was always 'looking for things that are not there' and commented, 'nowadays my memory is such that I can only remember the distant past'. This was not as serious as it sounded – she was merely slightly forgetful about names and dates – but was all part of her discontent with the present and preference for the past. Nothing would induce her to try to focus on what she could do to make the present and the immediate future more attractive – all suggestions for those holidays in the sun she had so loved, and from which she had so often drawn inspiration, were rejected. Kits and Olive urged her to go to Portugal with them, but she refused, and wrote to a friend, 'secretly it would bore me to sit in the sun by a pool'. She stayed at Kilmarth, clinging to her 'routes', and steadily losing weight because she no longer had any appetite. By July, she was down to seven stone and her doctor ordered X-rays – 'and finally an awful thing being plunged up the arse'. She went to Plymouth hospital for this and awaited the results nervously. These showed nothing physically wrong, 'it is all due to stress . . . worrying over that bloody Bridge and being rung up endlessly . . . and having nothing to write'.

This was the crux of the whole problem: it was now five years since she had written any fiction, two years since she had written any non-fiction (she did not count her autobiography) and she had never in her life gone so long without an idea. Everyone who knew her was aware of her great fear that she had dried up creatively – she talked about it freely, constantly asking what could she do. But it drove her mad when well-meaning people suggested stories to her which she might like to write – it was simply no good giving her the bones of a story and telling her to write it. Writing, as she had constantly pointed out, came from sources deep within her and these were empty. Her misery grew as she trailed aimlessly round Kilmarth with her dogs. She did not believe that her writing life had come to a *natural* end, nor would she accept the situation. On the contrary, the desire to write was as strong as ever, the need as urgent. Without writing, one whole side of herself was denied expression and she suffered terrible frustration. Nothing pleased her – even the visits of the young Browning boys were not as successful. Freddie, once 'bliss', was twelve and Robbie ten – they were changing into that species, the teenager, for whom she had little love, and she became as critical of them as she once had been of Tessa's children. Only Ned, at seven, and Grace, a delightful three-year-old, were still in the world of Peter Pan and likely to give her any pleasure.

That winter was the worst she had ever spent. Frank Price died in December and then, in the April of the following year, 1978,

Ellen died, just as Daphne had convinced herself that her dearest friend was recovering.[4] Her letters became increasingly full of rage about every topic she mentioned and especially the state of the country – 'Oh! if only the army would take over and have a military dictatorship.' Esther, living in the cottage next door and seeing her every day, was more aware than anyone that 'Lady B', as she always called her, was changing. She seemed lost, even when following her 'routes' so rigidly. Everything ticked over on the surface – the occasional visitor, such as the BBC radio producer John Knight, who came to do a piece on her grandfather George du Maurier's novel *Trilby*, could still find her charming and pleasant – but Esther knew it was all a façade. Without any writing to do, Lady B's 'No. 2' was making itself felt in other small ways. Once she would not have thought of interfering in the running of the house, in which she had no interest, but now she wandered into the kitchen and hung about looking critical. There were trivial complaints and a less harmonious atmosphere. Esther realized that without writing Lady B had no purpose in life and that it was bad for her to be alone so much, but she could not be persuaded to see more people. She was no frail, elderly lady who could easily be organized and manipulated – the control of her own life was vitally important to her and she would never surrender it unless some crisis took the decision out of her hands.

But the crisis, when it came, turned out to be of her own making. For four years, from mid-1977 to mid-1981, she battled with depression and waited with increasing desperation for the urge to write to return – or rather, the inspiration to feed this urge. Her daughter Flavia thinks that she was taking the pill Halcion[5] at this time, but it seemed only to increase her anxiety and sense of disintegration, making her more panic-stricken than ever about her inability to write. The publication of *The Rendezvous and Other Stories* in 1980 was a sign not that her imagination was once more fertile but that it was sterile: only three of the fifteen stories were 'new', and these were not new in the true sense. All three – 'No Motive', 'Split-Second', and 'The Rendezvous' – had been written many years before and roundly condemned by Victor Gollancz. At the time, Daphne had accepted his judgement, but now Victor was dead no one at Gollancz, not even Sheila, had the same influence. Daphne wanted these stories printed in a collection, together with some from her early work, to appear in the same volume as 'a writer's notebook kind of book', which would be about the genesis of *Rebecca*, and some of the articles she had written over the years. Jon Evans at Gollancz expressed reservations in an internal memo about the whole venture – 'surprised the author now wants to unveil so much apprentice work, some of which is very banal . . . the biographical pieces work well but the item on Romantic Love is trivial . . . the tone's wrong . . . seems something basically wrong about the whole thing.' There was indeed, but Gollancz bit on the bullet and published. Not, however, in one volume: *The Rendezvous and Other Stories* came out in 1980, *The Rebecca Notebook and Other Memories* a year later. In a preface to the 'new' short stories, Daphne said she had included earlier ones to show something of her development as a writer.[6] In fact, since none of her best stories from her strongest collections appeared in this volume, all it showed was an apparent *lack* of development. But she was pleased and felt in circulation again.

The pleasure was as short-lived as her delight had been that one of her grandchildren was married in the summer of 1978 and another generation would continue the du Maurier/Browning lineage of which she was the proud matriarch. Tessa's daughter, Marie-Thérèse (Pooch), married Nigel Defty. Daphne had become fond of Pooch, after being unsympathetic to her earlier, and felt her marriage was going to be a great success. She went to the wedding, in London, a great gathering of the clan. Even Tod was included, very old and now unable to make the journey to Cornwall, but mentally and verbally as vigorous as ever. Daphne had also managed a trip to see Oriel Malet in Normandy, and in the spring of 1980 went with her local friends Mary and Philip Varcoe[7] to the Scilly Isles. This was an unusual step for her – she had only ever been on holidays with her family, apart from those with Clara Vyvyan so long ago – but she liked both Varcoes very much and they urged her to come. She seemed to enjoy herself, but complained of exhaustion on her return. She had laryngitis and was taking 'anti-biotics and some pink medicine . . . on top of the various pills he gives me for nerves'.[8] She was grateful

Maureen Baker-Munton was there on one of her regular visits 'and will stay for a while . . . I don't feel ill or anything, just heavy and sleepy and keep spitting up green stuff'. Her letters were full of sentences like 'I have a wretched feeling my writing days are over' and 'I fear my imagination cell is dead'.

She was still walking regularly up and down 'thrombosis hill', but in spite of the exercise could not sleep even with sleeping pills. She would wake up at three in the morning and lie there until it was light, feeling worn out before the day began. A consultant came from Truro 'and pummelled me about', but his opinion was the same as her doctor's: there was nothing wrong with her body. Her condition was caused by 'nervous anxiety' and she was told to stay on the prescribed pills. She wrote about these to Bunny Austin – 'I think one of the reasons I am so down when I awake is due to the Mogadon tablets my doctor tells me to take . . . I sleep OK but awake, as I have said, very early and have this very depressed feeling . . . I have to take a tiny tablet called Largactil and a different tablet called Prothiaden, or Profiaden, I can't read the spelling . . . then about 11.30 at night before the Mogadon I have to take two more Profiadens, one big 75 mg and the smaller 25 mg.' These were 'to help me out of this neurosis . . . there is no reason for my anxiety-depression except that I can't write books any more, or stories, which . . . has been my life'.⁹

Throughout the latter part of 1980 and the first half of 1981 she often reported that she was 'lying in bed with my mind going round and round' and had 'bad nerve spells . . . which get me het up and worried for no reason'. One of these spells was over her car. She loved her little automatic red DAF – 'I love it almost as much as the two dogs' – and when the garage said it was not going to pass its MOT she was distraught. No other make would do – it would be 'torture' to have to have any other car. Kits scoured Cornwall but no other red automatic DAF could be found, and she had to have a Ford, which was 'insupportable'. A psychiatrist came to see her, a woman, but although Daphne rated her 'very good' she did not feel greatly helped. Instead, she wondered why she was alive at all. In July 1981 she fell on the stairs and was sent to Fowey hospital where she stayed three weeks, resting. On 11 August, Esther took in her breakfast as usual then went to Par to do some shopping. She returned an hour or so later to find Lady B standing at the top of the stairs and heard her say she had taken some tablets and would she send for the doctor. The doctor came and, though Daphne had only taken what amounted to a small overdose, had her admitted once more to Fowey hospital. It was a calculated cry for help.

Chapter Twenty-five

Many years before, in 1960, Daphne had written to her cousin Nico Davies that she understood why his brother Peter had committed suicide, 'being myself, constantly and for no earthly reason, a potential suicide'. Her opinion was that suicide arose not from despair but from anger. But just before her own apparent suicide bid, she had come out strongly against the taking of one's own life. Writing to Bunny Austin, about a friend of his who was suicidal, she wrote: 'I want you to tell your friend who is suffering from depression *never* to try and take his or her life, because I am quite certain that *that* would not take him or her into a happy land, but would keep them bound to haunt their former self, and hover like a ghost around their life on earth, even when the body has been burnt or buried.' The idea that this body might be reincarnated in another guise she thought foolish – 'it would mean God was stingy in creating souls ... like a pupil retaking O-levels.' These views would seem to indicate that taking a few extra sleeping pills and then telling Esther to call the doctor was very far from being a real suicide bid.

Whatever it was, Daphne's action had to be taken seriously and something had to be done. Kits came down the following day and took his mother from Fowey hospital to the Duchy, a private hospital in Truro. He stayed two weeks, until his mother was well enough to come home, and then Maureen Baker-Munton came, followed by Oriel Malet, until Flavia took over. But after Flavia left, and Kits and Olive had been there again, there was another panic attack and in November Daphne was once more back in the Duchy hospital. Her feelings she put into a poem:

They said it was not my body but my brain,
Had ceased to function in its normal way,
So back to hospital I went again, Doctors
Would find out what had gone astray.

A week of tests. Results? I am not told, but
Appetite has gone, has ceased to be. The sight
Of food appals me, hot or cold, the character sitting here
No longer me. I walk around the block, then
Come inside, no reason to exist or to reside upon
This planet here, myself has fled to unknown stars
Far lower than this earth.

Dear God, did you intend this from my birth?

By now the trouble was also physical – she had a chest infection
and, while in hospital, had a coronary. All three children came
down, and so did Maureen, to whom Daphne had written a
pathetic little note asking her to come. There was no doubt that
Daphne was very ill – she was too exhausted to talk, or be talked
to, and lay there, white and fragile-looking. Her weight was only
6st 5lbs, and she looked as though she lacked the strength to fight,
as well as the will. There were anxious discussions among the
family about what should be done if and when she recovered.
Clearly, she could not be allowed to go on living alone. Even with
Esther near at hand it was no longer safe. But nobody wasted any
time suggesting she should be moved from Kilmarth – everyone
knew that was out of the question. It became a matter of trying
to work out how she could be kept in her home yet be properly
looked after: the obvious solution was to engage some kind of
nursing care to back up the help Esther already gave. When
Daphne had regained some strength and was ready to return home
just before Christmas, this new regime was ready to be put into
operation. Nurses had been hired through a local agency and they
would live in, full time, for the foreseeable future, supervised by
Esther.

The first nurse employed, the head of the agency herself, visited
Daphne in hospital and then went home with her. It was naturally

a very difficult home-coming, even though softened by the arrival of Flavia and her new husband, General Sir Peter Leng, for Christmas. Daphne had never wanted anyone to live with her – she dreaded the idea – but now she had no option. If she wanted to stay at Kilmarth she had to be looked after properly and that meant a nurse-companion. But it irritated her that she was obliged to submit to this new arrangement, especially since she considered there was nothing really wrong with her, she was 'just a bit down' and now thought she probably always would be. Bunny Austin annoyed her by trotting out the old MRA philosophy by which she had once been so attracted and she gave him short shrift – 'don't tell me to listen to God . . . no message comes from God, though I say, dear God help me.' Nor did she want to go to the MRA nursing home – 'I don't want to go anywhere, so please stop urging me . . . I am not so bad I need healing.' What she did need was a return to writing, but she was in the process of facing up to the fact, finally, that she would never write again. The void had to be filled, and the only way to fill it was to impose even stricter 'routes' upon herself and on her nurses.

These nurses worked shifts, with two of them usually alternating over a ten-day period. Any hope of one nurse staying full-time was found to be impractical – the 'routes' were too severe: not many women could face the door of Kilmarth being shut for the night at four-thirty in the afternoon. Then there was their patient's temperament: from being always so pleasant in manner, Daphne was now inclined to be irritable and to betray all the understand-able strain of being a very private person suddenly robbed of her privacy. She was perfectly aware these nurses were costing her a great deal of money – around £500 a week – and because this appalled her she treated most of them as servants out of whom she was determined to get her money's worth. She had small but effective ways of doing this if she took a dislike to a nurse. She would wait until they were settled by the fire and then ask for some item to be brought to her which involved a trip to another room; when it had been brought, she would wait until the nurse was comfortable again before making a similar request – this would go on all evening. But there were nurses with whom she developed a real relationship and in them she inspired the same affection and admiration she had roused so often in her life. Having them as companions did not seem such an intolerable imposition. They had to follow her 'routes' – each day was set in a rigid pattern from which no one could deviate – but once they had got used to these and accepted them, half the battle was won. Any upset in 'routes' caused great distress – even a meal five minutes late was a cause for criticism. Monday was the day for a walk in the Menabilly grounds, Tuesday the day for visiting the Varcoes' house, and so on.

Yet Daphne was certainly not senile or in any way not in control of her own life, and the most successful nurses were those who appreciated this. Margaret Robertson, who stayed almost a year (and returned later on two more occasions), quickly learned that her patient must be allowed to take the lead and that however frail she looked she had a will of iron. Margaret was from Yorkshire and this gave her two topics of conversation which sparked Daphne into animation: one was Whitby, which Margaret knew well and which was where George du Maurier used to take his family on holiday, and the other the Brontës, all of whose books she had read and liked to discuss. Margaret, who had some psychiatric nursing training, discovered that Daphne much preferred talking about her grandfather's novels to her own and, in fact, often denied having written some of her own. She found this strange, but came to the conclusion that this denial was a form of self- inflicted punishment. Daphne acted towards her writing past as though it were a person who had died – she was bereaved and the grief of the loss was too terrible to talk about. Talking about *Wuthering Heights* or *Trilby*, on the other hand, she always enjoyed, and through these conversations Margaret established a rapport which led her to discover other sources of amusement for her patient. One was dancing, which she managed to slip in as a new 'routes'. She would play records Daphne had mentioned loving – 'A Nightingale Sang in Berkeley Square', for example – and encourage her to dance. Round and round Daphne would waltz, by herself, sometimes singing too, and this was such excellent exercise as well as therapy that Margaret would try to extend it – but no, dancing was to be half an hour and not a minute longer: that was 'routes'.

If establishing some rapport with Daphne proved possible for Margaret, getting her to eat did not. It was a constant struggle for all the nurses. They had to resort to all kinds of tricks and sometimes even these failed to induce her to let anything pass her lips. Some of the nurses tried straightforward bribery: if Daphne would eat, then she could have her evening glass of whisky. If she would not, then it was hinted that it might be denied her (though it never, in fact, was). Naturally, with a woman as strong-willed as Daphne, this led to unpleasant clashes and resulted in predictable tensions. But, fortunately, the majority of the nurses found more subtle ways of tempting their patient to eat enough to put some weight on her, and one nurse in particular solved the problem. This was Terry Jones, who took over soon after Margaret Robertson left. She was with Daphne for four years and left for good only when she emigrated to Canada. Terry was Cornish and to Daphne's delight was studying for her Bardic examination while she was with her. She would enlist Daphne's help, constantly asking her what the Cornish for certain words was and teaching her others, so that there was some real mental stimulus. Of even more value was Terry's attempt to treat her patient's depression differently. She urged her instead of depending on pills to do breathing exercises – down the two of them would go to the beach and stand facing the sea taking deep breaths. This was good for the 'rattle' Terry could hear in Daphne's chest, a legacy of attacks of emphysema, which she had suffered from until she stopped smoking,[1] five years before.

Gradually, during Terry's regime, Daphne's physical health improved. She put on weight again until she was 8 stone and became more settled. Except for the constant changing of relief nurses, 'routes' were adhered to in a satisfactory way and she appeared to accept that she would never again live on her own. Her attachment to the nurses, successful in winning her over, was strong – both Margaret and Terry were invited to make their permanent home with her and she was extremely upset when each of them left, since they themselves had become 'routes'. The family and her close friends came and went, conscious that without Esther next door the system would not be workable. Esther provided them with a kind of insurance policy: any nurse who might try to exploit the situation would soon be found out and dealt with by Esther – so much so that it was made clear to all of them by the agency that it was as important to get on with Esther as with Lady Browning. In all, during the next eight years, there were eight nurses, including one male nurse, who alternated two-week shifts backed up by extra companion helps, who did not necessarily have any training. However bleak the set-up may have looked from the outside, there was no doubt that Daphne was very well cared for and that her wish to remain in her own home and be as independent as possible was being honoured, even if at her own expense.

It was obvious that at a more or less constant £500 a week for nursing help, as well as the cost of running Kilmarth, the money Daphne had saved from her royalties was not going to last forever. By 1986, when there had been no new book for five years, the situation she herself had envisaged, in which she would have spent all her capital and be dependent on the royalties from old books which were dwindling, was rapidly approaching. Vast sums had been claimed by the taxman, generous help given to all her children and some others of her family and friends, more still spent on both Menabilly and Kilmarth, and though she could never be called poor, it was suddenly alarming for those who supervised her financial affairs to realize that an outlay of £25,000 a year on nurses plus another £10,000 at least on general expenses plus paying for grandchildren's school fees – at her own insistence – amounted to a tremendous drain on her resources. The income from America was steady but could not be altered. Daphne's interest in business affairs was still avid, but during her stay in hospital in 1981 she had given Maureen's husband, Monty Baker-Munton, in whom she had implicit trust, power of attorney.[2] With the family's approval, he approached Gollancz with the suggestion that some collection of Daphne's stories should be published to mark her eightieth birthday, and so her last book, *Classics from the Macabre*, was published in July 1987 and earned her an advance of £7,500. She refused to let anyone write an introduction – and was positively hostile to some of the names Gollancz suggested might write one, such as Iris Murdoch.

In spite of the comfort of 'routes' and of her two dogs, and in spite of all the small pleasures she enjoyed – music, walking, television – there was now an undeniable pathos about Daphne's life. She retreated more and more into herself, and there was the unmistakable impression of a strong person trying to cope with the loss of what had been her real life: her writing. She was marking time and knew it. When her children were with her, particularly Kits of course, she made great efforts to be the old Bing, but with others she did not always bother. Some old, local friends were cut out of her life – she shrank from them and even acted as though she were afraid of them.[3] Her determination not to cling to her children, which she had expressed from the age of fifty onwards in the strongest terms, meant that she turned more and more to the Baker-Muntons. She had known Maureen forty years and Monty nearly as long, and they were a link with Tommy – she thought of them both as capable and devoted to her and she had always needed such unquestioning devotion. It was only the memory of this kind of devotion that persuaded her to make one of her very rare outings from Kilmarth to visit Tod, who had come to end her days in the Trelawney Nursing Home at St Miniver. The choice of this Cornish rather than London nursing home was made simply because it would be near to Daphne and she might be able to see her, but Daphne was extremely reluctant to visit. Esther persuaded her, pointing out how much poor Tod longed to see her, though it was touch and go right up to the last moment whether she would actually go through with the visit. Esther drove her to the home, with Daphne resentful and constantly on the edge of demanding to turn round and go back. When they arrived, Esther was told to leave her with the ninety-five-year-old Tod for precisely twenty minutes and then collect her. Tod, of course, was enraptured at the sight of her visitor, who promptly lay down on the bed and settled into a waiting position while Tod gazed down at her adoringly. At the end of the twenty minutes Esther came for her and, once in the car, Daphne declared she was never going again: the strain had been unbearable and she could not stand a repetition. Soon afterwards, when her sister Angela was in hospital with peritonitis, there was no question of Daphne visiting her, although she was greatly concerned.

Since Daphne would now go nowhere except to visit Veronica Rashleigh, Mary Varcoe, Angela and two other near neighbours, everyone in the small circle around her tried hard to bring people to her. They were all aware how much she needed the monotony to be broken up and how rewarding the result could be. Esther sometimes even brought in one or two fans who turned up to see her, if she thought they would amuse her for a while; and she noted what a good effect these brief encounters could have, even if afterwards Daphne would claim to be exhausted. She also tried to keep Daphne's interest in her fan mail alive, though she was no longer up to writing letters herself. Esther had, in fact, become as much a secretary as a housekeeper, and they would have afternoon sessions together, going through the letters, with Esther trying to get Daphne to write a few words of her own, though she could no longer use a typewriter and her handwriting was shaky. Yet the devotion of her fans touched her and she could still laugh at the more absurd questions: why, for instance, did Frank Crawley (in *Rebecca*) have an Adam's apple and was it heavily significant, in view of this, that the main crop at Manderley was apples? . . . Young fans pleased her most, especially if they were men. A German student, Thomas David, who began writing to her in 1985, saying that together with Edgar Wallace she was one of the best, became a regular correspondent, even though Esther did all the writing. It was only to people from the far past that Daphne would now put pen to paper herself – for Dorothy Sheppard, the maid at Cannon Hall, she would still write brief messages and send her love, and to Bunny Austin she would scrawl a few lines. The rest of her once lively correspondence was over.

But the telephone was heavily used, with each member of the family having 'routes' calls, as well as Angela's daily 9 a.m. call. The Browning boys no longer stayed at Kilmarth for their summer holidays, nor did they come for Christmas – the noise and disruption was too much, even in a spacious house like Kilmarth, and so from 1981 onwards Kits and family stayed in a rented house in Fowey. The days of Daphne relishing her matriarchal status were over. She became a great-grandmother just before she was ill in 1981, when Pooch had a son, but she could be interested only for so long in both grandchildren and children. She would long to see them and be pleased when they came, but in a very short time she was retreating behind her newspaper or going off to watch television without paying her visitors much attention – there was no more sitting around exchanging amusing anecdotes, mocking and mimicking gleefully, relishing the family style. She ate her meals, when in company, with great speed, then was capable of leaving the table abruptly and marching off. In her thick jacket and the postman-style cap to which she had become attached she looked as though she had settled into one last part and didn't care what anyone thought. She looked eccentric and sometimes, in spite of her frailty, a touch threatening. She could still stride into a room, on days when she felt energetic, and impress with the force of her personality, but on the whole the inhabitants of Par and Fowey, where she went to shop with her nurse-companion, saw her as a sadly diminished figure from the woman who, in her youth, had attracted every eye. Her face now, to the casual observer, had a shuttered look and in repose seemed blank – only for those she had known since Ferryside days was there a smile. But by then, the mid-eighties, there were few who came into that category. Both locally and further afield, her friends were dead. Foy Quiller-Couch,[4] Clara Vyvyan, Ellen Doubleday, Karen Prescott, Tod, Ferdy, Carol Reed, Frank Price, Jack Wolfenden – so many of those who had meant most to her, apart from her family, were gone. Only her sisters connected her to the past, and of the two it was only Angela whom she saw regularly. Like Daphne herself, Angela had someone looking after her and suffered from many painful ailments (in contrast to Daphne herself, who was physically very fit). But even Angela found her sister was becoming less and less interested in anything and that conversation was limited.

One thing Daphne *was* interested in was her own memory. She had a poor memory, from 1981, for names and dates, but there was no evidence of senility or Alzheimer's disease – she still knew her own family and those around her, could bath, feed, and dress herself, and suffered from no more than the kind of memory depreciation common to old age. But she became over-anxious when she discovered a lapse in her memory and could not rest until she had remembered whatever it was she had forgotten. She would write down on scraps of paper what she wanted to recall, and when she had either remembered or found out the answer through asking others she would be triumphant. Her memory was important to her and so was the ability to think clearly. Thinking, she once wrote, had always been near to praying in her opinion and she had taken to visiting the little chapel she had had made in Kilmarth for her Catholic grandchildren. She would kneel there, apparently lost in thought, and content. Her religious beliefs had always been idiosyncratic – at one time she declared herself to be almost a pagan, at another that she believed in 'something' but not anything taught by the established church. At times of grief she had been known to enter a church, and at others to refuse because she could not bear churches. Her conviction that there was life after death in some form, however, was one to which she held fast, and this became a religion of a sort, as well as a comfort. She had a Catholic missal by her bed, which she read regularly, and though there was no talk of God or any formal praying – only with Tommy had she ever prayed – it was obvious she had some kind of faith in a spiritual life.

There is no doubt that, cared for as she was, and with a constitution as strong as hers, Daphne could have lived to be as old as Tod, but at the beginning of 1989, as she approached her eighty-second birthday, she appeared to make the decision to take matters into her own hands and give up living. There was no question of suicide: she simply gave up without taking any positive action. In the spring she began not eating again. She secreted food instead of eating it and fooled her nurses with some success. Even when they realized what was happening, they could not force her to eat – she just closed her mouth and shook her head. She would drink Complan, but that was all, and after a month of this she was down to six stone again. Margaret Robertson came back from Ireland – having always said she would come in an emergency – and was shocked at the state in which she found Daphne. Maureen Baker-Munton, arriving soon after Margaret had returned, was equally distressed to find Daphne weak and wretched and even frightened. When it came to the time for Maureen to go, Daphne was more pathetic than she had ever seen her, and not even the promise that

Maureen would return the following month for her birthday was any consolation. On Sunday 16 April, after six weeks of virtually no food, Daphne initiated what was clearly meant to be a series of farewells. The weather was wild, with winds sweeping in from the sea and the rain lashing against the windows. It was not 'routes' to go out on a Sunday afternoon to Menabilly, but she insisted Margaret should take her to Pridmouth beach. They drove to the track leading to it and, struggling against the cold wind, went down on to the beach where Rebecca met her death. Daphne stood for a while, watching the crashing waves, and then asked to be taken to the house, to see Veronica Rashleigh, an unheard of break in 'routes' – Menabilly was only visited on a Monday. After that, they made another call on a nearer neighbour to Kilmarth before she would agree to go home. On Monday, there was a further disruption of 'routes'. Saturday was the day for visiting Angela at Ferryside, but Daphne asked to be taken to see her and then on to Mary Varcoe's, her Tuesday 'routes' visit. All who saw her during that day were awed by this skeletal figure, moving slowly but with such determination, utterly tragic and pathetic. By Tuesday night, 18 April, Margaret and Esther were in no doubt that Daphne was winning the battle to will herself to die.

She went to bed that night after strictly observing 'all routes'. At eight-thirty the next morning, taking in her breakfast on the dot as usual, Margaret found the light still on and Daphne's eye-shade still in place across her eyes. She had died in her sleep. This was not the death she had hoped for – 'when my time comes, let me go out like a light, swiftly' – but nor was it, in the final stage, so very different. She had been in control right up to the end, and control was what so much of her life had been about. Strong, determined, she liked to dictate the terms in every aspect of her life, even if behind the façade of complete control there was a part of herself she had never tamed, but to which she had never given full rein. In her death, as in her life, she tried to be in command.

The funeral was on 26 April. Only the immediate family, together with the Baker-Muntons, Esther, and Margaret Robertson, attended the crematorium service, and then the Baker-Muntons joined the family for the thanksgiving service in the tiny

Tregaminion chapel at the gates of the Menabilly estate, which was filled with white camellias, Daphne's favourite flower. Her grandchildren Freddie and Grace Browning each gave a reading. Then, in the evening, there was a last dinner at Kilmarth.

Tributes poured in from all over the world and the obituaries were long, prominent and widespread. Attempts to assess the literary worth of Daphne du Maurier in its entirety took second place to recalling the impact of one novel, *Rebecca*, but at least the general consensus of opinion was that this had earned its place among modern classics. She was portrayed as a recluse, who had shut herself away in Cornwall and shunned fame, and as an immensely wealthy woman who had made no use of her riches. Her life was judged privileged and fortunate but largely uneventful. And most common of all was the tag attached to her name: 'the world's most popular romantic novelist'. This was a misinterpretation only because the very word 'romantic' has become so debased; in its original meaning, as a teller of stories, it was perfectly accurate. *Rebecca* and much else of her work is romantic as *Wuthering Heights* and so many other great novels are romantic, possessing a spirit of adventure, mystery and excitement. This was the spirit which imbued all her work; it was the very reason why she was so widely read. She cared about writing stories which would hold the reader's attention and make them want to know what happened next. She had no desire to be admired mainly for the quality of her prose, which was sometimes awkward, but wanted instead to create an atmosphere of tension the reader could not resist. And this she did many times over.

Her writing career, properly beginning in 1931 with the publication of *The Loving Spirit*, and effectively ending in 1977, spanned a time of great change in literary fashions and tastes and in the growth and importance of women's fiction. For a while, Daphne was flowing with the tide, but after the publication of *The Scapegoat* in 1957 her kind of novel, as she herself realized, was no longer in sympathy with the trend towards the realistic fiction she hated. She had it in her to change and produce something different but not the desire: she wanted to stay true to an older tradition. Her writing self, that 'No. 2' which caused her so much trouble, demanded escapism, not reality, and it was only obliquely, and especially in her short stories, that she was able to give expression to it. This distinction – between her living self and her writing self, between the person she was on the outside and the quite different person she knew herself to be on the inside – was one she herself made repeatedly. When she was able to balance the two selves, she was happy, as she was in the thirties, but when the two separated, as they began to do towards the end of the fifties, she was miserable, and the strain of juggling these two different personae brought her near to breakdown. In the mid-seventies, when her writing ability left her, it became tragically clear that her 'living' self could not be content, or even survive, on its own. Never was there a clearer case of a writer who 'lived to write', or of a writer for whom life came to have no meaning and little joy without writing.

Daphne du Maurier, Dame of the British Empire, a world-wide and enduring bestselling author for nearly fifty years, had a loving family, devoted friends, and everything, it would seem, a woman could possibly have wanted, but if she could not write all this seemed worthless. Her novels and stories gave pleasure to millions, and among them were at least three worthy of a place in any literary canon – *Rebecca*, *The Scapegoat* and *The House on the Strand* – but what they gave to *her* was more important. Through writing she lived more truly than she did in her daily life – it gave her satisfaction, release and a curious sense of elation. As her early editor Norman Collins so astutely said, 'No one ever imagined more than Daphne.' And it was the fire of her imagination which warmed and excited her millions of readers, and still does.

Afterword

Daphne du Maurier's children warned me, when I began this biography, that I would find their mother 'a chameleon', an opinion constantly repeated by those who knew her well. Everyone described to me how, the moment she met new people, she would try and adapt to them.

This desire, and willingness, to adapt herself to others is to a considerable extent reflected in her letters. The tone changes, sometimes quite dramatically, according to the recipient, even when she is imparting the same information or relating the same anecdotes. She liked to make each correspondent seem especially favoured and drew them into a little conspiracy against everyone else. Not a single member of her family or any of her closest friends was safe from caustic comments and ridicule. She gave people what she thought they wanted and was untroubled by the idea that this might amount to calculated double-dealing and hypocrisy.

Yet she emerges from her letters as more consistent in her attitudes and opinions than this description might suggest. Her outward behaviour might vary but her inner self remained the same. Often, she felt she was outside her bodily self, describing how she looked down from above and saw herself laughing and chatting in a way her inner self found quite extraordinary. Her whole life seemed to her an act, except when she was totally alone.

This was why writing was so important to her. The gap between reality and fantasy was often narrow, and when the two became confused so did she. In the case of Ellen Doubleday, fantasy came to take over at times and brought Daphne nearer to that schizophrenic state she feared. What was going on in her head spilled over into her life and she could, and did, cast real people as the creatures of her fantasies. Then she wrote about them.

Only once in her life did this work the other way. Gertrude Lawrence began as a fantasy creature in *September Tide* and then stepped from Daphne's fantasy into her life. Daphne found that when she was with Gertie she did not need fantasies because, for a very short while, Gertie fulfilled them. She could be her inner self with Gertie as she could with no one else, however much she loved them. She found that 'something' for which she had been searching as a child. When Gertie died, she lost it forever.

This 'something' was undoubtedly partly sexual. As she admitted to Ellen, her relationship with Gertie became physical and this made a difference. But she was ambivalent, even then, about her own sexuality. The fury she felt at being thought a lesbian was because she truly did not see herself as such: she thought of herself as 'a half-breed', attracted to both men and women, as she told Frank Price, bisexual himself.

In many ways, she reflected the sexual judgements of her era. During the twenties and thirties, when she was growing up, women who were lesbians were thought of as women who should have been born men. If two women were in a lesbian relationship there was always speculation from outsiders as to 'who plays the man'. Today a lesbian would define her sexuality differently; a man is precisely what she would not wish to be. A lesbian is now simply a woman who loves women, and to whom intimacy with a man is abhorrent.

How abhorrent it was to Daphne is difficult to judge. All her pronouncements on this subject were made in late middle and old age. But there is some evidence that she disliked the final consummation of the heterosexual act. What she preferred was 'spinning' which, put plainly, meant foreplay. After the death of Gertrude Lawrence sex and 'spinning' both stopped. The significance for her work was immense: post-1952, after Gertrude Lawrence died, fantasies took over as a substitute for life, and the fantasies themselves revealed deep emotional disturbance.

What was distressing for her children was to discover, as a result of letters to Ellen Doubleday (made available after this biography was originally completed), that their mother had not told them the truth about Gertrude Lawrence. She spoke freely to them, when they were adults, about Christopher Puxley, but never explained her devastation when Gertie died. So far as they could judge, her attitude to homosexuality was tolerant but, at the same time, she did not approve of it. Told that some man she admired was gay, she would say regretfully, 'Oh, he *isn't* is he?'

This attitude sprang from her father's detestation of homosexuality. Daphne could never have admitted to him any 'Venetian tendencies', which made denying and concealing them vitally important. Gerald, in his poem to her, told Daphne she should indeed have been a boy. If he hated homosexuality, where did that leave a girl who knew she had 'Venetian tendencies'? Condemned, more than most, to subterfuge.

The success with which Daphne maintained this subterfuge was striking. To her children, she was a mother who seemed happy and content. The revelation that she was so tortured for much of her life has been a shock. They cannot quite believe in such deception and are tempted to wonder if perhaps this is another instance of fantasy, that perhaps their mother was merely inventing and dramatizing, and none of this inner life need be taken seriously.

I think it should be taken very seriously indeed. The controlling of her 'No. 2' persona, of the boy-in-the-box, was no fantasy. Daphne battled with it all her life and the result is seen in her work. It may have tortured her to feel she was two distinct people, but it also fuelled her creative powers: without 'No. 2', that boy-in-the-box, there would have been nothing. In the letter she wrote in 1957 to Maureen Baker-Munton, which is printed in full in the Appendix following, Daphne herself stresses how her work gave her release from thoughts, images and ideas which disturbed her. Her great fear, she acknowledges, was 'a fear of reality'. Her whole life's work was an attempt to defy reality and create for herself a world far more exciting and true than the one in which she lived. We have her own word for it that when her ability to do this left her, and reality at last confronted her, her life was not worth living; the death of the writer was indeed the death of the self.

Appendix

This letter has been quoted from in the text but is of such significance that I feel it should be made fully available.

It is to be remembered that it was written shortly after Daphne's husband, referred to as 'Moper', had had a nervous breakdown and while Daphne herself was in a state of shock and struggling to avert her own breakdown.

Mena.   July 4th, 1957

Dearest Maureen,

I would have written before, but have been going through such a turmoil of psychological politics since the weekend, and trying to get at the understanding of all these troubles that I have not been able to write to anyone, or pay a bill, or do damn all, except swim to keep the health stable, and sit with Gran to keep the mind stable. First, I do thank you from the bottom of my heart and Bim[1] too, for being such bricks of friends to go up and cope as you did, and to start to help unravelling the knot. It was like being faced with a great jigsaw puzzle, or a pack of cards, and trying to fit the right bits into the right squares, and get the suits of cards straight. I think if we, every one of us, have patience – and watch our dreams (!) – and apply the dreams to the waking day, the business will get straight and everyone will be the better and the more understanding for the blow-up of the boiler. I did what you advised, and did rather an Oxford Groupy sort of thing, and wrote a great long letter to Moper,[2] saying how to blame I

1 Monty Baker-Munton.
2 Tommy, Daphne's husband.

420

had been for so much of his unhappiness during the past years, and came clean about the Puxley man, and then tried to explain in easy language for him to grasp how my obsessions – you can only call them that – for poor old Ellen D and Gertrude – were all part of a nervous breakdown going on *inside myself*, partly to do with my muddled troubles, and writing, and a fear of facing reality. This fear of reality came to the fore twice, once with the horror of going into the witness-box for that *Rebecca* case, and the fear mainly because I had written *Rebecca* about my feelings of jealousy re him and Jan Ricardo, and I was so terrified of that coming up in the Box and making publicity that I was nearly off my rocker. I did, I am sure, break down in Ellen's house once the case was over (though if you remember, its outcome was still undecided), but because I wanted someone to understand and to love at that moment, I turned bang to Ellen, who was suddenly a symbol for the terrific reliance and love I had had as a kid of 18 for that French Ferdie [sic] person. (For the understanding of that relationship, read again *The Parasites*, and Bing's[3] three inner selves, Maria, Niall, Celia, were the three people I know myself to have been. Niall, the boy, was the one who turned to Ferdie, and later to Ellen and Gertrude.)

So, during all those years from '47 to '52, I was neglecting Moper because I was trying to work out the problem of Niall. I had let him swim out to sea once, but the book did not say if he was drowned, and I did not know either. He was not drowned. He came to life again as Philip Ashley in *My Cousin Rachel*, and here I was identifying myself with my boyish love for my father, and my boyish affection for old Nelson Doubleday, and suddenly was overwhelmed with an obsessional passion for the last of Daddy's actress loves – Gertrude – and the wife of Nelson, Ellen.[4] They merged to make the single figure of Rachel, and I did not know if this figure was killing me or not, or if it had killed my

3 Daphne's nickname.
4 This could be misunderstood: Daphne is referring to Philip's boyish affection and hero worship of his cousin Ambrose, who was modelled on Nelson Doubleday, without the slightest suggestion of any sexual undertone. She identified in *My Cousin Rachel* with Philip, cousin of an older man who died leaving a widow about whom he had mixed feelings. But Philip had no mixed feelings about Ambrose, any more than Daphne had about Nelson.

father and Nelson. The symbol behind the living woman can either be the Healer, or the Destroyer. In the book I killed both, and Philip Ashley was left to his solitude in his Mena. The only thing to do was then to write out the many problems in yet a different way, and the short stories were written. Monte Verita is myself and Moper, and myself going to the mountains to learn the truth, and Moper waiting for me, and finally dying without ever having learnt that the person who had gone to the mountains had not the perfect beauty of mind and body he wanted in his wife, but had a leprous face (learning the truth can give a person the appearance of disease, and leprosy can eat away the body and the mind. If you try to reach the gods you can destroy the body – leprosy).

The Old Man was Moper's jealousy of Boo,[5] and his unconscious wish to destroy him. In the end he kills his son, and possesses his mate again. But that is not the whole significance of the story. The real significance is that Moper must not kill his own begotten son, but kill the petty jealous *self* which is his hidden nature, and so rise again. This is the truth behind Christianity, and all the religions.

All those stories have inner significance for problems of that time. *The Apple Tree* is what that Puxley person went through with his wife, though she did not die. *Kiss Me Again, Stranger*, is the warning I had about poor Gertrude's death. And so on, and so on.

Then we get this urge to go to Greece by me, and I would think it chimed in with Moper's first urge towards—.[6] (Me in the meantime having done *Mary Anne*, once again a try-out of the basic problem. Here, I and Gertrude, identify ourselves together, although I am the centre character which she could have acted. I found, on research, that Mary Anne's life could have been mine in reverse. Married to a drunkard (Puxley) and then meeting the C-in-C Duke of York (Moper), etc, etc. But in that life Mary Anne ruins the Duke, and gets him to resign from being C-in-C by witnessing against him in the House of Commons. Tie-up here once more. I could have witnessed against Moper in the Case in

5 Kits, Daphne's son.
6 Name of Tommy's mistress.

America, but did not. End, they parted resentful and hating each other, he died full of dropsey never having really achieved the top, and she ended in France, with her children married and bored with her. Not our answer!

And so to Greece. My fearful urge to consult the Delphi oracle, that has not given answers for two thousand years! Went to Delphi, but of course no answer, only the Greek words over the temple door 'Know Thyself'. For the past four years have been trying to do this! Read every Greek thing under the sun, and found, to my great interest, that the original Daphne had two myths. First myth was that, afraid of men, she was chased by Apollo and to save herself from waxing,[7] called to her father – a river god – to turn her into a tree. Could be my story. Daddy-complex, and don't forget that the tree of life in Norse mythology is Ygdrasil![8]

Second myth: Daphne not a nymph, but a priestess of the original oracle which was held by Gee, the Earth Mother. (Gee. Odd, this.) To save the oracle – matriarchal and devoted to goddess worship – from being seized by a man and turned over to patriarch society, she called on Gee, the Earth goddess, to turn her into a laurel. Another tree. And after that, the oracle was held by Apollo and by Gee, and worshipped by the devotees of each until patriarchal society overwhelmed the matriarchal society, Gee was suppressed and forgotten, and finally, as history tells us, even the wise Know Thyself Apollo was chucked for later religions.

OK. This established. I knew I had to write something, nothing to do with Greece. But if I waited, just as Daphne, the priestess, waited until she was in a trance and the goddess prophesised [sic] through her, something would emerge. In the meanwhile, the torments of hell because I felt no one I had ever loved was real (except the family). In other words, the tribe, the original social group were real, nobody else. Then the urge to go to France, to find out about forebears, and take Jeanne (Moper backing out.—[9]). Went, and found the *verrerie*, and forebears, and at the same time began *The Scapegoat* seed. Came back, and began to

7 Code for making love.
8 Name of Tommy's boat.
9 Name of Tommy's mistress.

write it, not knowing what it was about, or what I was doing. It is my story, and it is Moper's also. We are both doubles. So is everyone. Every one of us has his, or her, dark side. Which is to overcome the other? This is the purpose of the book. And it ends, as you know, with the problem unsolved, except that the suggestion there, when I finished it, was that the two sides of that man's nature had to fuse together to give birth to a third, well balanced. Know Thyself. The one man went back home having been given a hint that his family, in future, would be different, would be adjusted; the other man went to the monastery, for a space of time, to learn 'what to do with love'.

Can Moper, and can I, learn from this? I think we can. What Moper learns in Weymouth Street now may be his turning-point, just as what I went to Delphi to discover, four years ago, was mine. But the dark side is not yet destroyed. We must be patient. And though I have worked out, these last few days, all the characters in *Scapegoat* and what they represent, I don't want to resurrect *Rebecca* in reverse. What is past is also future. I wrote as the second Mrs de W. twenty-one years ago, with Rebecca a symbol of Jan. It could also be that the Sixpence[10] in Fowey is the second Mrs de W. and I – in Moper's dark mind – can be the symbol of Rebecca. The cottage on the beach could be my hut. Rebecca's lovers could be my books. Mrs Danvers, devoted, could be Tod, the old devotee. And Moper, in a blind rage, shoot me as Maxim shot Rebecca, and put my body in *Yggie*, and take *Yggie* out to sea, and then the old tragedy be re-enacted, and when he married, as he would in time, some younger Sixpence, be haunted by my ghost. *Or*, the present Sixpence, a symbol of Jan, be taken out to sea and killed, because what has happened is that some old ghost of Jan is resurrected that had been buried, just as Rebecca's body was discovered in the boat and brought to the surface. The evil in us comes to the surface. Unless we recognise it in time, accept it, understand it, we are all destroyed, just as the people in *The Birds* were destroyed.

I haven't been able to explain this to Moper, of course, he

---

10 Code name for girl in Fowey with whom Daphne believed her husband to be having an affair.

simply could not take it in, and may never take it in. But I want you and Bim to keep this letter, as a witness of my belief, and if you have a typewriter, some time make copies for future family reference. Also, it might help you both in your own lives. I believe that I have got myself adjusted now with the family, *all* of whom, even Peter, is coming up to scratch. Flave and A are back. I have prepared Flave, who seized the situation in a moment, with her rather deep insight, whereas Tess is more practical. Boo is also prepared, but of course not fully yet. We have all got to cope in future, but so must Moper, eventually too, and not just be the man who takes, and takes, and takes. His sweet good side must come and balance him.

At the moment, there is a brief plan that Peter may bring Kits here for his Long Leave, and I come up with them (July 15th – Tessa's birthday – perhaps Moper go to her for it, and see Paul?) and then I bring Moper down her again for anniversary, if he is well enough to come. Because for all our sakes, we must know that dark side, which I don't think he has shown to — —, might conceivably come up if he comes here and sees Sixpence, with me here. Something berserk might snap, with that revolver, and that Tommy gun, and the arrows. I am not talking madly. I know. And I shall have to discuss this with doctors. Meanwhile, Gran, whom I thought was dying, is gradually better, and so dependent on me that it's torture, so I can't just chuck her to Ferryside, but must see that it's done in the right way. Angela still nervy, but her broadcast has given her confidence. Tod still a major problem, but I may learn how to deal with that one too. No more for the moment, too absolutely spent. I write to you both because I think you both understand.

Lots of love,
Bing

Works of Daphne du Maurier
(with first publication)

The Loving Spirit, Heinemann, 1931.
I'll Never Be Young Again, Heinemann, 1932.
The Progress of Julius, Heinemann, 1933.
Gerald: A Portrait, Gollancz, 1934.
Jamaica Inn, Gollancz, 1936.
The Du Mauriers, Gollancz, 1937.
Rebecca, Gollancz, 1938.
Come Wind, Come Weather, Heinemann, 1940.
Frenchman's Creek, Gollancz, 1941.
Hungry Hill, Gollancz, 1943.
The Years Between, Gollancz, 1945.
The King's General, Gollancz, 1946.
September Tide, Gollancz, 1949.
The Parasites, Gollancz, 1949.
*The Young George du Maurier: A Selection of his Letters,
    1860–1867* (ed.), Peter Davies, 1951.
My Cousin Rachel, Gollancz, 1951.
The Apple Tree, Gollancz, 1952.
Happy Christmas, Todd, 1953.
Mary Anne, Gollancz, 1954.
Early Stories, Todd, 1955.
The Scapegoat, Gollancz, 1957.
The Breaking Point, Gollancz, 1959.
The Internal World of Branwell Brontë, Gollancz, 1960.
Castle Dor, J. M. Dent, 1962.
The Glass Blowers, Gollancz, 1963.
The Flight of the Falcon, Gollancz, 1965.
Vanishing Cornwall, Gollancz, 1967.
The House on the Strand, Gollancz, 1969.

Works of Daphne du Maurier

Not After Midnight, Gollancz, 1971.

Rule Britannia, Gollancz, 1972.

Golden Lads: Anthony Bacon, Francis and their Friends, Gollancz, 1975.

The Winding Stair: Francis Bacon, his Rise and Fall, Gollancz, 1976.

Echoes from the Macabre, Gollancz, 1976.

Growing Pains: The Shaping of a Writer, Gollancz, 1977.

The Rendezvous and Other Stories, Gollancz, 1980.

The Rebecca Notebook and Other Memories, Gollancz, 1981.

Classics from the Macabre, Gollancz, 1987.

Notes and References

CHAPTER ONE

1 There is an account of these liaisons in *Gerald*, Daphne's biography of her father (Gollancz, 1934), and in *Gerald du Maurier* by James Harding (Hodder & Stoughton, 1989).

2 Arthur Llewelyn Davies was the second son of John Llewelyn Davies, the brilliant scholar who was Honorary Chaplain to the Queen and a radical who supported women's suffrage. His sister Emily founded Girton College, and his daughter Margaret was a co-founder of the Women's Co-operative Guild. Arthur was called to the bar in 1891, aged twenty-eight, and married Sylvia du Maurier – the union of two very different families.

3 The games Gerald played with his daughters are well documented in Daphne's autobiography *Growing Pains* (Gollancz, 1977), and in Angela's *It's Only the Sister* (Peter Davies, 1976).

4 The first house in Hampstead lived in by the du Mauriers was 4 Holly Mount, then they moved to Gangmoor House, facing Whitestone Pond on the summit of Hampstead Hill; a year later, in 1870, they settled at 27 Church Row (where Gerald was born in 1873) and from there went to New Grove House, where they stayed twenty-one years.

5 Mrs Beaumont also at one time wrote articles on household and domestic subjects for *The Bystander*, the magazine edited by her son.

6 Letter to Pucky (Ellen M. Violett, second daughter of Ellen Doubleday), 7 October 1948.

7 Gerald himself finally volunteered, in 1918, at the age of forty-five, and was accepted by the Irish Guards. He was a disastrous soldier (amusingly described in *Gerald* – see note 1 above) and was luckily still being trained when the Armistice was declared.

8 There is no date on this poem, but it is likely it was written around 1920.

9 There is a description of 'Eric Avon' in *Growing Pains* (see note 3 above). Daphne claimed there were 'no psychological depths' to this invented character, who was Captain of Cricket at Rugby and shone at everything. She played the Eric Avon character in games until she was fifteen.

10 Letter to Ellen Doubleday, 10 December 1947, quoted more extensively in Chapter Fourteen.

11 Maud Waddell's surname, with the emphasis on the first syllable, was pronounced by the du Mauriers as 'Waddle'. This made them think of a waddling walk, which in turn led to the thought of toddling and toddle, and was shortened to Tod: a typically convoluted way of bestowing nicknames.

12 Frederick Lonsdale was the successful playwright of the 1920s and early

1930s. He met Gerald in 1904 and they were friends from then onwards. The two of them worked many times together and used to sit up all night smoking, drinking and playing cards. There is an entertaining description of the du Maurier and Lonsdale families holidaying together in Frances Donaldson's biography of her father, *Freddy Lonsdale* (Heinemann, 1957).

13 Tod was an accomplished painter of watercolours. When she decided she hated Australia, she paid for her passage home, first-class, by selling her paintings. She was elected to the Royal Watercolour Society and also the Société des Artistes and had her work exhibited in both London and Paris.

14 Letter to Pucky (Ellen M. Violett – see note 6 above), 23 August 1949.

15 Daphne considered that J. M. Barrie understood Gerald better than anyone else and that this understanding went into the creation of the part of Will Dearth in *Dear Brutus*. (Recording, 'Portrait of Gerald', made for the centenary of Gerald's birth in 1973, BBC Sound Archives.)

CHAPTER TWO

1 Patricia Hastings, who was at Camposena with Daphne, has provided me with information about the school.

2 To describe a man as 'dago-like' shows Daphne as a creature of her class and time, and was not seen by her as derogatory, though it undoubtedly was. In a similar way she refers to Jews and Negroes without stopping to think about the terms she uses. This could be interpreted as being anti-semitic or anti-black, but, in fact, she was neither. Later in life she was tremendously pro-Israel and also strongly against apartheid, and signed petitions to that effect.

3 Letter to Ellen Doubleday, December 1947.

4 Gerald du Maurier hated homosexuality, and when *The Vortex* was staged in 1924, which dealt not with homosexuality but with an ambiguous mother–son relationship, he used it to protest against the theatre becoming besmirched with 'filth'. The play's author, Noël Coward, replied with a spirited defence, and though this did not change Gerald's mind, the two became, if not friends, at least tolerant of each other.

5 Letter to Ellen Doubleday (see note 3 above).

6 Daphne always had dogs from now onwards, all of them West Highland terriers (except Bingo, half-Spaniel half-Sheepdog). There was Mouse, Moray and Bibby, whom she had for ten years each, and finally Mac and Ken, who survived her. She was devoted to her dogs, lavishing affection upon them, but disciplined them very strictly.

7 A board game, rather like ludo.

CHAPTER THREE

1 There is a description of going to Cornwall as a child in the prologue to *Vanishing Cornwall* (Gollancz, 1967).

2 Daphne records in her memoir *Growing Pains* that she had to be led from her seat in tears after watching Gerald in *Dear Brutus*.

3 Recorded by Angela du Maurier in her first volume of autobiography, *Old Maids Remember* (1966), where she describes her father as a 'mixture of Mr

Barrett and a schoolboy brother' and reflects that his conversation with his daughters was often 'strangely bawdy'.

4 Described by A. L. Rowse in *Quiller-Couch: A Portrait of 'Q'* (Methuen, 1988).

5 Daphne told her son this.

CHAPTER FOUR

1 The best description of Daphne finding Menabilly is given by her in an article called 'The House of Secrets', written in 1946, for a book entitled *Countryside Character*. This later appeared in *The Rebecca Notebook and Other Memories* (Gollancz, 1981).

2 Gerald's first film was *Escape* (1930), made on Dartmoor, which proved a gruelling experience. He followed this with *Lord Camber's Ladies* (1932), made by Alfred Hitchcock, in which he starred with Gertrude Lawrence. The money he earned got him out of financial difficulties but, compared to the income from lending his name to a brand of cigarettes – 'Du Maurier cork-tipped' – it was extremely hard work and he detested the experience.

3 For Carol Reed's career see *The Man Between*, a biography by Nicholas Wapshott (Chatto & Windus, 1990).

4 Daphne's real feelings towards her mother are given in a letter to Ellen Doubleday, January 1948, quoted at length in Chapter Fourteen.

5 The trip with Otto Kahn is described in *Growing Pains*. Daphne tells, with great relish, how she avoided her host's unwelcome attentions by stripping her clothes off and diving naked into the water. Later, he offered to buy her a fur coat, but she asked for a dagger instead.

6 Clara Vyvyan was forty-five when Daphne, aged twenty-three, met her. Her husband, Sir Courtenay, was still alive and they were both great gardeners. Four years previously she and a friend, with two Indian guides, crossed the divide from Canada to Alaska, collecting and pressing wild flowers for Kew Gardens.

CHAPTER FIVE

1 Mentioned in *Growing Pains*.

2 Daphne uses this simile – that sex is like a game of tennis – frequently in her correspondence.

3 The first print-run for *The Loving Spirit* was 2,300 and the advance £75; for *I'll Never Be Young Again* it was 2,000, and the advance £125; and for *The Progress of Julius*, the last novel published by Heinemann, 4,000, with the same advance.

4 Angela's *The Little Less*, dealing with a lesbian friendship, was turned down. It was eventually published in 1941.

5 Both Daphne (in *Gerald*) and Angela (in her two volumes of autobiography) describe scenes with Gerald near to the kind portrayed in *The Progress of Julius*.

Notes and References

1 Why a boy named Frederick was called 'Tommy' nobody can now remember, but he was called 'Boy' in the army – 'the boy Browning' – to distinguish him from his father, who was also serving in 1916. After his father died, 'Boy' stuck, and those who did not know assumed Browning was called this because of his extremely youthful appearance well into middle age.

2 Tommy became very attached, not just to George (who was best man at his wedding), but to the entire Hunkin family. He backed George Hunkin's boatyard and later, with Daphne, bought it. George was a regular visitor to tea later on, and his wife's sister, Mrs Hancock, known as 'Hanks', was the Brownings' cook in the late 1940s and early 1950s.

3 Volumes I and II of Lt.-Col. Sir Frederick Ponsonby's *The Grenadier Guards in the Great War 1914–1918* has details of Tommy's battalion's action.

4 Mr Hubert Browning, Tommy's cousin, described this incident to me in a letter.

5 Laila Spence made available to me a copy of Guy Westmacott's memoir, privately printed in 1979.

6 Argument still rages among the contemporaries of both Tommy and Jan over who broke off the engagement. I am inclined to believe those who say that Tommy did.

7 Daphne describes how she and Tommy met in *Growing Pains*. Mrs Hunkin informed her that Major Browning wished to meet her and later she brought Daphne a note. It said their fathers were once 'fellow members of the Garrick Club' and that, since he heard she was recovering from an appendix operation, he would like to take her sailing. She accepted.

8 Leo Walmsley (1892–1966) was best known in the 1930s for his autobiographical novels. *Three Fevers* (1932) was greatly admired by Daphne and she wrote to Tod that she wished she could write like Walmsley. He lived in a derelict army hut, overlooking a creek of the River Fowey, with a young actress who later became his second wife.

9 Tommy reminded Daphne of this in a letter written on their thirteenth wedding anniversary, quoted in Chapter Twelve.

10 Angela's nickname was Puff, shortened from Puffin, and Jeanne's was Queenie. Daphne herself was known as Bing, and later also sometimes as Track, and Tray.

11 'Chink' was a controversial figure in the army during the Second World War, when he felt he was made a scapegoat for everything that went wrong with the Eighth Army in the Desert Campaign. He was a friend of Ernest Hemingway and was reputed to be the prototype for the hero in *Across the River and Into the Trees*. He was demoted in 1943, and afterwards allowed his home to be used as an IRA training ground. See *Chink* – a biography by Lavinia Greacen (Macmillan, 1989).

12 It was thought at the time by fellow officers in the Grenadier Guards that Tommy had, in marrying an actor's daughter, rather let the regiment down. Lord Carrington remembers his father being disgusted with those who said so.

13 Lt.-Col. Frederick Henry Browning CBE died in 1929 at the age of fifty-nine. He was a great sportsman – rackets and cricket – at Oxford, and after taking his degree went into business, becoming chairman of Twiss, Browning

and Hallowes. He was on the board of the Savoy Hotel. During the First World War he worked in Intelligence and was afterwards attached to the Foreign Office for services at the Versailles peace conference. He was an immensely popular man, though rather overbearing in his behaviour to his gentle wife Nancy.

14 Why there were no Brownings at this unconventional wedding nobody knows. Tommy's mother was neither abroad nor ill at the time and neither was Grace, his older sister. He was very fond of both his mother and sister and of his cousins, which makes their absence strange. Since both Mrs Browning and Grace liked Daphne and were delighted at the marriage, their absence was certainly not a mark of their disapproval.

CHAPTER SEVEN

1 'Daddy's old horrors' can only be a reference to Gerald's drinking. Daphne quotes him in *Gerald* as saying, 'Too many whisky and sodas, that's my trouble. They give me the horrors.' How serious his drinking was, and whether it continued all his life, she does not say. Whatever the truth, his 'horrors' never prevented him working, and he never drank before a performance. The form the 'horrors' took was that 'he put his hands over his eyes and [would] stand and tremble and hold on to Mo or one of his children . . . until . . . the terror, fear and loneliness were gone' and he had stopped hearing voices in his head. (*Gerald*.)

2 The name 'Tessa' came from Margaret Kennedy's *The Constant Nymph*, and not, as sometimes believed, from *Tess of the D'Urbervilles*.

3 Grace Browning, sixteen months older than her brother, never married. She was an indefatigable worker for the Girl Guide movement (she was Commissioner for Westminster), and Chairman of the National Association of Training Corps for Girls, and was awarded the OBE in recognition of her work for this organization.

4 It was a surprise to Daphne's children to discover that she had ever driven after her marriage. They had assumed that their father, who adored his cars, would not let her drive.

5 Letter to Foy Quiller-Couch, 14 April 1934.

6 Letter to Pucky (Ellen M. Violett), 12 January 1949.

7 Victor Gollancz to Daphne, 15 March 1961.

8 For accounts of Victor Gollancz's life and work see *Victor Gollancz* by Ruth Dudley Edwards (Gollancz, 1987), and *Story of a Publishing House: Gollancz 1928–1978* (Gollancz, 1978) by Sheila Hodges (née Bush), Victor Gollancz's secretary, who became Daphne's editor.

CHAPTER EIGHT

1 *Jamaica Inn* is the only one of Daphne's books for which there is no record of the first print-run. The production book covering 1936 is missing from the Gollancz files.

2 Not only did Daphne never sew, she also was proud to tell her daughters that she had never even lifted an iron. Their domestic skills were a constant source of amazement to her.

Notes and References

3 Oscar Yerburgh, whose stepfather was sent to Alexandria to command the Coldstream Guards, lived in the house after the Brownings left. He and his family 'adored the lovely house and garden' and thought Hassan 'gracious, tactful and silent-moving'.

4 Queen Anne's Mansions was a block of flats in Queen Anne's Gate, off Petty France, St James's, where flats could be rented by the week or month.

5 Once she was back in England Tessa became very fond of Grace Browning and received from her, during her childhood, a great deal of the affection not bestowed on her by her mother.

6 This was the beginning of Daphne's long history of taking sleeping pills. Medinol was a mild sleeping drug, but later she moved on to stronger ones. These are not usually named in her letters and papers, but simply referred to by their colour, but in the late 1970s and early 1980s she does name some (see Chapter Twenty-four).

7 This 'psychological side' was more significant than anyone realized. As Daphne related to Michael Thornton many years later (see the *Observer*, April 1989, for Thornton's account of this) and to Maureen Baker-Munton (letter, July 1957, quoted in full in the Appendix, p. 420) the starting point for *Rebecca* was her own jealousy of Tommy's one-time fiancée, Jan Ricardo. Jan Ricardo married in 1937 and died during the war (she threw herself under a train), but Daphne was still haunted by the suspicion that Tommy had found the beautiful, dark-haired, glamorous Jan more attractive than herself.

CHAPTER NINE

1 A. J. Cronin's *The Citadel* had had a first print-run of 30,000 in June 1937.

2 The film producer David Selznick bought the film rights to *Rebecca*. Alfred Hitchcock, who had directed *Jamaica Inn* in 1939, was under contract to Selznick Studios and was given it to direct. Daphne was not pleased because she hated what Hitchcock made of *Jamaica Inn* (see p. 144), but *Rebecca*, made in 1940, delighted her, though she lived to regret a carelessly drawn-up contract, which meant that in future years she did not receive royalties from the very successful TV adaptations.

3 For Frank Buchman see *Frank Buchman: A Life* by Garth Lean (Constable, 1985).

4 Daphne knew perfectly well that Victor Gollancz loathed MRA, and she had been afraid of his contempt. What she did not realize was that Victor's business sense made him look on anything his most successful author wrote with indulgence.

CHAPTER TEN

1 Daphne called Henry 'Christopher' and herself 'Jane' – nicknames derived from *The Loving Spirit*. 'Jane' was a shortened form of 'Janet', the novel's heroine. Christopher is her grandson in the novel.

2 Quoted in Angela's autobiography *It's Only the Sister*.

3 Peter Howard was a journalist who wrote for Express Newspapers. He investigated MRA in 1940 and became a convert, writing a book, *Innocent*

433

Men, in which he gave the facts as he saw them. On publication he was forced to resign.

4 A sulpha drug (sulphathiazole) made by May & Baker. These drugs were used to treat bacterial infections before the introduction of antibiotics in 1941.

5 Daphne once wrote to Ellen Doubleday that, although at the time of writing *Frenchman's Creek* she had seen Puxley as being like the pirate, later on she realized that the pirate was really the man she would have liked to be.

6 Margaret Eglesfield always called Browning 'Major', which is the rank he held when she was first engaged by Daphne.

7 Not quite all the people. Mrs Puxley, mother of Henry ('Christopher') and John, was still alive and objected to the way in which real people from the Puxley family had been used. She disapproved especially of how the women were portrayed.

8 Published in the USA in 1942, and in Britain, by Todd Publishing Group, in 1953.

CHAPTER ELEVEN

1 This huge tax bill was the first of many and at this point Daphne had no accountant. After the war, when inflation began, she was in the surtax bracket, which rose to 80 per cent. Until trusts were set up for her children in the early fifties she was shocked to find most of her earnings going in tax. Tessa remembers her mother white-faced when she received this particular tax demand.

2 An entailed estate or house can, in fact, be sold, so long as the proceeds of any sale are paid to the trustees of the settlement and become subject to the same trusts.

3 But it was also based on someone else's real life story, and Daphne caused a good deal of offence in Cornwall for using it. John Rathbone, MP for Bodmin, was reported missing in 1940. His wife was returned unopposed to Parliament to fill his place, when his death was confirmed. In 1942 she remarried and shortly afterwards it was rumoured that her first husband was, after all, alive and a prisoner. The rumour turned out to be untrue.

4 Daphne herself wrote the first draft of the screenplay of *Hungry Hill*. It was then taken over by Terence Young and Francis Crowdy. The film appeared in 1946, starring Margaret Lockwood, Dennis Price, Michael Denison, and Jean Simmons.

5 All descriptions of the interior of Menabilly in this chapter are taken from Flavia Leng's as yet unpublished MS 'Dreaming of Manderley'.

6 The other two girls were Violet and Joyce Hooper.

7 Flavia Leng's MS (see note 5 above).

8 Tommy's letters are all written in a strange mixture of Cornish dialect (or his version of this) and code words and phrases. It seemed confusing to stay absolutely faithful to this and so I have kept the exact sense but 'translated' the so-called dialect, and the code.

9 The beret was actually maroon but was invariably described as red, and the paratroopers as 'red devils'. The insignia of the British Airborne Division was a light blue Pegasus against a maroon background. Tommy paid great attention to such details.

Notes and References

CHAPTER TWELVE

1 Flavia Leng's MS (see Chapter Eleven, note 5).
2 Tommy originally estimated that the new boat he had in mind would cost £3,000. He wrote in March 1945, asking Daphne to back him to that extent. In May 1946 he finally bought an old fishing-boat to convert (named *Fanny Rosa*) for £1,050, but then found that the cost of conversion and furnishings brought the total to £6,500. By the time the boat had been brought home from Singapore, the final cost was almost £8,000, 'but I assure you, you will get value for money'.
3 Letter to Mlle Fernande Yvon (Ferdy), 12 September 1946.
4 The Whitelands House flat in Chelsea originally belonged to the mother of Grace Browning's friend Helen MacSwiney. Tommy took over the lease after the war.
5 Letter to Ferdy (as note 3 above).

CHAPTER THIRTEEN

1 Tod went on frequent holidays, so the letters to her still continued at intervals.
2 Tommy had eight teddy bears. Every Christmas he gave them new silk bows, a different colour each year.
3 Letter to Tod, 18 October 1942.
4 Daphne did, at least, visit the school and took Tessa there on her first day.
5 The film of *The King's General* was never made. In 1958, Daphne received a telegram from Zoltan Korda, brother of Alexander, saying that he intended to start shooting in the spring. He sent Daphne the script, which she disliked; it suggested Elizabeth Taylor for the heroine, which horrified her. She met Korda in London, but once more *The King's General* was shelved. (All this was related in letters to Michael Thornton.)
6 Ellen George McCarter was born in 1898 in New Jersey, into a well-to-do family. She had a typically society-girl education. A great beauty, she married Atwood Violett after the First World War and had two daughters. In 1931 she divorced her husband, and married Nelson Doubleday the following year. She was a great reader and the ideal publisher's wife. During the war she and her husband offered shelter to many English authors and publishers and their families, including Daphne, who had turned it down.

CHAPTER FOURTEEN

1 Letter to Ellen Doubleday, 10 December 1947.
2 Ibid.
3 Ibid.
4 Letter to Maureen Baker-Munton, 4 July 1957 (see full text in Appendix p. 420).
5 She did. Judge Swan took until January 1948 to make up his mind, but finally said, 'I am convinced there was no copying,' and dismissed the complaint with costs to the defendants.
6 Nickname for Mrs Hancock, who still came in to cook sometimes.

7 Letter from Ellen Doubleday to Daphne, 5 December 1947.
8 Letter to Ellen, 10 December 1947.
9 Letter to Ellen, 13 January 1948.
10 Letter to Ellen, 4 February 1948.
11 Letter from Ellen, 9 February 1948.
12 Ellen kept a carbon of her unsent paragraph in the letter of 20 March 1948. She kept carbons of all her letters and treasured every scrap Daphne sent (now the Ellen Doubleday Collection, see copyright note).
13 Letter to Ellen 21 February 1948.
14 Both Ellen and Nelson were moved by what Ellen was to call Daphne's 'titanic capacity for giving of herself' (letter to Daphne, 18 August 1948). Daphne herself described keeping a vigil over the exhausted, sleeping Ellen in the hospital where Nelson was treated (letter to Ellen, 15 July 1948).
15 Letter to Ellen 15 July 1948.
16 Letter to Ellen, 9 August 1948.
17 Letter to Ellen, 28 October 1948.
18 Kits came downstairs one day and, asked if he had seen his father, said yes, he was in his room 'moping'.
19 Letter to Ellen, 2 September 1948.
20 Letter to Pucky (Ellen M. Violett), 23 August 1949.
21 Letter to Ellen Doubleday, 18 November 1948.
22 Ibid. These comments on Gertie and the memory of Gerald's comments assume an extra significance in view of Daphne's assertion in the letter of 4 July 1957 to Maureen Baker-Munton (see Appendix p. 420 (cf. p. 435)) that Gertie was 'the last of Daddy's actress loves'.
23 Letter to Ellen, 7 December 1948.

CHAPTER FIFTEEN

1 Letter to Ellen Doubleday, 27 February 1949.
2 Letter to Ellen, Easter Day 1949. The postcard from Gertrude Lawrence was copied out in this letter (see below in text).
3 Ibid.
4 Ellen would have liked Daphne to write Nelson's biography. Daphne was initially attracted to the idea, saying she would like to do for Nelson what she had done for Gerald, but decided she would not be able to do what she thought biography should do – 'give all the truth' – because it would hurt Ellen if she went over 'times of unhappiness . . . and personal things . . . it is often hard for a family to take'.
5 Letter to Ellen, 7 July 1949.
6 Letter to Ellen, 21 July 1949. Tessa remembers that her father also sang and danced. Tommy was a good dancer, though his speciality was a Russian Cossack dance.
7 Letter to Ellen, 9 August 1949.
8 Letter to Ellen, 28 August 1949.
9 Letter to Ellen, Thanksgiving Day 1949.
10 Letter to Ellen (no date), November 1949.
11 Ibid.
12 Letter to Ellen, 22 February 1950.
13 Daphne edited a volume of George du Maurier's letters and wrote an

Notes and References

introduction to it (*The Young George du Maurier: A Selection of his Letters 1860–1867*, Peter Davies, 1951).

14 Letter to Ellen, 22 February 1950.
15 Ibid.
16 Letter to Ellen, 13 July 1950.
17 Postcard to Ellen from Gertrude Lawrence, November 1950.
18 Letter to Ellen, 9 August 1951.
19 Letter to Ellen, 14 June 1951
20 Letter from Ellen to Daphne, 19 June 1951.
21 Letter to Ellen, 14 June 1951.
22 Letter from Ellen to Daphne, 19 June 1951.
23 Letter to Ellen, 9 August 1951.
24 Letter from Ellen to Daphne, 25 September 1951.
25 Letter to Ellen, 1 October 1951.
26 Letter to Ellen, 6 December 1951.
27 'The Birds' was filmed in 1963, with Alfred Hitchcock directing. Daphne hated the film and couldn't understand why Hitchcock had so distorted her story.

CHAPTER SIXTEEN

1 Letter from Ellen Doubleday to Daphne, 19 June 1951.
2 Letter to Ellen, 3 July 1951.
3 'Cinders' was Daphne's nickname for Gertrude.
4 Pucky (Ellen M. Violett), Ellen Doubleday's second daughter by her first marriage, was in the car and overheard this interchange.
5 Letter from Ellen Doubleday to Daphne, 5 June 1952.
6 Letter to Ellen, 13 July 1952.
7 Letter to Ellen, 8 August 1952.
8 Ibid.
9 Clara Vyvyan wrote a book about her walk from which these quotations are taken: *Down the Rhône on Foot* (Peter Owen, 1955).
10 Letter to Victor Gollancz, 10 September 1952, Modern Records Centre, Warwick University.
11 She asked Ellen to send her 'two rubber girdles' from America and was extremely pleased with the slimming effect.
12 Peter de Zulueta (1928–82) came from an old Catholic Spanish family who lived in England. His father, who died when Peter was fifteen, had been attached to the Spanish Embassy. His mother came from Grimsby and Peter went to work in a family business there from 1959–65, after he left the army.

CHAPTER SEVENTEEN

1 Clara Vyvyan also wrote about this holiday: *Temples and Flowers* (Peter Owen, 1955).
2 Letter to Victor Gollancz, 18 May 1953, Modern Records Centre, Warwick University.
3 Daphne used the word 'pathetic' here in a different sense from the usual.

437

She meant that she and Flavia did not need other people and could stand on their own. Later, she used 'pathetic' in the usual way when she applied it to Tommy in his last few years.

4   Tessa has no memory of asking her mother actually to be in the room for the birth, and she was not. But she certainly asked Daphne to be in London for the birth, and she came up just in time to take Tessa to the nursing home. Peter, Tessa's husband, was serving with the army in the Canal Zone at the time, and Daphne took over his role. She was very supportive and caring, and this marked a change in her relationship with Tessa.

5   Oriel Malet wrote an amusing account of this: *Jam Today* (Gollancz, 1956).

6   Brian Johnston and his wife, Pauline, clearly remember Tommy coming to supper and sinking down into an armchair, with a sigh, declaring, 'I'm slowing down,' and seeming very tired and depressed.

7   Letter to Bridget Graham, 1 February 1955.

8   Gollancz's files (all quotations from letters to and letters from Sheila Bush are taken from these files, which are contained in folders marked with the titles of the du Maurier novels).

9   Monty Baker-Munton (b. 1922) was a Spitfire pilot in the war. Maureen met him in Kandy after he had been flying in Burma, but it was not until the early fifties that she got to know him in London. He was working by then in his family's business (they were maltsters). He was taken by Maureen to Menabilly, and Daphne decided at once that he was utterly reliable and trustworthy. He married Maureen in July 1955 and from then on became as devoted to the Browning family as she was.

10 *The Scapegoat* was filmed in 1959. In spite of Alec Guinness in the lead and Bette Davis in a supporting role, not to mention a script by Gore Vidal (with Robert Hammer, who directed), the film was not a great success and Daphne was bitterly disappointed.

11 Letter to Ken Spence, 17 October 1957.

12 Letter to Maureen Baker-Munton, 4 July 1957 (see Appendix p. 420).

CHAPTER EIGHTEEN

1   Letter to Foy Quiller-Couch, 3 November 1957.

2   Daphne knew, all the same, that Angela had borne the brunt of caring for their mother.

3   Letter to Evie Williams, 23 October 1957.

4   One of them was 'The Rendezvous', which appeared in the collection of that name, published in 1980, after Victor's death.

5   Letter to Victor Gollancz, 14 November 1955, Modern Records Centre, Warwick University.

6   As above, 2 September 1952.

7   Letter to Ken Spence, 25 August 1958.

8   Daphne began writing to Symington in February 1957 and their correspondence continued until May 1960.

Notes and References

CHAPTER NINETEEN

1 Richard Pegler, of the London firm Spicer & Pegler, became Daphne's accountant in 1949 and continued to handle her finances until the early sixties. He became ill before his retirement and this worried Daphne, with some justification.
2 Letter to Elizabeth Divine, 7 July 1956.
3 Daphne took over the narrative in Chapter XVII of *Castle Dor*, though she also added some extra dialogue earlier. It was published by Dent in 1962 with a preface by Foy Quiller-Couch.
4 Daphne, in fact, had only just stopped 'touching it up'. Discussing her looks in this letter (to Evie Williams, 13 May 1960) she criticized her daughters for 'already touching up their hair', when she had been doing so for the last five years.
5 Kits was now sharing his Whitelands flat with a friend and each of them paid £4.50 rent. This letter (to Evie Williams) is a typical example of Daphne's exaggerations over her financial plight. She makes it sound as though Kits contributed nothing and lived in isolated splendour.

CHAPTER TWENTY

1 During his hospitalization in 1957, Tommy's liver was discovered to have been damaged, and he was not supposed to drink alcohol. He greatly reduced his intake but never managed to abstain completely.
2 Tommy had developed thrombosis in his left foot. He finally had to have a lumbar sympathectomy in order to try to restore the circulation in his leg and to prevent gangrene developing. It failed. Amputation of the foot was then the only option.
3 Instead she wore black and white for a year.

CHAPTER TWENTY-ONE

1 She wrote an article about being a widow, which appears in *Rebecca and Other Memories*.
2 Sent to her by Michael Thornton in April 1963. He was preparing an article about her.
3 This spirited but not necessarily reliable version of the meeting with Philip Rashleigh was given in a letter to Michael Thornton, 21 April 1965.
4 Foy Quiller-Couch and Clara Vyvyan were still great friends of hers. In 1955, Foy had moved into Trelowarren (Clara's home), into the main house, with a Mrs Hanson (niece of Octavia Hill), whom she had looked after since the death of her parents. Clara remained at Trelowarren, in a wing of the main house.
5 Letter to Elizabeth Divine, 24 March 1966.
6 Letter to Grace Browning, 21 March 1965.

Notes and References

1 This comment, in a letter to her agent, Curtis Brown, is puzzling. The budget for the *Vanishing Cornwall* film was £9,000, and Doubleday put up half of that.

2 This overdraft incident was due to a delay in the transfer of some money. Daphne knew perfectly well there was no real problem but enjoyed dramatizing the situation.

3 The King's Road in Chelsea, London, is full of antique shops.

4 It was Sir John Wolfenden who persuaded her to go.

5 Letter to Bridget Graham, 8 May 1969. Bridget and her husband Michael Graham lived at Polpey, Par, near Kilmarth, and became friends of Daphne's after she moved there (though Michael had known the du Maurier girls ever since they came to Fowey).

6 She told no one about the honour. Even her children learned of it from the newspaper.

7 Daphne wrote to 'my pin-up boy', Harold Wilson, congratulating him when he became Prime Minister. She also wrote to Mary Wilson, who replied that on the first day at 10 Downing Street she had felt like the second Mrs de Winter in *Rebecca*. Daphne sent Mary Wilson copies of her books and received a volume of her poetry in return.

8 There was a short correspondence with Peter Bessell over Rhodesia. Daphne was very anti-Ian Smith, and was indignant that Bessell appeared to want to come to terms with him.

9 It was Foy Quiller-Couch who had aroused Daphne's interest in this fund. Foy was an indefatigable worker for the National Trust and between 1929 and 1937 had raised money to buy cliffs between Polruan and Polperro (mainly Lantivet Bay).

CHAPTER TWENTY-THREE

1 Made into a highly successful film, of which Daphne greatly approved, in 1973, with Nicolas Roeg directing and starring Julie Christie and Donald Sutherland.

2 See Chapter Six, note 11.

3 Fans had never troubled her much at Menabilly – though the children remember American soldiers during the war coming to try to have copies of *Rebecca* autographed – but at Kilmarth she was more accessible. Some persistent fans became a serious problem in the next decade.

4 John Reece was their sales representative for Cornwall. He used to take copies of her books to Daphne for her to sign, as many as a thousand at a time.

5 Letter to Bridget Graham, 25 February 1972.

6 Letter to Livia Gollancz, 7 April 1972.

7 Letter to Karen Prescott, 8 November 1975.

8 'Nim' was code for 'urinate', 'pal' for 'defecate'.

9 Letter to Evie Williams, 14 May 1974.

10 Daphne kept a diary of the two visits to France she made while researching the books on the Bacons.

Notes and References

11 The American money was finally brought over and the full tax paid. The figure given by her agent is the sum before tax.

CHAPTER TWENTY-FOUR

1 She enjoyed, though, Lady Antonia Fraser's 'Rebecca's Story', written for *Harpers and Queen* in September 1976, and contributed a witty epilogue to it herself. But, in spite of telling Antonia how amused she was by the story, she wrote to her agent saying that this could go too far and they would 'need to watch out'.

2 Letter to Michael Thornton, 18 July 1974.

3 Jim Orr was equerry to HRH Prince Philip.

4 Ellen treasured and kept every letter, note and postcard Daphne ever sent to her, except for the very last letter she received while she was dying. Somehow, in spite of her weakness, she managed to keep this with her in her last days, but after her death there was no trace of it.

5 Dr Luther says that to the best of his recollection he never did prescribe Halcion for Daphne, and certainly never prescribed it for anyone as a tranquillizer. It is always possible, of course, that Daphne obtained Halcion without her GP's knowledge from another source.

6 These early stories have an interesting history. A Mr T. Todd gathered together, from magazines, eighteen stories written by Daphne between 1927 and 1930 and, with her permission, published them in 1955, when he had started up his own publishing firm again after the war. In 1965 he offered them back to her if she would donate £100 to any Cornish charity. She agreed and paid £100 to Operation Neptune. Some of them then appeared in *The Rendezvous and Other Stories* in 1980.

7 Philip Varcoe took over the management of Cornwall Mills from his father during the war. He knew Tommy and through him met Daphne. From 1975 onwards Daphne visited the Varcoes at Lanescot weekly.

8 Letter to Henrietta Stapleton-Bretherton, 26 May 1980.

9 Mogadon is a brand-name for Nitrazepam, an effective sleeping drug to combat early waking. It can be habit-forming and its effectiveness may become weaker with time. In those over sixty, as Daphne was, it can cause forgetfulness, a side-effect of all sleeping drugs.

Prothiaden is a brand-name for Dothiepin, an anti-depressant used widely for the treatment of long-term depression. The average adult dosage is 75–150 mg daily. The most serious side-effect is the possibility of causing dangerous heart rhythms.

Largactil is a brand-name for Chlorpromazine. This was the first of the anti-psychotic drugs marketed in the fifties. It has a general tranquillizing effect and is usually used in the treatment of schizophrenic mania and similar conditions. (See *The British Medical Association Guide to Medicines and Drugs*, ed. Dr John Henry, MB FRCP, published 1991, Dorling Kindersley.)

CHAPTER TWENTY-FIVE

1 Daphne was never a heavy smoker. The maximum number of cigarettes she ever smoked in one day was eleven, but her usual intake was six. Each

441

cigarette was carefully fitted in to her daily routine and became 'routes'. She had no difficulty giving up.

2   Monty Baker-Munton was appointed trustee by Daphne in 1960; in company with other professional advisers he gave investment advice from 1961; he helped over alterations to Kilmarth and monitoring of the costs in 1968; and in 1976 he liaised with Curtis Brown, Daphne's agent, over publications. To give him power of attorney in 1981 was the logical conclusion of all the trust Daphne placed in him. In her will, he, together with her son, was appointed literary executor.

3   Mary Fox, friend of the du Mauriers from their joint Hampstead days and their neighbour in Fowey from the war onwards, moved to Lostwithiel, eleven miles away, in 1983. Daphne visited once then said it was too far to be included in 'routes'. Mary visited her for a while but finally discontinued the visits because she did not feel entirely welcome. Bridget Graham felt similarly spurned.

4   Foy went into a home in 1982 and from there to the asylum at Bodmin, where she died in March 1986 of senile dementia.

Index